MICHELANGELO AND THE REFORM OF ART

Michelangelo was acutely conscious of living in an age of religious crisis and artistic change, and for him the two issues were related. Concentrating on Michelangelo's lifelong preoccupation with the image of the dead Christ, Alexander Nagel studies the artist's associations with reform-minded circles in early sixteenth-century Italy and his sustained concern over the fate of religious art in his own day. Understood within the context of reform, Michelangelo's art reveals an artistic and religious culture where self-conscious archaism mingles with aggressive innovation, and ambivalence regarding the role of images yields radical aesthetic experimentation. A reassessment of Michelangelo's work, this revisionist study sheds new light on High Renaissance and Mannerist art as a whole.

Alexander Nagel is assistant professor of art history at the University of Toronto. A recipient of a Getty Postdoctoral Fellowship and a grant from the Social Sciences and Humanities Research Council of Canada, he has published articles on various aspects of Renaissance art in the *Art Bulletin, Burlington Magazine,* and *Zeitschrift für Kunstgeschichte.*

MICHELANGELO
AND THE REFORM OF ART

ALEXANDER NAGEL
University of Toronto

CAMBRIDGE
UNIVERSITY PRESS

PUBLISHED BY THE PRESS SYNDICATE OF THE UNIVERSITY OF CAMBRIDGE
The Pitt Building, Trumpington Street, Cambridge, United Kingdom

CAMBRIDGE UNIVERSITY PRESS
The Edinburgh Building, Cambridge CB2 2RU, UK
http://www.cup.cam.ac.uk
40 West 20th Street, New York, NY 10011-4211, USA
http://www.cup.org
10 Stamford Road, Oakleigh, Melbourne 3166, Australia
Ruiz de Alarcón 13, 28014 Madrid, Spain

First published 2000

Printed in the United States of America

Typeface Bembo 11/13.5 *System* Quark XPress™ [HT]

A catalog record for this book is available from the British Library

Library of Congress Cataloging-in-Publication Data is available

ISBN 0 521 66292 3 hardback

For Weronika

Contents

List of Illustrations

Acknowledgments

Research for this book began during my graduate studies, and this means that it is particularly indebted to my mentors. I am grateful above all to John Shearman and Joseph Koerner, the advisors of my doctoral thesis, where I first explored several of the issues treated here, and to my other principal teachers, Jim Ackerman, Howard Burns, James Hankins, and Henri Zerner. In more recent times, I have benefited greatly from dialogue with my colleagues at the University of Toronto, Jeffrey Hamburger, Matt Kavaler, Michael Koortbojian, Evonne Levy, William McAllister Johnson, Alina Payne, Philip Sohm, Brian Stock, and Natalie Zemon Davis. For comments and contributions offered throughout my work on this book, I am grateful to Gadi Algazi, Michael Allen, Leonard Barkan, Fabio Barry, Lisa Bessette, Erin Campbell, Stefano Cracolici, Elizabeth Cropper, Neal Dolan, Jill Dunkerton, Marvin Eisenberg, Reginald Foster, Christoph Frommel, Gisèle Gordon, Paula Hayes, Philine Helas, Michael Hirst, Peter Humfrey, Bernice Iarocci, Merlin James, Bernhard Jussen, Sarah Lawrence, Jean-Claude Lebensztejn, Thomas Lentes, Stuart Lingo, Maria Loh, Thomas Mayer, Larry Meyer, Andrea Nagel, Pablo Nagel, Elisabeth Neumann, John O'Malley, Marjorie O'Rourke Boyle, John Paoletti, Andréa Picard, Beatrice Rehl, Sheryl Reiss, Elizabeth Sears, Leo Steinberg, Jack Wasserman, Chris Wood, and Alexi Worth.

I am also grateful to several sources of support during my research, including a Harvard University Travel Grant in 1990, a Lemmerman Foundation Grant for study in Rome in 1991, and a Mellon Foundation Grant for dissertation completion in 1992. A Getty Postdoctoral Fellowship in 1995–96 allowed me to expand my research significantly beyond the scope of my doctoral thesis. I wish to thank Marta Hallett, Ronald Nagel, and Claudia Nagel for their support, both logistical and moral, during that crucial year. The ideal conditions of a research fellowship at the Max-Planck-Institut für Geschichte at Göttingen in 1997 allowed me to bring the book into its present form. Throughout my work on this book, I have benefited primarily from the resources and assistance offered by the libraries of Columbia University, the University of Toronto, and Harvard University. I owe a special debt of gratitude to Susan Halpert, librarian at the Houghton Library at Harvard, who has offered unstinting assistance from beginning to end. I would also like to express my gratitude to the Bibliotheca Hertziana in Rome and the Warburg Institute in London, on whose freely offered resources I have relied extensively throughout my research.

INTRODUCTION

Michelangelo's Work as an Art Historian

By Michelangelo's time Christian images had strayed far from their origins. This is not simply a judgment of modern-day historians; it was a matter of concern for Michelangelo and his contemporaries, who were acutely conscious of living in a time of dramatic, even volatile, artistic change. The spectacle of artistic change in this period is familiar to us. It features centrally in the most influential accounts of Renaissance art from Giorgio Vasari's time on, where it has almost without exception played a central role in narratives of progress. If recently published art historical surveys are any indication, this approach to the period is no longer very compelling to most scholars, and it has come under direct attack by several. And yet, as the naming of Vasari and the very word rinascita suggest, the preoccupation with change and progress is itself a legacy of the Renaissance and cannot very well be thrown entirely out of accounts of the period. Our detachment from this legacy gives us instead a different purchase on its Renaissance origins. Something similar could be said about other familiar legacies, such as modern conceptions of art and artistic genius. As they come under revision in our time, it has become possible to write very different histories of art and its functions in the Renaissance – ones that, for example, pay greater attention to the nature of workshops, the role of patrons, and the institutions and codes within which art functioned. And yet our understanding of the period would be incomplete if the question of new conceptions of art and the artist did not play some part in it. Again, the point is not to throw them out but to approach them as historical problems, now that they are no longer cultural assumptions.

In the Renaissance artistic change meant primarily changes in traditions of Christian art. Change did more than move art forward; it also promoted a retrospective sensibility. The awareness that art had a history informed the practices of the artists' workshops even before the history of art had become a preoccupation of writers. Giorgio Vasari wrote at the end of the *Lives of the Artists,* first published in 1550, that he was greatly helped by notes on the history of Florentine art compiled by Michelangelo's teacher Domenico Ghirlandaio – an indication that by the end of the fifteenth century the manual and oral traditions of the workshops were themselves being committed to writing.[1] As a pupil of Ghirlandaio's and then a protégé of the household of Lorenzo de' Medici, Michelangelo had been exposed both to the practical art historical lessons of the workshops and to the historical interests of the humanists in the Medici circle, a circle that included that most sophisticated philologist Angelo Poliziano, tutor to the Medici children and advisor to the young Michelangelo.[2]

This combination made of Michelangelo an especially acute observer and critic of the history of art, a skill colorfully illustrated in Vasari's account of Michelangelo's experiments in forgery. The best known example is that of the *Sleeping Cupid,* which the artist not only sculpted in the antique manner but artificially distressed, revealing a sensitivity both for the style of the antique and for the process by which it comes down through history. In a less famous passage, Vasari also recounted that Michelangelo was an expert forger of drawings, revealing that Michelangelo's historical attentiveness was not limited to works of remote antiquity. Vasari said that he imitated the styles of the old masters *(maestri vecchi)* so effectively that no one could tell the difference between the copy and the original. Again, stylistic accuracy in copying the model came with an awareness of its status as a relic: Michelangelo "tinged them and aged them with smoke and various other means, making them look dirty so that they appeared old."[3]

Michelangelo's preoccupation with past art was rooted in the tradition-conscious Ghirlandaio workshop and can be understood as an extension of the standard apprentice training in the study of earlier masters. But Michelangelo's experiments developed these practices into something close to their opposite. In the traditional training, the apprentice sketched after drawings in the workshop and after public works to learn his craft, under the tacit assumption that the models were relevant and adaptable to present needs. When he made a copy of an older work, the apprentice of course strove to make it as accurate as possible. In conforming to his model the apprentice was in fact shaping himself, literally incorporating himself into a craft and a tradition. In Cennino Cennini's manual for painters, written about 1400, the first thing the apprentice is instructed to do after learning to prepare materials is to draw, and that means to "take pleasure and pains in constantly copying after the best masters" – but not too many masters, as that would be distracting. Instead, he advised the apprentice to concentrate on one master, because "it will be against nature if you do not get some grasp of his style and his spirit."[4]

When Michelangelo made a forged copy of an older work, he also strove to make it as accurate as possible, but it was an accuracy of a different kind. If the workshop copy presupposes that the model is assimilable and adaptable in the present, the forgery presupposes a gap between model and copy. The workshop copyist is shaped and informed by his model – Cennini adopted metaphors of filiation to describe the relationship. The forger, instead, begins with the acknowledgment that the style of the earlier work is foreign and (thus) must be recreated by artificial means – that it must be forged and not just imitated. The workshop copy concentrates directly on the earlier work's content; the forgery, rather, treats the earlier work as an object, an artifact and a document that must be reproduced, stains and all. Workshop copies are intended to integrate the pupil into a corporate structure and into a tradition. Forgeries, instead, celebrate the artist's individual *ingegno,* setting him or her apart from, and in some sense above, tradition. In what is only an apparent paradox, the ability to imitate exactly the work of others signals a freedom from the weight of tradition.[5]

The drawings that Michelangelo copied belonged to a fairly remote past – they were old enough to require "smoked" forgeries – and this implies that they were also stylistically remote. Michelangelo's practice as forger was predicated on a sharp awareness that the works of the past belong to the past and are to be appreciated accordingly. It sprang from a developed, quasi-scholarly interest in the documents of the history of art, an interest that anticipates the art historical writing of the later sixteenth century. As Anthony Grafton has shown, the work of the forger is closely entwined with the work of the critic. The forger not only provokes the critic to make more careful distinctions among sources but also often provides the critic with the methods for doing so. And this is why the critics best equipped to detect a forgery have so often been the ones most sorely tempted to produce one.[6]

Although none of Michelangelo's forged drawings is known to survive, from other evidence we gain some idea of how his historical intelligence worked – where, for example, he drew period lines in the art of the past. The clearest evidence comes in the much-studied drawings after Giotto's and Masaccio's frescoes, among the artist's earliest drawings (Figures 1–4).[7] Usually a contentious lot, Michelangelo scholars have in the case of these drawings offered a remarkable show of unity, joining to celebrate the young draftsman's emendations of the models. They have observed that Michelangelo gave greater texture to the garments, a greater sense of the presence of the body underneath, and a more solid and natural posture to the bodies themselves.[8] At times the Vasarian bias becomes explicit. Writing about the drawing after Giotto, Bernard Berenson declared: "It is not surprising that [Michelangelo's] figures are better articulated and have more vibration and tremor of life than the originals, so much we expect from a boy genius at the end of the Quattrocento."[9]

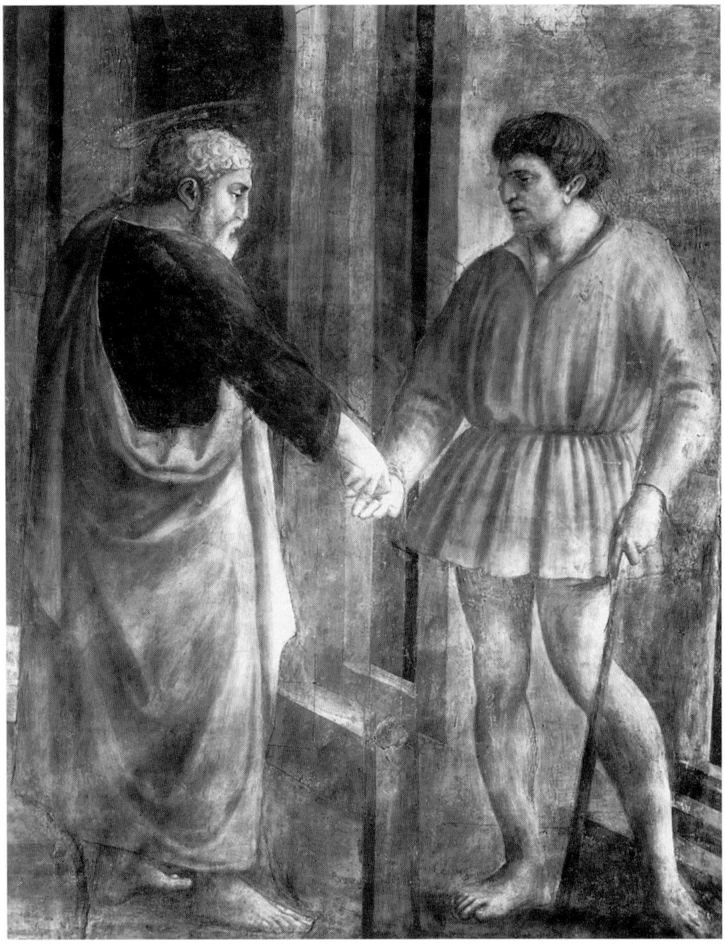

1. Masaccio, *The Tribute Money, detail of Saint Peter and the Tax Collector.* Fresco. Brancacci Chapel, Santa Maria del Carmine, Florence, Italy. Alinari/Art Resource, NY.

Vasari's progressivism is no longer the air we breathe, and it is possible to put these drawings in a different light. Without disputing any of the earlier observations, it is possible to reframe them by asking different questions: Rather than asking, "How do these drawings move beyond the past?" we might ask, "How do they approach the past?" If we do, an insufficiently noticed difference between the two drawings emerges with extreme clarity. Michelangelo takes an aggressive, "wholesale" approach to Masaccio's *St. Peter.* He makes subtle changes to every part of the figure, reconstituting it in a new, ampler style. The relations between the figure's extended arm, back, and neck, for example, have been thought through from scratch, resulting in a subtle but complete reinterpretation of the figure's posture – a reinterpretation with important implications for the subject's significance, because it directly concerns the issue of Peter's will and obedience. Michelangelo has made the figure so much his own that if we had no evidence whatever of the existence of Masaccio's fresco, we would not necessarily know that this drawing was a record of it.

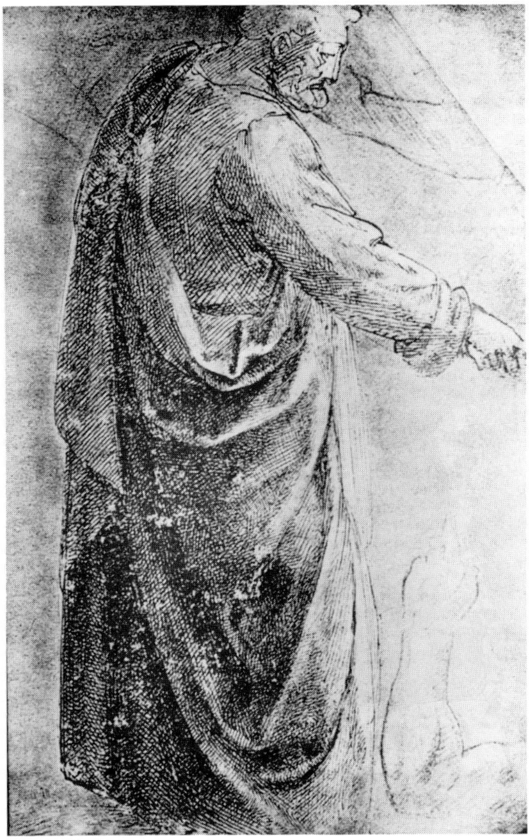

2. Michelangelo, *Copy after Masaccio's Tribute Money.* Drawing. Staatliche Graphische Sammlung, Munich, Germany.

How different from the approach taken to Giotto! Rather than reformulate Giotto entirely according to contemporary stylistic dictates, Michelangelo's principal intention was to *preserve* the characteristic features of Giotto's figures. He deliberately abandoned a "modern" figure style, such as he used in the drawing after Masaccio, and instead preserved the small head, the small shoulders, the high waist, and the barrel-like form that are characteristic of the Trecento model. The approach stands in stark contrast to a slightly later drawing, after the very same group in the fresco, by Michelangelo's contemporary Baccio Bandinelli (Figure 5). Here the Trecento features are almost entirely suppressed and the proportions, postures, and expressions are translated into a contemporary language.[10] If we had no record of the existence of Giotto's fresco we might not know that Bandinelli's drawing was a record of it, whereas we would very likely be led in that direction by Michelangelo's drawing: It is both clearly of the late fifteenth century and clearly after a Giottesque model.

To appreciate the significance of this fact, it is worth considering some of the difference between imitation in the apprentice's training and imitation in literary education. The imitation of classical models was the basis of education in medieval grammar schools no less than in humanist curricula. This imita-

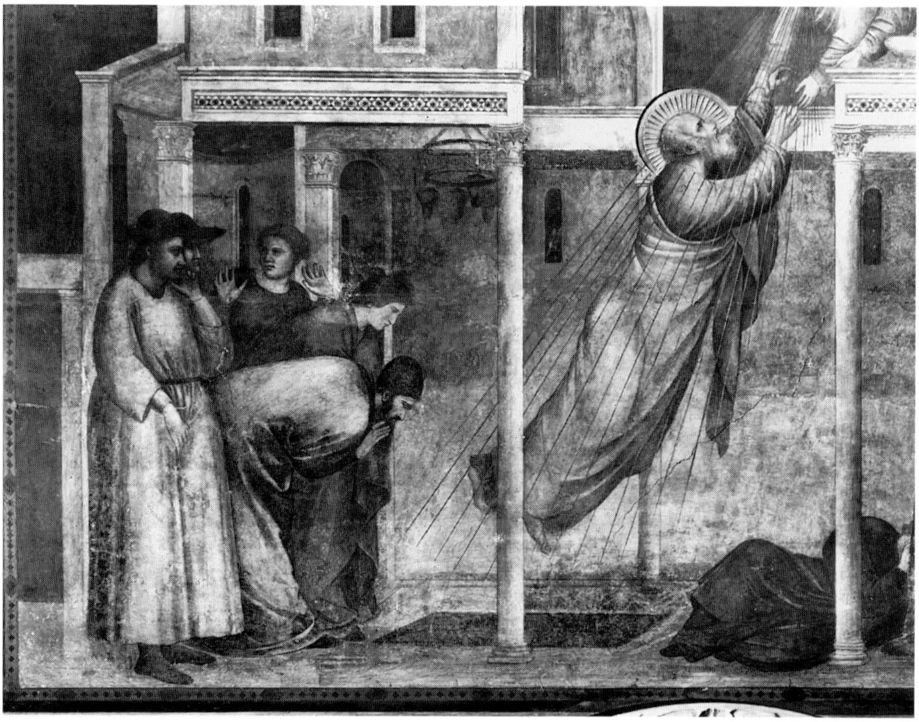

3. Giotto di Bondone, *Ascension of St. John the Evangelist, detail of group at left*. Fresco. Peruzzi Chapel, Santa Croce, Florence, Italy. Alinari/Art Resource, NY.

tion could be quite mechanical. Memorization was a significant fact of life for the student, and often, in the days before photocopying, students even had to be their own scribes, literally copying out their readings into what would be their own private textbooks.[11] Of course the ultimate purpose of imitation was to use the classical texts as models in a more abstract sense, for example as models of syntactical or poetical structure, or as models of organization, for example of the parts of an oration. Needless to say, those wanting to imitate Cicero more closely also could, and all too often did, insert his exact turns of phrase into their compositions.

Art students were both closer and farther from their models. That witty and irritable sixteenth-century English school master Roger Ascham railed against students of letters, who, although they had the excellent models of Plato and Cicero before them, did not imitate these as faithfully as painters, those lowly artisans, routinely imitated their models. "For surely the meanest painter," he said, "useth more wit, better art, greater diligence in his shop in following the picture of any mean man's face than commonly the best students do, even in the best university, for the attaining of learning itself."[12] But in fact students would have had trouble following Roger's advice, because textual imitation that is too faithful is in danger of becoming simple duplication in ways that painting can never be. It is something like a digital process: A perfectly transcribed or excerpted text is, by definition, the *same* text, because in texts, as opposed to images, it is possible to have what Nelson Goodman has called sameness of spelling.[13] The one great exception, of course, would be Jorge Luis Borges' Pierre Mesnard, who rewrote verbatim chapters 9 and 38 and part of chapter 22 of the first part of Cervantes' *El Quijote* but did not transcribe them: He reproduced them, miraculously, after steeping himself in Cervantes' culture.

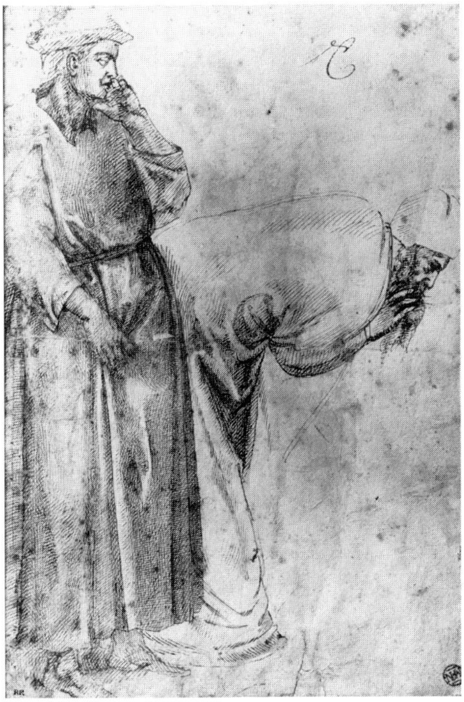

4. Michelangelo, *Drawing of two figures (after Giotto)*. Drawing. Louvre, Paris, France. Giraudon/Art Resource, NY.

In the case of art, where despite the best efforts of theorists there is no grammar but only objects, there is no such thing as sameness of spelling, and we have something closer to analogue copying. Copyists have to follow the lines of the model with their hand, and that means, especially in the case of drawings, reenacting the physical performance that produced the original. This is a physical process of assimilation of a special kind, and it deserves the kind of rigorous study that textual imitation has received. I want to make only one simple point about it here, and that is that when the model is a remote one, when the effort of copying involves a conscious warping of one's own style – and in this period the word *style* really meant stylus, or the pen – then the process raises some pressing questions. In reproducing the strokes made by the original artist, I relive them as a series of decisions, decisions that were natural for the artist and are not for me. It is not just that the artist's individual style is different from mine. It is that the entire period style, the very premises on which the artist worked, are different. The strange quality of a sleeve, therefore, and my resistance to it, prompt questions about the otherness of those times generally. If those questions preoccupy me enough, I might consider taking the next step, from archaizing drawing to outright forgery.

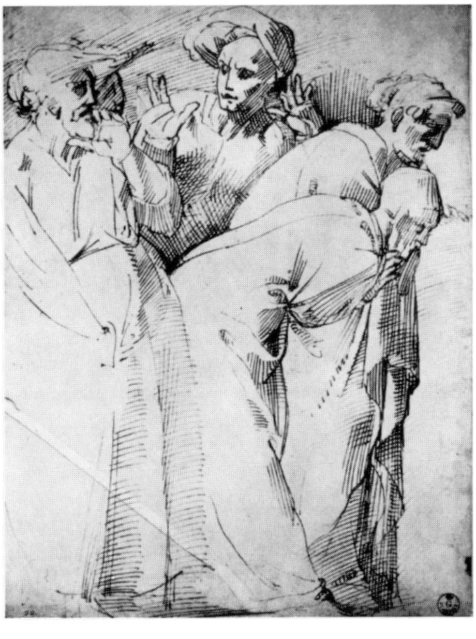

5. Bandinelli, *Copy after Giotto's Ascension of St. John*. Drawing. Uffizi, Florence, Italy.

Again, this is not to deny that Michelangelo also made the emendations to Giotto that previous scholars have observed; it is simply to give them a different significance. His application of the cross-hatching technique learned from his master certainly gave a new pliability to the folds and (thus) a stronger sense of the presence of the leg underneath. But this tendency to emend remained subordinated to the quite novel commitment to acknowledge and imitate the features of a style distant from his own. Michelangelo could not completely refrain from altering the model in the direction of a modern figure style; on the other hand, he did not go so far as to reshape the figures entirely in his own manner, as he did in the drawing after Masaccio, and as Bandinelli did in *his* drawing after Giotto.

In sum, Michelangelo wrestled with the father but paid homage to the grandfather. Critics have consistently dated the drawing after Giotto earlier than the drawing after Masaccio, as if the only way to register the difference between the two drawings within a Vasarian schema is as a development in Michelangelo's own artistic progress. But to suggest that Michelangelo should first have been Giottesque and then have become Masaccesque would be to take the dictum "ontogeny recapitulates phylogeny" to absurd extremes. The more reasonable conclusion is that there was a historical horizon in Michelangelo's view of the art of the past, and Giotto lay on the far side of it. It was the same frontier that was perceived fifty years later by Giorgio Vasari and that he placed between the first and second "ages" of his *Lives.*[14]

Vasari articulated his tripartite scheme, as it were, theoretically, in his three prefaces.[15] But he also occasionally dramatized it in the narratives of the *Lives.* Perhaps the most obvious instance occurs in the life of Perino del Vaga. Perino, fresh from the workshop of Raphael, returns to his hometown, Florence, to spread the gospel of the new Roman grand manner. It is, of course, in the Brancacci chapel that Perino's colleagues gather to engage in "the praise and blame often bandied about among artists." Perino claimed that the Roman painters had surpassed Masaccio's style and proposed to do a fresco next to one by Masaccio to prove his point.[16] He never gets around to doing it, but simply the intention to do so reveals an effort to demonstrate art historical periodization through the method of compare and contrast, long before Heinrich Wölfflin made left and right transparencies into an apparently indispensable institution of art historical pedagogy. Wölfflin was of course working within a well-established discipline and in a classroom. Perino's proposed fresco would have been quite a departure from contemporary practice – it was a work made not on commission but for the purposes of critical demonstration – and in the time before the art history classroom, the demonstration had to be done in paint, on the traditional church wall, and with the permission of the convent's prior.

The Perino anecdote is tantalizing in that it seems to document a form of artists' shoptalk that has gone largely unrecorded, but it remains very much a story of Vasari's, designed to dramatize the scheme of the *Lives.* (On which wall would Perino have painted the proposed comparison fresco?) In the drawings by Michelangelo, we see the scheme articulated and dramatized by Vasari taking practical shape more than fifty years earlier. I want to insist on this. In these drawings Michelangelo does not simply exemplify Vasari's culminating third era but goes some way toward working out the historical scheme itself. In the drawing after Giotto, what began as a workshop copy, an act of assimilation into a tradition, became instead its very opposite, a critical acknowledgment of historical distance. In this, if anything, lies a claim to epochality, for a retrospective sensibility is one of the distinguishing features of much of what we call High Renaissance art. This book argues that the awareness that art had a history pervaded Michelangelo's work, and that it is a key to understanding its relation to the critical religious culture of the sixteenth century.

In his *Vite d'Artisti,* Giovanni Battista Gelli, a contemporary of Vasari, gave several accounts of Michelangelo's appreciation of the art of the Trecento and early Quattrocento. He wrote that when Michelangelo was in Florence he was reported to have gone to the Bardi chapel in Santa Croce to admire Giotto's fresco of the *Death of St. Francis,* remaining in front of it for three or four hours at a time. Gelli also mentioned a fresco attributed to Giotto on the piazza of the Gianfigliazzi, "where Michelangelo was on several occasions seen to be gazing fixedly."[17] What about these outmoded works captivated Michelangelo's interest? The instances discussed above show that Michelangelo's admiration for these works was different in quality from that which he gave to works produced by immediate predecessors and contemporaries. The latter formed the ground upon which and against which he shaped his own style, whether they offered something he wished to emulate (Masaccio, Jacopo della Quercia, Donatello) or to resist (Niccolò dell' Arca, Francesco Francia, eventually Leonardo da Vinci).

On the other hand, the fact that Giotto's frescoes lay on the far side of this horizon does not mean that Michelangelo's admiration for them is to be simply thrown together with his admiration for antique sculpture. Michelangelo's reception of the antique was in fact closely connected with the polemics of contemporary style. Michelangelo aspired to equal and surpass the figural style of antique art; it was the measure against which he judged his own work and those of his contemporaries. Trecento art, especially Trecento painting, was not a model in this sense. Michelangelo would have been the first to acknowledge that the figural style of these works was not something to which he or his contemporaries aspired. The deliberate warping to which he subjected his own style in his efforts at imitation and forgery gives the measure of how far removed they were from his stylistic concerns. Michelangelo approached Giotto with a sense of formal estrangement caused by temporal distance. No artist who makes deliberately archaizing drawings after the old masters, let alone outright forgeries, could claim to belong to an unbroken tradition in the way that, say, Cennino Cennini did circa 1400, when he claimed a direct lineage back to Giotto and asserted that "he [Giotto] had more finished craftsmanship than anyone has had since."[18]

And yet there Michelangelo was in rapt admiration before these works, a fact that forces us to qualify our understanding of art historical attitudes in this period. Michelangelo was capable of admiring these works as effective and powerful works for their own time, and in this sense to be awed and fascinated by them. The recognition of distance need not diminish fascination, as the writings of art historians abundantly attest. And yet it would be a mistake to ally Michelangelo's attitude too closely with the enthusiasms of modern art historians. For whereas post-nineteenth-century historians confront all periods of history, even recent history, with a developed set of disciplinary tools, Michelangelo lived a historical process that was itself marked by a new reflexivity about historical processes. The continuity of tradition – whether understood in religious, political, or social terms – was a topic of passionate debate in the years around 1500. Tradition was in a state of disrepair, provoking efforts both of suturing and of wholesale fabrication. In the terms of Pierre Nora, retrospective continuity was ceding place to the illumination of discontinuity, and the work of history was being called upon to supplement the processes of memory.[19] Much of what is most characteristic of early sixteenth-century art and culture derives from this intermediary position, at once part of tradition and disjoined from it, and it is little wonder that this critical climate should have produced stunningly forceful interventions in cultural interpretation and historical thought. We see such interventions in the debates concerning a national language and literature, in the prolific political self-examination undertaken in Florence and Venice, in the growing concern over religious reform, and of course in the emerging discipline of the history of art.[20] For these reasons, medieval art provoked Michelangelo's art historical attention in a way that antique art did not. It had become antiquated within generational memory, undergoing a Gadamerian process whereby temporal distance becomes a productive condition of cultural interpretation.[21]

We can gain a better grasp of Michelangelo's attitudes toward the art of the past by turning to the views of Vasari, who very clearly articulated the principle of appreciation from a historical distance. Vasari was keenly aware that he was writing for an aggressively modernist artistic culture. Anticipating that many of his readers would find it "ridiculous to compare the old artists with those of this age," he defended himself on several occasions by urging an appreciation of the works produced in the first age – that is, in the Duecento and Trecento – in view of the time in which they were made: "But those who take into consideration the nature of their age, the scarcity of artists, the difficulty of obtaining good assistance, will consider them not merely beautiful, as I have said, but miraculous. . ." For this reason, he said, "my intention has always been to praise not simply, but, as they say, relatively [*non semplicemente, ma come s'usa dire, secondo che*], and to have respect for the places, and the times, and other similar circumstances."[22]

It is worth stressing how specific this attitude was to the realm of the visual arts. No one felt it necessary to qualify their praise of the great Trecento poets in the terms of *secondo che,* despite the fact that it was widely recognized that their language was antiquated. The distinction between Latin and vernacular literature, for which there is no analogue in the visual arts, made it possible to celebrate the Trecento vernacular poets as superior models to which modern poets should aspire. The classic statement was made by Pietro Bembo in his *Prose della volgar lingua* of 1525. According to Bembo the Italian language had increased in refinement only until Petrarch and Boccaccio: "After this point no one has been seen to reach this level, let alone to surpass it. And this is to the great shame of our century."[23] Petrarch and Boccaccio could be held up as ideal models in the realm of vernacular literature just as Virgil and Cicero were in the realm of Latin literature. There was no parallel to this in the contemporary criticism of the visual arts: The antique was an ideal model but the art of the immediately preceding centuries was clearly inferior to the art of the present day. The contrast was clearly drawn by Giovan Battista Gelli toward the middle of the sixteenth century. Gelli argued that, in contrast to painting, which after Giotto progressed with "one foot in front of the other" up to the perfection of Michelangelo, in poetry Petrarch achieved such perfection that "after him it appears that no one has been able to surpass him, or even equal him."[24] Thus, Gelli could proceed to give an extended reading of Petrarch's poem on Simone Martini's portrait of Laura as a marvel of poetry for contemporaries to study and imitate, but about Simone Martini himself he could only say that "there is no evidence that he was as famous [as Polycleitus], and apart from that one does not see much art in those works of his that have come down to us."[25]

A passing remark by Giovanni della Casa indicates that Vasari's *secondo che* was something of a standard view among *intendenti* by the middle of the sixteenth century. In his book of manners, the *Galateo,* he called Giotto "not only master, but without any doubt a singular master according to those times [*secondo quei tempi*]."[26] The attitude is well dramatized in another story of Vasari's, where again the protagonist is Perino del Vaga. Upon seeing a Madonna fresco by Giotto in old St. Peter's in danger of being destroyed, Perino had it removed from the wall and placed in a safer part of the church, surrounded by a new frame and other pieces of Trecento memorabilia – a restoration assemblage clearly motivated by the commitment to see the art of the past in the context of its time, or *secondo quei tempi*. According to Vasari,

Perino intervened out of piety, *"per pietà a quella pittura."*[27] The word *pietà* meant both pity and piety,[28] and here both meanings are at play in a way that is characteristic of sixteenth-century cultural attitudes: The old religious devotion originally commanded by Giotto's Madonna has been compounded by the historian's veneration for an old work under threat of extinction. It is difficult to say when one kind of *pietà* superceded the other, and around 1500 the two kinds mingled quite a bit. In 1500 we are still a far cry from the cultivated disenchantment of the seventeenth-century doctor Thomas Browne, who was able to say, "Now one reason I tender so little Devotion unto Reliques is, I think, the slender and doubtful respect I have always held unto Antiquities."[29]

The element of pity in the historical piety explains why Vasari's attitude toward the Duecento and Trecento is generous but condescending, offering something like a handicap clause that makes allowances for the disadvantages of earlier times. But for Vasari these allowances do not change the fact that the work of the earlier periods has been superceded "in this time, which is at the apex of perfection." The earlier works can be appreciated *secondo che,* according to those times, but it would not be of any particular use for a modern artist to go back to them.[30]

Michelangelo went beyond Vasari's principle of period tolerance by returning, on several occasions, to medieval models in his own art. For example, in his *Medici Madonna* in the Florentine church of San Lorenzo Michelangelo followed the unusual composition of a venerated Trecento icon in the same church (see Figures 62 and 64).[31] Somewhat later, in the drawing of the *Pietà* for Vittoria Colonna, (see Figure 93) he introduced a Y-shaped cross, which, as Michelangelo's biographer Condivi has informed us, was based on the cross "carried in procession by the Bianchi at the time of the plague of 1348, and afterwards placed in the church of Santa Croce, at Florence."[32] This is only one of the drawing's archaizing features, which are discussed in chapter 6.

Evidently, Michelangelo did have reasons to go back to the forms of the Trecento. These and several other examples discussed in this book indicate that Michelangelo went back to earlier forms not in spite of their remoteness but because of it. And what made them both remote and worthy of emulation was their aura of authentic religiosity. The point is underscored by the fact that neither the San Lorenzo icon nor the Santa Croce cross could be considered signal artistic monuments in the way that Giotto's paintings were. If they were valued, it was for their status as venerable cult images. But here venerable would have two meanings, just as Perino's *pietà* had two meanings. Antiquarian veneration compounded traditional religious veneration, without simply replacing it – another instance of the intermediary position of sixteenth-century culture. The acknowledged remoteness of these works demanded that they be understood *secondo quei tempi,* and that in turn meant that if one were to go back to them, as Michelangelo did, it was *for* their perceived historical significance, *for* the social and religious value they were believed to have held in their time. In other words, Michelangelo was engaged in a form of the social history of art.

And yet this was hardly the view of the academic historian. For a certain brand of reform-minded person in the sixteenth century, the works of the thirteenth and fourteenth centuries were emanations of a more religious time and thus guides to the restoration of religion in the present day. Their cultic power was, paradoxically, bound up with their remoteness. Where modern historicism recognizes distance and goes about reconstructing and visualizing the past, archaism recognizes distance and yet remains committed to the possibility of a physical conjunction with the present, of injecting the presence and power of the original in the here and now. Archaism is a strain that runs through several aspects of reform thought in the sixteenth century, and is one of the prime sources of its peculiar pathos.

The association of old art and religious authenticity produced some interesting wrinkles in sixteenth-century aesthetics. There were those who defended the simplicity, even the perceived awkwardness, of the early art as itself a sign of its purer spirituality. In his *Dialogues on Painting,* written in the 1540s, the Portuguese painter Francisco de Hollanda described a commission given to him by the queen of Portugal to copy the miraculous image of Christ in the Sancta Sanctorum. One of the interlocutors asks him, "[D]id you do it with that severe simplicity which the old painting has and with that fear in those divine eyes which in the original seem to belong to the very Saviour?" Hollanda is then accused of being a poor friend to Vittoria Colonna, also one of the interlocutors, because he has not shown her "a thing that was so much to her liking."[33]

Other sources confirm that Colonna, Michelangelo's close friend from the 1530s, had a strong interest in the "St. Luke" Madonnas of Rome. In one poem about them she admitted that their artistry is "lacking" (*manco*) and "imperfect" (*imperfetto*) but defended these qualities as features of a humble style (*modo umil*) with special spiritual effectiveness. At first she proposes that the painter produced an imperfect work owing to his inability to contain the divine immensity of such a subject, but then she suggests, more interestingly, that it was the result of choice: The painting's defects result from a deliberate restraint on the part of the painter. The painter was "perhaps disdaining [*forse sdegnando*] the grave lights and proud shadows of art," she says, knowing that the humble act ascends to God. Made without the blandishments of art, the painting humbly offers only the *alto dissegno,* the essential schema or design.[34] In proposing that earlier artists engaged in intentional simplification Colonna was echoing a point already made by Hieronymus Emser in his 1522 treatise against the Wittenberg iconoclast Andreas Karlstadt, where he gives the idea a socio-economic twist. Having seen "quite simple images" in many old cloisters and collegiate churches, he argues that this "was not done because of any decline of art (for in earlier times there were no doubt capable painters, although they were not so common as they are now)" but for two reasons: Because people back then preferred to give the "vast amounts of money which we spend on pictures today" to the poor, and because they were aware that "the more artfully images are made the more their viewers are lost in contemplation of the art and manner in which the figures have been worked."[35]

Of course, Colonna and Emser were projecting a sixteenth-century predicament back onto the making of the early images. It was the sixteenth-century artist who had to exercise restraint in order to preserve the piety and authenticity of religious art. The problem arose in the sixteenth century as a corollary to the growing awareness that "modern" aesthetic ideals were not necessarily compatible with religious purposes. No one was clearer about this than the Dominican theologian Giovanni Andrea Gilio, who in 1564 declared that the "old customs" had been "changed and ruined by the caprices of modern painters [*la consuetudine . . . che poi è stata mutata e guasta dai capricci de' moderni pittori*]." He defended the old cult images, "which to modern eyes look vile, awkward, lowly, old, humble, without skill or art" as *"imagini oneste e devote."*[36] He prized in particular their frontality, what he called their *prosopopea,* a feature to which he attributed an almost anthropological significance.[37] In a frontally oriented image, simplicity and directness inhere in the work as structurally embedded virtues; the forward-facing figure assumes the ethical responsibility of clear public address. By contrast, for Gilio the self-involved contorsion of the *figura serpentinata* was the emblem of modern decadence, the fetish of the modern artistic cult of virtuosity and individualism, the hothouse fruit of an elitist preoccupation with the pursuit of difficulties accessible only to the few.[38]

Gilio conceded that at times the old images "deserve rather to be laughed at than to be marvelled at," but he proposed a compromise – a *regolata mescolanza* – that would eliminate the errors of both the old and the new art.[39] A similar point had already been made by Vasari, in a passage that introduced the 1550 version of his life of Fra Angelico, where he held up the Dominican artist as a *juste milieu* between the artistic deficiencies of medieval art and the religious indecorousness of the nudes of his own day.[40] As it happens, for Gilio Michelangelo was the prime offender among modern artists. Proposals for the reform of art in this period were many and not necessarily compatible. Despite their shared concerns, Michelangelo's tortured efforts to reform religious art failed to convince the Counter-Reformation theologian. And yet Gilio's views help us to understand what Michelangelo saw in Giotto. It is likely that Michelangelo appreciated Giotto's works, similarly, as examples of high artistry not divorced from authentic religious meaning and purpose, and it is possible that he believed this unity to be characteristic of that more "integrated" age. Such a judgment would not have been out of line with contemporary constructions of Florence's "communal" past, which was invoked in similarly idealized terms throughout the constitutional crisis of the Savonarolan years, and again during the revived republic of 1527–30.[41] Different as they were, both Girolamo Savonarola and Niccolò Machiavelli believed that social cohesion and religious belief went together, and both looked to the past to demonstrate the point.[42]

The array of meanings attached to the word *rozzo,* an adjective often applied to medieval art in the sixteenth century, gives some idea of why medieval images should have held appeal for reform-minded sixteenth-century critics. When one called a work of art *rozzo* one generally meant that it was crude and imperfect, but one could also mean that it was unfinished, rough in the sense of a sketch or *abbozzo.* Thus it was possible in the sixteenth century to see the old images described by Vasari and Gilio as *rozze* not merely in pejorative terms but in a more sympathetic light as first efforts or sketches that in later periods were brought to refinement, as if the early works offered the preliminary outlines that were later colored in.[43] The sixteenth-century art and literary critic Vincenzo Borghini said that all works of nature are "imperfect, rough, harsh, etc. [*imperfette, rozze, acerbe, ecc.*] and that time smoothes, matures, and refines them [*e che il tempo le dirozza, matura e affinisce*].[44] In the poem discussed above, Vittoria Colonna suggested a similar idea: The old cult image was *manco* and *imperfetto* because it had not received the pictorial refinements [*i gravi lumi e la fiera ombra*] that would have given it finish, holding instead to the firm and virtuous lines of the *alto dissegno.* First or archaic works, according to Borghini and Colonna, are like unfinished works. The corollary of this notion is that the strata of the individual work of art offer an archeology, a physical epitome of the history of art. The conceit could be manipulated in other ways: In a dialogue of 1490 the humanist Paolo Cortesi compared the rough Latin of Dante to "an old painting [*veteri pictura*], in which the colors have lost their splendor, but the outlines [*delineamenta*] still please."[45] Here history strips away rather than adds, but the result is the same: The old image lacks color and refinement, presenting simple but satisfying outlines.

By the middle of the sixteenth century, a period haunted by a sense of decadence and belatedness, the simple lines of the old images came, in many people's eyes, to possess a positive value. It is a premise of this book that such an archaizing taste often went hand in hand with a preoccupation with reform, a preoccupation that is by definition backward-looking. The idea of renovation went hand in hand with the idea of returning to an earlier age. Thus, in a typical flourish of reform rhetoric, the humanist Jacopo Sadoleto could say in 1528 that Pope Clement VII was "the author of a new age, of new times, new institutions, new morals, but nonetheless, the newness of these would draw as near as possible by imitation to that holy and pious antiquity [of the early Church]."[46] From the beginning of Christian thought this process of reform has been associated with the visual arts, and specifically with the physical work of artistic restoration. In describing the reform of man and his restoration to the image and likeness of God, the Greek fathers continually compared it to the process of cleaning a painting that has been marred but not completely ruined by the addition of unsuitable colors and by the accumulation of dirt.[47] Augustine compared the reform of man to the restoration of a deformed sculpture, a task that only God, "the artist who shaped it," could accomplish.[48] In our period, the Dominican Girolamo Savonarola, whom Michelangelo heard preach, invoked an architectural metaphor: Drawing the distinction between earthly things that grow old and divine things that are not subject to time, he compared the contemporary Church to an old building in need of repair.[49]

A conception of reform as restoration leads to modes of archaism that go well beyond the simple quotation of old models. It makes experiments with the very structure of the work of art into a mode of archeological investigation. This book concentrates on aspects of Michelangelo's work that reveal a consistent preoccupation with processes of excavation, recovery, and remembrance. It begins with a highly unusual experiment in altarpiece painting, in which the narrative of Christ's *Entombment* becomes a means of thematizing the relation between viewer and cult object as one between present and past, thus making the problem of distance – and the means by which it is bridged – central to the picture's subject. Such a "subjective" address to the viewer was unusual in altarpieces and yet very much in line with certain strains of humanist and reform-minded piety. Pushing this experiment further, in later treatments of the theme Michelangelo moved beyond painting and its official public functions altogether to the "subsoil" of drawing – a more withdrawn and less regulated realm, which he attempted to make into an alternative category of religious art in its own right. Finally, he transplanted these efforts to the realm of marble sculpture, whose greatest virtue in Michelangelo's eyes lay in identifying the making of the work of art with the process of excavation – to the point where, in his final work, the *Rondanini Pietà,* the process yields an archeology of the Christian image. The fact that virtually all of these works remained unfinished can be explained circumstantially in each case. But it can also be seen as a natural concomitant of this conception of art. If art is excavation, then it is a reversal of the finishing process, and the result will be marked by an unfinished quality whether it is literally finished or not.

To put it another way, in these works theme is inseparable from structure. That all of these experiments involved the image of the dead Christ, I argue, is not a coincidence or the result of an inscrutable artistic preference. It was a significant choice, first because a restored emphasis on Christ's sacrifice, in opposition to the quasi-polytheistic saint worship of the late Middle Ages, was a battle cry of reformers of all stripes. At a basic iconographic level, therefore, the return to Christ involved the removal of the later accretions of hagiographic piety and the restoration of an "originary" Christocentric emphasis in Christian art. More specifically, the theme of Christ's Passion and entombment was significant for Michelangelo because the process of death, interrment, and resurrection was itself an allegory of stripping, digging, and restoration. Michelangelo was not alone in drawing this parallel. In the opening address to the Fifth Lateran Council, in 1512, the famed Augustinian preacher Giles of Viterbo argued that the Church suffered evils because Christ periodically withdraws from it, but like Spring after the ravages of Winter, like resurrection after death, Christ would return and effect its reform.[50] Powerfully joining Michelangelo's artistic process and his preoccupation with reform, the subject became for Michelangelo a lifelong preoccupation bearing all the traits of an obsession.

How did Michelangelo reform this central subject of Christian art? In Michelangelo's view, the artists of his day had become overly distracted by the afflictions suffered by Christ, lingering with perverse relish on the wounds and blood that disfigured Christ's mortal body, on the many circumstantial details of his torture and martyrdom, and on the wild lament of his mourners. He countered this enormously widespread trend with a typically humanist *repristinatio*: Removing the blotches of blood and the wounds from Christ's body like so many overpaintings and disfigurations, Michelangelo offered instead a pristine and radiant dead Christ based on the models of antique sculpture. This was more than a stylistic preference. It was fundamentally a restoring of theological perspective, for it turned attention away from the immediate story of tragic suffering and death to the ultimate victory that resulted from Christ's sacrifice. This, too, was a preference shared by prominent advocates of reform. Gian Matteo Giberti, the celebrated reforming bishop of Verona during the second quarter of the sixteenth century, ordered the blood depicted spouting from Christ's hands removed from paintings of the *Crucifixion,* because it was unfitting to show Christ in an agonizing state when he triumphed over death, was resurrected, and ascended into heaven.[51] Michelangelo – and Giberti for that matter – found this more high-minded emphasis in the art of earlier times. For Michelangelo, the early days were identified with the time when sculpture still dominated religious art, and painting had not yet fallen prey to the distractions of an excessive naturalism.

Michelangelo's effort to conscript antique pagan statuary into a project of Christian reform was in many ways typical of the humanist culture that prevailed in papal circles in the early sixteenth century. And yet Michelangelo's theological commitment and sophistication led him to some unusual solutions even within this cultural milieu. This book argues that bacchic mysteries were an especially important part of Michelangelo's effort to purify Christian art and to restore its theological emphasis on the mystery of Christ's sacrifice.

To modern eyes the effort to restore the spirituality of Christian art by recourse to bacchanalia may seem hopelessly abstruse and even overtly fraudulent. But to take such a view is simply to rehearse the condemnations of Counter-Reformation critics and to fail to see these works in the context of early sixteenth-century humanist culture.

Michelangelo incorporated the animations of antique sculpture in an effort to reinvest the narrative expressiveness of contemporary Christian art with spiritual and theological significance. This involved a highly motivated adaptation of what Aby Warburg called antique "pathos formulas," one that differed markedly from the practices of several other antique-inspired Renaissance artists. Where other artists found in antique art models of purposeful narrative action, Michelangelo found bodies possessed by forces larger than themselves. Michelangelo's efforts were designed to reanimate a "dead" Christian art on the one hand while harnessing and neutralizing the demonic forces of pagan art on the other. Christian *repristinatio* was to accompany what Warburg called the aesthetic detoxification [*aesthetische Entgiftung*] of pagan art. The result was an art as disjoined from both of these traditions as it was deeply informed by them. It is one of the recurrent arguments of this book that Michelangelo's much-vaunted independence from the antique was not simply an assertion of artistic originality and modernity but the result of approaching pagan themes within a Christian context, and specifically within a culture of reform.

This book studies several ways in which art historical sensitivity was bound up with religious concerns in the sixteenth century. Michelangelo was acutely conscious of living in an age of religious crisis and rampant artistic modernization, and for him the two problems were related. The art of the Duecento and Trecento was separated from Michelangelo's time by a history of volatile artistic change. The most significant change, one that concerned Michelangelo particularly, was the rise of panel painting, which in Italy came to predominate over sculpture at the center of Christian worship. One of the decisive strengths of the medium of painting was its great amenability to formal and technical innovation. Foreigners were quick to notice the taste for change in Western art of the late Middle Ages. More than one Byzantine visitor, for example, was astonished at what appeared to be the rampant license allowed to Western painters and expressed grave concern over the dangers it posed to Christian tradition and orthodoxy.[52] Alarms were of course also sounded in the West, most often by attentive clerics of a reform-minded or observant persuasion who arose periodically to castigate novelties and abuses in the making and use of images.[53]

By 1500, however, artistic developments threatened a break with the tradition of the Christian image altogether. In Hans Belting's view, the artistic developments of this period mark the end of the era of the Christian image on the eve of a modern and secular "era of art."[54] It is possible to raise objections to this view – by pointing out, for example, that cult images continued to be produced and venerated long after 1500 – but it is certainly true that the period around 1500 is marked by a crisis in several traditional categories of religious art, that it saw the emergence of new forms of secular art, and that these developments raised important questions about the traditional functions of images. The watershed was especially clear in the north, where the Protestant Reformation brought a long-standing debate over the role of images violently to a head.

The situation in the Protestant north was critical enough to call for clear resolutions about images, ranging from outright abolition to new and careful codification. The situation in Italy, however, remained ambiguous, especially before the Counter-Reformation. But it would be inaccurate to claim that concerns were not present, just as it would be inaccurate to claim that they had not been present in the north before Martin Luther. Clerics, humanists, patrons, and artists in Italy continued to believe in the religious vocation of art, even as its nature and status was changing. As a result, Italian art of the period is filled with implicit but acute concerns over the functions, history, and legitimacy of religious images. Crisis is not just the fact of dislocation but the perception of dislocation itself, and is thus inseparable from the act of criticism.[55] Such "critical" concerns appear in the work of artists as diverse as Michelangelo, Raphael, Fra Bartolommeo, Andrea Sansovino, Giovanni Bellini, Tullio Lombardo, Lorenzo Lotto, Rosso Fiorentino, Jacopo da Pontormo, Parmigianino, and Jacopo Sansovino, among many others. They go, in other words, straight to the heart of our conceptions of High Renaissance art and give it a stranger appearance. In contrast to the progressivist view, which sees it as a culminating period of harmony and classical perfection, this view of the period reveals a more anxious art of disjunction, compensation, projection, and desire – and as a result casts a sharper light on the new forms of artistic and historical self-awareness that mark the period as a whole. It helps to explain why what we call the High Renaissance was such a brief episode and was so quickly followed by the strange experiments of the art of the 1520s and after. The career of Michelangelo makes it necessary to see this history as a continuous one.

Although several of the artists of this period can be linked to reforming circles, only in rare instances can their works be said to originate in anything like a reform agenda. Consequently, they do not answer to the methods used to study the art of the Protestant north or the campaigns of the Counter Reformation, and no doubt this is why they have so far eluded thoroughgoing study along these lines. This book, which studies one artist's response to the problem, is intended as a start in this direction.

Michelangelo's response emerges most clearly in his lifelong preoccupation with a type of image known in the period as *imago pietatis,* and commonly known today as the Man of Sorrows. One of the most popular cult images of the late Middle Ages, it consists of the frontally presented dead Christ, shown in formats ranging from bust length to full length. The figures surrounding Christ varied, but one feature of the image remained decisive: The image stood as a general symbol of Christ's Passion and sacrifice, and was not linked to any one episode in the Passion narrative. Images of this sort had become distinctly old-fashioned in advanced artistic circles by 1500 in Italy, and Michelangelo's versions of the figure are typical of their time in that they attempt to introduce the figure within a consistent narrative setting. And yet the fact that he preserved the figure at all, returning to it obsessively throughout his life and often in the face of extreme compositional and structural difficulties, suggests a deliberate interest in preserving an earlier tradition of religious art within "modern" artistic conditions. This conscious effort of preservation becomes especially clear in Michelangelo's later treatments of the theme, which show overtly archaizing features. These works have for too long been understood in isolation, as the creations of Michelangelo's brooding genius. Michelangelo's preoccupation with the *imago pietatis* reveals not only an awareness of artistic and cultural change but also a concern over its effects on religious traditions and institutions. Idiosyncratic and personal as they are, his works confront issues of central importance to reformers and humanists of the period.

My focus has led me to pay a good deal of attention to the *Entombment* in the National Gallery in London (see Figure 6), a work that aroused much interest in the late nineteenth century and then fell into relative obscurity until recent times. As the work is not mentioned by Vasari or Condivi and is first recorded, as far as we know, in the seventeenth century, its place in the Michelangelo corpus has been open to debate.[56] Nonetheless, the great majority of scholars has favored the attribution to Michelangelo and placed it in his early period. The list includes Jakob Burckhardt, Jean Paul Richter, Gustavo Frizzoni, Bernard Berenson, Adolph Goldschmidt, Aby Warburg, Carl Justi, Henry Thode, Adolfo Venturi, Johannes Wilde, Cecil Gould, and more recently Howard Hibbard, Michael Hirst, and John Shearman.[57] The fact that the panel remained obscure is due in large measure to the fact that it was excluded from the Michelangelo corpus in Charles de Tolnay's highly influential five-volume study, published between 1943 and 1960. As it happens, Tolnay then reversed himself after the picture's cleaning, but the habit of excluding the work from consideration has persisted.[58]

Michelangelo is a sacred cow, still, and this means that debates about his corpus acquire a vehemence usually reserved for religious disputes. The question of attribution is not a central concern of this book, but because it has proven impossible entirely to avoid it is perhaps appropriate to state the creed I follow. It is my belief, and a premise of this book, that the question of attribution cannot be convincingly argued on stylistic grounds alone but must be addressed in the context of a larger historical inquiry. This means taking into account the larger questions that affected cultural production generally (e.g., the debates concerning imitation, or the comparison of the arts), as well as taking into consideration the array of patronal modes and tastes and the institutional contexts within which art functioned. It also means taking into account how such concerns are mediated at a level closer to formal structure, through such questions as decorum, function, format, and genre. Connoisseurship pursued in the absence of such an inquiry has extremely dubious value, especially for works of art produced in the sixteenth century and earlier. The aspects of the London painting that most strongly suggest Michelangelo's authorship have to do with the work's conception – not only its innovative narrative structure but also its interpretation of the status of Christ's body between death and resurrection and its reception of the Man of Sorrows tradition. Any serious study of the painting must also take into account the work's place in the history of the altarpiece, as well as its relation to Michelangelo's late *Pietàs*. These questions have received limited attention, if any, in previous studies of the painting. The first questions are addressed in the first part of this book; the last question is a recurring concern of the second part.

When the painting is understood in light of these questions, it is possible to see its many unusual – not to say awkward – features as something other than violations of the standards of artistic "quality" cherished by modern connoisseurs. They can be understood, instead, as part of a (frustrated) effort to respond to the threat of generic disruption, a threat that Michelangelo perceived as a crisis in a tradition of religious art. Similar things could be said about several drawings that have discomfited Michelangelo scholars and that here are interpreted as experiments motivated by consistent preoccupations in Michelangelo's art. By the same token, however, the analysis offered here puts certain drawings that are now widely accepted in a more dubious light. Thus, this book offers something to upset everyone. I can say only that I have based my judgments not merely on a personal sense of the artist's style, but on a set of criteria deriving from a historically informed interpretative framework. Michelangelo's experiments with the Passion subject constitute a fervent *parti pris* in a period debate, a debate rife with theological and ideological implications. Of course, such a framework does not guarantee correct attributions, and about several I remain unsure, but it does provide a reasonable basis for debate and thus, I hope, a useful alternative to the arguments from dogma and authority that characterize so much traditional connoisseurship.

The first part of this book studies tensions between developments in history painting and traditions of religious art in the fifteenth century. I focus on the theme of the entombment of Christ, which by the later fifteenth century had become a kind of proving ground for ambitious history painting, and I focus on altarpieces, which until the end of the fifteenth century constituted the principal venue for large easel painting. The *Entombments* by Michelangelo and Raphael were deliberate efforts to adapt this theme, and this conception of painting, to the altarpiece format. They offer a commentary on the status of this central institution of Christian image making in an era that saw its predominance thrown into question by the rise of new conceptions of art. Their responses to the problem, studied in chapters 3 and 4, involve quite novel interpretations of the traditional functions of altar painting, which I attempt to show are consonant with some of the more innovative strains of humanist thought in the period. The generic tensions confronted in these works preoccupied a whole generation of painters to follow, including Pontormo, Rosso, and Titian, and provide a historical basis for understanding the archaism of Michelangelo's late works.

The second part of the book studies Michelangelo's withdrawal from the traditional categories of religious art. In chapters 5 and 6, I study Michelangelo's return to the theme of the Man of Sorrows in the realm of the presentation drawing, a new type of drawing made as a finished work in its own right and presented as a gift. I argue that the new category represented for Michelangelo an alternative to the public and institutional realm of church art, specifically of altar painting. Efforts to reinvent the traditional cult image as a work of art, these works on paper culminated in the *Pietà* drawing for Vittoria Colonna of circa 1540. On the basis of Michelangelo's letters and poems and the writings of Colonna and members of her circle, I argue that the new and rarefied conception of art embodied in the presentation drawing served as a privileged model for the spiritual hermeneutics promoted in this reform-minded milieu.

The late *Pietà* sculptures, studied in chapter 7, belong to a later phase, when the hopes of this milieu had been dashed and it had become harder to believe in the exquisite marriage between aesthetic tastes and spiritual sensibility embodied in the presentation drawings. The late *Pietà* sculptures are the fruits of a more reclusive position, removed even from the interpersonal dynamics of the presentation drawings, and lie completely outside the artistic categories known in the period. The most private of works carried out in the most public of media, monumental marble sculpture, their irony is greater and their archaism more overt. I argue that they embody a series of reflections on the relation between sculpture and the history and nature of Christian cult images, and I attempt in this way to connect issues raised in the *paragone* debate to reform concerns prevalent in the period.

PART ONE

HISTORY PAINTING AND CULT IMAGE IN THE ALTARPIECE

CHAPTER ONE

Transport and *Transitus*

HISTORY AND FIGURE

A frieze of tightly pressed figures fills the foreground, almost entirely screening the landscape behind (Figure 6). Upon closer observation, the figures on this shallow proscenium settle into clear spatial relationships. Nestled between three figures, one behind and one on either side, the naked body of Christ occupies the center of the picture. The triangular grouping around Christ extends to include two figures (one of them not yet painted) kneeling on a strip of bare ground in front. Anchored in the lower corners of the picture, the two kneeling figures mark the outermost poles of an arrangement whose surface symmetry reflects a symmetry disposed in depth. The disposition of the figures leaves the central foreground clear, affording the viewer a frontal, virtually unobstructed view of the figure of Christ. The symmetrical relationships initiated in the painting are completed in the person of the viewer, who is placed, almost ceremonially, at the bottom of the steps, directly opposite Christ, an analogy to his front-facing, full-length figure. In its basic structure, this composition posits the presence of the person standing before it. The viewer, one might say, is its organizing principle.

This state of affairs is complicated by the fact that we have here not a simple grouping of sacred figures, a *sacra conversazione,* but rather the depiction of a biblical story. The design of the painting thus insists on the relation that links the story to the viewer. It implies, even, that in this relation lies its sacred purpose and significance. Such a claim falls in line with a venerable exegetical tradition according to which sacred events, though embedded in history, also contain what exegetes typically called a "mystery," "figure," or "sacrament" – a spiritual meaning that lifts the event out of history and connects it to the

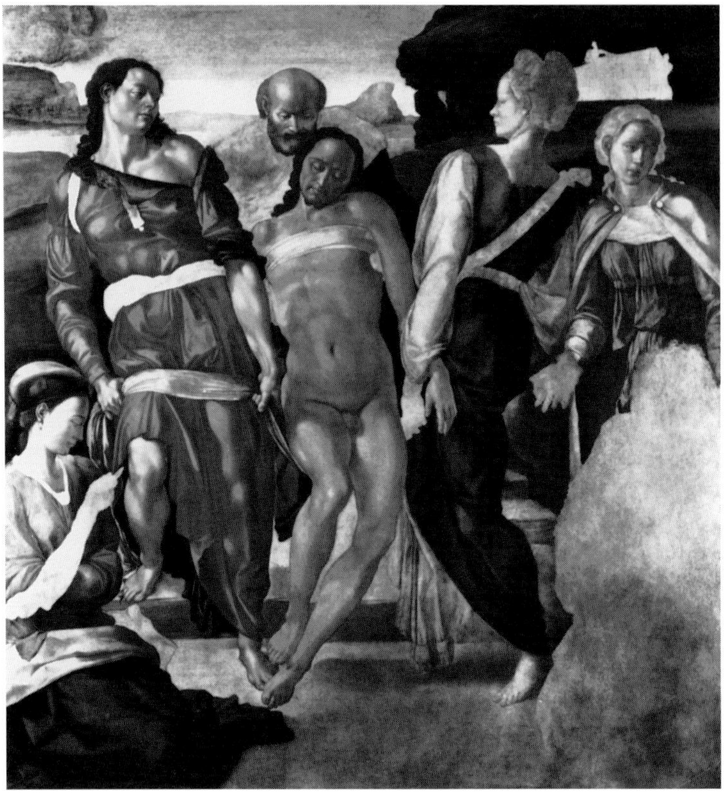

6. Michelangelo, *Christ Carried to the Tomb.* Panel. National Gallery, London, England.

larger scheme of Christian belief.[1] In a sermon of 1496, the Dominican reformer Girolamo Savonarola claimed that this connection between history and "figure" was what most clearly distinguished sacred history from secular history and from poetry. Sacred scripture was written not only to record names, places and dates – that is, to document what occurred historically – but also to have a further, deeper meaning – in Savonarola's words, *"per significare altro."* He called this deeper meaning the *senso allegorico* (a term that here refers to all the levels of exegetical interpretation beyond the literal, and not only to the allegorical level in the strict sense). He pointed specifically to the absence of this dimension in the history of the ancients: "Look at Livy – his writings don't signify future things, but only describe what occurred in the past. . . No other writing except sacred scripture has allegory – not even poetry, as some say." Sacred history is unlike poetry, he argued, because it has the literal, historical level, the *verità di storia,* that is missing from the *favole* of the poets. It is unlike pagan history, because it also has levels of higher meaning. This meaning "is shifting and can be taken in many ways, that is, it does not stay still like history [*il qual senso è vago e puossi pigliare in più modi, ita che non sta fermo come la istoria*]."[2]

The idea that figural meaning "moves" was something of a commonplace. We find it also in a treatise on the celebration of Easter by Paul of

Middelburg, the compatriot and correspondent of Erasmus who served as physician and astrologer at the papal court. He applied the idea to argue for a finer distinction: that moveable feasts, such as Easter, are figural in a way that feasts fixed to a specific date, such as Christmas, are not. His explanation of the distinction, debatable as it is, offers a concrete example of figural thinking at work circa 1500:

No mystery or sacrament is signified by the day of Christ's Nativity; instead, it is merely denoted that on that day Christ was born. Easter/passover (*Pascha*) however contains a mystery and sacrament, because it signifies a passing over or across (*transitum*) – is in fact the phase of the Lord's passage. It prefigures Christ's passage from death to life and our liberation from the devastating devil.

In drawing this distinction Paul was, of course, contravening a long-standing tradition of highly figural exegesis of the Nativity and of other events marked by fixed feasts. His argument thus stands as a useful reminder of the flexibility with which these principles were applied, and as a warning against overly systematic accounts of figural thought in this period. Nonetheless, his fundamental principle that figural meaning involves movement is a quite orthodox one. For Paul the principle was epitomized by the concept of *transitus* at the heart of the word *Pascha,* for an event contains a mystery when it is "figurative of future things and rememorative of things past." For Savonarola, figural meaning "does not stay still," for Paul it is "moveable," and it is this quality that connects Christ's historical sacrifice and resurrection "backward" to the sacrifice of the lamb and the salvation of the Jews at Passover, and "forward" to its reenactment in every Mass, where its benefits touch the faithful through the sacrament of the Eucharist.[3]

Michelangelo's *Entombment* confronts the question of Christ's sacrifice directly and interprets it in a manner that is in several respects typical of developments in late-medieval Christian devotion. The work does not merely point to an objective theological dogma or truth but rather locates its significance in the effective relation between the biblical subject and the viewer's individual experience. The mystery at the heart of the painting's theme consists in the viewer's becoming conscious that the sacred event has occurred "for" him or her. The painting develops this emphasis in ways that bear especially close affinities to trends in humanist religious thought, as I attempt to show in chapter 3. The painting's claims were, however, conceived and realized through means specific to traditions of image making, and not simply by a direct application of theological or humanist principles. Accordingly, the following chapters are devoted to clarifying these "intra-artistic" processes. Such an analysis is necessary to understand the painting's significance, because a dialogue with a tradition of Christian image making informs the painting's thematic content, which has in part to do with the relation between present and past forms of worship.

The figures carrying Christ are shown in the process of moving backward, away from the viewer. They are beginning the climb up a series of steps toward the tomb that is being prepared in the distant background. This fundamental point about the painting's narrative organization is not readily apparent, a fact due in part to the painting's unfinished state. We see only the silhouettes of the figures opening the tomb in the background, and only the bare underdrawing of the steps leading to the tomb. We are also missing crucial details in the mechanism of Christ's support structure, not to mention the key foreground figure of the Virgin on the right, who was meant to be shown kneeling with her back to us. But there is a more fundamental reason for the difficulty in reading this picture. Such a mode of narrative movement, a combination of frontal orientation and retrogression away from the viewer, is extremely rare in Renaissance painting. It is likely that many contemporaries also would have had difficulty in identifying the painting's subject. The first thing they would have seen was the figure of Christ, and they probably would have called the picture a *Cristo morto* or a *pietà*. Nonetheless, a great deal of thought was put into the picture's narrative structure, and it deserves careful study.

The frontal orientation and symmetrical structure interfere with the impression of movement, an effect that is strongly reinforced by a studied avoidance of figural overlapping. Although it is an extremely crowded composition, almost every limb shown in the painting meets but does not trespass the contour of the neighboring figure. Look, for example, at the points of contact between the profiles of the carriers and of those figures closer to the margins. These outer figures, in turn, just meet the picture edge at several points, without spilling beyond it (a point that would have been clearer before the cropping of the panel). These were deliberate decisions and carry significance. The figures perform their actions, and yet they are locked into a surface structure that resists the logic of movement through space. They act in the open space of history, and yet the relations among them are controlled by an order that operates at the level of the two-dimensional image – that is, at a level "external" to the history, and beyond the awareness of the actors themselves.[4] This "external" level has to do instead with the image's objective existence as an altarpiece. In making the historical actors conform to dictates at the level of surface and framing, Michelangelo in effect adapts the actions of sacred history to the structural realities of a ritual setting. But it is not as if we first have the history and then its ritual adaptation. For Michelangelo, such an adaptation was always already implicit in sacred history, and this is what makes it sacred and not secular. The "fit" between the represented scene and the formal organization of an altarpiece suggests that there is an inherent relation between the historical event and the ritual structures of Christian worship. The painting's entire thematic structure is designed to confirm and celebrate this relation.

The subject's dual nature as *historia* and *figura* affects the very attitudes of the figures, which are worth observing in some detail. The figure of the dead Christ is a calm center surrounded by effort and struggle. Those around him strain upward, but his figure describes a relaxed curve against their strict isocephaly. They pull and hoist, evidently struggling under great weight, and yet Christ's figure seems to rise by itself, from the toes upward, weightless and flamelike. This ambiguity turns on the toes of the left foot, which seem to be pushing, ever so slightly, against the ground.[5] His limbs are passive, pushed and turned amidst the jostling, and yet a hint of torsion gives the sense of a body controlled from within. Christ's body is held up to view, almost inadvertently, in the midst of the carrying, and yet it presides, ambiguously enthroned, in the center of the composition. Christ assumes an unwitting majesty in death. The historically contingent episode has resolved itself into a structure inviting formal worship.

The work of carrying is distributed among the three figures immediately surrounding Christ. Standing two steps above the others, the older man behind bends down and, biting his lip, pulls Christ up by a strip of cloth stretched across the chest and under the arms. At the head of the group, he concentrates on steering the body and steadies Christ's upper torso with his (still unpainted) left hand. The other two figures support the greater part of the weight, using another sheet slung under Christ's thighs. St. John, in red to Christ's right, steps backward with his right foot onto the first step. He pulls the cloth upward with his left hand and with his right locks it over his upraised right thigh.[6] The posture of the figure to Christ's left is more difficult to read, but it is in fact a version of St. John's, turned in the opposite direction.[7] She also takes the cloth in her (unpainted) left hand, and, stepping upward with her right leg, presumably locks it over a concealed, upraised right thigh in the same way St. John does. Even the triangular form described by her robe's neckline, together with her sash, mirror the corresponding features in the figure of St. John.

Michelangelo established a sort of division of labor between the three figures who are carrying and the three who are lamenting, keeping the latter at a significant distance from the body. The carriers serve as buffers around Christ: The bodies of the other three merely touch the outer profiles of the figures making up this inner sanctum. Only the hem of the Magdalene's robe makes contact with the body of Christ – appropriately enough, given the Magdalene's legendary associations with Christ's feet.[8] The standing figure to the extreme right is the farthest, physically and psychologically, from the rest of the scene, and remains significantly outside the symmetrical structure formed by the other figures. The relation of her head to her shoulders indicates that she has turned away from the central group. With a gesture of renunciation she has given up watching the event and casts a tear-clouded gaze out of the right edge of the picture (Figure 7). Her face does not express distracted grief of the kind favored by the antique-inspired artists with whom Michelangelo was especially affiliated, such as Donatello (Figure 8). It shows

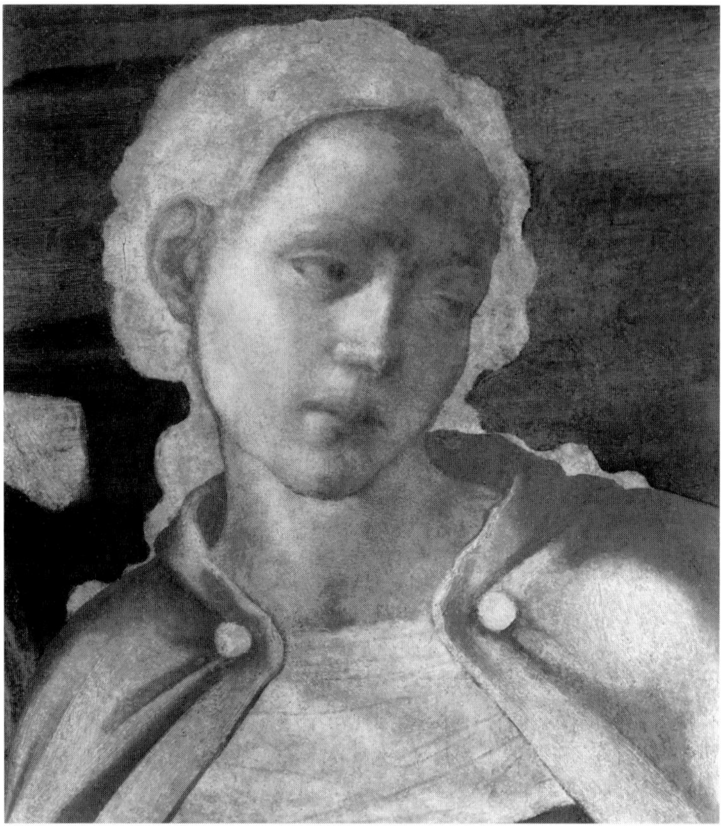

7. Michelangelo, *Christ Carried to the Tomb, detail of head of female figure to right*. Panel. National Gallery, London, England.

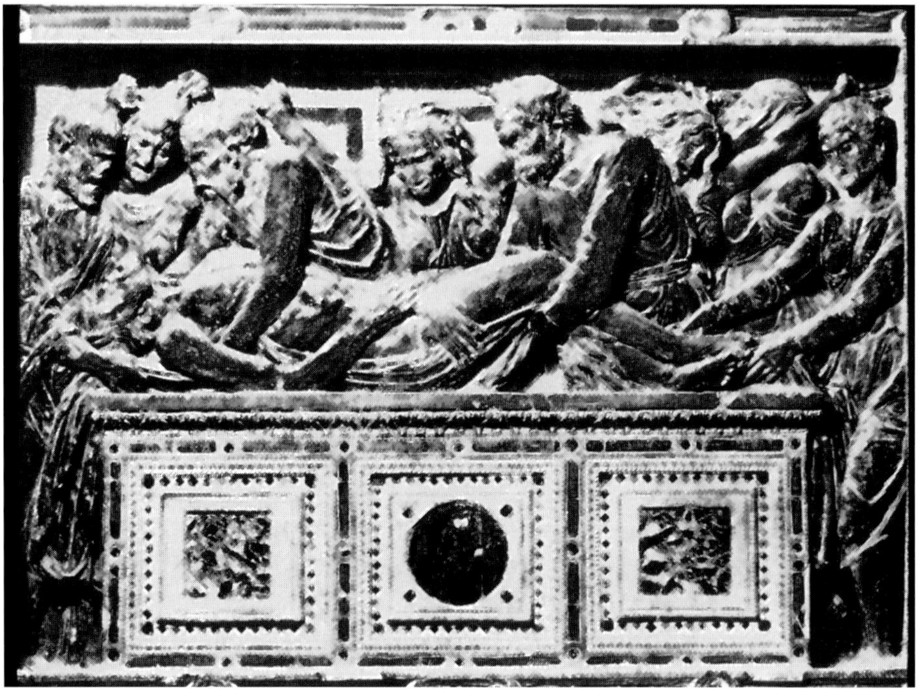

8. Donatello, *Entombment*. Bronze. Sant'Antonio, Padua, Italy.

instead a more muted attitude, suggesting absorption within thought or memory. The figure kneeling on the left also diverts her attention from Christ but fixes it on a specific object: A drawing in the Louvre informs us that she was to hold the nails of the Crucifixion in her left hand and the crown of thorns, before her eyes, in her right[9] (Figure 9). Finally, the figure on the right, unpainted but certainly intended to represent the Virgin Mary, was to be shown kneeling with her back to the viewer and, probably with joined hands, gazing directly upon Christ. A drawing in Siena after the painting, although it contains misreadings, gives some sense of the intended posture of this figure[10] (Figure 10).

These are three different kinds of gaze, and they express three different attitudes. It would be misunderstanding their significance, however, to read them, in the spirit of Alberti, as varied dramatic responses to the action at hand. They are emphatically undramatic and are hardly responses.[11] Whatever their differences, they share the quality of a sustained attitude, a state of mind not bound to the single, unrepeatable moment. The gaze of the standing figure drifts away from the scene and out of the picture. She

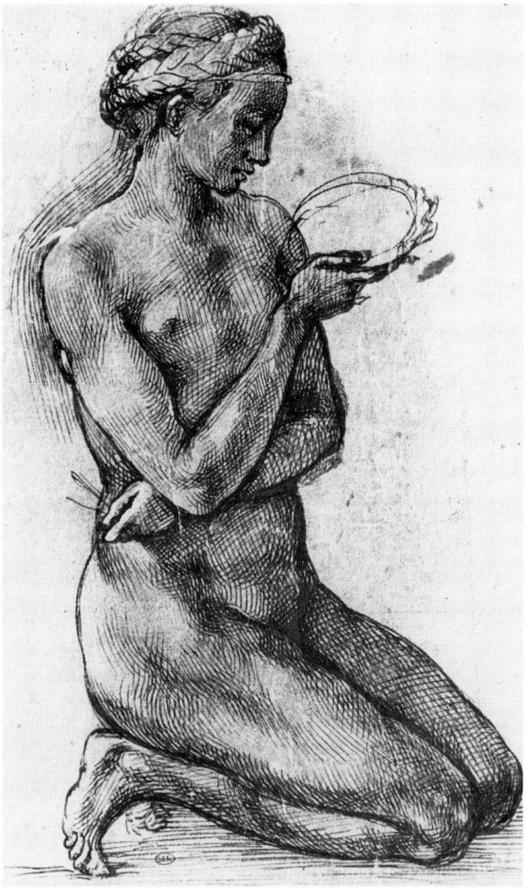

9. Michelangelo, *Woman on Her Knees.* Drawing. Louvre, Paris, France. Giraudon/Art Resource, NY.

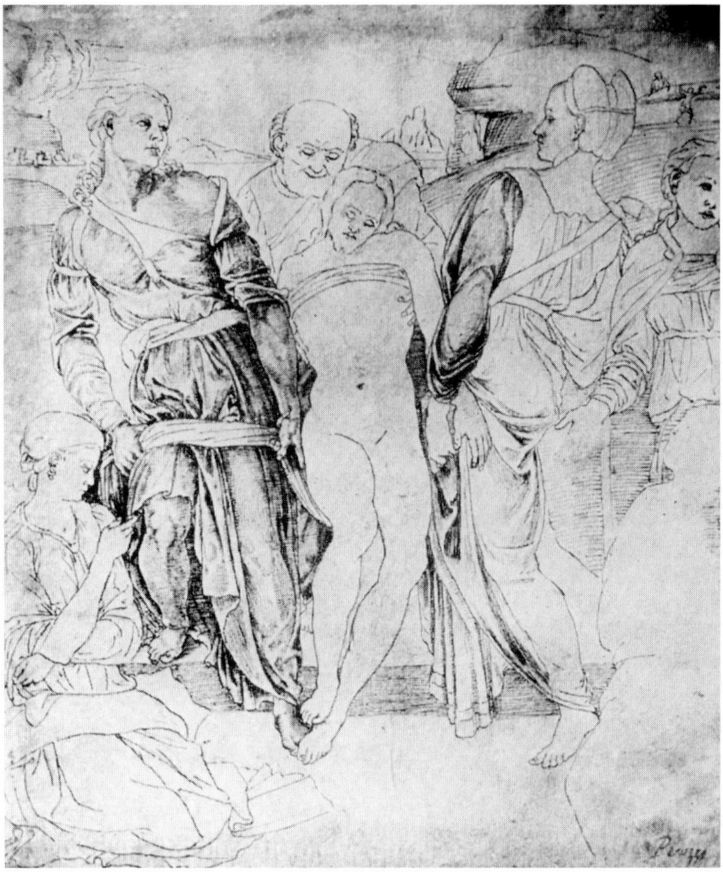

10. Copy after Michelangelo's *Christ Carried to the Tomb* (Fig. 6). Drawing. Biblioteca Communale, Siena, Italy.

has turned away from the outward event and into a world of private thought. The figure kneeling on the left, her gaze perfectly perpendicular to the main axis of attention, also ignores the action and contemplates instead the artifacts left in its wake. Even before the historical Jesus has passed out of the scene, she initiates a mode of reverence that was to be formalized and perpetuated in the cult of relics. The Virgin, finally, attends directly to the focus of the scene but does the most to suspend its narrative effect. Christ, having presumably just been taken from her lap, is now set before her at viewing distance, like a cult image, and she settles significantly into an attitude of worship. Of all the figures, her position and attitude most resembles that of the posited worshipper before the painting. The dictates of dramatic unity have thus given way to modes of contemplation not strictly anchored in historical time. They have, indeed, more to do with the viewer's time: They are states that could be expected to continue during the viewer's own contemplation of the image.

If we take it in strictly narrative terms, this painting depicts an intermediate moment, rarely represented in earlier art: After the deposition and lamentation, but before the entombment proper, this is the moment "between stations" in which a group of bearers has formed and begins to break away from the remainder of the group that had been lamenting over Christ.[12] As the carrying group begins the slow procession up the hill, two (unpainted) figures in the background lift the slab off the tomb that is to receive the body. The work's novelty and significance, however, lies not only in the representation of a rare subject but also in the means by which the subject is staged, for the frontal orientation of the composition places a special burden on the role of the viewer. The viewer finds him- or herself placed just beyond the mourning group from which the body is being separated, and placed, at the bottom landing of the steps, directly opposite Christ. To attend to the painting is to acknowledge that you are implicated by its subject.

John Shearman noted that the adoption of a "situated" point of view was a strategy typical of medieval devotional texts such as the *Meditationes vitae Christi,* which exhort the devotee to imagine him- or herself present at the sacred event. In this panel, accordingly, we are offered "the experience of the rupturing group seen from within."[13] In contrast to a lateral composition, which asserts the self-sufficiency of the scene and reports it to the viewer as if in the third person, here the narrative structure incorporates a direct second-person address to the viewer.[14] But, pace Shearman, it does not "include" the viewer in the event so much as it interprets and thematizes the relation between the biblical event and the viewer situated in the here and now. The drama of separation interprets the relation between viewer and image. This relation *is* its subject, and it gives the viewer a special responsibility: Christ is being drawn away, and we remain where we are. History is, as it were, receding from the present.

ANCIENT TRAGEDY AND CHRISTIAN LAMENT

The many unusual features of the London *Entombment* result from an effort to bring a new conception of history painting, derived from antique models and explicitly articulated by Leon Battista Alberti, into alignment with the traditions and conventions of the altarpiece. In book 2 of his treatise *On Painting,* Alberti laid down the principles of what he considered "the great work of the painter," the *historia.* The mark of the Albertian *historia* is consistency – consistency of material, proportion, gesture, and theme. Consistency is guaranteed by a careful construction from part to whole: From the surfaces to the members, from the members to the bodies, and from the bodies to the entire composition. Surfaces are rendered through circumscription, which transfers complex three-dimensional shapes to the two-dimensional surface of the panel. For this task Alberti recommends the use of the veil, or squared window. When he moves on to members, he first addresses the problem of proportion and anatomy. Again, these are technical questions; they concern the rigorous application of procedures for guaranteeing accuracy.

Alberti appeals to another level of artistic judgment when he discusses, at greater length, the problem of gesture and appropriateness to function. This discussion extends to include his treatment of bodies. "We must ensure," he says, "that all the members fulfill their proper function according to the action being performed." He proposes an ancient work of relief sculpture, representing the carrying of the dead Meleager, as a paradigm of this principle (Figure 11):

They praise a *historia* in Rome, in which the dead Meleager is being carried away, because those who are bearing the burden appear to be distressed and to strain with every limb, while in the dead man there is no member that does not seem completely lifeless; they all hang loose; hands, fingers, neck, all droop inertly down, all combine together to represent death. This is the most difficult thing of all to do, for to represent the limbs of a body entirely at rest is as much the sign of an excellent artist as to render them all alive and in action.[15]

The example is artfully chosen to illustrate a limit case of the *historia*: It embraces the full spectrum of bodily expression, from the inertness of death to the activity of life. "A body is said to be alive," Alberti continues, "when it performs some movement of its own free will. Death, they say, is present when the limbs can no longer carry out the duties of life, that is, movement

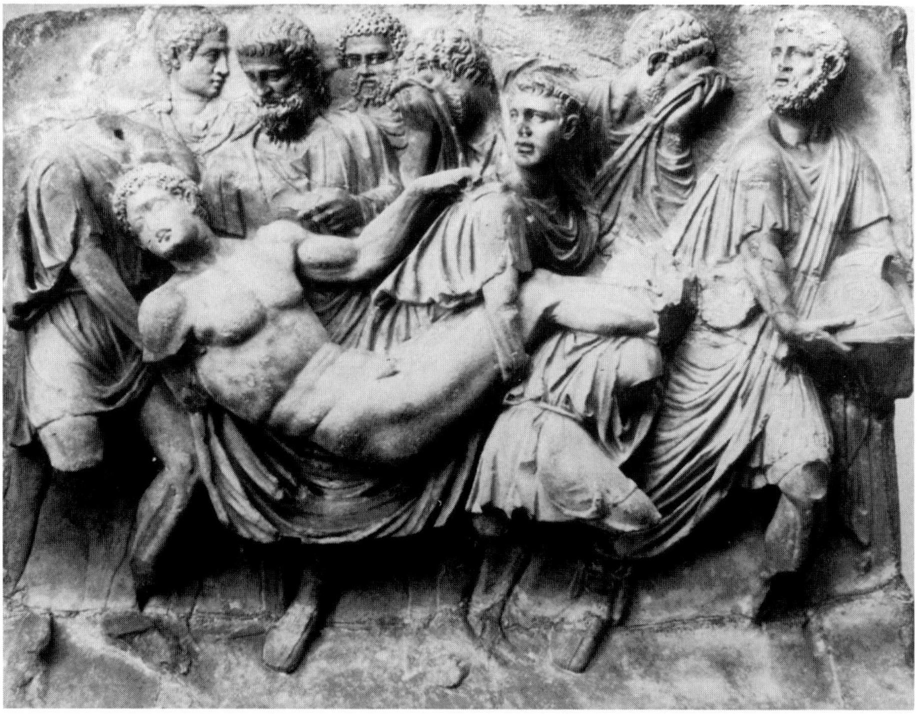

11. *The Carrying of the Dead Meleager.* Marble. Palazzo Doria-Pamphilj, Rome, Italy.

and feeling."[16] He then goes on to assert that the expression of feeling through movement is the primary task of the *historia.*

The tragedy of Meleager lies in the loss of that capacity to "carry out the duties of life" in one who was especially well endowed to perform great actions. The scene of his carrying is to be praised, in Alberti's view, because it dramatizes this loss. Meleager's inert limbs "all combine together to represent death": His body is the very sign of the incapacity to perform actions and express feeling; it represents the extinction of the capacity that makes up the *historia.* The theme of the story is the burden of that incapacity on the living: "All alive and in action," the accompanying figures "strain with every limb" to support the burden. At the most fundamental visual level, the typical antique composition – a frieze of vertical figures intersected by one horizontal – is organized by the opposition between life and death.

The historical interest of Michelangelo's London *Entombment* derives in large measure from the effort to adapt this conception to a Christian context. For a thoughtful Christian artist this adaptation could not be an easy one. The radical opposition between life and death embodied in the scene of the carrying of the dead Meleager did not square cleanly with the theology of Christ's Passion. Both the inertness of the dead Meleager and the efforts and lamentations of the living place dramatic emphasis on the irreversibility of the hero's death. The lateral orientation of the composition confirms this effect by insisting on a transitory, one-way movement out of the scene. These effects are in implicit opposition to the "figural" understanding of history developed in medieval biblical exegesis, discussed briefly above. As we saw, according to this conception historical events occur within chronological time but they also play a "suprahistorical" role within the entire Christian eschatological scheme.[17] Viewed according to this scheme, these events *had to happen* in order to fulfill their role within the figural structure of history. As a consequence, excessively to lament pitiful episodes in sacred history – for example, the expulsion of Adam and Eve or the death of Christ – is to lose sight of their ultimate meaning and importance within Christian eschatology.

This conception stands in implicit contrast to the principles of ancient tragedy. Tragedy occurs when the hero is brought down by adverse circumstances, by forces not entirely within his or her control. These external forces make it possible even for a good and heroic person – for example, Oedipus or Meleager – not to succeed in living a good life. As Martha Nussbaum has shown, ancient tragedy finds its vocation in the gap between being good and living well and on these grounds was roundly condemned by Plato. The poets, he claimed, "speak wrongly about men in matters of greatest moment" when they show the lives of good and just people being brought down in this way.[18] For Plato, a truly good person is not susceptible to this sort of serious downfall: There is no gap between being good and living a good life, and therefore tragedy teaches a falsehood.

As Nussbaum has argued, Aristotle's ethics allowed for this gap, and this made him a more sensitive critic of tragedy. That a good person could be brought down by misfortune was, he recognized, the key to tragedy's ability to arouse the emotions of pity and fear. Pity stems from the belief that the person is good and thus did not deserve the suffering.[19] Fear stems fundamentally from an identification with the hero's vulnerability, from an awareness that similar misfortunes may be visited on us. These emotional responses are not fundamentally altered even when the tragic event is understood to be part of the hero's "fate." The fact that a tragic occurrence was determined by the gods does not diminish its truly disastrous and irreversible consequences, and thus its capacity to arouse pity and fear. All of this applies to tragic events in history as well, although there, Aristotle pointed out, the effect is lessened because the events of history are more idiosyncratic, less generalized, and thus not as well suited to the process of identification.[20]

The tragic emotions do not entirely apply in the context of Christ's Passion. Tragic fear, for example, depends on identification with the hero and the attendant feeling that a similar fate could befall oneself. For such identification to develop, the hero must be mortal and, though good, not entirely perfect – conditions that are notably disrupted by Christ's special status as both man and God. There was, on the other hand, a strong equivalent to tragic pity in the late-medieval tendency to dwell on the torture and abuse inflicted on the innocent Christ. But the pitiful aspect of the Passion was, as Christian preachers and theologians repeatedly insisted, only one part of the story, for through this mortal suffering Christ achieved victory over death and brought the promise of redemption to humankind. It was, therefore, a peculiarly Christian view of history that could see events such as the expulsion of Adam and Eve from paradise, or Christ's Passion, at once as wholly lamentable and as occasions for theologically informed joy.[21]

This is not to say that Christian art, drama, and devotional literature did not pursue dramatic effects – specifically in the expression of lamentation – that sorely tested the limits of this conception. Already in the eleventh century, the propagation of the image of the dead Christ on the cross in Byzantine art was cause for much controversy and hand-wringing. The papal legate Cardinal Humbert of Silva Candida, visiting Constantinople in 1054, expressed outrage that the Greeks should venerate an "image of a dying man" on the cross. He did so because he believed that after death the body of Christ was separated from the Holy Spirit and thus was like the body of any man. The Byzantine theological tradition, on the other hand, had in various ways affirmed belief in the continued efficacy of the Holy Spirit within Christ's dead body, a belief that won the day in the west only with the advent of scholastic theology. The new image thus became a polemical means of asserting the dual nature of Christ, and Byzantine theologians strained their poetic abilities in an effort to explain how the image of a dead body also represented the living god.[22] The figure of the dead Christ, of course, won the day in the west as well as in the east, and by the late Middle Ages it had become a pervasive feature of art, drama, and devotional literature. From the thirteenth through the fifteenth century artists and writers strove to offer ever more effective descriptions of Christ's afflicted body and the lament of his mourners. In the process, of course, the original insistence on the mysterious presence of the Holy Spirit within the dead body receded from view, a state of affairs that by the early sixteenth century produced a fresh round of objections from concerned clerics. Gian Matteo Giberti, the prominent reforming bishop of Verona during the second quarter of the sixteenth century, ordered interventive restorations of paintings of the crucifixion showing blood spouting from Christ's hands, because he believed it was unfitting to show Christ in a state of agony when he had triumphed over death, resurrected, and ascended into heaven.[23]

Such interventions remained rare before the Counter Reformation. In other cases we must match the objections to the works of art. Niccolò dell'Arca's famous sculpture group of the *Lamentation* in Bologna, for example, insists on the tragedy of Christ's death to a degree that stands in potential conflict with the theologically informed attitude just described (Figure 12). That Christian thinkers of the period were capable of identifying the danger in these terms is demonstrated by a Good Friday sermon of 1496 given by Girolamo Savonarola. He complained of a form of piety – especially popular among women, he implies – that saw only pain and suffering in the Passion: "These women would like to cry with the Virgin, but don't think that she cried the way people say." The sadness of the Virgin, Savonarola argues, was

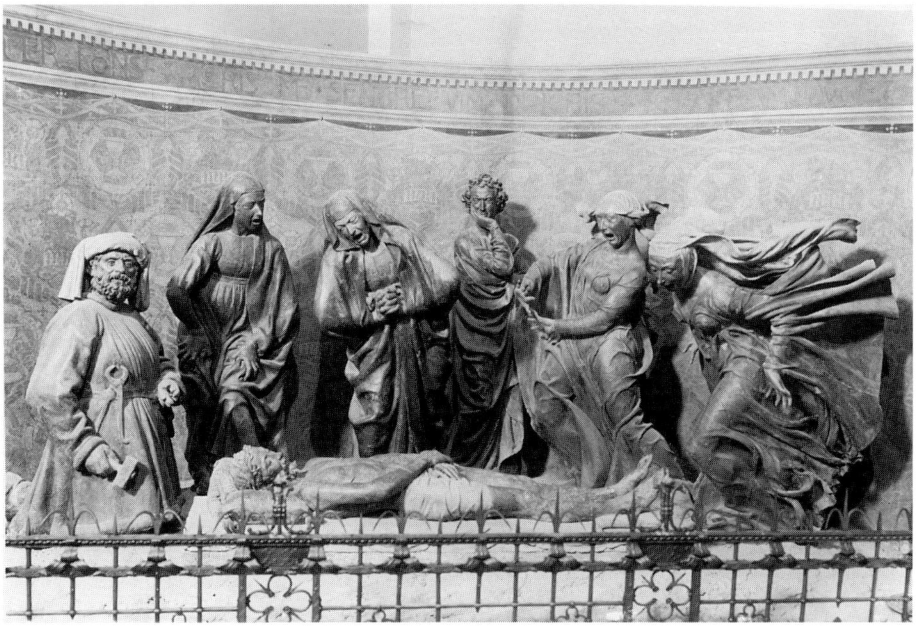

12. Niccolò dell'Arca. *Lamentation*. Marble. Santa Maria della Vita, Bologna, Italy. Alinari/Art Resource, NY.

tempered by her understanding of the place of these events within the Christian scheme of redemption. The tendency of "these women" to see the Virgin solely as a grief-stricken mother stemmed, in Savonarola's view, from a crippling eschatological myopia. His position rested on solid Christian authority: On the Gospels first of all, which are notoriously reticent about the Virgin's lament, and on a long tradition of Christian polemics against excessive, "pagan" forms of lamentation going back to St. Paul.[24] Placing himself in this tradition, Savonarola explained how it was possible for the Virgin to be paradoxically both happy and sad:

> And don't think that [the Virgin] walked through the streets screaming, her hair wild, or with indecent carriage, because she could command her sensible side not to feel pain. She went directly behind her Child, but with dignity and great modesty, shedding a few tears; she did not appear entirely sad, but happy and sad, in such a way that men marvelled at her, because she did not behave as women normally do. Nor is it true that she was consoled by Mary Magdalene; she rather consoled the Magdalene. She did not need to be consoled by the other women; instead, she consoled them by saying: Be strong, let him suffer; this is what has been prophesied.[25]

Savonarola was not the only one to mount this criticism at the time. In the opening pages of his early sixteenth-century treatise on the Passion, the popular theologian and preacher Pietro da Lucca railed against those writers and preachers who write inanities about the Passion, such as depicting the Virgin as "a woman driven insane by her excessive pain, going around from house to house and to all those places where her beloved son had been taken. . ." In doing so, he says, they "insult the perfect knowledge, modesty, and patience of the irreprehensible Mother of God," who "with so much charity wanted that her only son should redeem human nature with his harsh death."[26] Neither Savonarola nor Pietro da Lucca referred specifically to works of art, but there can be little doubt that they were aware of similar abuses in images of the period. As Savonarola spent his novice years in Bologna, in fact, it is very likely that he had direct knowledge of Niccolò dell'Arca's celebrated group. In any case, the passage just quoted gives a good idea of what he would have thought of it. Evidence presented in the following chapters will suggest that on this point Michelangelo held very similar opinions. This is not to say that his solutions would have pleased his partisans in the debate.

The principles voiced by Savonarola were heeded more often in the arena of the altarpiece. Although no clear set of rules existed to prescribe the altarpiece's functions,[27] its close association with the altar naturally encouraged an emphasis on those features of the subject that connected it to the scheme of redemption celebrated in every mass rite. That is, altarpieces were more likely to stress the "figural" significance of biblical events. This is evident, for exam-

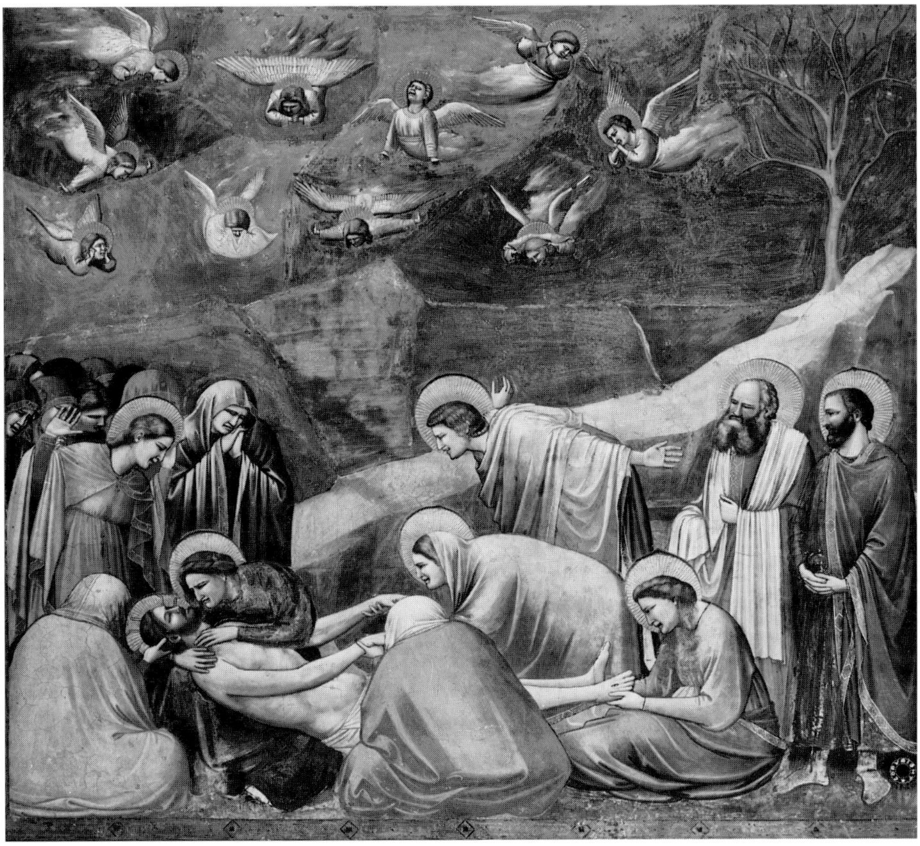

13. Giotto di Bondone, *Lamentation*. Fresco. Scrovegni Chapel, Padua, Italy. Alinari/Art Resource, NY.

ple, when one compares Giotto's *Lamentation* fresco from the Arena chapel (Figure 13) to the closely derived panel from the church of San Remigio now in the Uffizi, usually ascribed to Giottino (Figure 14). On an independent panel, the narrative scene is isolated from the serial structure of the fresco cycle. Hans Belting pointed out that the structural autonomization of the narrative subject on a single-field panel made it the focus of sustained attention different in quality from that which it received as a "station" within a sequence.[28] Belting did not elaborate on this suggestion, which touches on a fundamental distinction of modern linguistic theory. Ferdinand de Saussure described two axes of language, the syntagmatic and the associative, which he suggested corresponded to two forms of mental activity. The syntagmatic axis is the "horizontal" combination or sequence of signs, such as we have in a sentence; the associative axis establishes "vertical" relations between any one of the units and other similar units of the system. Saussure adopted the example of architecture: This Doric column stands in contiguous, "syntagmatic" relation to other parts of the building, such as the architrave, but it can also be compared to other types of columns, such as Ionic and Corinthian, in a relation of potential substitution, an associative relation, what later semioticians would call a paradigmatic relation.[29] Roman Jakobson developed the distinc-

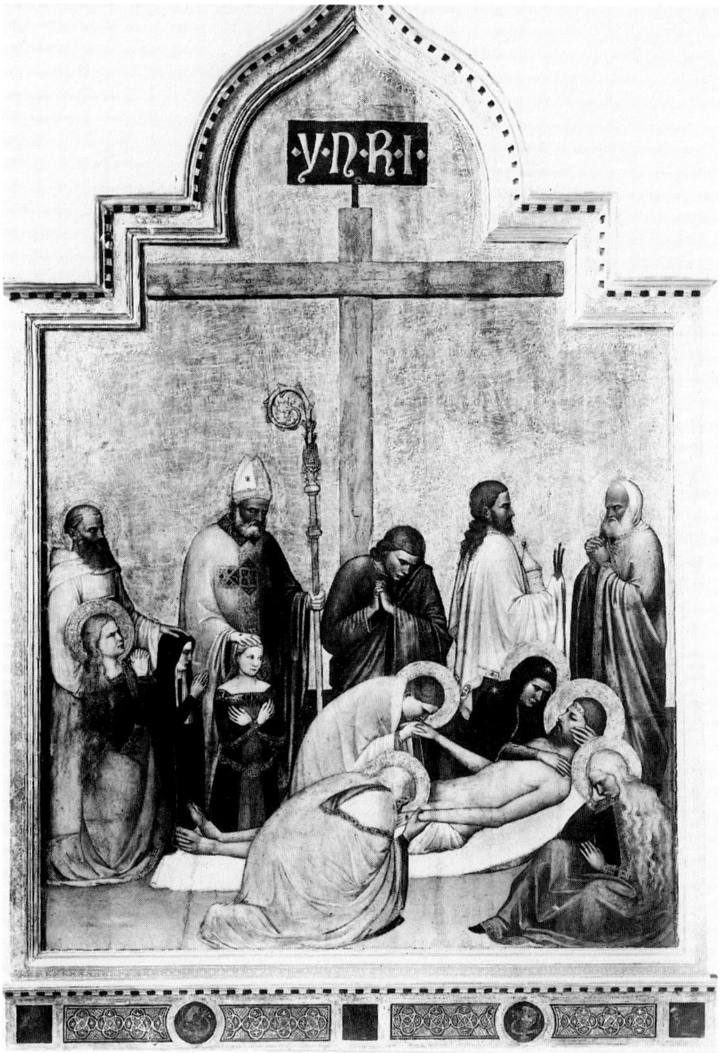

14. Giottino, *Lamentation*. Panel. Uffizi, Florence, Italy. Alinari/Art Resource, NY.

tion into one between the metonymic (syntagmatic) and the metaphoric (associative) and suggested its application to a wide array of cultural expressions – pointing, for example, to the preference for metaphorical or associative relations in Romantic literature, in contrast to the metonymic or syntagmatic proclivities of Realist narrative.[30]

The distinction can also be found in Christian ritual and thought, for example in the contrast between the literal level and the allegorical levels, or between history and figure, in biblical exegesis.[31] Giotto's fresco cycle in Padua offers a rich combination of both modes of signification: One can read it "horizontally" as a chronological sequence, and one can also read it "vertically" and find figural, or paradigmatic, associations that connect chronologically disparate scenes.[32] Large-scale narrative painting on panel, as it developed in fourteenth-century Italy, brought the two functions together in a newly condensed relationship.[33] Giottino's panel in the Uffizi, based on Giotto's fresco, provides a very clear case in point. As A. M. Birkmeyer showed, the image suppresses the temporal and geographical references of the historical narrative: The landscape setting of Giotto's fresco is replaced by a gold ground and a neutral stage. The great cross that occupies the gable structure "is less the Cross from which Christ has been taken down, than, in the symbolic sense, one of the *arma Christi*."[34] Moreover, on the left side of the cross appear patron saints and donors "of later days." These features break open the internal consistency of the historical narrative and facilitate its "suprahistorical" application in the context of Christian ritual. The historical actors, particularly the Mary at Christ's feet, serve as models or "figures" of prayer and devotion for the Christian worshippers kneeling near her – a relation of similarity that stood at the basis of a widespread late-medieval devotional strategy that Frank Büttner has termed *imitatio pietatis*.[35] The painting is thus designed specifically to operate at what biblical exegetes designated as the third or "tropological" level of meaning, by which the biblical event is connected to the heart and mind of the worshipper.[36]

Similar principles are at work in Pietro Perugino's Uffizi *Lamentation*, painted for the church of Santa Chiara in 1495, although here we see them adapted to the conditions of late fifteenth-century painting (Figure 15).

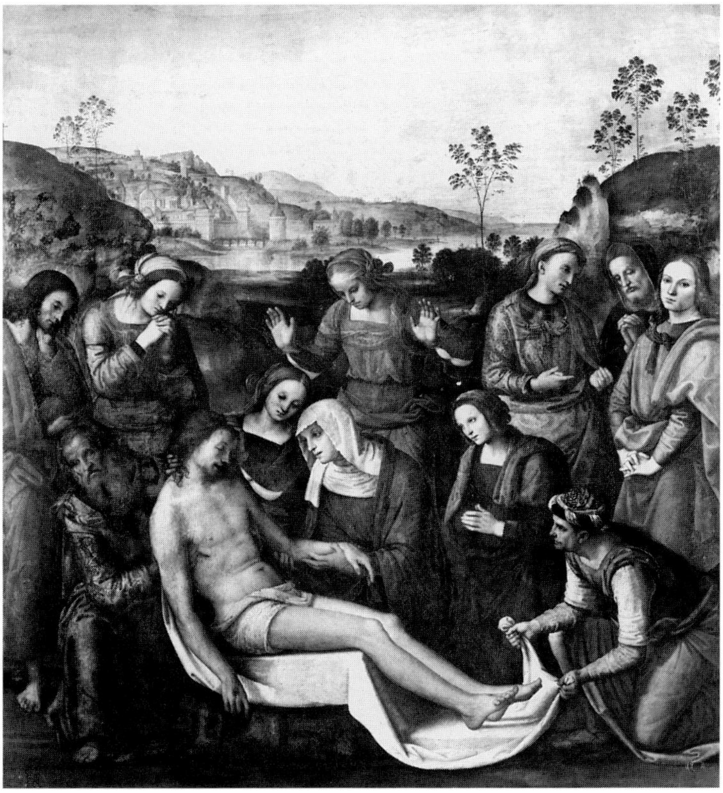

15. Pietro Perugino, *Lamentation*. Panel. Galleria Palatina, Palazzo Pitti, Florence, Italy. Alinari/Art Resource, NY.

Disruptions of internal historical consistency such as we find in the Giottino-attributed panel would have been considered archaic in Perugino's time, and so Perugino opted instead for a more gentle expressive restraint throughout. Active, "momentary" gestures – especially gestures of dramatic lamentation – are muted or entirely absent, and subsidiary relationships among the figures are kept to a minimum. Almost every figure establishes a separate and meditative relationship to the dead Christ, who is shown propped on a square (altar-like) block covered with a white (altar cloth–like) winding sheet. The muting of lament assimilates the attitudes of the historical actors to the worshipful activity of the viewer before the painting's real altar. This altarpiece's obedience to the principles voiced by Savonarola might be more than coincidental, as the principal patron of this church is known to have been associated with the Dominican preacher.[37]

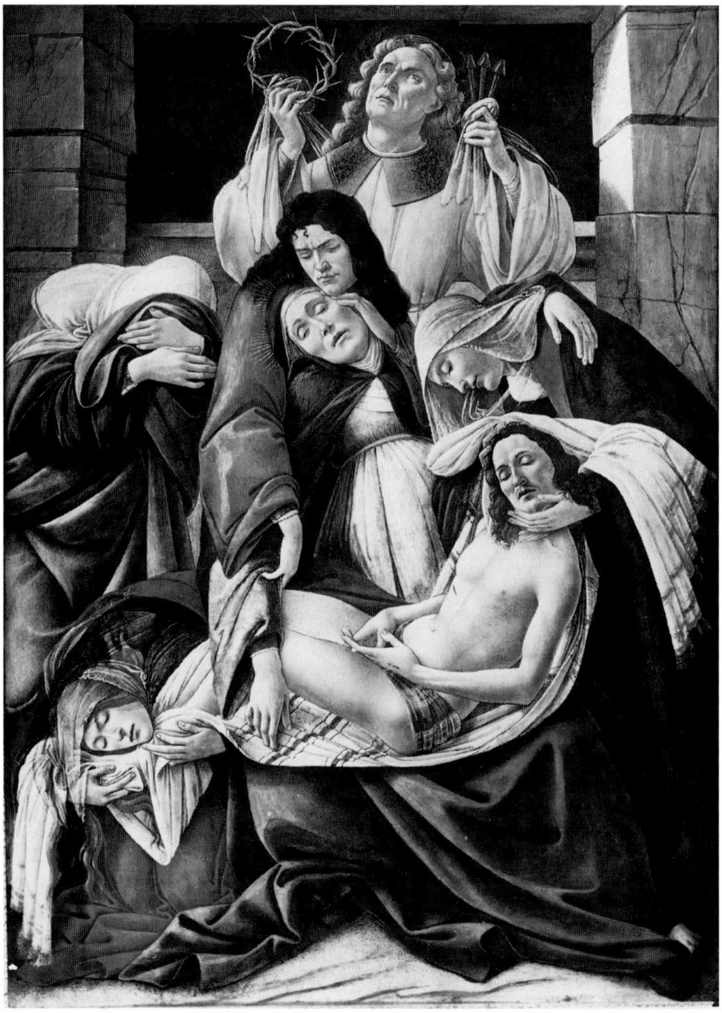

16. Sandro Botticelli, *Lamentation*. Panel. Museo Poldi Pezzoli, Milan, Italy. Alinari/Art Resource, NY.

Things are stretched to a point of greater tension in Sandro Botticelli's *Lamentation* in the Poldi Pezzoli Museum in Milan, which is informed by a much stronger interest in antique-inspired expressive motifs, or what Aby Warburg called pathos formulas (Figure 16).[38] The painting shows several dramatic gestures of lamentation, at least two of which have distinguished antique pedigrees: The woman to the right cradles Christ's head just as Andromache held the dead Hector in the *Iliad,* and the figure to the left veils her face – a motif invented by Timanthes to express unimaginable grief, for which he was celebrated both by ancient writers and by Alberti.[39] Even while introducing these motifs, however, Botticelli manages to maintain a significant degree of emotional restraint. We see no wild hair, no flailing limbs, no screaming faces of the kind seen in other *all'antica* works, such as those by Donatello (see Figure 8) and Niccolò dell'Arca (Figure 12). The faces, with the exception perhaps of the figure at the top, conform to the prescriptions for measured lament voiced by the church fathers and repeated, in Botticelli's day, by Savonarola. Viewed in this light, the Homeric and Timanthes-derived motifs may perhaps be read as instances of a very refined sense of decorum: They are highly expressive antique motifs that could be considered not to violate the theologically informed code of lamentation.

All of these works are focused on the immobile body of Christ, a feature that facilitated their participation within "figural" structures appropriate to the liturgical context of altarpieces. The challenge was of an entirely different order in the case of Alberti's proposal for a *historia* modeled on the scene of the carrying of the dead Meleager. The crucial difference lies in the representation of movement, which emphasizes both historicity and irreversibility. This much is suggested, at least, by the fact that nothing like it was attempted on the principal panels of altarpieces during the fifteenth century.[40]

THE ALTARPIECE AS A DOMINANT FORM

Alberti's challenge was indeed taken up in the fifteenth century, but within the more experimental and flexible medium of engraving, in Andrea Mantegna's famous print of the *Entombment,* where the Meleager model is adapted to the Christian subject (Figure 17). Large, public panel painting was controlled by more formal conventions than was the new print medium, and thus it offered greater resistance to this conception of history painting. A revealing example of the reception of the Alberti–Mantegna tradition within this format is offered by a Foppa-school panel in Pavia, where elements of Mantegna's composition are clearly quoted but are adapted to a more conventional *Lamentation* formula (Figure 18). This state of affairs was due in large part to the generic control that the institution of the altarpiece

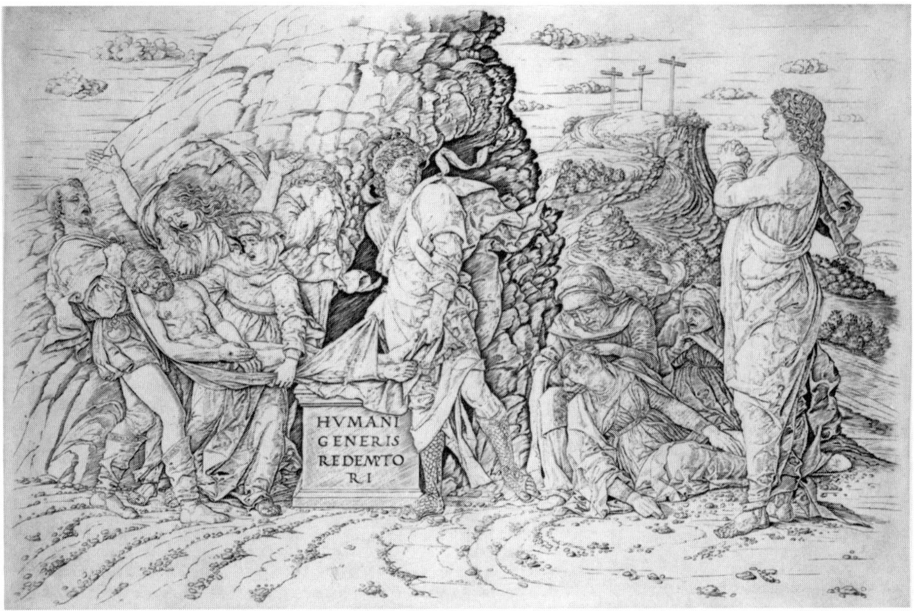

17. Andrea Mantegna, *Entombment.* Engraving. Rosenwald Collection, © 1999 Board of Trustees, National Gallery of Art, Washington, D.C., U.S..

exerted over the format. This is not to claim that large panels were not occasionally, and even quite often, painted for other purposes. It is to argue that the altarpiece fulfilled the role of the "dominant" in the sense intended by Roman Jakobson:[41] Not only was it, in most places, numerically the most common type of painting done in this format in the fifteenth century[42] but it was, more important, governed by a set of conventions that were more coherent and powerful than those controlling any other venue for large panel painting.

The dominance of the altarpiece is most clearly demonstrated in the morphological development of the format: It was through the metamorphosis of the altarpiece that panel painting developed, in the 1430s, the familiar form of the rectangular picture surrounded by an independent frame, the *quadro,* which then became the paradigm for easel painting as such.[43] No one would deny that there were square and unified panels before the 1430s, and in other categories besides the altarpiece. But, as Max Ernst once said, *"Ce n'est pas la colle qui fait le collage."*[44] The crucial structural claim for the later history easel painting was not the square shape of the panel per se but the idea that the pictorial fiction is notionally independent of the material structure of the picture. This idea was first systematically asserted through the application of mathematical perspective in altarpieces of the late 1430s and early 1440s, such as those by Fra Angelico and Domenico Veneziano.[45] It is what crucially distinguishes these experiments from other paintings on rectangular formats, such as *spallièra* painting.[46] In the new brand of altarpiece the rectangular format was not imposed by the furniture but was an abstract delimitation of the pictorial field. It represented an arbitrary cutoff, a slice through the pyramid

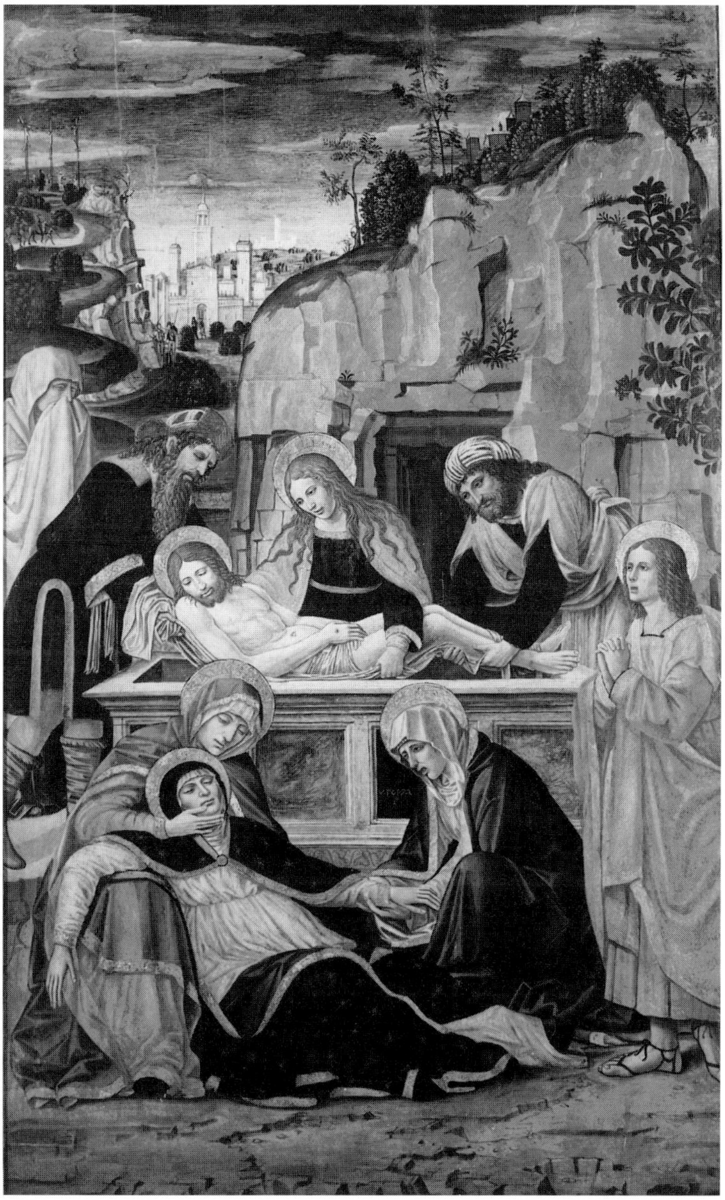

18. School of Vincenzo Foppa, *Lamentation*. Panel. Malaspina Gallery, Pavia, Italy.

of vision, a cropping of a notional reality that exists independent of it. Later, once the format was established and the notion of the "picture" had become normative, the claim of pictorial autonomy came as a matter of course without the need for rigorous perspectival constructions.

But formats were not independent of institutions. The main venue for the new kind of picture until the early sixteenth century was the altarpiece, and this fact determined the uses to which the format was put. The dominance of the altarpiece was so strong that it affected the nature even of nonreligious painting carried out in this format: It has been observed that altarpiece conventions are at work in Luca Signorelli's now-lost *Pan,* as well as in Botticelli's *Primavera* and *Birth of Venus.*[47] New kinds of painting had first to lay claim to the surfaces of large panels, and this meant that they had to contend with the resistance posed by the conventions of the altarpiece.[48] Whether strictly derived from him or not, several features in line with Alberti's other proposals for painting, such as those concerning perspective and proportion, were introduced into altar painting of the fifteenth century, but not the conception of *historia* embodied in the Meleager model. When Michael Baxandall correlated Albertian principles with the rise of the rectangular, single-field, perspectivally constructed picture format usually referred to as the Renaissance *pala,* he might have added that a significant aspect of Alberti's proposals for painting was held back even in this format.[49]

Michelangelo's unfinished London *Entombment* was an ingenious, and ultimately frustrated, effort to effectuate this merger. His fundamental move was to adapt the lateral conception to a structure of frontal presentation that would conform to altarpiece conventions of frontality and symmetry. This was not merely a formal question. Such a solution not only brought important changes to the treatment of the theme but also occasioned a reevaluation of the very function of the altarpiece. Before embarking on this argument, however, it is necessary to address some reasonable initial doubts. Given the obvious differences between Michelangelo's painting on the one hand and the Meleager–Mantegna tradition on the other, what is there to connect it to these precedents, or to Alberti's proposals, at all? Why not simply see it in relation to the often-cited panels by Fra Angelico and Rogier van der Weyden (see Figures 25 and 30, discussed below) to which it is compositionally closer? The main feature that connects Michelangelo's panel to the tradition discussed in this chapter is the preoccupation with ideas of conveyance and trajectory, and thus with the mechanics of support and carrying. This dynamism sets it apart from Fra Angelico's and Rogier's panels, which both show a stationary group. The concern with figures in movement was, moreover, as Warburg saw, bound up with the revival of antique figural formulas, a concern that is largely absent from Fra Angelico's and Rogier's panels. Moreover, there is a good deal of evidence, as I attempt to show in chapter 4, to suggest that Raphael himself responded to Michelangelo's panel in the making of his own *Entombment* now in the Borghese Gallery, and thus understood it in relation to the tradition of Meleager, Alberti, and Mantegna.

But there is even more direct evidence: A nude pen study that Michael Hirst has plausibly connected to the London panel shows, I believe, Michelangelo working directly from Mantegna's print (Figure 19).[50] It reveals Michelangelo's efforts to adapt Mantegna's lateral composition into a new configuration. Pointing to the pose, and above all to the downward gaze cast over an upraised shoulder, Hirst proposed that the drawing reveals an early idea for the figure of

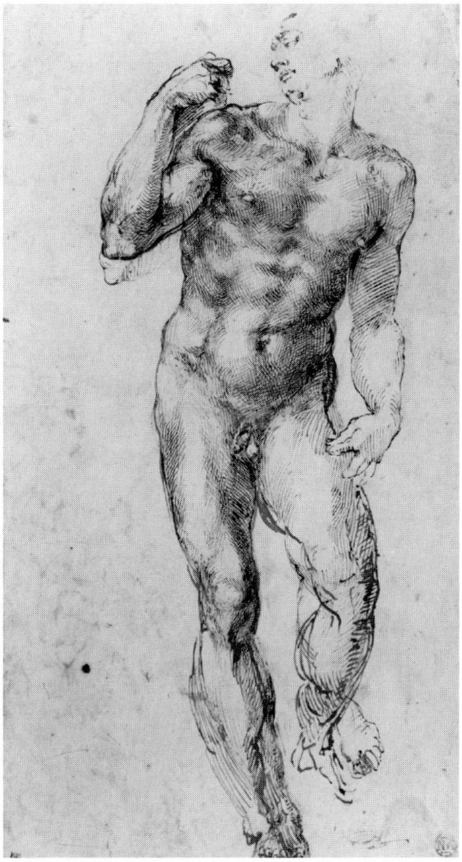

19. Michelangelo, *Male figure study.* Drawing. Louvre, Paris, France. © Réunion des Musées Nationaux.

St. John, to Christ's left in the painting. The drawing was, however, clearly made before Michelangelo had definitively settled on the frontal conception of the theme. The figure is derived from the crucial central turning figure in Mantegna's print. Like that figure, Michelangelo's stands on his right leg and is shown poised between a frontal orientation and a lateral direction. The figure seems to be designed to be holding the winding cloth in his right hand and locking it over his right shoulder. His head is turned to gaze back over this shoulder, presumably at the body of Christ. This motif was preserved, in reverse, in the final painting, where the figure was put on the other side of Christ. In the drawing, however, the implied slinging of the winding cloth over the shoulder makes it unlikely that the figure is engaged in a backward movement, as it was finally worked out in the painting. Rather, the figure is shown looking over his shoulder while stepping forward. This progression is equivocal: The stepping leg shows several pentimenti, which alternate between an oblique and a frontal view. The drawing is probably not operating within a fully worked out conception: It shows Michelangelo attempting to think it through, as it were, from this turning figure outward. He was exploring the opportunity for torsion and movement occasioned by the motif of carrying but had not yet resolved its implications for the larger composition. It is hard to imagine, for example, what this figure's posture implies for the body of Christ. A lateral position, with the body enclosed lengthwise in the winding cloth as in a hammock, seems to be the most likely possibility, although it is not made clear.[51]

In the painting, the composition has been organized so that Christ is presented upright and frontally. The resulting solution offers effective resistance to several basic Albertian principles. First, as we have seen, Michelangelo subverted the primary lesson of the Meleager model by qualifying the emphasis on the deadness of the body: Christ is being carried with great effort and strain and yet he is shown upright, without wounds, and ambiguously suspended. Second, Michelangelo qualified Alberti's conception of the picture as an open window through which we see figures freely moving in space. In contrast to Mantegna's print, where we see complex figural overlappings, here the figures are kept from overlapping by an external imperative that operates at the level of the picture surface. Third, the figures who are not carrying are suspended in undramatic attitudes: One turns away, the other meditates, and the third assumes an attitude of veneration. These are barely movements and do not conform to Alberti's principles for dramatic response. Fourth, and most important, Michelangelo broke open what Alois Riegl called the internal unity (and thus the temporality) of the narrative, and produced an "outer unity" or "coordination" with the viewer.[52] This structural reformulation transformed the historical episode of the transport of Christ into a figural *transitus* that moves over and across history.

The resistance to the Albertian model in Michelangelo's panel results from the effort to accomodate Alberti's conception to the implicit demands of altar images and, thus, to the ritual setting of Christian worship. The key move was to adapt the subject to altarpiece conventions of symmetry and frontality. The frontal presentation of Christ, in turn, overtly attaches the image to the tradition of the Man of Sorrows (or, as it was known in the period, *imago pietatis*) – a cult image tradition with archaic associations to the Christian altar and to the mystery of the Eucharist.[53] Michelangelo responded directly to two significant adaptations of this tradition, a predella panel by Fra Angelico in Munich and a larger panel by Rogier van der Weyden now in the Uffizi, both of them Medici commissions (see Figures 25 and 30). These works are noteworthy – and were evidently appreciated in their time – for having adapted the traditional image in light of developments in modern narrative painting. Michelangelo's painting pushed this effort further, by attempting a more complex narrative staging and incorporating an explicitly antique-inspired idiom of figural movement – in short, by coordinating the Man of Sorrows tradition with the demands of the Albertian *historia* as illustrated, for example, in Mantegna's engraving. The resulting solution not only brought radical changes to the conception of history painting proposed by Alberti but it also offered a critical reevaluation of the function of the altarpiece and a poignant commentary on the status of this central institution of Christian image making circa 1500. To understand this critical response, it is necessary first to examine the panels of Fra Angelico and Rogier van der Weyden in relation to their respective traditions.

CHAPTER TWO

Man of Sorrows and Entombment

FRA ANGELICO AND THE MAN OF SORROWS IN ITALY

The image of the Man of Sorrows was transmitted to the West via Byzantine icons that began to be imported in large numbers in the twelfth and thirteenth centuries.[1] The Byzantine examples, such as the famous mosaic in Santa Croce in Gerusalemme (Figure 20), typically show a figure of the dead Christ represented upright but not nailed to the cross and thus not attached to any one episode of the Passion narrative. The image fuses the upright image of the Christ of the Crucifixion with the image of the lying Christ on *epitaphioi,* or altar cloths.[2] In its bust-length format it also resembles icons of the Pantocrator. The paradox of Christ's dead but standing figure expresses a mysterious divine efficacy within the dead body, suggesting the life-giving virtues of Christ's sacrifice. The Byzantine Man of Sorrows was one of several images developed to meet the changing demands of the Eastern Passion liturgy, which from the eleventh century on had been greatly enriched by a series of new texts and rites. Its "synthetic" qualities enabled this single image to serve for the various readings and prayers that composed the new Passion services.

After it was introduced into the West with the importation of Eastern icons, the image soon achieved enormous popularity. Commonly called *imago pietatis,* it brought a new physical and emotional immediacy to the representation of the mystery of Christ's sacrifice. The image was, indeed, quite early and quite often associated with the sacrifice of the Mass.[3] The reality mysteriously present in the bread, in its daily offering on the altar, was commonly visualized by late-medieval mystics in the form presented by this image. At the elevation of the Host, for example, a vision of Christ appeared to the thir-

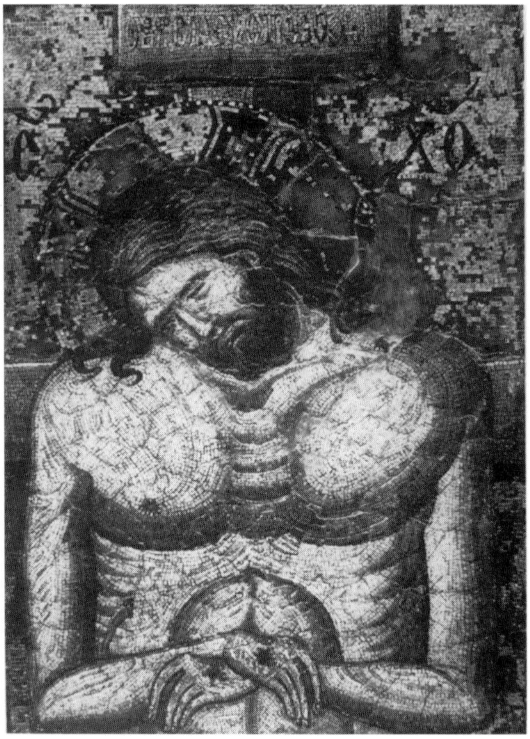

20. *Man of Sorrows.* Mosaic. Santa Croce in Gerusalemme, Rome, Italy.

teenth-century mystic Angela of Foligno under the aspect of the *imago pietatis*: "The image of the blessed Lord and crucified one appeared to me, as if just taken down from the cross."[4]

The image thus made the appeal to the emotions a powerful vehicle of Christian dogma.[5] In reviewing the double meaning of the word *pietàs* in its association with this image, Hans Belting showed that the image encapsulated key elements of the Christian doctrine of redemption: *pietàs* refers, reciprocally, both to the empathetically aroused piety of the beholder and to the mercy of the Redeemer. The exploration of empathy-inducing effects was thus from the beginning a constitutive part of the image's meaning and function, and this in turn encouraged its remarkably free and open-ended development.[6] From the original Byzantine bust formula, it was expanded throughout the fourteenth and fifteenth centuries by the inclusion of additional figures and gestures, and by the introduction of increasingly aggressive devices of pictorial staging.[7] The elaboration of illusionistic and rhetorical devices was, indeed, the logical consequence of the claim to immediate visual experience celebrated by the image. It is thus not possible to explain the development of the image, every step of the way, by reference to specific theological prescription. As the theologian Giovanni Andrea Gilio said with great clarity in 1564, it is difficult to give a hard and fast reason why images should be so and not otherwise, because apart from Guillaume Durand's *Rationale* "we do not have any rule or law, except what the custom of painters [*la consuetudine de' pittori*] before Michelangelo has demonstrated."[8] Changes resulted from processes internal to the practice of image making and were then canonized and standardized by patterns of patronage and reception.[9] This was true even in cases where the changes carried important theological consequences, as Gilio recognized and as we shall see below. The following account of the reinterpretation of the image before Michelangelo must therefore proceed by direct analysis of the images themselves, studied in relation to their respective traditions.

The Eucharistic associations of the Man of Sorrows image were made explicit, and given widespread currency, by the legend of the Mass of St. Gregory. The linking of Gregory with the mystery of the Mass probably derived from the popular tradition that he was the first author of the *Ordo Romanus.*[10] According to the legend, Christ appeared on the altar of St. Gregory the Great in response to his prayer for a sign to convince an unbeliever of the truth of the Eucharist. The icon in Santa Croce in Gerusalemme (see Figure 20), despite the fact that it was a relatively recent import, was soon claimed to be the image originally commissioned by St. Gregory the Great in commemoration of the event.[11] On the basis of this legend, huge indulgences were attached to the Man of Sorrows image in the late Middle Ages: In the fourteenth century seven *Pater nosters*, seven *Ave Marias* and seven short prayers called the "prayers of St. Gregory" said in front of the *imago pietatis* obtained a true pardon of 6,000 years in Purgatory; by the fifteenth century the sum had been inflated to 46,000 years.[12] Before the advent of the Man of Sorrows image, however, the Gregory legend existed in a different form: In the thirteenth-century *Golden Legend,* for example, Christ's real presence in the sacrament is manifested by the appearance of Christ's finger upon the altar.[13] Emile Mâle, betraying the iconographer's tendency to make images dependent on texts, asserted that the legend of the miraculous Mass does not appear in the *Golden Legend.*[14] It does, but in this earlier version that has nothing to do with the visual tradition of the Man of Sorrows, and that thus cannot be adduced as a textual source for the image. The miraculous legend was visualized in the form of the Man of Sorrows only in the course of the fourteenth century – that is, after the importation of the Byzantine icon formula – and it was only then, through the proliferation of images depicting the miracle, that the legend achieved its vast popularity. In other words, the image gave new form and life to a legend, which in turn elaborated an account of the origin of the image.[15]

The identification of the Man of Sorrows with the consecrated Host of the Mass led to its frequent use on altarpieces, where it remained, however, confined to subordinate zones.[16] Often called a *pietà,* the image was commonly found in the predellas and upper registers of Italian altarpieces.[17] An early example of the Tuscan type, Simone Martini's Pisa polyptych of 1319, corresponds to the model of the Byzantine bust-length panels with Chirst's arms crossed over his chest. In a slightly later predella by a follower of Bernardo

Daddi (Figure 21), the figure of Christ is shown in half length, with his arms held open and his outstretched hands taken by St. John and the Virgin. The flanking Virgin and St. John were a part of the earliest Italian Man of Sorrows images.[18] The Daddi school predella, and many others that are similar in composition, "motivated" the presence of the two flanking figures by linking them to Christ via gestures drawn from narratives such as the deposition.[19] Christ's open-armed pose and the attitudes of St. John and the Virgin, for example, show similarities to the monumental sculptural groups of the late thirteenth and early fourteenth centuries.[20]

In the Daddi-school panel (see Figure 21) we also see the half-length format "rationalized" by having Christ submerged from the waist down in a sarcophagus. This feature, another effect of the tendency toward narrative contextualization, was to become a standard element of Man of Sorrows images in Italy throughout the following century.[21] It carried special implications when used on altars, and especially when placed in the predella immediately above the altar, as it often was in Italian altarpieces. In this position, the Man of Sorrows image was assimilated to representations of the Mass of St. Gregory, where the figure of Christ was often shown with his upper half rising up from the back of the altar (see Figure 28). The idea of immersion was quite explicitly explored in countless sacrament tabernacles, where the half-length figure of Christ is shown submerged in the recess containing the Host, an eloquent means of asserting his consubstantiality with the sacrament. These ideas came together in altarpieces that carried a sacrament tabernacle in their principal fields, such as a mid-fifteenth-century Veronese example in the Isabella Stewart Gardner Museum[22] (Figure 22).

In most Florentine altarpieces of the fifteenth century, however, the Man of Sorrows appeared in the predella, which, in contrast to the windowlike principal field, was understood to belong to the physical framework of the altarpiece itself and thus to be in more direct physical relation to the altar below. In the predellas of several late-Quattrocento altarpieces in the church of Santo Spirito in Florence, the Man of Sorrows is shown half submerged in a tomb that is not

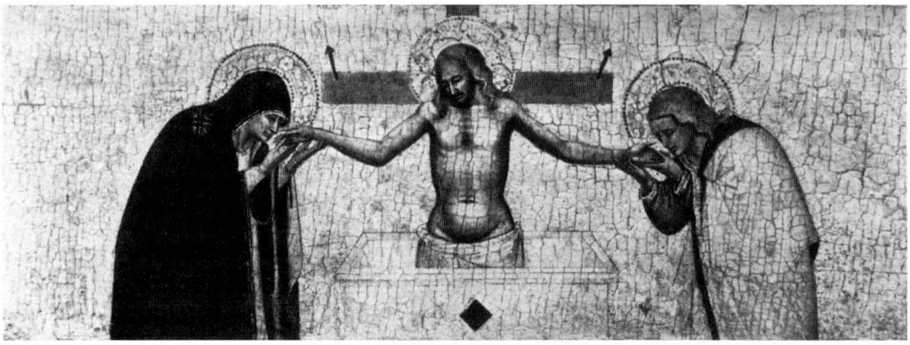

21. Follower of Bernardo Daddi, *Man of Sorrows*. Predella panel. Formerly Lycett Green Collection, London.

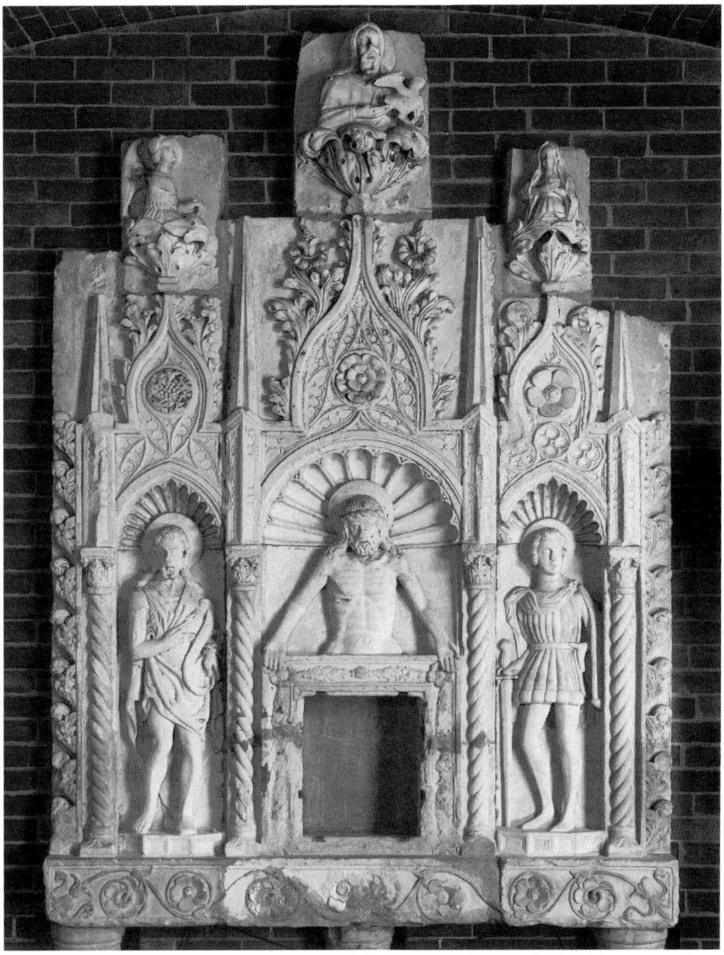

22. Bartolomeo Giolfino, *Tabernacle altarpiece with Man of Sorrows.* Marble. Isabella Stewart Gardner Museum, Boston, U.S..

oblong, as one would expect a tomb to be, but blocklike and squarish – indeed, strikingly similar to the real altar in front of it (Figure 23). These altars, like almost all from the period, themselves have a square recess carved into their top surfaces. This recess, often described by liturgists as a *sepulchrum,* was designed to hold the relics that were necessary for the altar's consecration.[23] Often pieces of the consecrated Host were added to the relics for the purposes of consecration; by the thirteenth century the Host was regularly used as a substitute in the absence of relics.[24] If the altar as a whole was not consecrated, the stone covering the *sepulchrum* served as the consecration stone and was meant to provide an area large enough to hold the chalice for the wine and the Host.[25] The precinct of the *sepulchrum* thus served both to contain and support the body of Christ. A woodcut from a Savonarola tract explicitly connects this element of the altar apparatus with the *imago pietatis*: It shows the Man of Sorrows standing on this very stone, the metaphorical tomb slab, effectively displacing chalice and Host with his physical presence (Figure 24). The image

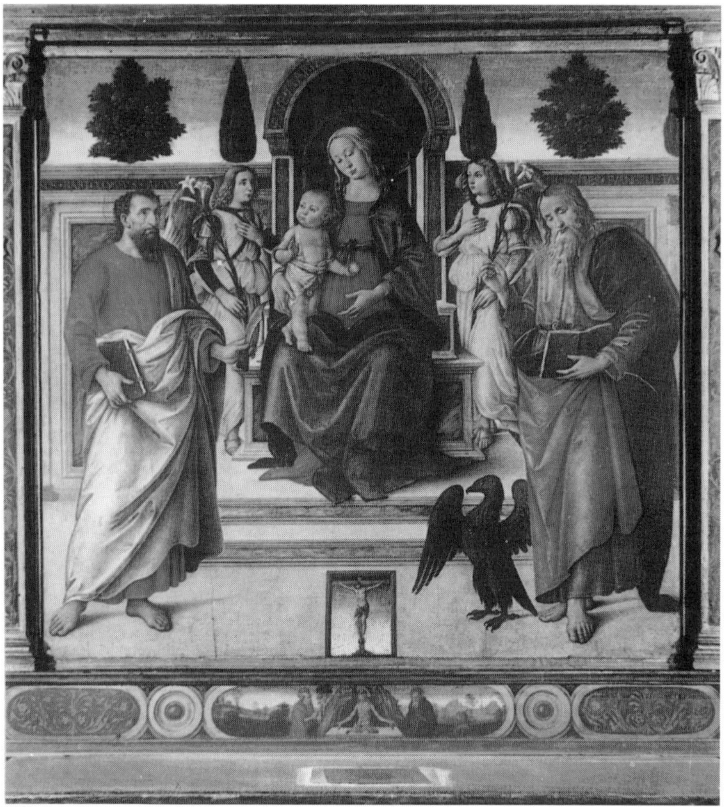

23. Master of Santo Spirito, *Madonna and Child and Saints.* Panel. Santo Spirito, Florence, Italy.

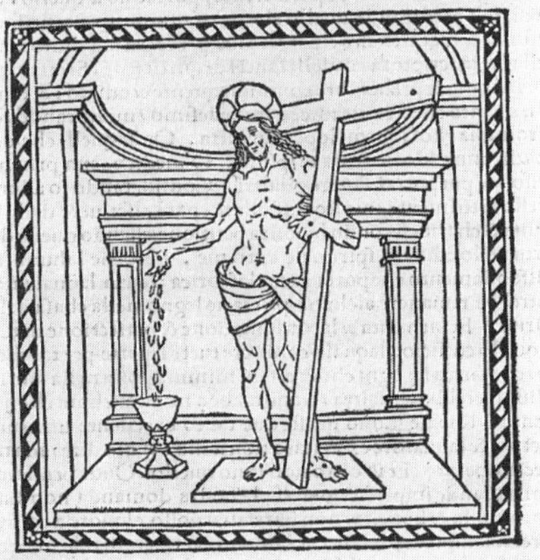

¶ Breue & utile tractato della Humilita / composto da frate Hieronymo da Ferrara dellordine delli predicatori.

GRande & intolerabile presumptione mi pare dilectissima in Christo Iesu / ingerirsi & insegnare ad altri quello / che per se lhuomo non intende / maxime nelle cose morali / & nella uia della uirtu: nellaquale non sipuo perfectamente esser docto / chi non lha in se medesimo per lungo & continuo exercitio prouata. Et molto piu nella uia della perfectione della uita spirituale e / insopportabile la / Superbia di choloro / che ardischono insegniarla ad altri / & mai non conobbono / non dico pur che habbino gustata in se medesimi una minima scintilla di quella. Si perche a tutti

a

24. Florentine, *Man of Sorrows.* Woodcut. By permission of the Houghton Library, Harvard University, Cambridge, Mass., U.S..

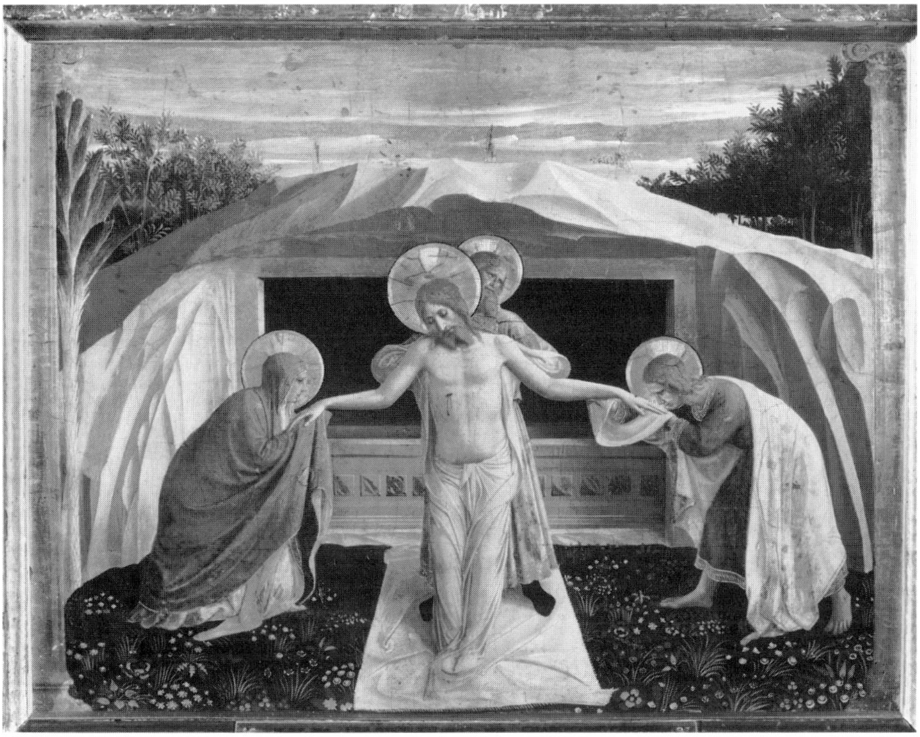

25. Fra Angelico, *Christ at the Tomb.* Predella panel. Alte Pinakothek, Munich, Germany. Scala/Art Resource, NY.

in the predella, therefore, claimed a direct analogy to the Eucharist consecrated on the altar before it.

Fra Angelico inherited and reformed this tradition in the central predella panel of the altarpiece he painted for the church of San Marco about 1440 (Figure 25). In the somewhat earlier altarpiece of the *Coronation of the Virgin,* painted for the church of San Domenico in Fiesole, Fra Angelico had introduced a largely conventional *Man of Sorrows* in this same position (Figure 26). In the *Coronation* predella, Christ is shown standing in the tomb surrounded by the instruments of the Passion. Before the tomb sit St. John and the Virgin, at a scale different from the figure of Christ, almost as part of the system of Passion symbols arrayed around him. In the central predella panel of the San Marco altarpiece Fra Angelico adapted the traditional Man of Sorrows scheme to stricter standards of scenic consistency: The figure of Christ is shown standing *before* the tomb, and the active presence of the other figures is "motivated" by the narrative of Christ's entombment.

Certain developments in contemporary painting already pointed in this direction. For example, in a nearly contemporary predella panel by the Master of the Osservanza, now in Dijon, the traditional half-length Man of Sorrows in the sarcophagus is set within the cave described in the Gospel texts. Christ is visible through a square opening, and St. John and the Virgin are shown sitting outside it. A larger panel by Filippo Lippi, in the Poldi Pezzoli Museum

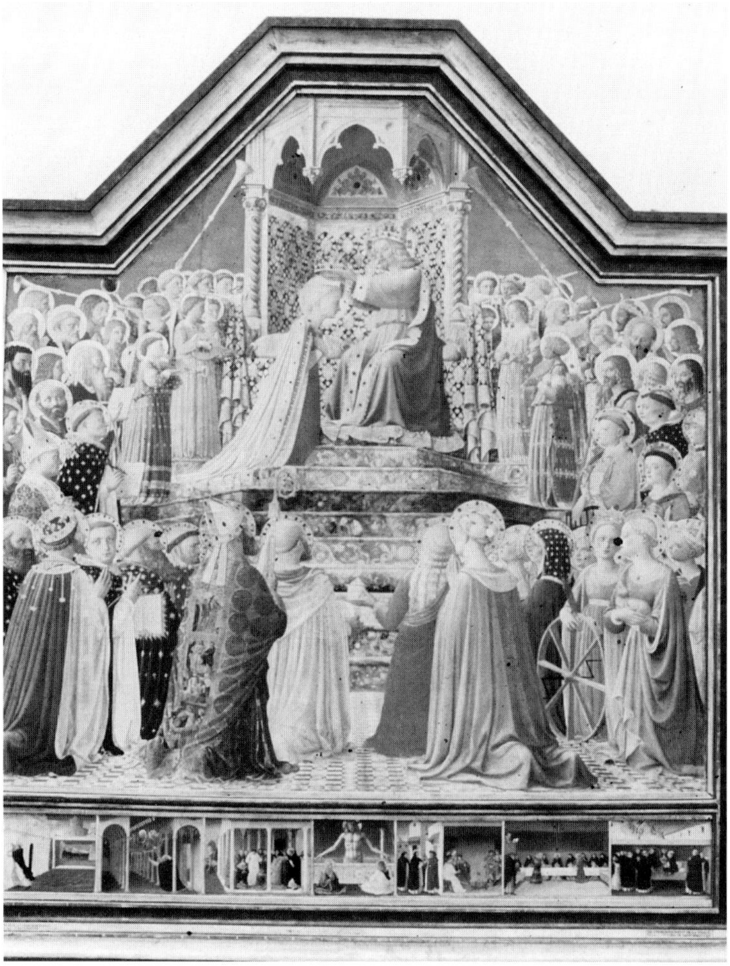

26. Fra Angelico, *Coronation of the Virgin,* detail of predella. Panel. Louvre, Paris, France. © Réunion des Musées Nationaux.

in Milan, shows the Man of Sorrows at three-quarter length, standing in the tomb but supported by John and Mary; the conception thus approaches a scene of entombment.[26] At the same time, and actuated by similar purposes, Jacopo Bellini was also experimenting with expanded narrative settings for the half-length *Man of Sorrows* (Figure 27). Significantly, he elaborated these experiments in his drawing books but did not attempt them in his formal finished paintings.[27] The "naturalization" of the *Man of Sorrows* into a consistent narrative pictorial conception corresponds in large measure to what Robert Suckale has described as a late-medieval *"allmähliche Depotenzierung des Zeichens,"* an *"umwandlung der Zeichen in eine immer stärker bildliche Form,"* a trend that he associated with an emerging conception of high art that was becoming increasingly differentiated from the visual forms of folk piety.[28]

Fra Angelico's San Marco predella took this effort to new lengths by transforming the *Man of Sorrows* into an entirely consistent entombment scene.

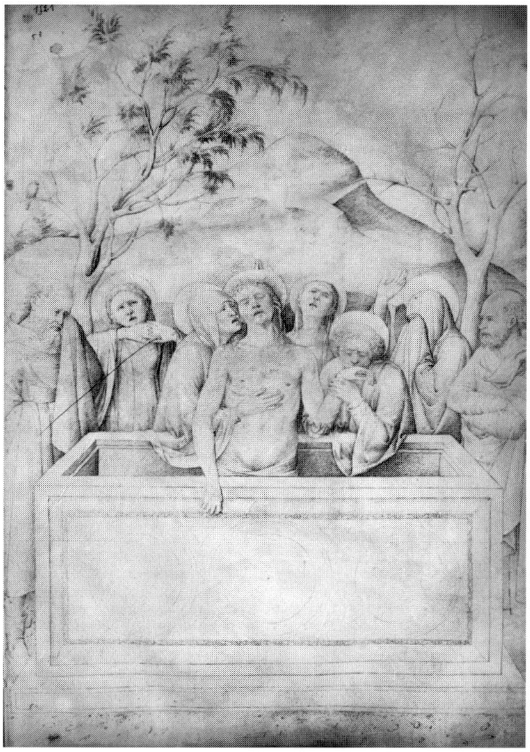

27. Jacopo Bellini, *Man of Sorrows-Lamentation*. Drawing book, f. 54. Louvre, Paris, France. © Réunion des Musées Nationaux.

The figure of Christ is shown frontally, in the pose derived from the deposition, his arms hanging open and his hands held by St. John and the Virgin, and is now supported from behind by Joseph of Arimathea. Most important, he is shown in full-length and before the tomb. In strictly iconographic terms the image would be categorized as an entombment, but its origins lie in the Man of Sorrows tradition, and this derivation is necessary to understanding its significance.[29] The figure of Christ, indeed, shows distinct vestiges of the half-length formula typical for Man of Sorrows images up to this time: From the waist down – that is, more or less at the level where Christ's body is intersected by the upper edge of the sarcophagus – the legs are concealed by the winding sheet. The upper half of the figure is then carefully delimited from the rest of the image: No part of Christ's upper body trespasses the limits of the dark rectangular window of the tomb. Even within the naturalistic setting of the scene, therefore, the original half-length Man of Sorrows is framed off, decontextualized.

The image's origin in the Man of Sorrows imprints it with sacramental associations. Beyond the body of Christ itself, the entire configuration of the scene preserves much of the presentational quality of the Man of Sorrows image. Joseph of Arimathea works to support the body, but the overall impression is one of an indefinitely extended halt before the tomb. The gestures of

St. John and the Virgin are adapted virtually unchanged from the Man of Sorrows image: Originally abstracted from the scene of the deposition and, as it were, held in suspension in the image of the Man of Sorrows, the poses have not been fully "reactivated" as functional gestures in this scene of entombment. The sacramental nature of the gestures only confirms the liturgical associations of the image as a whole: The body is touched only by hands covered with cloths, just as the sacred elements are handled during the Mass rite, and the sheet in which Christ is wrapped spreads into an almost perfect rectangle on the ground, a striking analogue to the cloth on which the celebrant sets the paten with the Host and the chalice with the wine – a practice we see clearly illustrated, for example, in Albrecht Dürer's woodcut of the *Mass of St. Gregory* (Figure 28).[30]

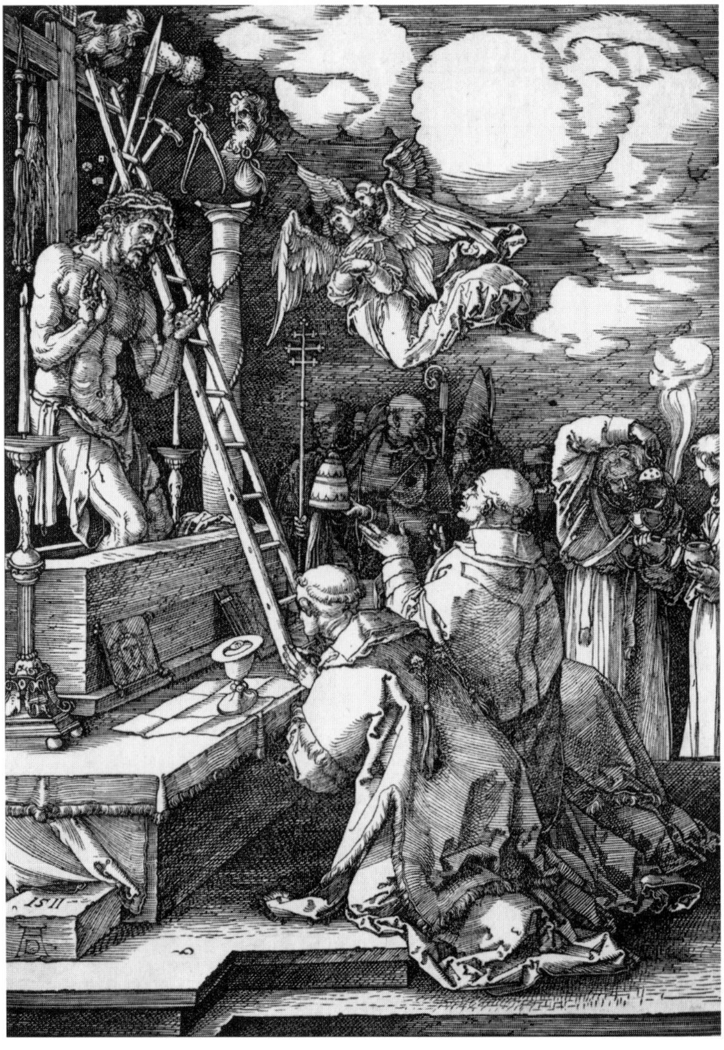

28. Albrecht Dürer, *Mass of St. Gregory.* Woodcut. Rosenwald Collection, © 1999 Board of Trustees, National Gallery of Art, Washington, D.C., U.S..

The fact that Fra Angelico's panel falls outside of established iconographic categories confronts the historian with special challenges. The work is an effort to reinterpret the form and significance of a traditional cult image within new pictorial conditions. The result was a novel approach to a central Christian mystery, and a new series of reflections on the role of representation in Christian art. Most artists, of course, simply adopted the new devices as novel means to traditional ends. For Fra Angelico, the adoption of a new pictorial regime committed to the representation of consistent historical settings made it necessary to find a new approach to representing the "figural" dimension of sacred events – and thus to come to terms in new ways with how such meaning works. Fra Angelico's discovery – one appreciated by Michelangelo – was to place rhetorical emphasis on controlled lapses in or subversions of the new claims to pictorial consistency. The usefulness of this device was recognized in the earliest monuments of perspectival painting. In Masaccio's *Trinity,* for example, the figure of God the Father "resists" the conditions of perspective that govern the rest of the fresco. He is viewed from dead in front (i.e., in orthogonal projection) from toes to head. His figure does not obey the vagaries of earthbound sight, embodied in and symbolized by the viewpoint-contingent system of perspective.[31]

In Fra Angelico, these challenges occur, for example, in material disruptions at the level of the picture plane, such as the "stains" to which Georges Didi-Huberman has drawn attention.[32] But they occur in other ways as well. In this predella panel, for example, the participation of the event within a suprahistorical structure is everywhere expressed by the subjection of the scene to a formality of design that is imposed, as it were, "from above." The contours of the figures, for example, conform to the shape of the rock behind, and Christ's winding cloth spreads into a rectangle reminiscent of a Eucharistic cloth. Ultimately – and, perhaps, inevitably – this dialogue between the natural and the artificial involves a metastatement about the status of the painting itself. The contents of the represented scene are not simply things we see through the arbitrary slice of the windowlike picture frame. Rather, they seem to "know" the picture frame exists. Here the statement is quite literal: The cave opening, down to the bottom of the sarcophagus, is exactly proportional to the rectangle of the panel itself. The elements of the historical event already contain the principle of its figuration. Did the picture frame determine the size and shape of the tomb opening, or vice versa? The question is undecidable, because the relation between the two occurs not within the causal logic of linear time but within the suprahistorical logic of figural associations.

It is no coincidence that this innovative predella panel stood under one of the first altarpieces to have been made in the modern Renaissance *pala* format, the altarpiece painted by Fra Angelico for the high altar of the church of San Marco in Florence circa 1440 (Figure 29). The experiments undertaken in the predella panel are of a piece with the revolutionary pro-

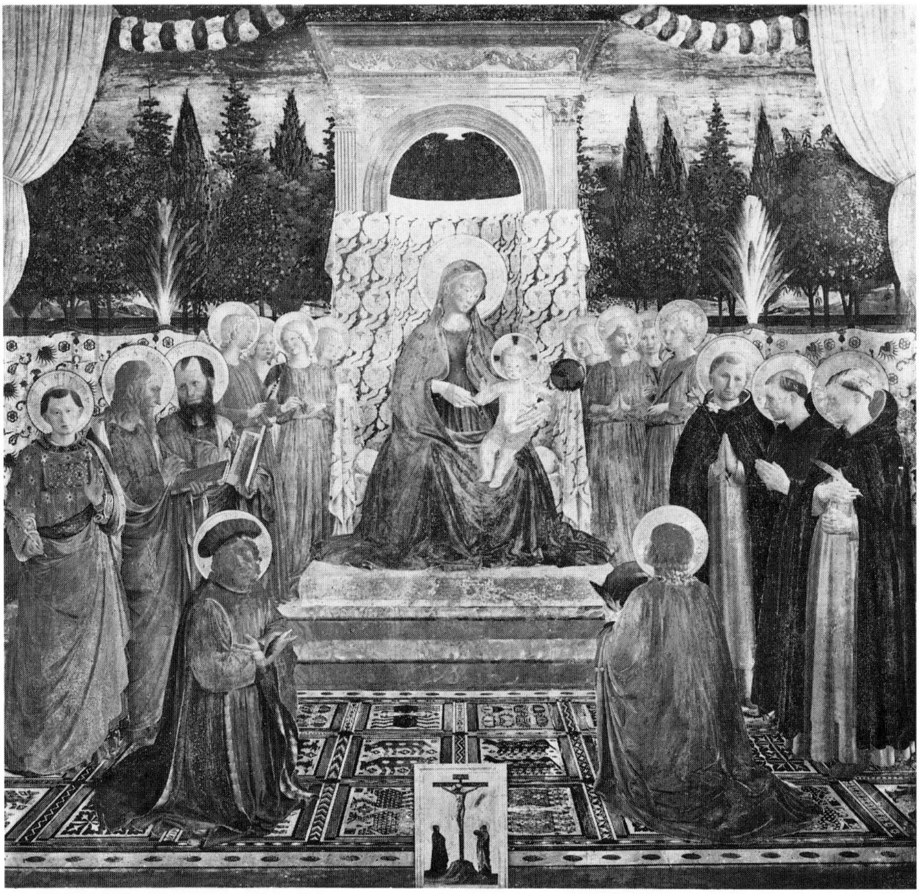

29. Fra Angelico, *Madonna and Child Enthroned with Saints. San Marco Altarpiece.* Panel. Museo di San Marco, Florence, Italy. Alinari/Art Resource, NY.

ject of the altarpiece as a whole. The altarpiece replaced Lorenzo di Niccolò's *Coronation* polyptych on the high altar of San Marco with a new conception of the altar image: The earlier gold-ground polyptych, an imposing piece of ecclesiastical furniture, was replaced by a unified and square panel, conceived in Albertian terms as a window. The new patrons at San Marco, Cosimo de' Medici and his brother Lorenzo, evidently chose to mark their patronage at San Marco, and more largely the new era of their patronage in Florence after their return from exile, with a consciously modern design program, whose centerpiece was a new high altarpiece done according to the rules of mathematical perspective.[33] After this type of altarpiece became standard (in accordance with the process that the Russian Formalists called "banalization"), painters often reverted to the traditional Man of Sorrows scheme in their predella panels. For this initial work, however, a greater pressure was evidently felt to modernize the predella in accordance with the claims of the rest of the altarpiece.[34]

ROGIER VAN DER WEYDEN AND THE NORTHERN MAN OF SORROWS

A strong and early response to Fra Angelico's predella panel came in Rogier van der Weyden's *Christ before the Tomb* now in the Uffizi (Figure 30). This panel was probably in Florence during Rogier's pilgrimage to Rome for the jubilee year of 1450.[35] In 1918, Karl Jähnig first proposed that Fra Angelico's composition served as Rogier's primary model.[36] The connection to Fra Angelico's full-length treatment allowed Jähnig to correct Adolph Goldschmidt's earlier proposal that Rogier's panel showed an *"Umbildung"* of the traditional Italian half-length formula of the Man of Sorrows into a full-length depiction with a realistic setting.[37] Goldschmidt's assertion was inaccurate but not insensitive: He had noticed in Rogier's panel, particularly in the upper half of the figure of Christ, with extended arms held by St. John and the Virgin, a link to the tradition underlying its immediate source, the Fra Angelico predella. As Jähnig remarked, the half-length formula was relatively rare in the north but, as we have seen, widespread in Italy.[38] Although it is possible that Rogier had an independent knowledge of this tradition, it is clear that he was responding primarily to its adaptation in Fra Angelico's panel.

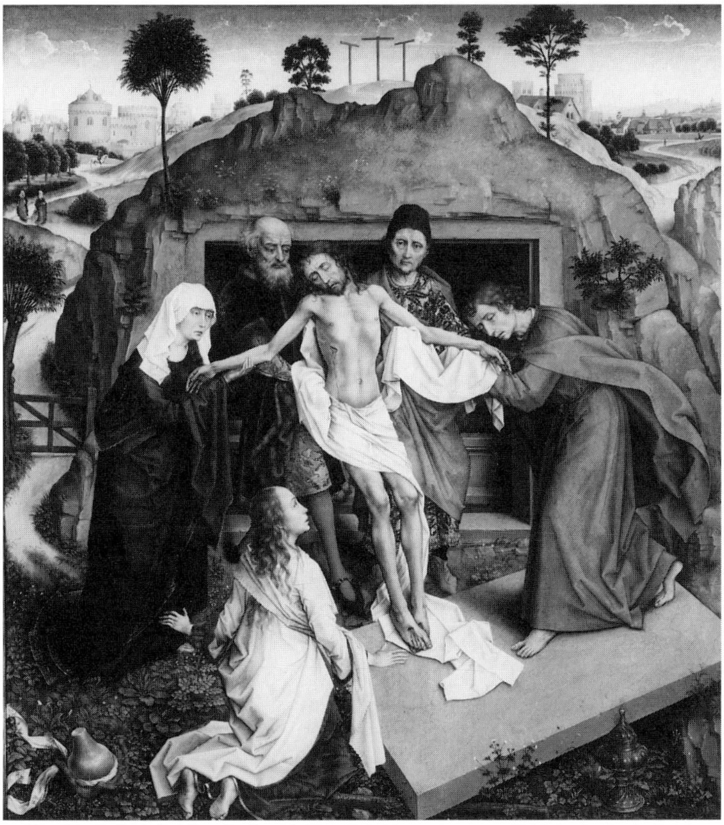

30. Rogier van der Weyden, *Christ at the Tomb.* Panel. Uffizi, Florence, Italy. Alinari/Art Resource, NY.

Rogier's response to Fra Angelico's efforts is best understood in light of earlier experiments with related problems in his own work. Even before this encounter, the two painters had struggled with similar problems, and the solutions they developed show some striking correspondences.[39] Both painters had, in the 1430s, attempted the considerable task of painting a complex narrative subject – in both cases the deposition – on the principal field of a monumental altarpiece (Figures 31 and 32). Although their solutions are markedly different, they both respond to a similarly perceived challenge: to reconcile a drastically widened scope of dramatic pictorial devices with the conventions and perceived functions of altar painting. As there was no established set of prescriptions for altarpieces in the period, these conventions were only implicit rules of decorum, and limit-cases such as these serve to bring them into light. Panofsky noted that Rogier's panel, now in the Prado, was a "painted critique" of Robert Campin's now lost *Deposition* altarpiece, whose composition is preserved in a copy in Liverpool.[40] In deliberate response to the sprawling composition of Campin's colossal altarpiece, Rogier contained his composition within a compressed, shallow box reminiscent of a *Schnitzaltar* and harmonized the movement of the figures by a series of circu-

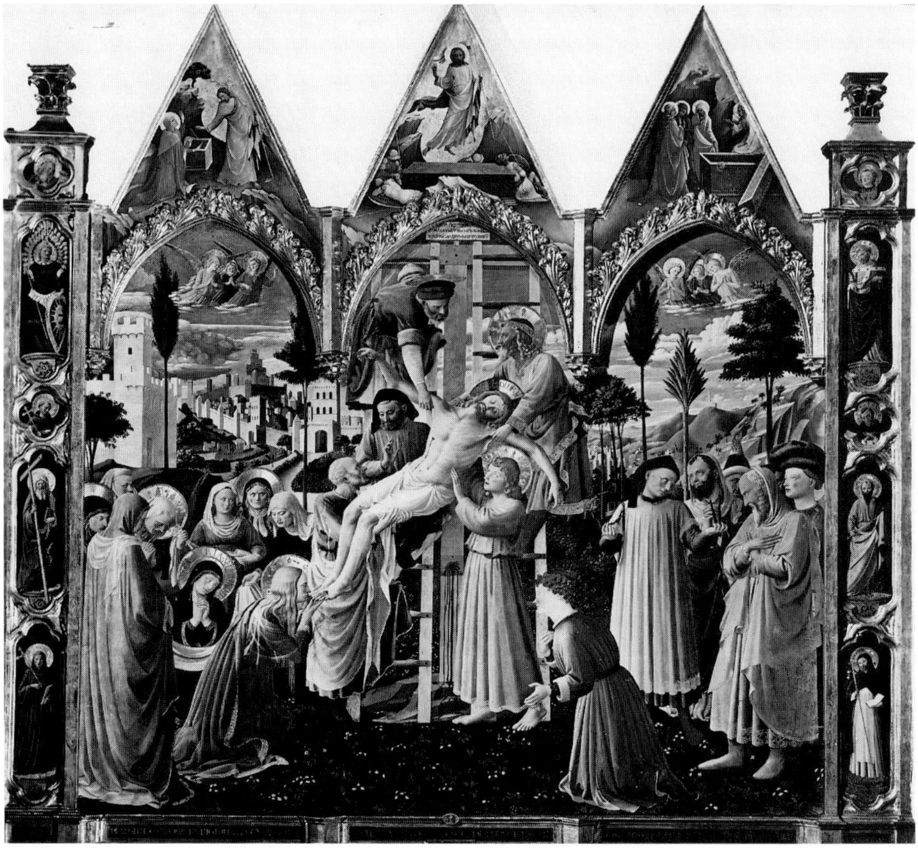

31. Fra Angelico, *Deposition*. Panel. Museo di San Marco, Florence, Italy. Alinari/Art Resource, NY.

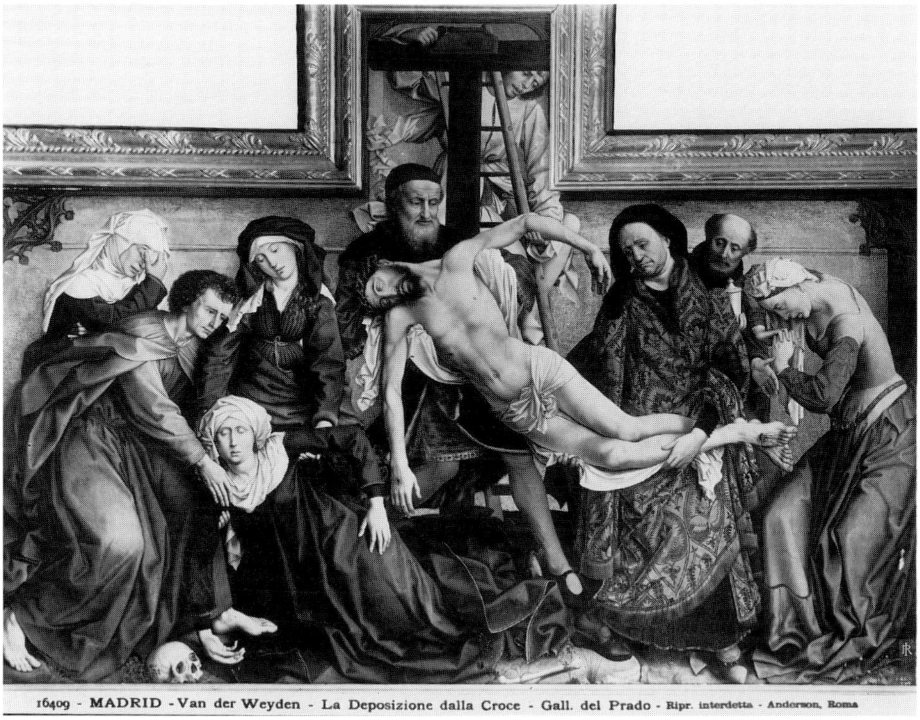

32. Rogier van der Weyden, *Deposition*. Panel. Museo del Prado, Madrid, Spain. Alinari/Art Resource, NY.

lating and intersecting rhythmic lines. Energy and movement is continually redirected inward and contained within the confines of a shrinelike space.

Fra Angelico's *Deposition* altarpiece addresses similar issues but offers a very different solution: The scene is set in an open landscape and contains many more figures, but a careful restraint is imposed on the action and gestures of the figures. Whereas in Rogier's *Deposition* the figures show a full range of emotional response, in Fra Angelico's work dramatic gesture is almost entirely contained within attitudes of contemplation: The figures cross their hands over their chests, join hands in prayerlike gestures, and kneel in worship. All action is accomplished with the quiet and efficiency of the movements performed at a Mass ceremony: The women at left lay the cloth over the Virgin's lap, preparing it, almost like an altar, to receive the body; in the center the men in gentle cooperation lower the body from the cross; on the right, a "congregation" is shown the instruments of the Passion and witnesses the event with quiet reserve. In both paintings, a gentle circulation of movement around the body of Christ has the effect of suspending the body in the center of the panel and counteracting the suggestion of its imminent removal.[41] If Rogier's panel is an implicit critique of Campin's triptych, Fra Angelico's altarpiece is a similarly critical response to Gentile da Fabriano's copious *Adoration of the Magi,* which stood on another altar in the same chapel (Figure 33). Both paintings, in other words, make the implicit but forceful argument

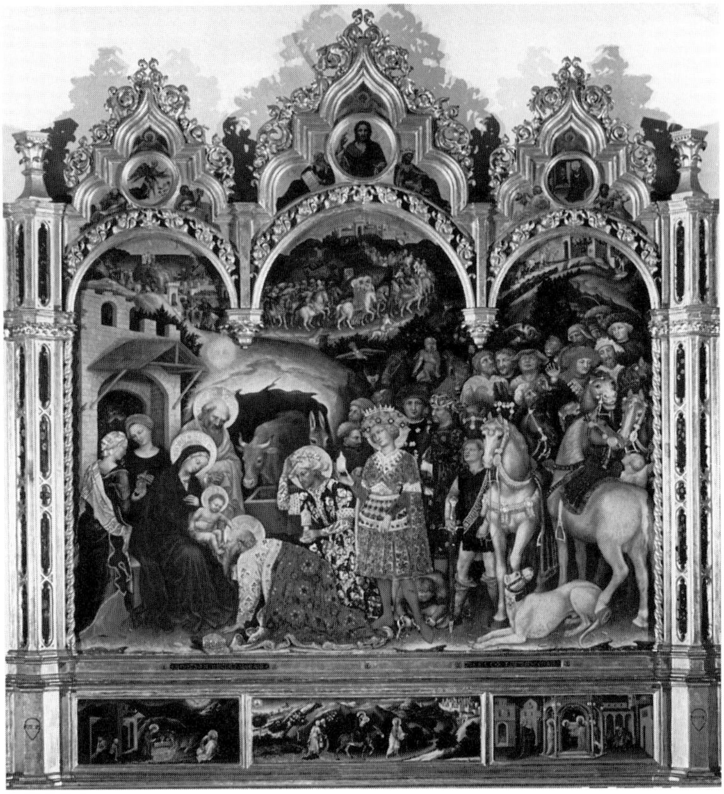

33. Gentile da Fabriano, *Strozzi Altarpiece: Adoration of the Magi*. Panel. Uffizi, Florence, Italy. Scala/Art Resource, NY.

that pictorial narrative needs to be used with special care on altar panels – that is, that it should be used to focus and reinforce devotional attention, not to disperse it.

The implicit dialogue between these two altarpieces continued in further works. In the 1440s Rogier experimented further with the format of the deposition in ways that can be understood as the inverse of Fra Angelico's experiment in the San Marco predella. A lost painting whose composition is preserved in several copies presents a close-up of the scene of the deposition, showing the three-quarter-length dead Christ with fallen arms surrounded by Joseph of Arimathea, John, and the Virgin[42] (Figure 34). The close-up device was a means of maintaining the intimacy and immediacy of the half-length devotional image within a pictorial regime that had made new claims to narrative consistency. Rogier's solution, in effect, restored the borrowings from the deposition that had become part of the image of the Man of Sorrows to their original narrative context. If Fra Angelico in his predella panel expanded a Man of Sorrows image into a narrative, Rogier cropped a narrative scene into the form of a Man of Sorrows composition. They are, again, complementary responses to the same problem: Fra Angelico expanded the setting while restraining action, and Rogier explored the drama while restricting the focus.

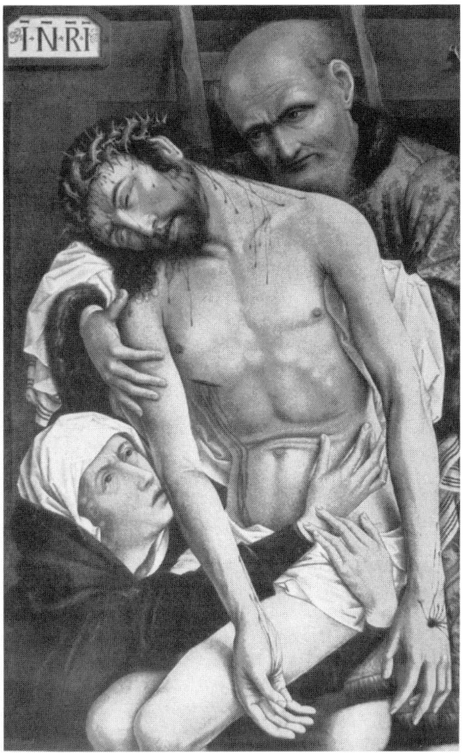

34. Copy after Rogier van der Weyden, *Deposition*. Panel. Formerly Fürstlich Hohenzollernsche Hofkammer, Sigmaringen, Germany.

Rogier was therefore well prepared to understand the nature and significance of Fra Angelico's innovation in the San Marco predella. He seized on the idea and adapted it to a full-size panel. Given the fact that Rogier's panel was, like Fra Angelico's altarpiece, commissioned by the Medici, the comparison between the two works has a historical basis: It is not difficult to imagine that Rogier's panel was commissioned, or at least received, in the spirit of a *paragone* – that is, as a characteristically northern response to the Italian model of the Medicis' favorite painter.[43] Rogier pushed Fra Angelico's innovation in new directions by incorporating a specifically northern conception of the full-length Man of Sorrows. The full-length Man of Sorrows had been developed in the late fourteenth century in France and was the result of a sharply different interpretation of the figure of the dead Christ from that which predominated in Italy.[44] In the Italian tradition, as we have seen, the mystery of the life-giving death was expressed through the image of the dead but upright, self-sustaining, and self-offering Christ. Even in the larger elaborations of the theme, for example, Lorenzo Monaco's panel of 1404 in the Accademia (Figure 35), Christ remains semi-active: The open arms of Christ are taken by St. John and the Virgin, but not simply for purposes of support; Christ virtually embraces the Virgin and proffers his hand to John, suggesting a somnolent will within the dead body.

The full-length conception developed in the north involved a greater emphasis on the effects of death in the figure of Christ. Tendencies in this direction were visible already on Italian soil. It was naturally enough an artist from northern Italy, Giovanni da Milano, who took up the theme in this more dramatic key and (consequently) expanded it to the three-quarter length. In his remarkable panel in the Florence Accademia, dated 1365, the effects of death in the figure of Christ are given new emphasis: Christ's mouth is half open and his arms, no longer capable of gentle, half-willed gestures, are rigid and cramped (Figure 36). The greater emphasis on the body's lifelessness in turn invites a more active participation on the part of the attendant figures. Christ is not left alone in the middle of the panel to support himself, as in the

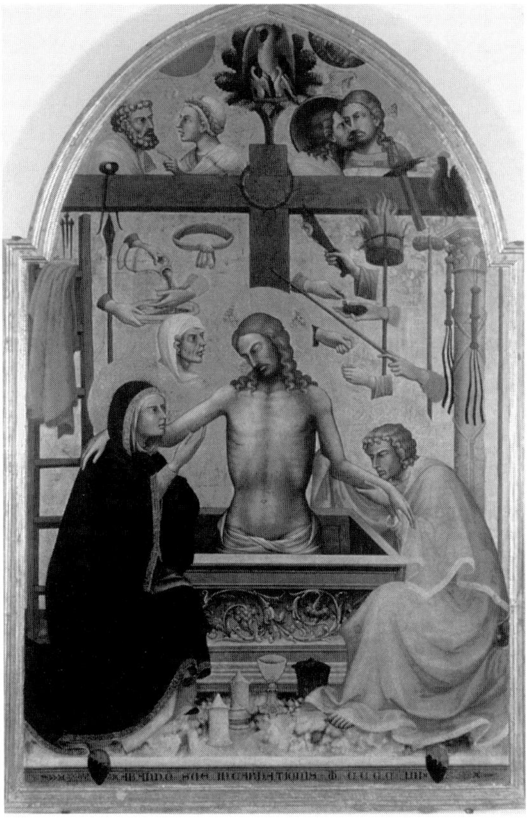

35. Lorenzo Monaco, *Arma Christi*. Panel. Accademia, Florence, Italy.

more traditional scheme; rather, the attendants now press around Christ, leaving no contour of his body exposed. The placement of the hand in support of Christ's underarm is a sensitive index of the new relationship: Christ can no longer be supported by his now entirely lifeless and fallen extremities but must be taken from a secure place under the arm, by which the torso itself can be held upright. This fact entails a closer relationship between Christ and the attendant figures and invites the introduction of a third figure lending support from above. The new configuration, moreover, necessarily leads to a change in format: It occasions the removal of the isolating precinct of the sarcophagus and with it, the limit of the half-length formula. The figures are now shown in three-quarter length and are clearly understood to be standing on a shared ground.

These innovations were not aggressively pursued in the following decades in Italy, where the half-length type remained predominant.[45] The direction indicated by Giovanni da Milano was pursued, instead, in the Burgundian tradition, which received and developed the Italian Man of Sorrows tradition beginning in the later fourteenth century.[46] One of the most distinctive features of the type as it developed in the north was the introduction of "suprahistorical" figures – God the Father or angels – in the composition. In the famous tondo ascribed to Jean Malouel in the Louvre (Figure 37), for example, Christ is shown fully dead, the oblique view giving dramatic emphasis to his hanging head and arms. He is shown in three-quarter length, and his lifeless body is supported by the figure of God the Father placed behind him, again with a hand placed in support of the underarm. In several other French works of the period, the figure of an angel fulfills this function.[47] Rather than having been mandated by theological authority, these iconographical innovations were, I believe, the result of an attempt to resolve a dilemma that had arisen within the open-ended development of the image itself. Christ had traditionally occupied a position at the apex of the composition, a position that expressed his lordship even in death, and thus the efficacy of his sacrifice. As artists, particularly in the French tradition, gave greater dramatic attention to his hanging and falling body, Christ's hierarchical superiority within the composition was ipso facto threatened. As we have seen, already in Giovanni da Milano's panel the increasing emphasis on the effect of death in the figure of Christ made it necessary to introduce an additional supporting figure above Christ in the composition. It was a natural response to the problem, but it diminished Christ's preeminent position in the image.

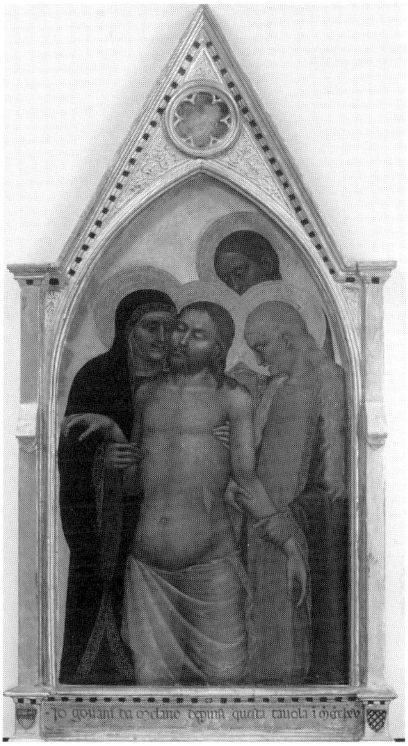

36. Giovanni da Milano, *Lamentation*. Panel. Accademia, Florence, Italy.

By giving this topmost position to an unearthly figure, God the Father or an angel, French artists preserved the sacramental significance of the image. The exalted figure above complements and compensates for the increased realism in the treatment of Christ's hanging body and thus confirms the efficacy of his sacrifice. Probably through the Burgundian tradition this idea passed into Netherlandish painting, where it was developed in several versions by Robert Campin (Figure 38). As Otto Pächt noted, Campin on the one hand intensified the naturalism of the image by concentrating on the coarse flesh and muscle of the Christ figure, and on the other formalized it, by making God the Father into a hieratic *Majestas* figure crowned with a tiara.[48] The scheme was adapted from the more traditional Trinitarian scheme of the "throne of mercy," with the seated God the Father holding the crucifix in his outstretched hands. The image as it developed in these traditions gave new

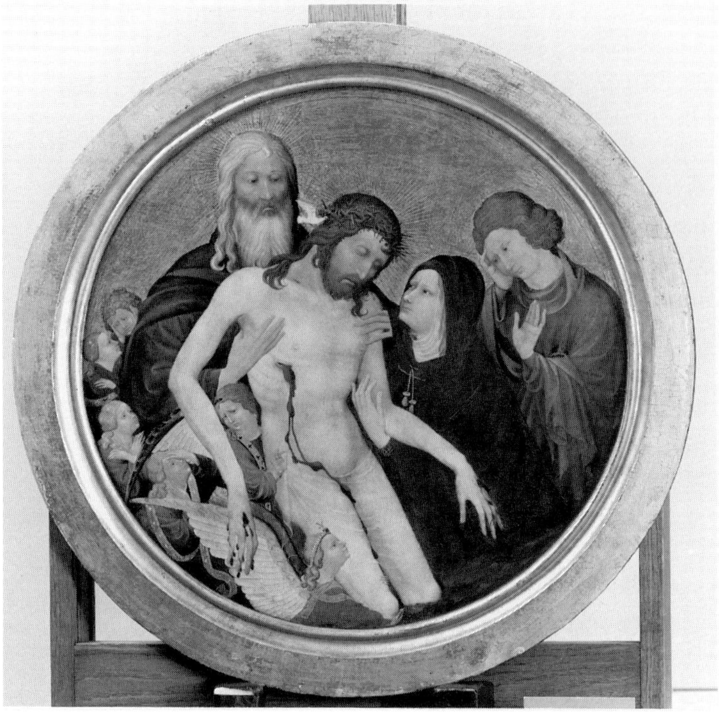

37. Jean Malouel, *Man of Sorrows-Trinity.* Louvre, Paris, France. © Réunion des Musées Nationaux.

visual expression to the appeal contained in the *Supplices* prayer of the Canon of the Mass:

We humbly beseech Thee, almighty God, let these offerings be carried by the hands of Thy holy angel to Thine Altar on high, in the presence of Thy Divine Majesty, that as many of us, as shall receive the most Sacred Body and Blood of Thy Son, by partaking thereof from this altar, may be filled with every heavenly blessing and grace, through the same Christ our Lord. Amen.[49]

The prayer, it may be noticed, is served equally well by the Man of Sorrows with angels, or *Engelpietà,* as by the compositions incorporating God the Father. I am not proposing the prayer as the source or impetus for the image; that would go entirely against the logic of open-ended development that I have attempted to trace here.[50] The content of the prayer, after all, had been just as well represented in the more rigid form of the throne of mercy, in which God the Father holds a Christ on the cross. The form of the image incorporating the broken, bleeding figure of the Man of Sorrows instead expands and develops the meaning of the prayer. It intensifies the theological message by the suggestion of a more immediate and affective relation between Father and Son, and thus of a more dramatic appeal to divine mercy.

Rogier's training in this tradition shaped his response to Fra Angelico's predella panel. In transforming the Italian half-length Man of Sorrows into a full-length figure supported by a venerable bearded figure from above and behind, Fra Angelico had strayed into territory more familiar to a painter trained in the Burgundian and Netherlandish traditions. But Rogier did not simply respond by producing a Netherlandish version of the Man of Sorrows; he also matched and surpassed Fra Angelico's panel in the field of narrative painting. He therefore deliberately avoided Fra Angelico's solution of placing one figure behind the dead Christ: To Rogier's northern eyes (if not to Fra Angelico's), that formula evoked the timeless vision of the Trinity images discussed above. Instead, he split the single figure into two historical actors, Joseph and Nicodemus, and left St. John and the Virgin in their places at either side. Everywhere Rogier has naturalized the formality of Fra Angelico's image, replacing the latter's strict frontality by an animating obliqueness. Drawing on Northern traditions, Rogier shows Christ's body to be dramatically lifeless, broken and turned at an angle. His feet are precariously perched on the edge of an obliquely placed tomb slab, replacing the neat rectangle of Fra Angelico's winding cloth. The slab itself is placed over a deep ravine in the earth underneath and is propped up by a thin log placed under the protruding corner. St. John, adapted from Rogier's other narrative compositions, echoes the oblique placement of the slab with his own diagonal movement. Fra Angelico's image is marked by confinement and closure: The cave blocks off the view of the horizon and any access to the landscape on either side, restricting all attention to the space between the tomb opening and perfectly proportional rectangle of the picture itself. Rogier's panel, by contrast, proposes an expansive and opening setting: A landscape emerges above the cave, extends around the cave and into the fore-

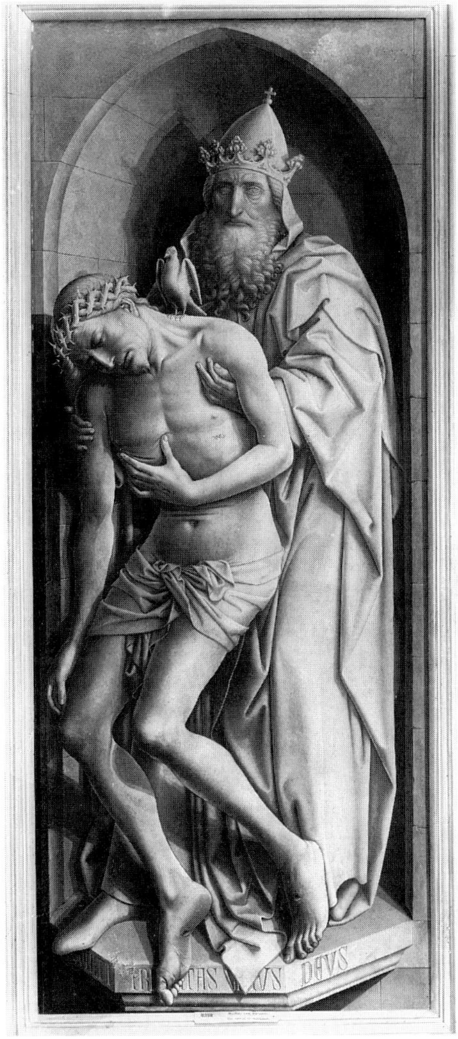

38. Robert Campin, *Man of Sorrows-Trinity*. Panel. Städelsches Kunstinstitut, Frankfurt am Main, Germany. Foto Marburg/Art Resource, NY.

ground, and gives the impression of extending beyond the confines of the picture. It also provides markers of a temporal trajectory, showing the city of Jerusalem, the empty crosses of Golgotha, and the path to the tomb in the foreground.

If Rogier elaborated on Fra Angelico's innovations with greater attention to narrative setting, he also deliberately preserved many of the features of the traditional Man of Sorrows scheme. The group is stopped before the tomb, and the mechanics of carrying and support are given less emphasis than are motifs of presentation and adoration. Nicodemus stands behind Christ but plays virtually no supporting role; he simply presents the body to the viewer. The Virgin and St. John, likewise, rather than playing the more actively engaged roles they do in other Rogierian compositions, here stay largely within the limits of the Italian Man of Sorrows scheme: They do not help in supporting the body but rather remain at Christ's extremities. Their gestures, in fact, bear a strikingly close resemblance to those found in Lorenzo Monaco's large panel of the *Man of Sorrows* discussed above (see Figure 35). Perhaps the unusually large size of Lorenzo Monaco's panel recommended it to Rogier's attention as he adapted Fra Angelico's conception to a full-size format. Rogier's solution thus stands in inverse relation to that of the earlier Prado *Deposition*: Instead of pursuing narrative energy and then containing it within a restrictive shrine structure, here he adopted Fra Angelico's approach of providing an open narrative setting but restricting dramatic movement within a paradigmatic figural structure. This structure was designed to preserve the image's fundamentally Eucharistic message. Rogier's panel was thus an effort to outdo Fra Angelico's panel in narrative complexity while retaining its sacramental significance.

In both Fra Angelico's and Rogier's panels the figures are stopped before the tomb and there is little indication of narrative progression. Indeed, what we see seems scarcely "motivated" by the story: The figures have, in the midst of a narrative setting, assumed a mode of gesture and presentation that conforms to the tradition of the Man of Sorrows. This is not merely a formal difference but is a difference in the nature of the image's function and address. The figures have stopped above all to present Christ in this form to the viewer: The viewer's gaze is addressed as a principle "external" to the history. What we see, therefore, is not so much a moment or an indefinite halt *within* the narrative as a suspension of the logic of the narrative itself. Rogier worked to soften this discontinuity: He showed a more complete setting and, most important, he introduced the foreground figure of the Magdalene, who looks in toward Christ from a point of view analogous to that of the viewer, thus offering an "internal" motivation for the frontal presentation of Christ. Her attitude implies a continuity between dramatic attention within the picture and the activity of the viewer before the picture. It is, in other words, a strong precedent for the solution adopted later by Michelangelo. But in what sense?

NARRATIVE AND ICON

In 1903 the relationship between Michelangelo's London panel and Rogier's panel in the Uffizi became the subject of public art-historical debate.[51] The point of the discussion was to demonstrate an as yet unnoticed episode of influence, and thus its purpose was to stress points of similarity between the two works. Adolph Goldschmidt pointed out, beyond formal similarities, a similarity in narrative conception: ". . .in both there is a certain unmotivatedness in the situation [*eine gewisse Unmotiviertheit der Situation*], a presentation to our gaze of Christ held completely upright, rather than as a horizontally carried body."[52] Goldschmidt failed to perceive that Michelangelo's panel offered a critique of the precedent on exactly this point. In contrast to Rogier's panel, we are confronted with a very precise and transitional narrative predicament, from which a "before" and an "after" can be clearly extrapolated. It is, as we have seen, a moment in between "stations," in which Christ has been withdrawn from the mourning women and has begun to be carried away to the tomb.[53] By turning this more transitional conception on axis with the viewer, the work makes the motif of frontal presentation – and thus the address to the viewer – an integral part of its narrative structure.

Michelangelo's staging is quite unique, but the idea of depicting this transitional moment in the narrative was not. The late medieval literature on the life of Christ had made it a habit of meditation and devotion to exercise the imagination in supplying the transitional episodes left out of the Gospel accounts.[54] In the late thirteenth-century *Meditationes Vitae Christi,* for example, we find an extended passage describing the lament and burial of Christ. It gives great emotional emphasis to the scene of Christ's separation from the Virgin, with whom the figures plead repeatedly to release the body for burial.[55] A later devotional text, Thomas à Kempis's *Meditationes Vitae Christi,* also dwells on this moment of separation and quite specifically enjoins the reader to visualize it from the point of view of the female mourners. "Consider," he says, "how sorely the loving friends of Christ then sorrowed, and especially the holy women, when they beheld Jesus taken from them, and shut up in the Sepulchre."[56] Both Fra Angelico and Rogier van der Weyden, in lesser known works, experimented with the more transitional episode of the departure of Christ along just these lines and, for both, this experiment occasioned the adoption of a laterally oriented composition. A panel by the school of Fra Angelico, now in Washington, D.C. (Figure 39), shows again the scene at the tomb, but this time within a more complete narrative setting.[57] Joseph of Arimathea and Nicodemus are shown carrying Christ toward the tomb at right, an action whose effect is to break up the immediately preceding scene of mourning. The picture is thus a step beyond the *Threnos,* the halt that had itself been introduced (on the basis of apocryphal texts) between the deposition and the entombment in Byzantine art.[58] It explores the following, final

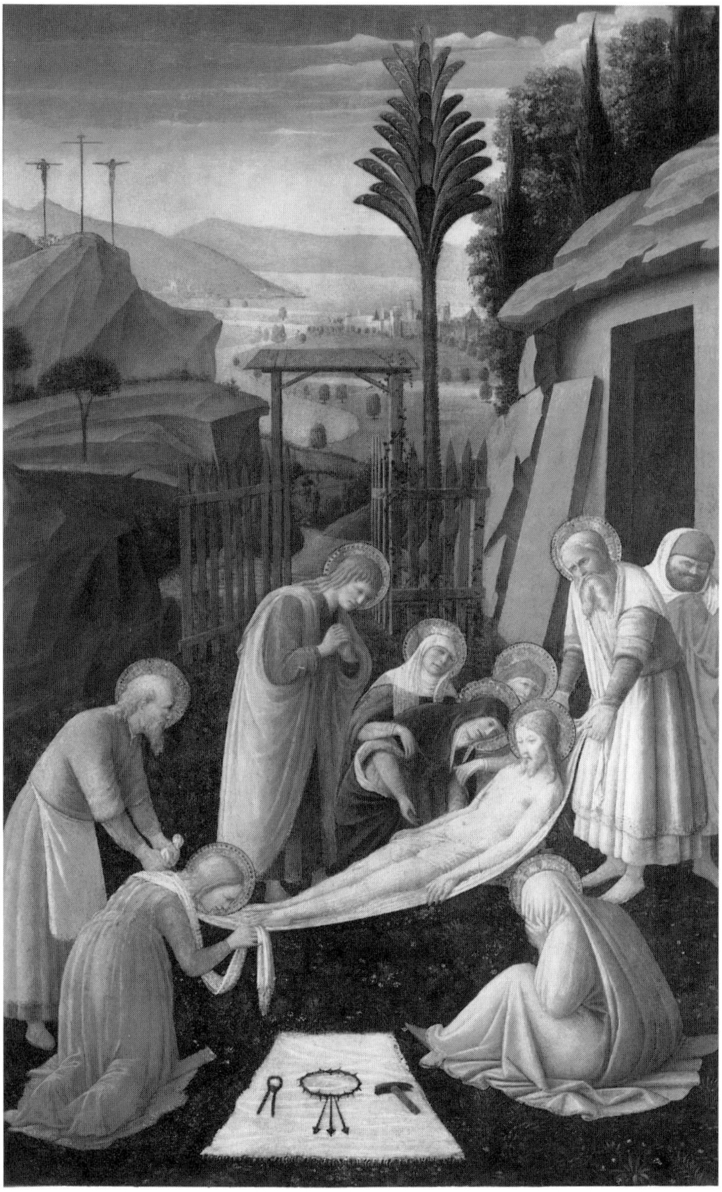

39. Attributed to Fra Angelico, *The Carrying of Christ to the Tomb.* Panel. Samuel H. Kress Collection, © 1999 Board of Trustees, National Gallery of Art, Washington, D.C., U.S.

moment of separation: The Virgin reaches for another kiss – that is, for a prolongation of the *Threnos,* but is held back as the body is taken away.

Fra Angelico's experiment yet again finds an analogue in the work of Rogier. A now-lost altarpiece, whose central and left panels are recorded in drawings in Paris (Figure 40) and (formerly) Leipzig, respectively, also concentrated on the moment of carrying.[59] Although the scene is situated closer to the cross than to the tomb, here again the Virgin is restrained while reaching for a last kiss, as Joseph and Nicodemus proceed with the body toward the

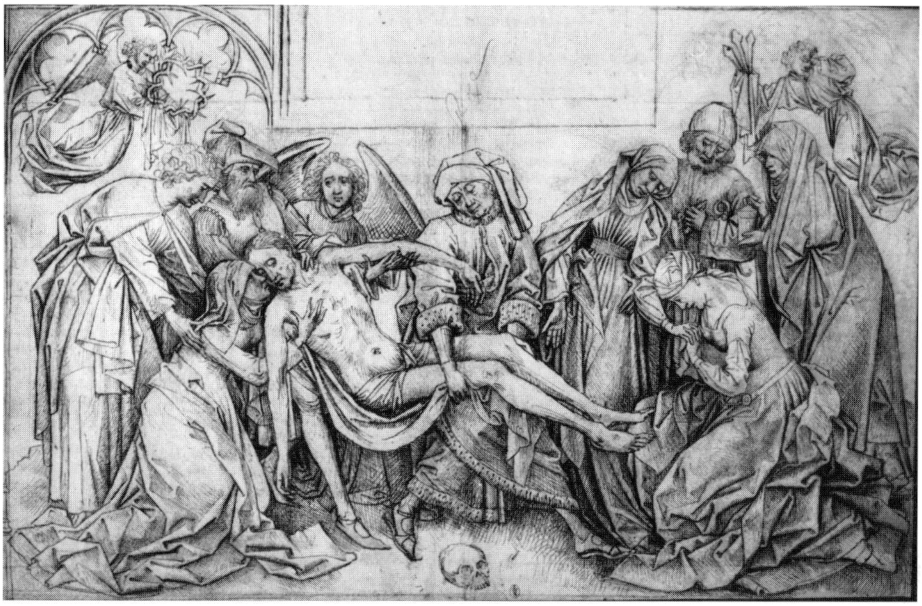

40. Copy after Rogier van der Weyden, *The Carrying of Christ to the Tomb.* Drawing. Louvre, Paris, France. © Réunion des Musées Nationaux.

right. The composition, in which Christ is entirely suspended in the air between the two carriers, shows some striking similarities to antique reliefs of the carrying of Meleager.[60]

In both of these works the more transitional conception involves a lateral arrangement and thus a departure from the mode of frontal presentation associated with the Man of Sorrows image. This is not merely a formal distinction. Art historians and semioticians have long recognized that lateral and frontal compositions involve different modes of address and thus different functional implications for images.[61] Before it became a concern of modern-day scholars, however, the distinction was the subject of implicit commentary and debate within the history of image making. In the Christian tradition, it lies at the basis of the never fully theorized distinction between representational images, or portrait-icons, and biblical scenes, or narratives.[62] Meyer Schapiro, noting a sharply different treatment of the two types of image in the same early medieval fresco cycle, suggested that they should be thought of as instances of different modes, like the modes of music or the genres of poetry. He went so far as to describe the eighth-century iconoclastic controversy as a conflict over the growing dominance of the icon mode over the episodic or narrative mode.[63] A similar distinction cropped up during the Western iconoclastic controversy of the sixteenth century, prompting moderates like Luther and the early Zwingli to claim exemption for images of the narrative kind on the grounds that they were less susceptible to idolatry.[64]

Luther did not invent the distinction between narrative and icon, which appears to have been a working part of the way people thought about images in the period. Orthodox polemicists who favored cult images made the opposite argument but used a similar distinction. The thirteenth-century bishop Luke of Túy believed the profile or "one-eyed" image of the Virgin to be a heretical degradation of her divine status. As Meyer Schapiro observed, Bishop Luke probably would not have objected to profile images of the Magi but could not accept the Virgin's demotion to the level of narrative action of the lesser figures. Luke similarly objected to the recent development of "three-nail" crucifixes, which twisted the traditionally frontal body of Christ in a way that he saw as a "derision" and an "insult."[65]

Luke offered early opposition to a late medieval trend away from the traditional portrait icons. He and other like-minded conservatives were alarmed not only by experiments with profile views, but also in a more fundamental sense by the increasingly assertive effects of illusionism. The shock was perhaps most strongly felt by foreign visitors to the West, who complained that the images in Western churches had lost all connection to their prototypes. Symeon, Bishop of Thessalonica, observed that "instead of painted garments and hair, they adorn them with human hair and clothes, which is not the image of hair and a garment, but the [actual] hair and garment of a man, and hence is not an image and a symbol [*tupos*] of the prototype." He was not claiming, of course, that the images in fact carried real hair and clothes; he was objecting to the prevailing ambition to make figures that looked real and not like images based on recognizable venerable prototypes, and in this sense his outrage was akin to Luke's. The Byzantine Church official Sylvester Syropoulos, in Italy for the Ferrara–Florence Council of 1438, declared, "When I enter a Latin church, I do not revere any of the [images of] saints that are there because I do not recognize any of them. So I make the sign of the cross and I revere this sign that I have made myself, and not anything I see there."[66]

A situation like this was bound to produce, even among the proponents of the new art, some thoughtful essays in archaism. Even if they would not have satisfied any of these critics, these efforts were informed by shared concerns. One very sophisticated effort of this kind was the dramatic close-up, which preserved the intimacy and frontal address of the icon without renouncing a highly developed conception of narrative art. In the last section, we saw this and related experiments in the work of Rogier and Fra Angelico, in both of whom a mastery of pictorial narrative was combined with a sensitivity for traditions of religious art. Later it was developed in the Venetian tradition.[67] In these and several other works we find what amounts to a form of implicit art criticism. Distinctions were made between different types of images, and different compositional modes, and the making of these distinctions involved interpretations of their efficacy and significance, as well as a certain degree of historical reflection, that goes well beyond the scope of contemporary writing on art. The series of paintings discussed here, for example, suggest a distinct awareness that frontal presentation is something worth preserving, that it embodies a link to certain traditional modes of attention and worship, and perhaps to tradition itself.

Such a critical attitude toward the nature and history of religious art was, of course, to become highly articulated in the debates of the Reformation and Counter Reformation. We see it, for example, in the *Dialogues* of Francisco de Hollanda, written about 1540, where he describes a commission he was given by the queen of Portugal to copy the miraculous image of Christ in the Sancta Sanctorum. One of the interlocutors asked him, "[D]id you do it with that severe simplicity which the old painting has and with that fear in those divine eyes which in the original seem to belong to the very Saviour?" Another interlocutor was Vittoria Colonna, Michelangelo's friend later in life, of whom it is said that such a thing was "much to her liking."[68] Colonna was known to have a developed interest in the "St. Luke" Madonnas of Rome, and wrote poems in which she extolled the virtues of their rough and simple style, or what she called their *"modo umil"*.[69]

Shortly thereafter, Giovanni Andrea Gilio was to offer a critical appreciation of medieval art, noting, for example, that medieval artists represented the crucified Christ with four nails because they could not manage the complexity of placing one foot over another. And yet like Colonna he defended the front-facing awkwardness of medieval artists, what he called their *prosopopea,* arguing that it was more "honest and devout" than the ingenious caprices of modern art, for him epitomized above all by the *figure serpentinate* of Michelangelo.[70]

Although it might well be considered a question specific to the concerns of visual artists, the special efficacy attached to the motif of frontal presentation was occasionally recognized by writers. For example, the poet and humanist Angelo Poliziano, artistic advisor to the young Michelangelo, used it in the context of a Good Friday sermon as a means of inducing a contemplative response to the figure of Christ. In the midst of a highly dramatic description of the events of the Crucifixion, Poliziano suspends the account and "opens" it to the contemplation of his listeners by presenting the dead Christ frontally, in a form that appears to be borrowed directly from the visual tradition of the Man of Sorrows:

> He who has been taken down from the Cross, with his arms spread, with his head bowed, with his heart open, calls you, my fathers, invites you to lament with him his most bitter pain. Accompany his holy wife, disconsolate widow . . . in kneeling and bowing and prostrating yourself before his holy feet.[71]

Poliziano's insertion of the Man of Sorrows, and the forms of attention appropriate to it, within the context of the Passion drama, finds several parallels in late Quattrocento Tuscan painting. Several of these works are elaborations either on Fra Angelico's San Marco predella or on Rogier's Uffizi panel.

They diverge from these models by showing not Christ at the tomb but the more transitional episode of Christ carried to the tomb, making the effort to preserve the front-facing Christ more problematic. For this reason they form the most significant strain of reception leading to Michelangelo's London *Entombment*. In a panel by the Master of San Miniato in Avignon (Figure 41), the figure of Christ held up by Joseph of Arimathea has been taken over almost literally from Fra Angelico's predella, but without the flanking structure that Fra Angelico himself inherited from the Italian Man of Sorrows tradition. Instead, Christ's arms are shown hanging straight down, and the lateral elements now suggest a temporal itinerary: The cross stands at the right and the tomb at the left. The scene is evidently understood to take place in between those two stations, but the insistence on the frontal presentation of Christ makes it unclear whether we are between deposition and lamentation or between lamentation and entombment. That we are witnessing the latter moment is suggested by the panel's derivation from Fra Angelico, and by the fact that the Virgin is being restrained by St. John, as if Christ were being taken away from her.[72]

A strenuous effort to preserve the frontal arrangement even while attempting a narrative of transitional movement, the panel reveals how high was the importance attached to preserving the frontal motif. It is not alone. We find a similar effort in a miniature by Gherardo and Monte in the Bargello Museum in Florence (Figure 42). The work was a Medici commission, as is indicated by the coat of arms at the top of the page, and it is therefore not surprising that knowledge of Fra Angelico's public altarpiece should be supplemented by

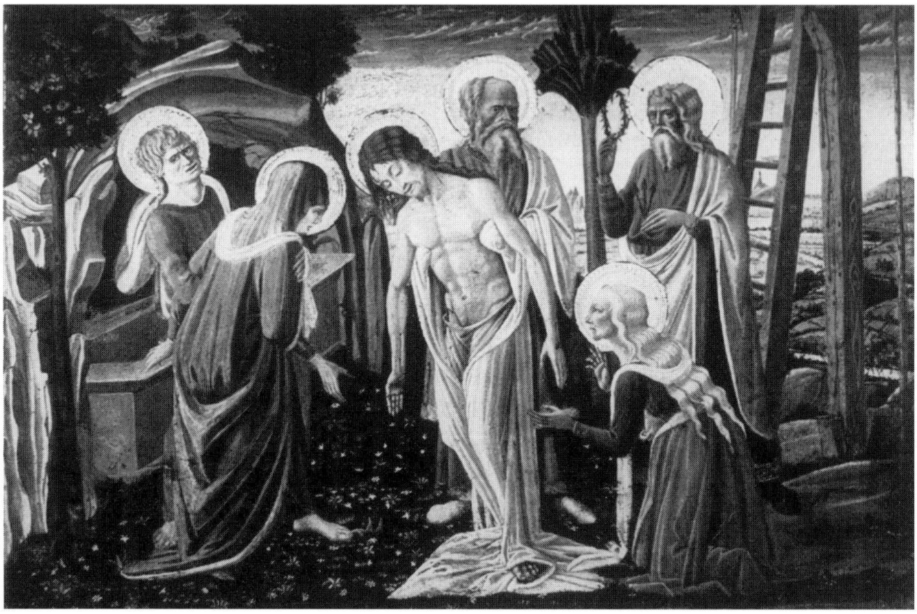

41. Master of the San Miniato Altarpiece, *The Carrying of Christ to the Tomb.* Panel. Palais des Papes, Avignon, France. Arch. Phot. Paris/CNMHS.

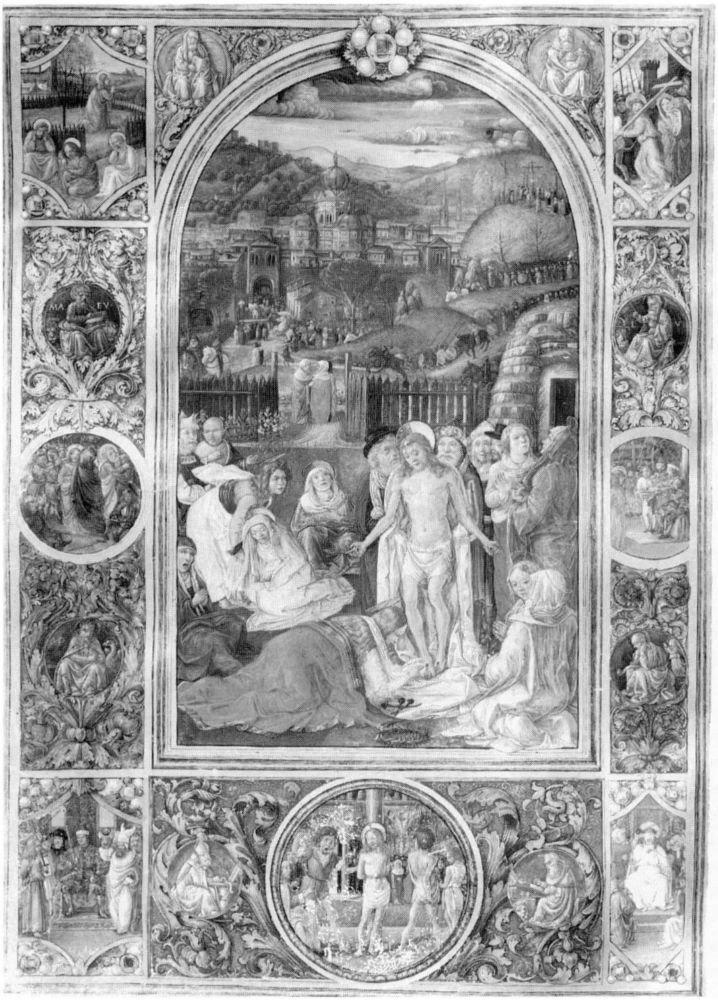

42. Gherardo and Monte, *The Carrying of Christ to the Tomb.* Miniature. Bargello Museum, Florence, Italy.

careful observation of Rogier's altarpiece, which was very likely in the chapel of a private Medici residence. The difference from both lies, again, in a more transitory narrative conception, where Christ is shown still at some distance from the tomb. Another adaptation of the Fra Angelico model, a predella panel by Bartolommeo di Giovanni also in the Accademia (Figure 43), explores the idea of transitory movement even more agressively by showing the actual process of carrying rather than mere gestures of support. The painter hit upon the device of a slinglike winding cloth that passes under Christ's thighs – the very same device later adopted by Michelangelo. It is indeed quite possible that Michelangelo knew this panel: It was the work of a fellow Ghirlandaio pupil, and it belonged to an altarpiece that originally stood in the church of San Marco, where Michelangelo had surely studied Fra Angelico's altarpiece and predella on the high altar.[73]

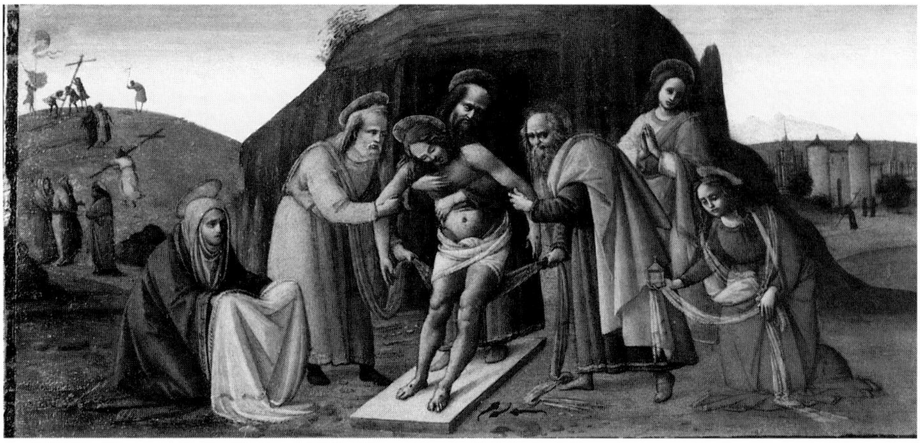

43. Bartolommeo di Giovanni, *The Carrying of Christ to the Tomb*. Predella panel. Accademia, Florence, Italy.

All of these paintings show evident efforts to preserve the frontal presentation of the figure of Christ inherited from the experiments of Fra Angelico and Rogier, but in adapting the conception to a more transitional narrative conception they invariably introduced a lateral or oblique axis into the frontal conceptions of their predecessors. Other experiments preserved the strict frontality of presentation, but always at the cost of a strict reduction of the narrative element. The more static scheme seems to have been preferred when it came to larger panels. In a panel by Cosimo Rosselli in Berlin, for example, the group has been placed *at* the tomb, here interpreted as a mausoleum-like structure. In a full-size altar panel by the school of Domenico Ghirlandaio in Dublin the scene is set before the more traditional cave, and the reduction of narrative emphasis is underlined by the presence of anachronistic saints.[74] This example proves, if proof were needed, that Fra Angelico's experiment was well known to the Ghirlandaio shop, where Michelangelo received his first artistic training.

The clearest alternative to the relatively convention-bound format of the altar panel was the medium of prints, and in many ways Michelangelo's painting was an effort to introduce the latest and most sophisticated experiments of the printed medium into panel painting. Besides Mantegna's *Entombment* engraving (see Figure 17), discussed in chapter 1, another important precedent in the investigation of a dramatic Passion narrative was offered by the *Great Passion* of Albrecht Dürer. The problem of transition in a narrative sequence was, indeed, what distinguished Dürer's series from its great predecessor, the series by Martin Schongauer. Rather than treating each image as a separate entity, in the paradigmatic tradition of the medieval "stations," he conceived the Passion as a continuous story, in which each scene contributes to the narration of the whole. This approach produced new and dramatic relationships between one scene and the next. In the sequence, the closest succession occurs between the scenes of the *Lamentation* (Figure 44) and the following,

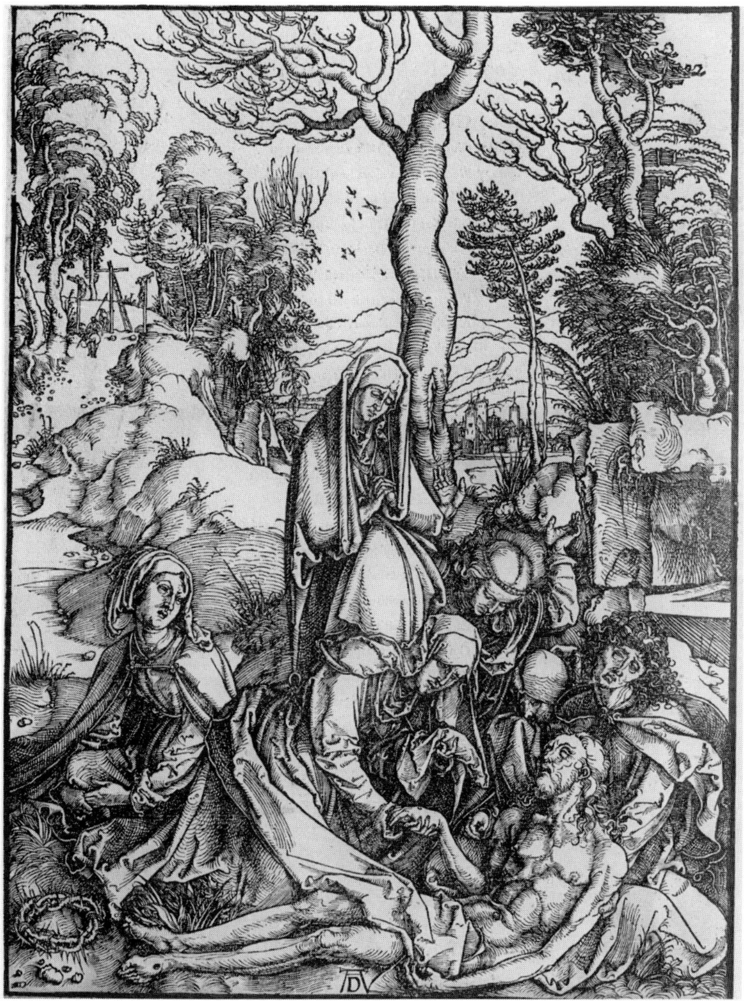

44. Albrecht Dürer, *Lamentation*. Woodcut from the Large Passion. Staatsbibliothek, Munich, Germany. Foto Marburg/Art Resource, NY.

quite novel scene of the *Carrying of Christ to the Tomb* (Figure 45), the last two scenes that belong to the group made before 1500.[75] Rather than being represented as two separate scenes, these images are treated as two moments of the same scene, virtually as frames within a cinematic sequence. In the earlier moment Christ lies in the foreground, his upper body held by St. John, and is lamented by the holy women; the tomb is already shown in the right background. In the next moment a larger crowd has assembled and the lamentation group has broken open: Three men have begun to carry Christ toward the tomb, which is in the same place as in the previous sheet; the lifeless Virgin has taken Christ's place in the arms of St. John, who watches the carrying group move away. The narrative ideas derive in part from a knowledge of classical reliefs, or Italian adaptations of them, which Dürer might have seen in Venice or Padua: The Italian derivation is virtually advertised in the female figure with upraised arms in the *Lamentation*.[76]

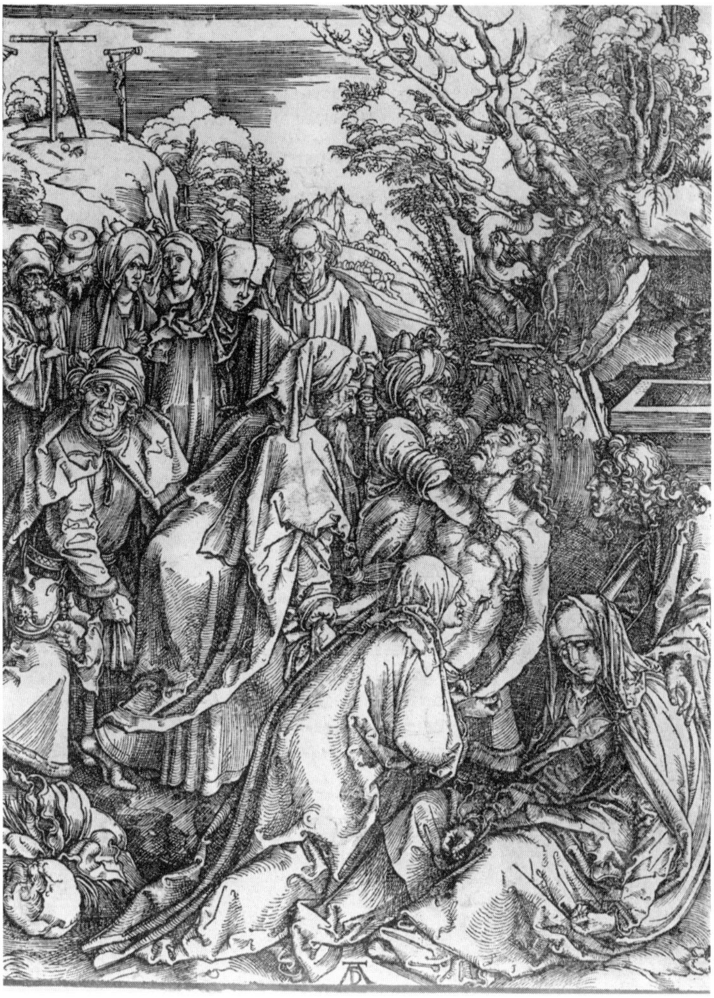

45. Albrecht Dürer, *The Carrying of Christ to the Tomb.* Woodcut from the Large Passion. Staatsbibliothek, Munich, Germany. Foto Marburg/Art Resource, NY.

The images and texts so far discussed show that late fifteenth-century readers and viewers were accustomed to imagining the scene of the carrying of Christ in all its transitions, and even to visualizing it from quite specific points of view. But though the scene had achieved some currency by this time in predella panels and prints, it was only rarely to be encountered on the principal panels of altarpieces. In this format, as we have seen, it was possible to find scenes of Christ at the tomb, such as Rogier's panel (see Figure 30), and the panels by Cosimo Rosselli and the Ghirlandaio workshop discussed above. A more common narrative subject in late fifteenth-century altarpieces was the lamentation, in which Christ's recumbent body is oriented laterally, a composition found in the panel for Santa Chiara by Perugino (see Figure 15). The greater prevalence of this compositional type meant that even the scene at the tomb was often given this form, as we see in Botticelli's Poldi Pezzoli panel (see Figure 16). Here again the narrative was stabilized by being focused on the immobile figure of Christ. In these cases, the paintings adopted the strategies of devotional texts such as the *Meditationes Vitae Christi*: the narrative scene was used as a means of contextualizing and thematizing the viewer's devotion on the central sacred figure, and the attitudes of the actors in the scene served as exempla of piety for the worshipper.[77]

And yet the very use of such scenes within liturgical and paraliturgical practice motivated a desire for increasing narrative animation in altarpieces of the period. Thus altarpieces of the deposition, something of a rarity in Rogier's and Fra Angelico's time (see Figures 31 and 32) became increasingly frequent toward the end of the fifteenth century.[78] Quite uncommon in this format, however, was the transitional scene of the carrying of Christ to the tomb, despite the fact that, as we have seen, it could be fairly widely found in predella panels, miniatures, and prints. Rogier van der Weyden's lost altarpiece (see Figure 40), discussed above, is a significant exception.

The London *Entombment* (Figure 6) can be understood as an effort to marry the new modes of narrative art with the conventions and traditions of altar painting, now clearly understood as conventions and traditions. It did so by drawing on a wider range of models of narrative composition and by coordinating the narrative structure with the frontal address to the viewer and thus the liturgical and devotional uses of an altarpiece. The key was to treat the drama of separation as a moment of visual confrontation. The transport of the dead body sets Christ at "viewing distance" for the actors within the scene, thus assimilating their activity to the gaze of the worshipper before the picture. The traditional narrative composition is turned ninety degrees, thus making the moment of dramatic confrontation coincide with the frontal address of the Man of Sorrows. The sequence of the narrative is not interrupted in order to hold Christ up to the viewer in a formal act of sacramental presentation; instead, Christ is shown almost inadvertently in the midst of the carrying, and his frontal orientation is motivated by the narrative itself, which interprets and articulates the transaction between viewer and image.[79] The *"Unmotiviertheit der Situation"* that Goldschmidt saw as a feature common both to this panel and to Rogier's Uffizi panel is in fact what Michelangelo most pointedly criticized in his precursor.

The effect is not unrelated to the strategies of the implied viewer developed in the tradition of the Venetian close-up, but there are important differences. In Mantegna's Brera *Dead Christ* (Figure 46), for example, the viewer is directly implicated by the "cropping" of the scene: What we see is understood as a fragment of a larger whole. By being given an intimate view, the viewer is by implication placed "inside" the scene, here directly at Christ's feet, in a position often occupied by historical actors and donors in more "complete" representations of the subject (as we see, for example, in Giottino's *Lamentation* [see Figure 14]). When the strategy is expanded to a full-size panel and a full-

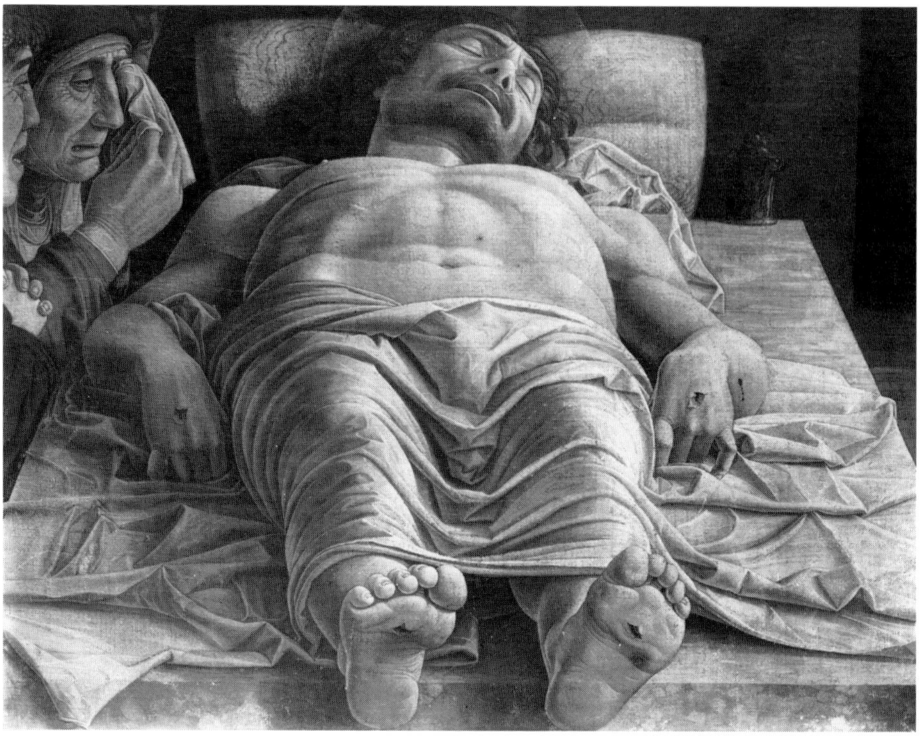

46. Andrea Mantegna, *Dead Christ.* Panel. Pinacoteca di Brera, Milan, Italy. Alinari/Art Resource, NY.

scale scene, as in Michelangelo's *Entombment,* the consequences are different. The scene is not presented as a fragment whose imagined setting includes the viewer. Rather, the narrative is complete, and at the same time it is organized "for" a viewer in the here and now. Sacred history is kept "whole," and yet its meaning is fulfilled in its relation to a contemporary viewer. The thematic structure, with its elegiac coloring, interprets the relation between the viewer and the subject as one between present and past. Christ is presented to the viewer as he is being withdrawn, making the idea of distance – and the means by which it is bridged – central to the picture's meaning. This emphasis bears affinities to certain strains in humanist thought, which are studied in the next chapter.

CHAPTER THREE

Humanism and the Altar Image

ARCHAISM AND ANTIQUE REVIVAL

Michelangelo's London *Entombment* marks a significant encounter between humanist culture and traditional Christian institutions circa 1500. It is typical of its time in that it was not merely the result of cultural change, but was itself a critical response to cultural change. The compositions of Fra Angelico and Rogier were developed as natural outgrowths from the Man of Sorrows prototype; they expand outward from the original formula, introducing a setting and additional figures. Michelangelo's painting proceeded in the reverse direction: It took a narrative conception based on classical reliefs and structured by a lateral composition, "turned" it ninety degrees, and (re)introduced the Man of Sorrows figure at its core. In this sense it was a more historically conscious gesture, an effort to restage and revive the figure of the Man of Sorrows within new artistic and cultural conditions. Michelangelo was aware of the Man of Sorrows as a category of image, and he was intent on preserving it. For the central group around Christ, Michelangelo seems, indeed, to have drawn directly on the full-length northern Man of Sorrows type, independent of its adaptation in Rogier's panel. A German woodcut from the late fifteenth century (Figure 47) shows the type as it was popularly available at the time.[1] The composition of the Man of Sorrows supported by three figures, which is commonly found in German art of the period, is strikingly similar to Michelangelo's core group.[2]

Michelangelo's gesture was deliberate and uncommon. The Man of Sorrows remained extremely rare on the principal panels of altarpieces, being traditionally reserved for marginal areas, such as predellas, upper registers, reverse sides, and wings.[3] Dagobert Frey saw this as a form of resistance, an

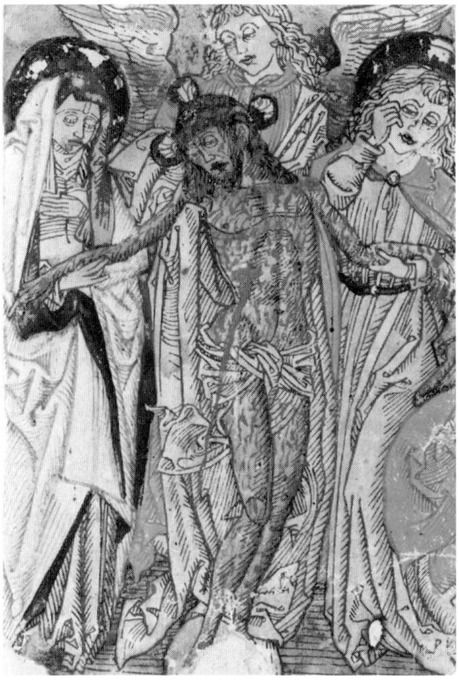

47. German, *Man of Sorrows*. Woodcut. Kupferstichkabinett, Staatliche Museen zu Berlin-Preussischer Kulturbesitz

uneasiness before what might have been a too powerful identification of the image of Christ with the real presence of the sacrament consecrated on the altar before it.[4] In support of Frey's thesis, one could point to many scenes of the *Miracle of St. Gregory* where Christ, appearing as the Man of Sorrows, seems to have materialized from out of the altar image. In a relief in the church of San Gregorio Magno in Rome (Figure 48), for example, the self-offering Christ is distinctly figured as an altar image that has come alive.[5] The Man of Sorrows as the principal image of an altarpiece appears natural in this representation, and yet it was quite rare in reality. Curiously, however, this tacit avoidance seems to have broken down, in both Germany and Italy, in the years around 1500. For example, a large middle-Rhenish panel dated 1503 in

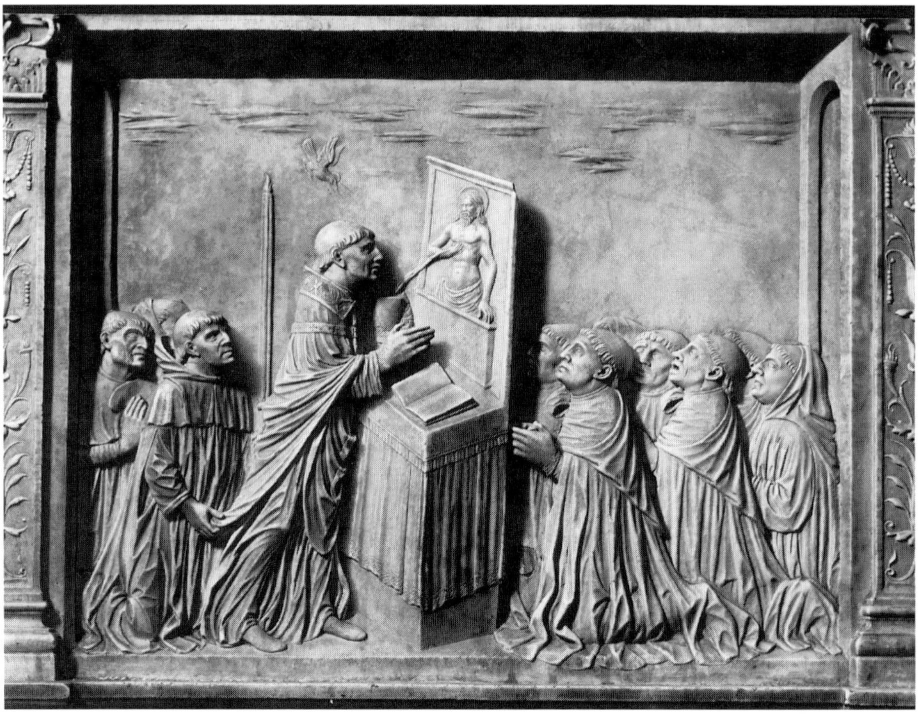

48. Luigi Capponi, *Mass of St. Gregory*. Marble relief. San Gregorio Magno, Rome, Italy. Alinari/Art Resource.

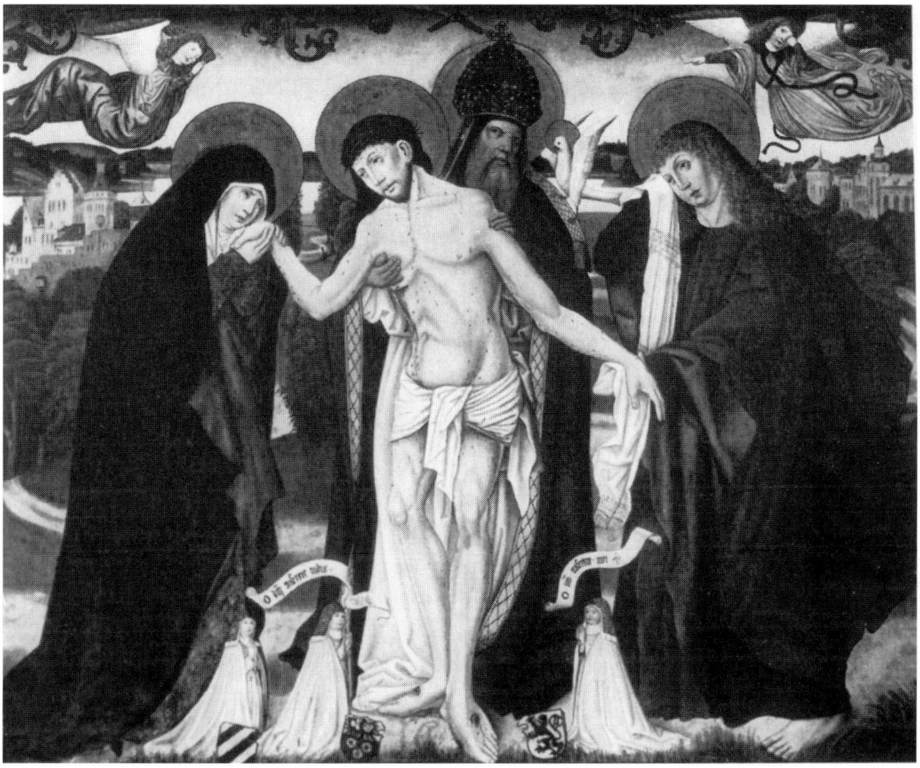

49. German, *Man of Sorrows-Trinity.* Panel. Städelsches Kunstinstitut, Frankfurt am Main, Germany.

the Städel-Institut in Frankfurt (Figure 49) shows the Man of Sorrows supported from behind by God the Father and held at either hand by the Virgin and St. John – a figural arrangement, again, very similar to the core group in Michelangelo's panel.[6] A slightly later and better known example is the sculptural group by Hans Daucher in the Fugger chapel in Augsburg.[7] In Italy, the subject appears toward the end of the fifteenth century in a number of altarpieces, especially in north Italy.[8] As unusual as its solution is, Michelangelo's panel is a part of a larger trend.

A parallel and not unrelated development was the increasing incidence of sacrament tabernacles on altars at this time.[9] As the Man of Sorrows was a favorite Eucharistic image, the two phenomena occasionally coincided, as we see for example in the early Venetian sacrament altar in the Gardner Museum in Boston discussed earlier (see Figure 22). But the two developments are related in a more fundamental sense. As Henk van Os and Peter Humfrey have observed, the rise of the sacrament altar bespeaks the emergence of a new doctrinal and Christocentric emphasis in altarpieces of around 1500, distinctly anticipating Counter-Reformation trends. In open contrast to the prevailing tendency to dedicate chapels to individual patron saints, the sacrament altar returned altar images to the central mystery of the Christian faith. It was in this sense an early instance of a largely cleric-driven, top-down effort to impose a theological agenda on altarpieces, in sharp contrast to normal practice, where altarpiece dedications were largely pragmatic and saint-oriented and were motivated by what Peter Humfrey has called "the vagaries of private devotional tastes."[10] Later to become a hallmark of the Counter Reformation, even in this earlier period the sacrament altar was promoted in distinctly reform-minded quarters. Girolamo Savonarola and the reforming bishop of Verona Gian Matteo Giberti were among the strongest early proponents of the practice of placing sacrament tabernacles on altars.[11]

The rise of the Man of Sorrows and of sacrament tabernacles on altars in the period around 1500 can be understood as instances of the "archaism of around 1500" noted long ago by Panofsky, and more recently analyzed by Hans Belting, Bernhard Decker, and Joseph Koerner.[12] For all of these scholars, this trend shows an awareness of artistic traditions that is characteristic of a mature and self-conscious artistic culture. The more recent literature has connected the phenomenon, further, to the increasingly acute concerns over the status and legitimacy of Christian images that arose in the years around 1500. To call the trends discussed above archaizing is, however, not to claim that putting sacrament tabernacles or Man of Sorrows images on altars was in fact a reversion to earlier practices. Archaism has less to do with historical reconstruction than with projection and compensation, and this is why its products appear so distinctly "modern" in retrospect. For concerned humanists and reformers, the sacrament altar and other forms of emphatically Christocentric imagery were forms of purification, means of restoring a clarity and doctrinal anchoring believed to have existed in the past, before the distractions and abuses introduced in later centuries. Michelangelo's London *Entombment* was a highly unusual and sophisticated instance of this trend, and must be understood in the context of a convergence of humanist thought and reform concerns in Italy circa 1500.

The complications arose from the fact that Michelangelo under took his effort of reform by recourse to the language of antique art, specifically to the array of gestures and motifs that Aby Warburg called pathos formulas. It was an effort that presupposed a critical distance from both the Christian and the pagan traditions, and it prompted special appropriations within the antique repertoire. Unlike many of his predecessors and contemporaries, Michelangelo was interested in the motifs of physical movement found in ancient art not only as Albertian *moti,* those outward gestures that express the inner emotions and thus make clear the motivations that make up a story. For Michelangelo, those motifs were not only expressive and denotative but excessive and purgative. They were not simply the expression of a motivated will, emotions manifesting themselves in instrumental action, but rather the manifestations of currents of suprapersonal energy passing through the human body. They were, in this sense, traces of the encounter between the human body and forces larger than itself. They were both a symptom of possession and a means of release.

Michelangelo's special receptivity to ancient art needs to be understood in its cultural context and not simply as an instance of the artist's inscrutable genius and originality. This book is an effort to see it as the result of approaching pagan art in a Christian context and specifically in a culture of reform. In Michelangelo's view, the Christian art of his day suffered from an excessive preoccupation with the literal details of Christ's earthly life and had lost touch with the spiritual sense of the Christian stories – what Paul of Middelburg called their mystery and their sacrament (see chapter 1). Rather than simply return to the archaic forms of the old cult images, however, Michelangelo drew on the ecstatic animations of antique sculpture in an effort to reinvest the narrative expressiveness of contemporary Christian art with spiritual significance. Moments of gestural excess beyond instrumental action, these gestures became, for Michelangelo, a means of pointing to the "figural" dimension that surpasses the literal level of the biblical story.

This meant contravening some powerful cultural trends. In his lifelong preoccupation with the theme of the dead Christ, Michelangelo avoided the model of the dead Meleager – the model that Alberti had held up as a classic example of the naturalistic depiction of a dead body and that had been enthusiastically emulated in the art of Donatello, Andrea Mantegna, Giuliano da Sangallo, Luca Signorelli, and others. In the place of the carrying of the dead Meleager, Michelangelo introduced the equivocal triumph of the stumbling Bacchus. For the wailing lament over the tragic hero he introduced the ecstatic participations of bacchic enthusiasm. He adapted the bacchic reliefs, especially those organized by motifs of frontal presentation and quasi-processional celebration, to the structures and institutions of Christian art. This effort is at work in the early *Entombment* and persisted all the way through the late *Pietà*s.

Michelangelo's interest in bacchic themes in this early work comes as little surprise, given the fact that the first work he made upon arriving in Rome in 1496 was the *Bacchus* (see Figure 54). The clearest example of the kind of antique work that served Michelangelo as a model in the London painting is a famous relief in the Vatican which shows the drunken Bacchus presented frontally and supported by two attendants (Figure 50).[13] The relief was well

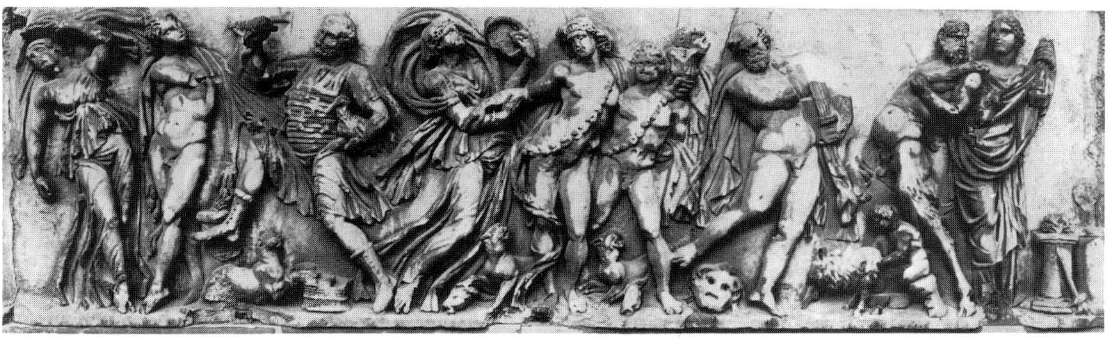

50. *The Drunken Bacchus with Attendants.* Sarcophagus relief. Musei e Gallerie Vaticani, Vatican City.

known to Renaissance artists from Pisanello to Guglielmo della Porta, and the compositional type was publicized in an engraving of 1506 by Jacopo Francia (Figure 51).[14] The central group around Bacchus shows a configuration almost identical, in reverse, to the central group in Michelangelo's painting: The swaying figure of the god is supported on one side by a male figure stepping back under the weight and on the other by a female figure in profile who arches her body, intertwining her arm with the god's. In several other ancient bacchic reliefs, this back-arching figure is shown facing in the opposite direction – that is, in the same direction as Michelangelo's figure.[15] The derivation from such a relief figure would, in fact, account for the curious absence of the far leg in the London painting.[16] The motif of the standing but unstable Bacchus supported by attendants would already have been familiar to Michelangelo from his days in the Medici household. It figured on a gem owned by Lorenzo de' Medici, which was in turn copied in one of the medallions in the courtyard of Palazzo Medici.[17]

Other features of the London *Entombment* bear close resemblances to the most famous modern rendition of bacchic themes at this time, Mantegna's bacchanal engravings. In the *Bacchanal with the Wine Vat* (Figure 52), for example, the figure asleep on the vat, sometimes identified as Bacchus, shows

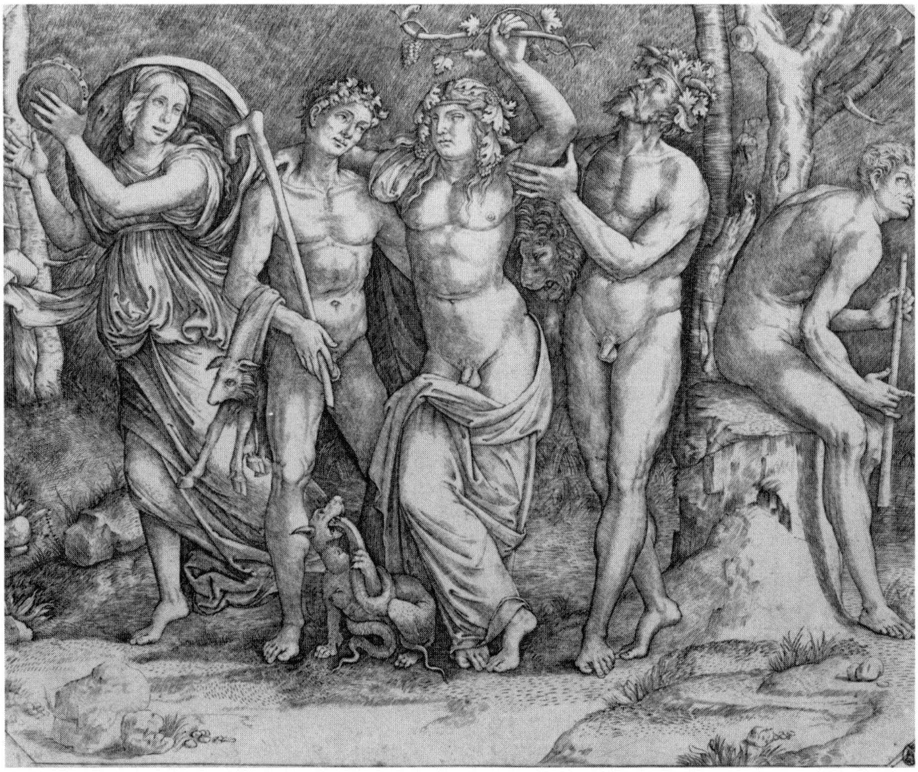

51. Jacopo Francia, *Bacchus and His Attendants.* Engraving. Rosenwald Collection, © 1999 Board of Trustees, National Gallery of Art, Washington, D.C., U.S..

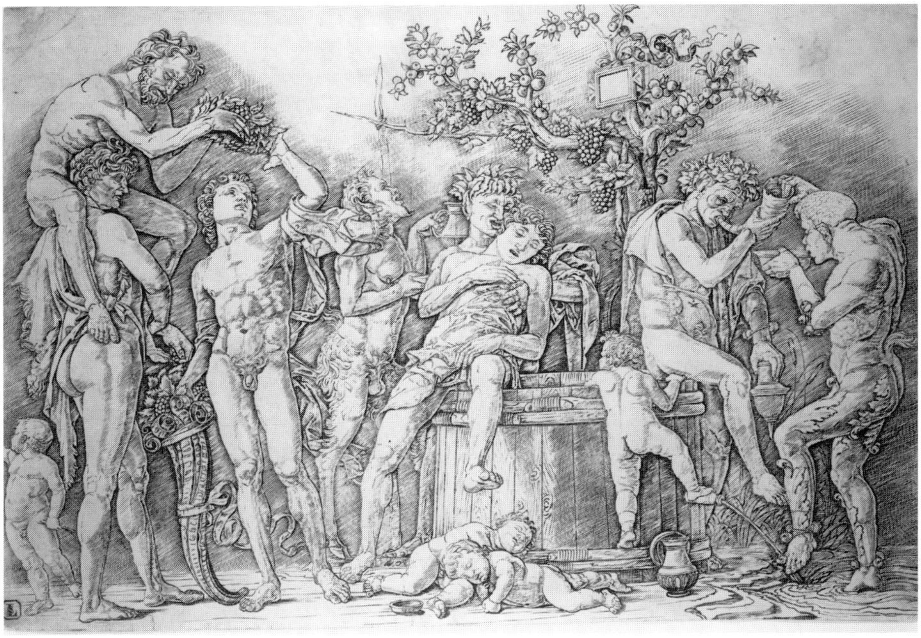

52. Andrea Mantegna, *Bacchanal with a Wine Vat.* Engraving. Rosenwald Collection, © 1999 Board of Trustees, National Gallery of Art, Washington, D.C. U.S..

a striking similarity to Michelangelo's Christ: His head is dropped on his left shoulder, his right arm is obstructed from the shoulder down, his foot just touches the ground, and his upper body is supported from behind in much the manner that Christ is supported in the painting. Mantegna's *Bacchanal with Silenus* (Figure 53), shows even closer parallels to Michelangelo's painting: The support structure around Silenus, right down to the strip of cloth slung under Silenus's thighs, is astonishingly close to what we see in Michelangelo's painting.[18]

The idea of incorporating bacchic motifs in Passion scenes was itself not uncommon in the period. Joshua Reynolds noticed the very same back-arching bacchante figure discussed above in a drawing by Baccio Bandinelli of the deposition. "This figure," he remarked, "Baccio Bandinelli . . . has adopted for one of the Maries, to express frantic agony or grief."[19] Aby Warburg was to make this maenad figure a central motif of his study of the revival of ancient "pathos formulas" in Renaissance art. He gave particular attention to its adaptation in Bertoldo di Giovanni's relief of the *Crucifixion,* a work made in the immediate orbit of the young Michelangelo, where the motif was used to express, in Warburg's terms, the "orgiastic mourning" of Mary Magdalene under the cross.[20] In these *all'antica* adaptations, the maenad figure is used as a means of intensifying the expression of lamentation and thus increasing the dramatic effect. The resulting solutions are, in other words, not far from the expressionism of Niccolò dell'Arca's *Lamentation* group discussed in chapter 1 (see Figure 12), which was itself informed by antique models.

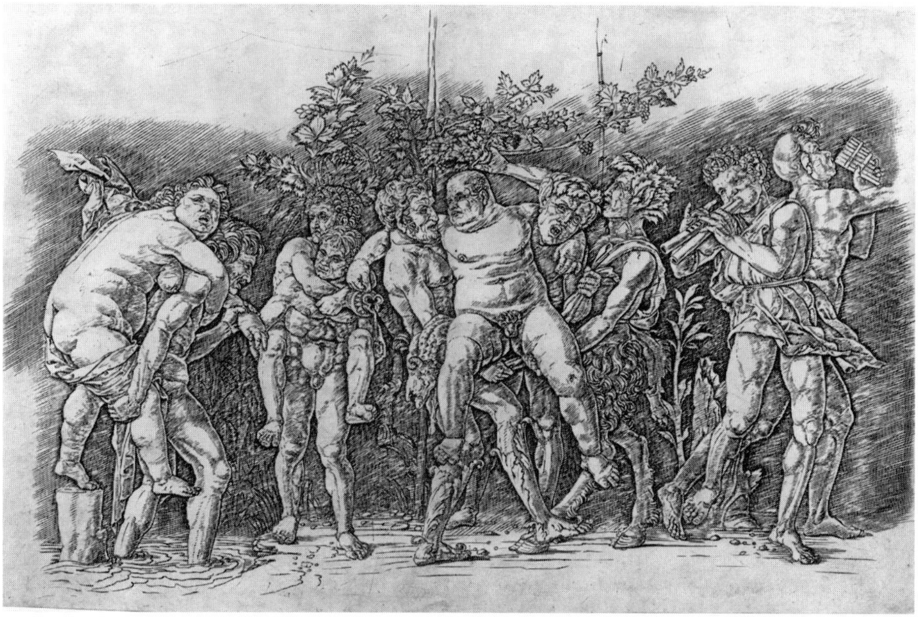

53. Andrea Mantegna, *Bacchanal with Silenus*. Engraving. Rosenwald Collection, © 1999 Board of Trustees, National Gallery of Art, Washington, D.C. U.S..

It has been noted, by Michael Hirst among others, that in his painting Michelangelo imposed a deliberate restraint on this sort of emotional drama.[21] In chapter 1 I argued that this restraint was part of a deliberate effort to draw attention to the sacramental significance of the sacred event, an implicit criticism of the widespread trend toward highly dramatic lamentations in the period that was in line with objections raised by Savonarola. In adapting antique motifs, Michelangelo proceeded in accordance with these concerns. The maenad figure was, for him, less an expression of "frantic agony or grief" than an enthusiastic and ecstatic participant in a divine mystery, an aspect of the figure's meaning that Warburg touched on in describing it as a form of "orgiastic mourning." The ecstatic figures who hold up the drunken Bacchus or Silenus were not simply involved in a mechanical act of support and carrying but were themselves receiving the influence of divine bacchic inspiration. By adapting such figures for his carriers, Michelangelo was able to transform a momentary narrative action into something closer to a processional, celebratory activity and thus to release the event from its narrow historical frame.

CHRISTENING PAGAN MYSTERIES

As we saw in chapter 2, the "signs of life" that were a characteristic feature of the traditional Man of Sorrows – his ability to stand upright, his half-open eyes, his half-willed gestures – all expressed a divine agency within the dead body and thus the promise of the benefits that derived from Christ's sacrifice. The figure's very front-facing posture was part of the message, for it epitomized the idea of presentation, of dispensation, and of self-offering. When a greater emphasis was placed on the deadness of the dead body, as in the Franco-Flemish tradition, this effect was "compensated," and the Eucharistic message preserved, by placing Christ's body in the care of God the Father or of angels. The image of the Man of Sorrows thus insisted on the liturgical, suprahistorical dimension of the Passion story. Michelangelo was intent on preserving this emphasis, with its theological implications, and he found in the swaying figure of Bacchus a means of preserving and reinterpreting its significance within the conditions of modern history painting.

The ability to remain upright while out of one's senses was one of the paradoxical privileges of bacchic inspiration. In one of the *Imagines* described by Philostratus, Comus, the god of revelry, appears "flushed with wine and, though standing, he is asleep under the influence of drink."[22] Erika Tietze-Conrat connected this passage to the youth standing erect and leaning on the cornucopia in Mantegna's *Bacchanal with the Wine Vat*[23] (see Figure 52). Michelangelo grappled with the issue concretely in his statue of *Bacchus,* now in the Bargello (Figure 54). The sculpture was made for Cardinal Raffaele Riario and was almost certainly the work that Michelangelo mentioned he was about to begin shortly after his arrival in Rome in 1496.[24] The letter clearly indicates that the sculpture was intended as a modern rival to ancient sculpture, well represented in Riario's impressive collection, and indeed the *Bacchus* is among the very first large-scale, freestanding statues since antiquity.[25]

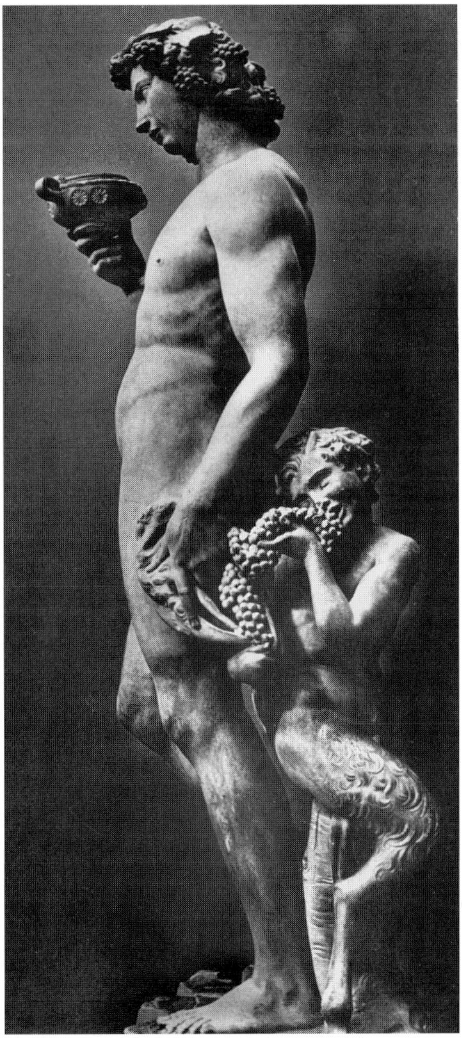

54. Michelangelo, *Bacchus.* Side view. Marble. Bargello Museum, Florence, Italy.

Little wonder, then, that in this work Michelangelo should have given special consideration to the "problem" of the freestanding figure. The sculpture is remarkable, and has often been criticized, for

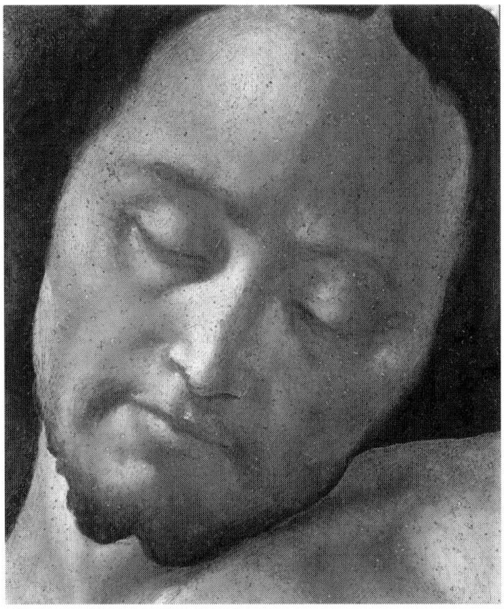

55. Michelangelo, *Christ Carried to the Tomb, detail of Christ's face.* Panel. National Gallery, London, England.

having pushed the representation of the effects of drunkenness to new limits. The soft, fleshy figure lurches forward and seems on the brink of losing his balance. As Wind explained, the representation was justified on the principle that the gods should be represented as filled with the power they dispense.[26] This made of Bacchus a special god, a god whose power is expressed in a paradoxical vulnerability. The passible quality of the god – in some legends Bacchus undergoes death and resurrection – made him a favorite in funerary contexts.[27] For Michelangelo these special qualities had concrete implications, for in affecting the god's bearing, they also affect his "status": Bacchus's drunken nature threatens his ability to remain upright – that is, to have a statue that stands and in this sense to be like other gods. Michelangelo was interested in Bacchus as the god of precarious uprightness, an aspect of Bacchus most recently emphasized by Marcel Detienne.[28] For Michelangelo, this aspect of the figure was important enough to demand a resourceful reinterpretation of the function of the "buttress." If in antique statuary the buttress typically served as a means of supporting the figure, here it serves the exactly opposite function of a counterweight: It is a tensile element that prevents the figure from falling forward.[29] Michelangelo's interpretation of the figure, in other words, draws acute dramatic attention to the question of its freestanding status, and in this problem, specific to statuary, lies an understanding of the nature of the god.

It is therefore not so surprising that these ideas should have come into play a few years later, when Michelangelo confronted the problem of reinterpreting the equivocally upright Man of Sorrows. Again, this was not simply a question of a borrowed motif. The problems of instability and support touch on the very status of the figure, and for Michelangelo this constituted an inherent affinity. Both Bacchus and Christ are equivocal figures, powerful in their vulnerability. Bacchus is sovereign in his drunkenness, and Christ assumes a majesty in death. Both hold themselves precariously upright, and in this liminal state dispense their benefits. As in the Vatican relief of Bacchus supported by attendants (see Figure 50), the attendant figures in the London painting struggle to maintain the god in an upright posture (see Figure 6). Christ is evidently dependent on the carrying figures, who labor strenuously under his weight, but at the same time he appears weightless, miraculously self-supporting.

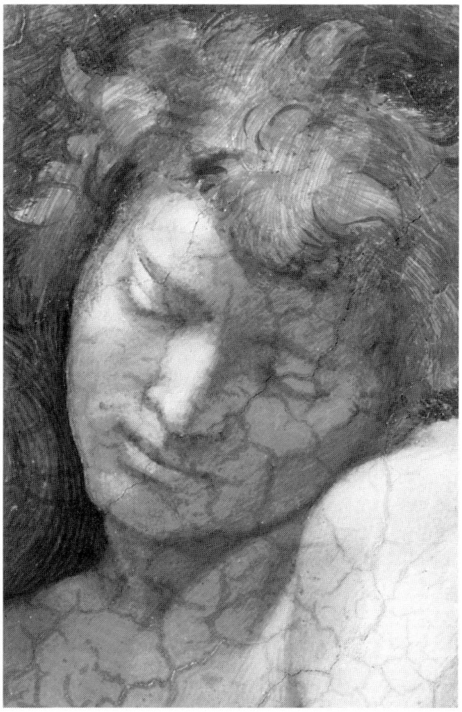

56. Michelangelo, *Creation of Eve,* detail of Adam's face. Fresco. Sistine Chapel, Vatican City.

We see no blood on Christ's body, no visible wounds, no signs of violence. Instead, Christ's body is soft, languid, and feminine, qualities often associated with Bacchus. Christ's face does not bear the marks of a violent death but instead suggests a slumber that is both peaceful and alert (Figure 55). In this sense Michelangelo's interpretation of Christ falls into a long medieval tradition that emphasized the "sweetness" of Christ's Passion, a distinct alternative to the emphasis on blood and gore prevalent in much late medieval drama and imagery.[30] For Michelangelo, Christ is not literally dead but rather in a sweet sleep. The strongest parallel to the face of Christ in the London painting within Michelangelo's oeuvre is the face of Adam in the scene of the *Creation of Eve* in the Sistine Chapel (Figure 56). This is the "deep sleep" into which God throws Adam before drawing Eve from him, as described in Genesis 2:21, one of the *loci classici* of patristic discussions of divinely induced ecstasy.[31] Another parallel to the London Christ can be found in the so-called *Dying Slave* in the Louvre, where as in London the swoonlike state is combined with an upright position (Figure 57). Although the interpretation of this work is still debated, a comparison with its pendant, the *Rebellious Slave,* reveals two significantly different responses to their bondage: Where the *Rebellious Slave* exerts physical effort in his struggle to break loose, the *Dying Slave* accepts, his body soft and languid as he surrenders to a deathlike swoon (which need not be identified with an actual death). As Adrian Stokes memorably put it, "He submits tenseless to his dream, yet sustains with the huge, refulgent orbit of his form the vigilance of light. His beauty is the one of a sea-cave's aperture that allows and withstands reverberating waves within. . ." The London Christ, similarly bound in strips of cloth, is also tender and accepting, and yet he too reverberates: Having taken into himself the effort and suffering of the world, he is vibrant and animated in sleep.

To put it briefly, Michelangelo put the dead Christ into an ecstasy. Christ was not simply dead but in a "transport" until the time of the Resurrection. We find this idea not only in the London *Entombment* but throughout the late *Pietàs*. The idea of associating Christian mysteries with ecstatic states, specifically, ecstatic drunkenness, formed a venerable tradition in Christian thought well before Michelangelo. An important source for the later development of notions of ecstasy was Plato's discussion of the good forms of madness, the blessings of heaven-sent madness, in the *Phaedrus.* There he outlined four types of madness, presided over by their respective deities: the inspiration of the prophet under Apollo, that of the mystic under Dionysus, that of the poet under the Muses, and that of the lover under Aphrodite and Eros. Through these means, the soul is led (back) to the experience of divine things normally beyond the ken of mortals.[32] The Jewish Philosopher Philo inherited this tradition and brought it to bear on the examples of ecstasy he found in the Old Testament, notably the swoon into which Adam was thrown when God drew Eve out of him (see Figure 56). In his discussion of ecstasy, Philo emphasized the soul's joy at leaving the body, celebrating ecstasy as a state where one is taken out of oneself and the soul tastes a higher knowledge – Philo invokes both Sophia and gnosis – belonging to divine things. His governing metaphor for this sort of spiritual frenzy, as Hans Lewy showed, was the oxymoron of *nephalios methē,* or *sobria ebrietas* (sober drunkenness), a notion that was to exert a deep influence on the Christian fathers in the East, most importantly Origen and Gregory of Nyssa, and in the West, most importantly Ambrose, Augustine, and Jerome.[33]

Ambrose described a new wine "pressed from that uncommon grape which, like the fruit in the barrel, hung in the flesh on the cross." This is the wine that "'makes happy the heart of man' [Psalms 103:15], that makes it drunk with sobriety [*sobrietatem inebriat*], that produces a steamy intoxication of faith and true piety [*crapulam fidei et verae religionis*]."[34] In another passage, Ambrose said that in the drunkenness induced by the Eucharistic wine "the body does not stagger, but remains upright, the spirit is not confused, but is sanctified."[35] Commenting on the mystery of the Eucharist, Ambrose invokes Song of Songs 5:1: "Eat my friends and become drunk O dear ones," which he interprets entirely in the spirit of *sobria ebrietas,* inviting the faithful to partake in the Eucharist, the *"mysticum dominici altaris convivium."*[36] In all of these cases, spiritual drunkenness is a benefit offered to and received by the faithful. Augustine, for example, invoked the metaphor of drunkenness to describe the enthusiasm of saints and martyrs, who forget their families and loved ones in the love of God: "Don't be surprised: they were drunk [*ebrii*]. What were they drunk from? You see, they took the goblet that would intoxicate them. . . So let us, brothers, become drunk 'from the rich overflow of his house' [Psalms 35:8]."[37] The idea was used in a Eucharistic context in at least one Renaissance altarpiece, by Moretto da Brescia in Santi Nazaro e Celso in Brescia, which was made for the altar of a confraternity dedicated to the sacrament (Figure 58). There we see the Man of Sorrows as a figure of the Eucharist, his blood pouring into the chalice. Solomon, the putative author of the Song of Songs, is shown on the right, holding a tablet inscribed with the same verse invoked by Ambrose: *"Comedite amici et inebriamini charissimi."* We find related ideas in a vision of Girolamo Savonarola, in which a bloody cross creates a river of blood like a fountain, and around the cross the faithful are removing their clothes and "bathing and becoming drunk in this blood."[38]

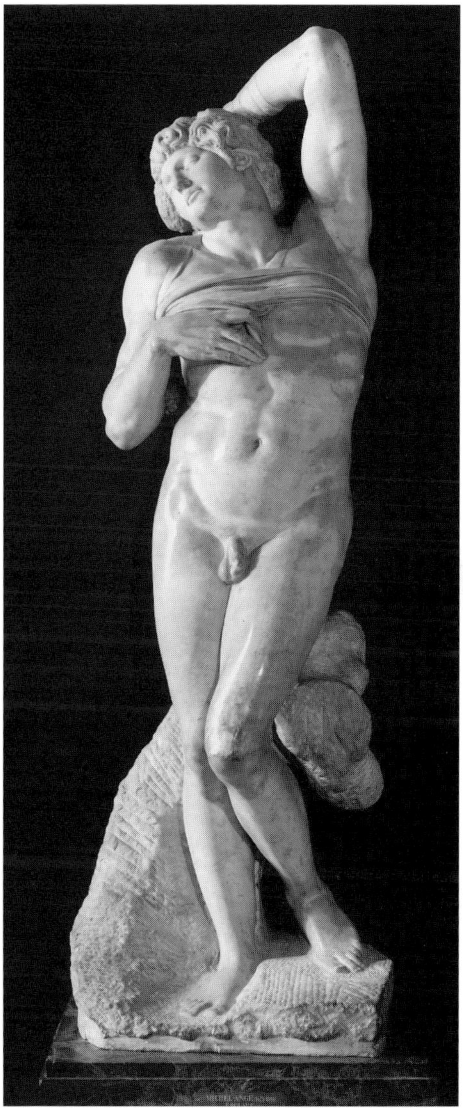

57. Michelangelo, *Dying Slave.* Marble. Louvre, Paris, France. © Réunion des Musées Nationaux.

This patristic tradition left a faint trace in the *Ovide Moralisé,*[39] but it was fully revived by the Renaissance humanists. The great novelty of the Renaissance revival of the tradition was its open invocation of the pagan sources. For good historical reasons, the Church fathers refrained from invoking Bacchus directly, but the Renaissance humanists, at a safer remove from pagan antiquity, felt no such inhibition. To borrow an expression from Marjorie O'Rourke Boyle, they openly christened pagan mysteries. The classic statement is the dithyrambic passage in Giovanni Pico della Mirandola's *Oration on the Dignity of Man,* where, invoking the same verse from Psalm 35 as St. Augustine, he enjoined his papal audience to mystical bacchic rapture:

> [L]et us be driven by the frenzies of Socrates, that they may throw us into an ecstasy as to put our mind and ourselves in God. . . . Thereupon Bacchus, the leader of the Muses, by showing in his mysteries, that is, in the visible signs of nature, the invisible things of God to us who study philosophy, will intoxicate us with the fulness of God's house.[40]

Marsilio Ficino, Pico's mentor, also had things to say on the subject of ecstasy. He took over from Plato's *Phaedrus* the four forms of madness or frenzy and expounded them with some variations throughout his career, consistently maintaining the *furor mysteriale* under Bacchus.[41] Invoking the same Psalm verse as St. Augustine and Pico (Psalm 35:8: *"Inebriabor ab ubertate domus tuae"*),

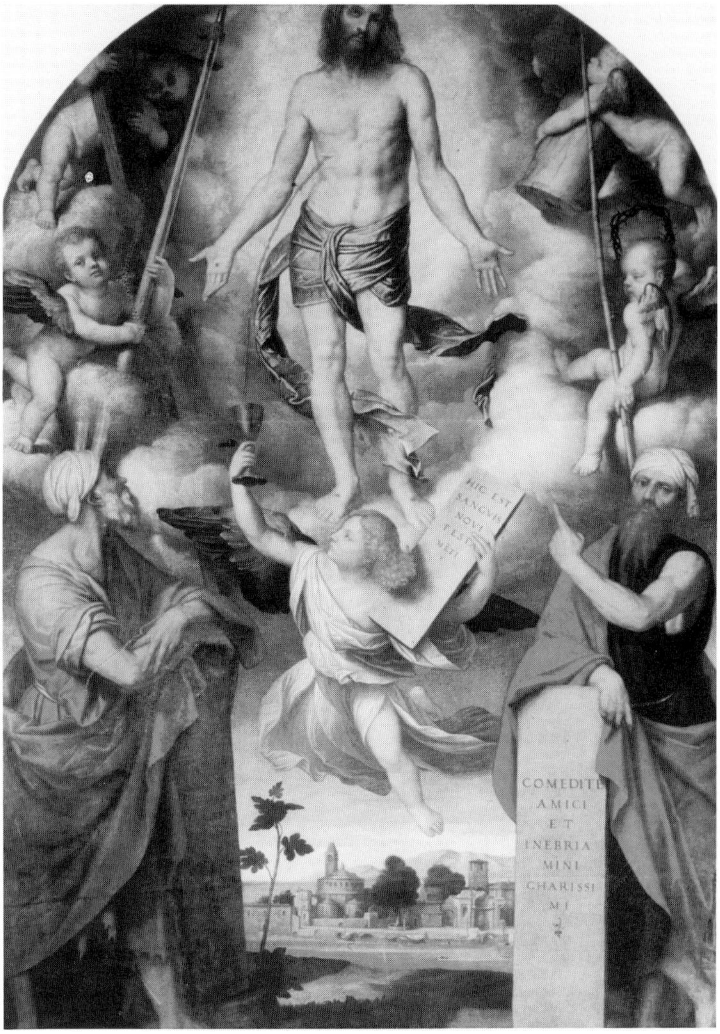

58. Moretto da Brescia, *Man of Sorrows with Moses and Salomon.* Panel. SS. Nazaro e Celso, Brescia, Italy.

Ficino defended the principle of the two types of drunkenness (*duplex ebrietas*), one the delirious earthly kind where the soul is put below itself and the other the divine kind where the soul is put above itself.[42] For Ficino, it was a felicitous and significant coincidence that the name Dionysus should have belonged to the Christian mystic he most admired, Dionysus the Areopagite, for modern scholars Pseudo-Dionysus. In Pseudo-Dionysus he found the spirit of the god Dionysus, which "was believed by the ancient theologians and Platonists to be the ecstasy of disencumbered minds, when they transgress the natural limits of intelligence . . . and rage, as it were, in a bacchic frenzy."[43]

Ficino also took up the theme of ecstatic transgression in a section of the *Theologia Platonica* (XIII, 2) where he deals with the vacations or alienations of the soul (*vacationes animae*), such as sleep, fainting, and wonder, in which the soul is temporarily released from the body and becomes susceptible to divine influence. In these states, when the body is softened and half dead, the vision of the soul becomes sharper, "since every time that it turns in one itself, it participates in celestial mysteries and in divine providence."[44] These ideas became common patrimony in humanist thought circa 1500. Giles of Viterbo, the Ficino admirer and noted papal preacher, also followed Augustine in likening the soul's illumination by love and divine grace to drunkenness, and like Pico he referred the metaphor directly to the mysteries of Bacchus, calling it a "furor Bacchi."[45] The theme of ecstatic drunkenness, applied in a Christian context, also played a very large role in the thought of Erasmus.[46]

We have come a far distance from Michelangelo's painting, and in order to get back to it it is important to observe that none of these writings connect the theme of inspired drunkenness specifically to Christ's Passion. The Church fathers and Renaissance humanists generally invoke the idea of spiritual drunkenness as a special privilege offered to the faithful. Even Moretto's painting (see Figure 58), which contains an image of the Man of Sorrows, invites the viewer/reader to delight in the joys of spiritual drunkenness, rather than actually depicting the figure of Christ or attendant figures as being under its influence. The idea of Christ himself drunk in the Passion comes up in late medieval Passion tracts, but without exception as far as I can tell these references are entirely negative, and without relation to the patristic tradition of *sobria ebrietas*. The tracts rely on language drawn from the mocking of the drunken Noah (Genesis 9:20–4) and of Jeremiah 23:9: "My heart is broken within me, all my bones tremble; I am become as a drunken man, and as a man full of wine."[47] Christ's drunkenness is presented not as a mystical virtue to be celebrated but as an accusation placed in the mouths of his persecutors: "'Why can't you stand up by yourself? We see very well that you are drunk.'"[48] The injustice of the accusations arouses pity for the abject Christ, not admiration for the mystical dispensations of Christ drunk in the Passion.

Closer to the positive construction is Augustine's typological interpretation of the drunkenness of Noah in the *City of God*. The drunken Noah prefigures Christ, who "was drunk and uncovered, that is, suffered in the Passion." But this was not a degradation, he argues, for in the words of St. Paul, I Corinthians 1:25, "'The weakness of God is stronger than men, and the foolishness of God is wiser than men.'"[49] But by far the most extensive description of the Passion in terms of ecstatic drunkenness comes from St. Jerome. In one of his commentaries on Psalm 80, he proclaimed, *"Dominus in passione inebriatus est* [The Lord was drunk in the Passion]" and asserted that in imitating Christ the saints are "daily drunk in the ardor of the faith." The specific identification of drunkenness with the physical violence of the Passion brings Jerome, of all the Church fathers, closest to invoking bacchic mysteries, when he concludes this passage with the enigmatic declaration, "There are many things to be said about the mystery of wine and drunkenness [*Multa sunt quae dicantur de vini mysterio et de ebrietate*]."[50]

Jerome was close to Michelangelo's conception in calling Christ drunk in the Passion, but there is a significant difference. Both Jerome and Augustine saw Christ drunk in his suffering – that is, in the abuse and tortures that he suffered in the Passion. In Michelangelo's painting, as in the later *Pietà*s, Christ is dead, his suffering over. The drunken ecstasy interprets not the violence and tumult of the Passion but the "transport" into which Christ is thrown after death. Michelangelo's lifelong engagement with the theme of the *pietà* and entombment can be understood as a sustained investigation into the ambiguous state of Christ's body in the interval between his death and his resurrection. As we will see, Michelangelo took several approaches to the problem, but one feature remained consistent: For Michelangelo, the dead Christ was not a mere corpse; he was suspended in a liminal, quasi-animated state, which Michelangelo interpreted variously as an ecstasy, a drunken sleep, or a transport. This is not so far-fetched a solution as it might first appear, for did not Augustine say that in an ecstasy the soul departs the body temporarily, leaving the body as if dead?[51] Did not Ficino call it a vacation of the soul, in which the soul "participates in celestial mysteries and divine providence?"[52] Ficino repeatedly described those in an ecstasy as tender (*tener*), soft (*mollis*), intact (*intactus*), and immaculate (*immaculatus*).[53] It is difficult to find better words to describe Michelangelo's Christ.

Both Ficino and Augustine were describing the experience of mortals taken out of themselves in an ecstasy. To apply this condition to the dead Christ entails some significant alterations. For mortals ecstasy and spiritual drunkenness are a means of becoming temporarily dead to the things of the world. They enter into contact with those divine things that are normally out of their reach and thus have a foretaste of the beatitude that awaits them on the far side of mortality.[54] In the case of Christ, who partakes of two natures, the reality of death is itself the brief interval. Our ecstasy is a form of little death; Christ's little death, which lasts only three days, is a form of ecstasy.

Such an interpretation of the figure of Christ affects the other figures, as we have seen. In the place of the pathetic expressions of lament that we expect to find in such a scene, we find instead forms of quasi-ritualistic participation; in the place of wild gesticulation, we find a solemn, meditative awareness. Above all there is restraint, and this means that even the bacchic elements are muted. Even the figures most closely modeled on bacchic prototypes do not quite rage in a bacchic frenzy; they are not quite caught up in enthusiastic participation. As we will see, Michelangelo let his bacchic hair down in his later experiments with the subject, which were undertaken in a more private sphere and in less regulated artistic formats. Here Michelangelo's main concern, as we have seen, was to respect altarpiece decorum, and above all to offer a clear alternative to the highly dramatic treatments of the subject that were the norm in contemporary art. Thus although there is a hint of a maenadic dance in the female figure to Christ's left, an almost ceremonial solemnity dominates and controls the painting. The effect of clamping is most evident in the way the figures are virtually locked into place by the tight surface structure and the elaborate bondage of sashes, belts, and winding sheets. The result is a somewhat awkward and unresolved work, an uncomfortable experiment that does not go far enough in any direction – and that has made Michelangelo connoisseurs uncomfortable to this day. It is not surprising that such an ingenious and frustrated effort should have been left unfinished. This initial failure introduces us to the tensions and frustrations that were to mark Michelangelo's lifelong preoccupation with the theme, right down to the final version of the Rondanini *Pietà*.

Michelangelo was not the only Renaissance artist who devised resourceful solutions to preserve the mysterious, sacramental significance of Christ's sacrifice under new pictorial conditions. The works of Fra Angelico and Rogier van der Weyden, studied in chapter 2, involved a delicate negotiation between the dictates of naturalism and an adherence to the Man of Sorrows tradition, understood as a link to the theology of the Eucharist. Closer to Michelangelo's time, perhaps the most conscientious modern artist was Giovanni Bellini. He made several adaptations of the Man of Sorrows image within narrative contexts and always took care to preserve theologically significant elements of the traditional image.[55] In open contrast to Mantegna, for example, he imposed a deliberate restraint on gestures of lament.[56] Bellini also found ways to allude to a supernatural efficacy within the otherwise naturalistically depicted dead Christ. In the *Man of Sorrows* of the upper register of the St. Vincent Ferrer polyptych, for example, he sharply emphasized the veins in Christ's arms. As the veins in the body are known to go flat at death, this anatomical "violation" indicates a mysterious virtue within Christ's dead body, and in this way served as a means of preserving the theological significance of the Man of Sorrows figure under new pictorial conditions.[57]

Michelangelo adopted a similar device in his early Roman *Pietà* (Figure 59), where Christ appears to be in a deep and animated asleep, and his limbs show pulsing, prominent veins.[58] From the London *Entombment* forward, Michelangelo engaged these concerns primarily in explorations of the mysterious implications of a powerless figure who remains upright, a problem he had confronted directly in his statue of the *Bacchus.* Little wonder, then, that he should have developed an interest in bacchic scenes generally, and specifically in the type of drunken figure about which Philostratus could say "though standing, he is asleep." Through these models Michelangelo found a means of emphasizing the life-giving qualities of the dead Christ, the latent animation in the limp figure – not his pitiful suffering, but an incipient radiance and beauty. The scene is thus understood less as a historical

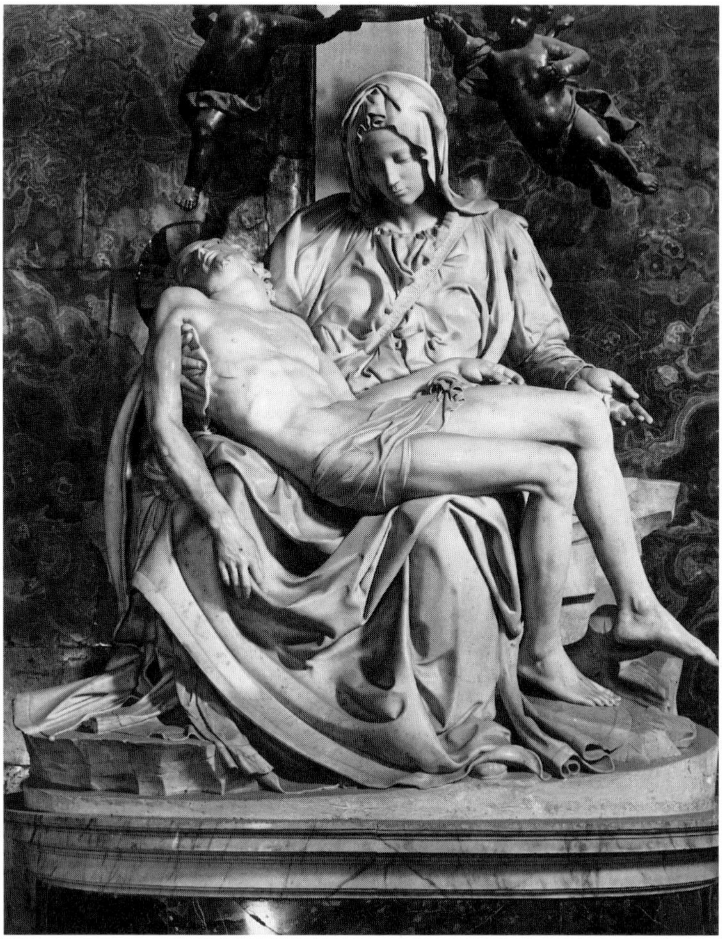

59. Michelangelo, *Pietà*. Marble. St. Peter's Basilica, Vatican City. Alinari/ Art Resource, NY.

moment of lament than as a ritual procession, a mysterious triumph. In her technical analysis of the painting, Jill Dunkerton observed that the flesh painting on the body of Christ does not quite reach the edge of the reddish undermodeling. The contours of the body thus "vibrate with a red-brown aura."[59] But the figure's auratic radiance is interpreted above all through the ideals of antique sculpture: Pristine and marmoreal, Christ is shown entirely nude and without wounds.[60] Adolfo Venturi interpreted the beautiful intactness of this "alabastrine nude" as a sign of Christ's coming resurrection, a suggestion that his death was no more than a sort of sleep before the awakening.[61]

Writers also found theologically inventive ways to assert Christ's animateness after death, and occasionally hit on solutions that came very close to Michelangelo's. The Dominican Raymond of Capua, writing at the end of the fourteenth century, embroidered on an established scholastic tradition when, recounting a vision of St. Catherine of Siena, he has Christ explain this mystery: "when my body was suffering and dying on the cross and when it lay there with all the life gone from it, it still had life latent in it and inseparably united to it all the time." And yet this latent virtue was so hidden that even the apostles, when confronted with the body, "all lost faith and hope." Christ specifies that although his body was no longer alive with the life it had received from its own soul,

it was still united to the unending life by which all living things live; and by virtue of this, at the time determined by all eternity, my own spirit was reunited with it [my body], with a much greater bond of life and vigor than it had had before, because it was endowed with the gifts of immortality and impassibility and other gifts which had not been granted to it earlier.[62]

We find related ideas in a fairly popular Passion tract written by the early sixteenth-century preacher and writer Pietro da Lucca. In describing the scene of the lament over the dead Christ, he asserted that already then "[s]igns of glory and victory" began to appear on Christ's body. "The dead and wounded and deformed body of the Lord," he said, "in one instant was made once again healthy, pure, and white [*sano, candido e bianco*], as if he had never received a wound or a blow." The five wounds, we are told, remained on Christ's body but only as a sign and testimonial. This transformation, it is important to note, occurs not at the resurrection but already before Christ's entombment. A little further on Pietro da Lucca asserted that although Christ's body was dead and separated from his soul, nonetheless "it was always united and conjoined with divinity."[63] As I show in part 2 of this book, related ideas were to play a major role throughout Michelangelo's later treatments of the subject, and they come up also in the work of Rosso Fiorentino. We also find very similar ideas in the Passion writings of Vittoria Colonna, Michelangelo's friend in this later period and herself the recipient of one of Michelangelo's most important treatments of the subject (see chapter 6).

Michael Hirst noted that the figure of Christ bears a resemblance to that of the Santo Spirito *Crucifix,* now in Casa Buonarroti:[64] In both, we find an entirely nude figure, the body beautifully intact and the face radiating peace and repose. The idea of representing a divinity fully nude was of course quite common in pagan antiquity but had very little precedent in Christian art. The ambivalence Michelangelo felt about it can be deduced from the present state of the London panel, where the genitalia are conspicuously missing in an otherwise fairly complete figure. Recent examination of the paint surface has determined that the genitalia were not painted and effaced later but were never painted at all.[65] The resistance must have been acute, for Michelangelo went so far as to paint the shadow cast by the missing genitalia on the left

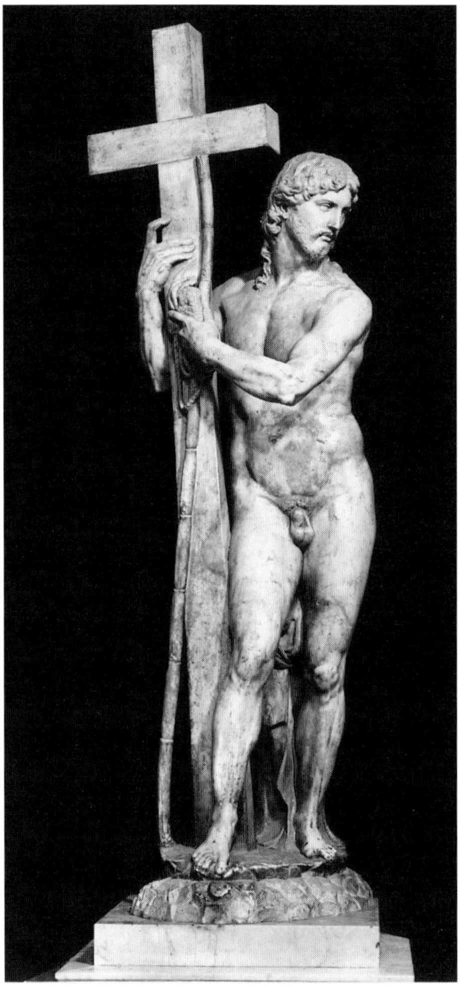

60. Michelangelo, *Christ*. Marble. Santa Maria sopra Minerva, Rome, Italy. Alinari/ Art Resource, NY.

thigh. As Hirst noted, the conception of the idealized nude Christ that we find in the London painting is not far from the statue of the *Christ* in Santa Maria sopra Minerva (Figure 60). Here the idea is overtly identified with the ideals of antique statuary and receives a distinctly triumphant interpretation, again despite the fact that the figure belongs to a type of Christ imagery in which the wounds and blood, the *ostentatio vulnerum,* traditionally played a prominent role.[66] In the painting the triumph is a more paradoxical one, because we do not have a Christ *sub specie aeternitatis* but a scene from the historical Passion: Christ is shown dead but unscathed, a victim of history and yet the embodiment of a divine perfection. The ideal beauty of the classical nude has been made to embody the suprahistorical principle in the Christian story.

The solution was well suited to the ethos of a papal culture that linked the renewal of the church to the myth of a new Golden Age explicitly visualized on the model of classical antiquity.[67] It was congruent, specifically, with the Roman humanist milieu one of whose epicenters in the late fifteenth century was the church of Sant'Agostino, a milieu to which Michelangelo was connected through his friend Jacopo Gallo as well as through his first Roman patron Cardinal Raffaele Riario, who was General Protector of the Augustinian Order. Beyond these circumstantial connections, we have documentation of an altarpiece commission from Michelangelo for Sant'Agostino in 1500, which Hirst and I have argued is to be identified with the commission for the London *Entombment*.[68] Michelangelo's sponsor for this commission was Jacopo Gallo, in whose villa Jacopo Sadoleto located his neo-Platonic dialogue *Phaedrus,* which offers a vivid depiction of this cultural milieu, and in the context of which Edgar Wind interpreted the *Bacchus*.[69] Giles of Viterbo, the most prominent figure at Sant'Agostino in the early sixteenth century, referred specifically to his friends concentrated at the convent when he said that although in other ages piety was combined with an unpolished manner and elegance tended to be impious, it was the achievement of his own age to marry piety and elegance.[70] The cultural optimism of the Roman humanist ambient in the early sixteenth century, which saw in the celebration of beauty, modeled above all on the antique, a path to spiritual enlightenment and Christian reform, was to last only a brief time.[71] Later decades saw the advent of a more circumspect and repressive culture, one less inclined to celebrate openly the marriage of pagan beauty and Christian spirituality. The developments between Michelangelo's early and later works, as we will see, respond quite dramatically to this cultural shift.

The revival of a medieval, Gothic tradition within a resourceful adaptation of the antique was identified by Wilde, and before him by Dvořák, as the characteristic feature of Michelangelo's early works.[72] It is in these terms that we can best understand the London painting's relation to the Roman *Pietà* (see Figure 59), which also interpreted a northern, Gothic form through the ideals of antique statuary.[73] The contract for the sculpture stipulated that it be "the most beautiful work of marble in Rome, and that no master living could do it so well" – in other words, that it be made to surpass both the ancient and contemporary sculpture of Rome.[74] Shearman has demonstrated that one of Michelangelo's primary antique models in this work was a type of Hellenistic Diana figure – and here again, as Shearman has pointed out, the reference to the antique prototype, a virgin goddess, is more than merely formal.[75] In a more general sense, the emulation of classical ideals guided a significant reorientation of the subject. In contrast to the traditional emphasis on Christ's broken body and the Virgin's bitter lament, Michelangelo offers an ideal, beautiful, pristine Christ in the tender embrace of an unusually youthful, beautiful, spouselike Virgin.

Here as elsewhere Michelangelo pushes the traditional subject away from dramatic sentimentality and toward a high-minded emphasis on the spiritual benefits of Christ's sacrifice, which find expression in the language of spiritual love. This was not merely a shift in style and interpretation but a departure at the level of format and genre. The work loudly announced its uniqueness in modern-day Rome, and its parity with the antique, in its status as a full-scale, freestanding piece of marble statuary – a highly unusual sight in Christian chapels at this time. In both the 1550 and 1568 editions of the *Lives,* Giorgio Vasari took special notice of its quality as a sculpture in the round (*"tutta tonda"*).[76] Jakob Burckhardt, in his history of the altarpiece, celebrated the *Pietà* as a "free-standing marble group of a type unprecedented in the Christian era" and called it "the final conquest of the Christian altar by antique statuary."[77] Whether or not Michelangelo's *Pietà* was intended to stand above the altar of its chapel, it certainly fulfilled its function as an unprecedented display of freestanding *all'antica* statuary in a

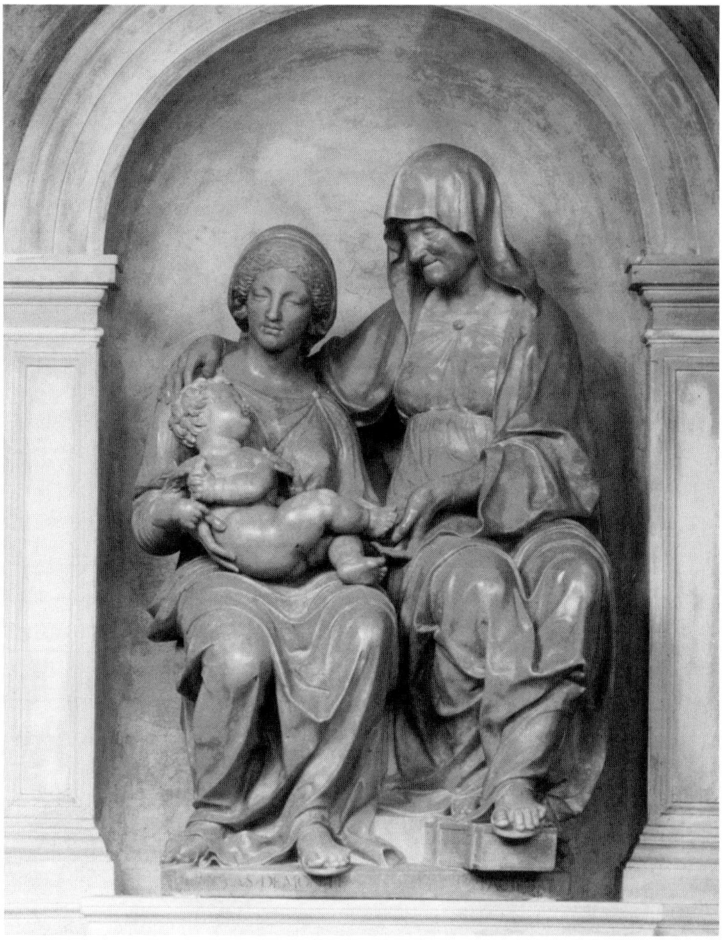

61. Andrea Sansovino, *St. Anne, the Virgin, and Child*. Marble. Sant'Agostino, Rome, Italy.

chapel setting. And it certainly set an important precedent for the subsequent trend of placing antique-inspired marble statues on Christian altars, a trend enthusiastically promoted in the following years by Andrea and Jacopo Sansovino. Andrea's *St. Anne* of 1512 (Figure 61) and Jacopo's *Madonna del Parto* of 1521 were, indeed, both made for the church of Sant'Agostino.[78] It is difficult for us, accustomed as we are to the polemics of the Protestant Reformation and to the reforms decreed by the Council of Trent, to imagine any relation between this spectacular revival of antique sculpture and a culture of religious reform. And yet for Giles of Viterbo, Prior General of the Augustinian Order from 1507 to 1518, the cult focused on Sansovino's *St. Anne* at Sant'Agostino was a shining example of that marriage of elegance and piety that he believed to be the great achievement of his age and the mark of an era of spiritual renewal.[79] The antique, even overtly pagan, allusions of this new brand cult image were, for this audience, an integral part of its deep Christian significance.

This is certainly the spirit that breathes through the *Coryciana,* the anthology of poems, many of them in praise of Sansovino's *St. Anne* group, that was dedicated to its patron the German humanist Johannes Goritz (Corycius), himself a friend of Giles of Viterbo.[80] In these poems Sansovino's sculpture is consistently celebrated as a triumph of Christian piety, an achievement that supercedes the achievements of antiquity. And yet the reference and return to antique forms remains, for the poets, the basis of its virtue and spiritual significance. In a poem by Jacopo Sadoleto, also the author of a poem on the recently discovered *Laocoön* group, Goritz is celebrated as the genius who has dared to "restore to our age ancient images."[81] The group is consistently praised as a Christian triumph over the pagan cults, and yet its virtues and Christian significance are continually described in pagan terms: The figures are referred to in the plural as "gods" and "deities," the Virgin is invoked as the queen of Mt. Olympus, and, in a poem by Baldassare Castiglione, the three figures are asked to distribute their gifts through the good offices of Ceres and Bromius.[82] Idolatry is a persistent theme of the poems – it is warned against by some, implicitly embraced by others – but one has the impression that this is above all a *topos* invoked by learned poets, not an indication that idolatry was a real possibility. The living and breathing sculpture, the sculpture inhabited by the deity, the efficacy of the sculpture in bringing the deity down to earth – these are well-worn themes of the epigrammatic tradition and were not likely to lead any of these poets to the truly idolatrous behavior that we find elsewhere in the period, such as in the cult of the Fair Virgin that flared up only a few years later at Regensburg.[83] The "cult" focused on Sansovino's *St. Anne* group instead revived the pagan cults in sublimated form; it was a new brand of elegant Christian piety that was as far from the original pagan cults as from the more recent "excesses" of Christian image worship. The freestanding marble statue, which inspired loathing in the Church fathers and fearful awe in the Christian Middle Ages, was here neutralized in an atmosphere of self-conscious and retrospective humanist spirituality. In the words of one of the epigrammists, Sansovino's work heralded "a new conception of statues.[84]

Michelangelo's revival of freestanding antique statuary in chapel settings continued after the *Pietà*[85] in the *Bruges Madonna,* the *Medici Madonna* (Figure 62), and above all in the Minerva *Christ* (see Figure 61). The concerns were also present in Michelangelo's early experiments in panel painting – in the London *Entombment,* as we have seen, but also in the *Manchester Madonna* (Figure 63). Here we see no description of setting – no landscape, not even a horizon – and the group of the Virgin and Child is treated as a freestanding block. These features clearly set it apart from other altar panels of the period, especially those containing elaborate architectonic settings. Even Francesco Granacci's *Rest on the Flight to Egypt,* with which it has

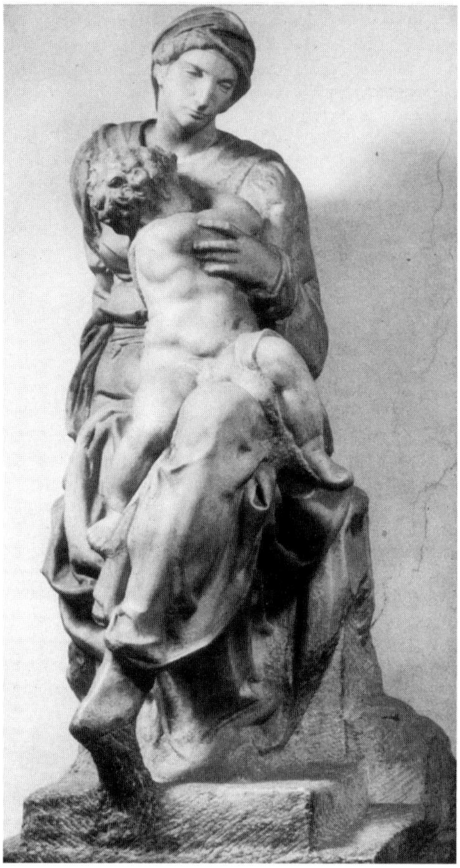

62. Michelangelo, *Medici Madonna*. Marble. San Lorenzo, Florence, Italy.

often been compared, appears cluttered when compared to the London *Madonna*.[86] In the face of widespread trends in contemporary altar painting, Michelangelo's painting represents a "return" to the figure, conceived in distinctly sculptural terms.[87]

The "sculptural" critique that here occurs within the medium of painting was later concretized in the sculpture groups of the *Bruges Madonna* and the *Medici Madonna* (see Figure 62), both of which incorporate specific motifs found in the earlier painting.[88] It might be argued that these works were carried out in marble simply in response to the requirements of the commissions or as the result of Michelangelo's personal preference for marble sculpture. The point remains, however, that in these works Michelangelo offered a departure from contemporary practice, proposing a strong, figure-centered alternative realized on the model of antique sculpture. In the case of an artist with strong religious convictions and a keen historical sensibility, such a departure could not but involve a significant critique, informed by an awareness of traditions of religious art. Michelangelo applied the principles of antique statuary within the context of Christian altars as a means of restoring the figural focus and simplicity of traditional icons and cult statues. But this was a restoration in a very new guise, well beyond obvious archaism. The complexity and novelty of the *Medici Madonna* (see Figure 62) are a far cry from earlier traditions of religious art. And yet here, where we would least expect it, it has been shown that Michelangelo modeled his group quite carefully on a Trecento icon venerated in the same church (Figure 64).[89] The similarities consist first of all in the subject of the breast-feeding Virgin but also in the treatment of the figures: in the twisted posture of the child and in the faraway gaze of the Virgin. Michelangelo's much-vaunted independence from the antique is, here and elsewhere, the result of a collision with traditions of Christian cult imagery. Michelangelo's "modernity" is crucially bound up with his archaism.

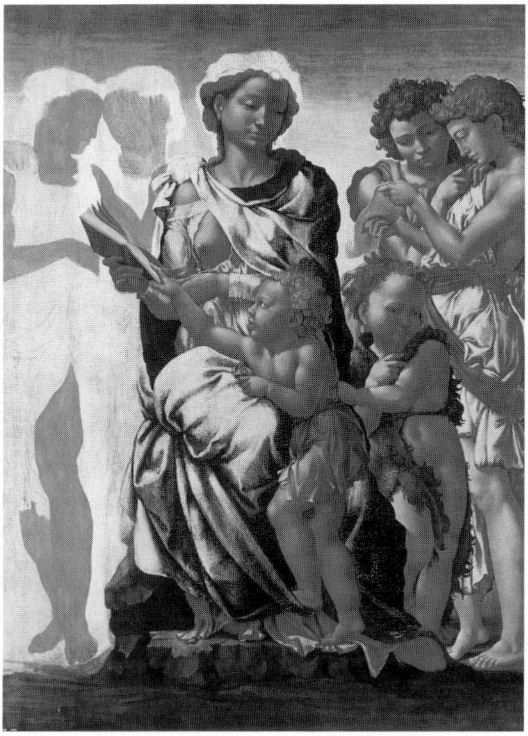

63. Michelangelo, *Madonna and Child with the Infant Baptist and Angels.* Panel. National Gallery, London, England.

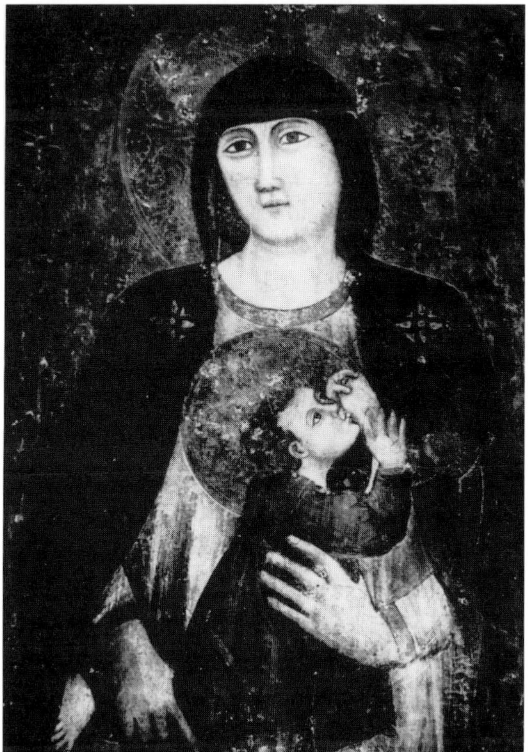

64. *Madonna of San Zanobi.* Panel. San Lorenzo, Florence, Italy.

THE PARADOX OF REFORM

The incorporation of antique sculptural models also occurred in the London *Entombment* (see Figure 6), and there, too, as we have seen, it involved a critique of trends in contemporary religious art. Antique revival and Christian reform went hand in hand, in a way quite typical of the culture of papal Rome in these years. Michelangelo found in antique sculpture the basis for an alternative both to the tradition of the "pitiful" dead Christ in late medieval art and to the more recent *all'antica* renditions (Donatello, Mantegna, Bertoldo), which interpreted it as a form of tragedy (see chapter 1). It was a natural link to draw: When Pietro da Lucca attempted to evoke the figure of the dead Christ that was no longer afflicted but once again miraculously pristine, he described the body as "sano, candido, e bianco," the same language used to describe high-quality marble, such as the "marmo carrarese novo candido e biancho" demanded of Michelangelo for the figures of the Piccolomini altar in 1504.[90] In the London *Entombment,* this thematic reinterpretation went hand in hand with a structural reorientation that served to maintain altarpiece conventions of symmetry and frontal presentation. Again, Michelangelo's respect for these conventions was more than a formal matter. This and later works were motivated by an awareness that frontal presentation was a link to a tradition of religious art and a key to its religious efficacy. Within a narrative work, a structure of frontal presentation connected the story directly to the here and now of Christian worship, effectuating and epitomizing the suprahistorical purpose and significance of the event. It brought the work quite concretely into dialogue with the protocols of frontality that governed ecclesiastical rites generally – rites whose purpose was, among other things, to draw the sacramental significance out of the events of sacred history. Even as he is being withdrawn from us, the radiant figure of Christ shines enthroned in the center of the panel; subject to history, he is also loosened from it and mysteriously presides over it.

In adapting the principles of history painting to these structures of frontal presentation, Michelangelo offered a solution, within the realm of altarpieces, to a problem that was also directly confronted by humanist scholars. As humanists with a developed interest in the study of secular history, they were compelled to give new critical attention to the question of what distinguished it from sacred history. I showed in chapter 1 that Savonarola, perhaps responding to the humanist climate of Renaissance Florence, had addressed the problem directly. He argued that Livy's histories were different from biblical history in that they did not have a figural dimension, or what he called "allegoria"; history, in Livy, does not "signify future things."[91] The humanists of Renaissance Rome pursued the distinction and, more important, developed rhetorical models that they felt were especially well suited to the nature of sacred history. For example, Aurelio Brandolini, a prominent humanist at

Sant'Agostino, declared in a Good Friday sermon delivered in the Sistine Chapel in 1496 that he was not describing the death of an ancient hero, such as Gavianus or Julius Caesar, but rather the death of the true God and Son of God. His crucifixion by those whom he had created, and for whose benefit he had assumed the flesh, went against all laws and norms (*"jus fasque"*): "This is something that no eloquence can attain, no ingenious acumen can penetrate, no breadth of mind can comprehend."[92] Unlike secular history, the events of sacred history resist logical or rational explanation; they can only be celebrated and marveled at.

John O'Malley demonstrated that the humanist preachers at the papal court, such as Brandolini, responded to the demands of their subject by deliberately applying the mode of epideictic oratory to the Christian sermon.[93] O'Malley showed that the choice of epideictic, exemplified in the sermon just quoted, found its most elaborate theoretical rationale in a treatise written by the same Brandolini, *De ratione scribendi*.[94] Epideictic or demonstrative oratory involved the distribution of praise and blame and was peculiar to ceremonial rather than legal occasions. Brandolini rather boldly defended the application of epideictic to the praise of God and asserted that it was especially well suited to describe what is beyond human comprehension, a primary concern of sacred oratory. The passage quoted above is one example of the application of epideictic in this sense. Epideictic was used to avoid the rationalistic tendency to lecture and dispute, and instead to "lead men to admiration and contemplation of divine mystery."[95] For this reason, as O'Malley pointed out, the epideictic preachers were especially fond of a celebratory language of visual presentation, inviting their audience to "look," to "view," to "gaze upon," to "contemplate" – *videre, aspicere, ante oculos ponere, contemplari*.[96]

Michelangelo's approach to sacred history is analogous to that adopted, and theorized, by Brandolini. Rather than describe the historical event as if it were the death of an ancient hero – *"aut Gavianum crucem, ut Tullius; aut Cesarem necem, ut Maro"* – he took care to preserve the dimension of mystery within the history by bringing the narrative structure into alignment with frontal modes of visual presentation that could be coordinated with the structures of ecclesiastical ceremonial. The very analogy with epideictic, however, suggests that this was a sophisticated rhetorical exercise and not a simple return to altarpiece conventions. Although Michelangelo's recasting of the Meleager-inspired composition was clearly motivated by a respect for the traditional functions of altarpieces, the incorporation of a new conception of pictorial narrative nonetheless produced a significant reinterpretation of those functions, and a powerful commentary on the status of the altarpiece as an institution circa 1500.

For one, the work elaborated a conception beyond the confines of established iconography, and as a result no longer strictly operated within the conventional categories of altar dedication. It is hard to imagine that this unusual composition, conceived through a resourceful combination of various traditions within the history of image-making, could have been determined by theological or patronal prescription (unless, of course, it was a cleric or donor with an extremely keen awareness of artistic tradition). The result defies iconographic classification: it is not a *Lamentation,* it is not a *Pietà,* and it is not strictly an *Entombment.* Even to describe it more precisely as a *Christ Carried to the Tomb* does not take into account the way the treatment of the theme – a frontally presented dead Christ directly implicating its viewer – determines its nature and significance. The specific organization of the painting is, in other words, crucial to the subject's meaning. More specifically, it expressly suspends the subject and demands that the viewer engage in the process of interpreting for him- or herself. The subject is completed in the experience of a viewer who assumes responsibility for his or her relation to it. This relation *is* the subject – and the very occasion of its "mystery."

The ideal of a sincere and internalized faith was, of course, not a new development in Christian thought. In the years around 1500, however, it was increasingly invoked in explicit opposition to the outward forms of worship institutionalized in official church ritual. It was a commonplace of reformist polemics at this time to condemn the increasingly elaborate ceremonial displays and the proliferation of masses and to exhort a return to a more sincere faith rooted in a direct relation to Christ and the Gospel. Savonarola (whose living voice, Condivi said, Michelangelo still recalled late in life) was one of the most pronounced critics of the excessive importance accorded to Church ritual:

> I have said it to you many times, the exterior divine cult is designated [*ordinato*] to the interior, and its entire order is then designated to God. . . . But those of lukewarm faith have done everything in reverse, because where everything is designated to and should be done for the glory of God, they have changed everything so that it is for their own glory, and they have made their own all those things which should be God's. The lukewarm priests and monks arrange these beautiful celebrations, hunt after bread, money and candles, and care little for the honor of God.[97]

In another place, Savonarola extolled the virtues of an "interior cult" and argued that "the good life does not consist in ceremonies but in being internally well oriented [*regulato*] toward God and toward one's neighbor." "Don't hope," he said, "in altar cloths or in chapels or in external things."[98] Here Savonarola was very close to the criticisms of reform-minded humanists.[99] The most influential of these at the turn of the century was Erasmus. In his widely read *Enchiridion Militis Christiani,* first published in 1503, the Dutch humanist declared:

I think there are far too many who count up how many times they attend Mass and rely almost entirely upon this for their salvation. They are convinced that they owe nothing further to Christ. Leaving church, they immediately turn to their former habits. I certainly do not hesitate to praise them for getting to Mass but I am forced to condemn them for stopping at this point. They have failed to let what takes place at Mass also take place in their hearts; the death of our Head that is there represented does not take place in their souls. . . . If you believe in what takes place at the altar but fail to enter into the spiritual meaning of it, God will despise your flabby religion.[100]

According to Charles Trinkaus, the shift from a celebration of the objective power of the sacrament to an insistence on its meaningful relation to the individual's conscience was closely connected to humanist literary and rhetorical ideals. A literary consciousness derived from the study of ancient letters served as the conceptual basis for a new understanding of Christian theology:

The very fact of [the humanists'] commitment to rhetoric, philology and the language arts led them to a new kind of religious emphasis. Since they were less interested in establishing technical theological niceties or the objective sacred significance of the sacraments than they were in moving their readers and listeners to a receptive and believing state of mind, they were led to stress in the very content of their dialogues and sermons this personal, subjective and psychological aspect of the meaning and importance of the sacraments.[101]

Michelangelo's painting was an analogous effort within the visual arts: The exploration of new devices of visual rhetoric, eliciting new forms of viewer response, produced a stronger emphasis on the relation between the Gospel message and the viewer's conscience. In fact, it gives this relation a pointedly elegiac coloring by interpreting it in historical terms: Standing before the painting, we are shown the Man of Sorrows as he is being withdrawn from us. The highly "subjective" address to the viewer, and even the elegiac tone, can be found elsewhere in Renaissance painting. We have seen, for example, that Michelangelo's experiments with the implied viewer were close to experiments with the dramatic close-up developed in the Venetian tradition of the private devotional image. This tradition was, in turn, given a more syncretic and elegiac flavor – and a less strictly devotional function – in the cabinet pictures produced in the circle of Giorgione. But all of these works operated outside of the parameters of church art. The significance of Michelangelo's panel lies in the introduction of these new pictorial strategies within the arena of the altarpiece, an effort that involved a reshaping, literally an internal reform, of the altarpiece's traditional functions. Earlier altarpieces had developed various forms of direct viewer address that supplemented the mediations of ecclesiastical ceremony and institutionalized prayer, but in this case the entire conception is predicated on the viewer's individual engagement with the image: the cooperation between viewer and image is necessary to the painting's thematic coherence. Put succinctly, the altarpiece's liturgical function has been completely absorbed and interpreted by its rhetorical structure.

In contrast to the tendency to seek the divine in outward objects and ceremonies, the London panel promotes an orientation inward. Whereas the old Man of Sorrows images granted huge indulgences when certain prescribed prayers were said before them (see chapter 2), in this panel the viewer's relation to the Man of Sorrows involves an engaged act of interpretative reading and a high level of self-awareness. The true mystery and benefit of Christ's sacrifice, it implicitly asserts, comes not through the saying of rote prayers before the image but through the viewer's reading of the painting and the consequent realization that Christ's sacrifice has occurred "for" him or herself. The painting is designed to promote this understanding by its own thematic means, with or without Mass rite and altar. Working under the auspices of humanist reform, Michelangelo arrived at the paradox of an altarpiece that no longer needs an altar.

After this strenuous and ultimately frustrated effort to reform altar painting from within, Michelangelo's later negotiations with the Man of Sorrows theme were undertaken in a private sphere, outside of the traditional categories of religious art. But the generic tensions confronted in Michelangelo's youthful painting preoccupied a whole generation of painters to follow. These efforts, which are linked to Michelangelo's panel by a shared theme and by a history of reception, clearly illustrate the fate of the altarpiece in an era that saw the rise of a modern conception of history painting, and thus provide a historical basis for understanding the archaism of Michelangelo's late *Pietà*s.

CHAPTER FOUR

The Altarpiece in the Age of History Painting

THE BURDENS OF THE ALTARPIECE

"Every true work of art has violated an established genre, and in this way confounded the ideas of critics, who thus found themselves compelled to broaden the genre."[1] Benedetto Croce might well have pointed to Raphael's *Entombment* of 1507, in the Galleria Borghese in Rome (Figure 65), as a classic illustration of his dictum. The work was commissioned as an altarpiece, and yet in its final form it presented a significant departure from the altarpiece tradition, proposing a conception of history painting that had not previously staked a secure claim to the format of large easel painting. The theme that Michelangelo had strenuously adapted to altarpiece conventions here produced a break with the altarpiece tradition altogether. This process of departure preoccupied Raphael during the preparation of the panel and informed his very approach to the painting's theme, which is centrally concerned with the problem of rupture and loss. And yet the fact that the painting marks a generic crisis complicates any effort to understand it historically. To approach this work according to the "normal" requirements of altarpiece painting as they were known in the period (*ante rem*) would be to ignore its own claims to historical novelty. But to treat it simply as a "history painting" of the kind familiar from later picture galleries is to impose upon it a category established only later (*post rem*), and whose very origins are part of the problem that requires study. The work demands, instead, to be studied historically (*in re*), as an instance of some of the transformations in the nature and status of painting that occurred in the opening years of the sixteenth century.[2]

The generic instability of the work is best illustrated by setting it within a history of reception. I argue here that Raphael's painting responded directly

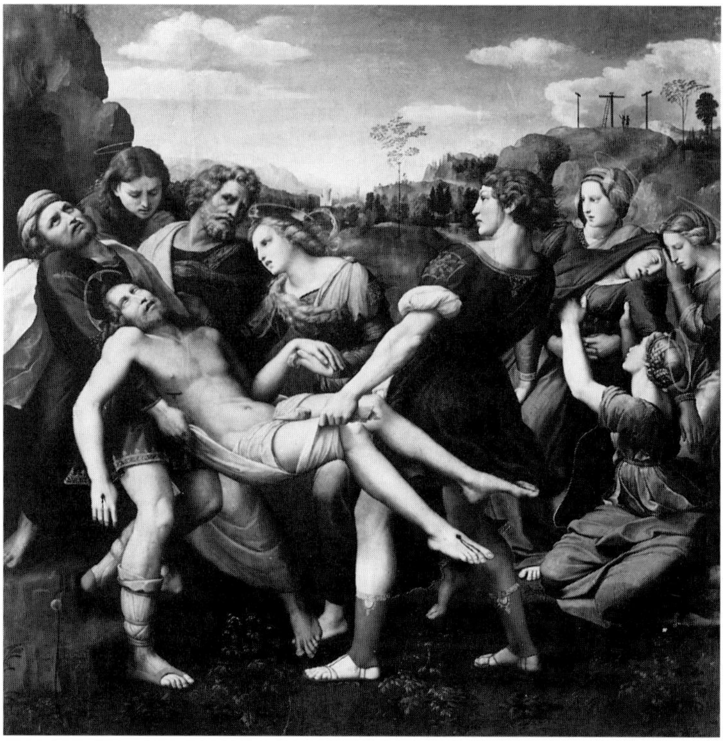

65. Raphael, *The Carrying of Christ to the Tomb.* Panel. Galleria Borghese, Rome, Italy. Alinari/ Art Resource, NY.

to Michelangelo's efforts in the London *Entombment* (see Figure 6) to preserve the altarpiece tradition while incorporating a new conception of history painting. Raphael's departure from the altarpiece tradition in turn produced a significantly "forked" history of reception: It was on the one hand recognized and ratified in Titian's *Entombment* in the Louvre (see Figure 76), which belongs firmly to the early history of the modern gallery picture, and on the other was resisted by Jacopo da Pontormo in the Capponi chapel (see Figure 77), where we see an effort to integrate anew the theme, and the new conception of painting it embodied, with the liturgical function and setting of altar images.

Raphael's painting introduced a conception of painting, articulated earlier in the fifteenth century by Leon Battista Alberti, into a format that until that time had been governed by the conventions and decorum of the altarpiece. Raphael did so quite deliberately, by carefully following Alberti's precepts on the depiction of members and bodies, as well as by depicting a theme – the entombment of Christ – that had become a paradigm of the Albertian *historia.*[3] As we saw in chapter 1, Alberti had proposed as a model for the history painter an antique representation of the carrying of the dead Meleager (see Figure 11), a challenge taken up in the more experimental and flexible medium of engraving by Mantegna, who adapted the model to the Christian subject of the entombment of Christ (see Figure 17). That it was not incorporated in altarpieces was, I argued, due to an implicit conflict with altarpiece conventions and traditions, a conflict clearly in evidence in Michelangelo's strenuous efforts to effectuate this adaptation. Raphael's altarpiece was not, in other words, simply intended as a better and grander altarpiece than those that came before it; rather, it heralded a departure from the altarpiece tradition as such, which it clearly confronted *as* a tradition.[4]

The goal of Alberti's treatise was to raise painting to the status of a liberal art; to this end it provided painting with a consistent set of procedures and principles. These principles were different from the kind of advice offered in, say, Cennino Cennini's *Libro dell' Arte,* in which the painter is told how to produce well-made, marketable goods and run an efficient, productive shop. Although Alberti's treatise had an important practical component, its main purpose was to supply painting with a set of aesthetic ideals. Indeed, according to Alberti, it was the mark of the true painter to put the ideals proper to the art of painting before any consideration of monetary profit. These aesthetic aims, and the means used to achieve them, were proper to painting conceived as an art. They applied whether the subject depicted was Christian or pagan.[5] Whether derived directly from Alberti or not, such a conception of painting as an art was essentially realized in the seventeenth-century picture gallery, where secular subjects could be found alongside religious subjects, all of them presented as illustrious examples of "history painting."

Before the gallery picture had become a dominant institution of art production, however, a protracted redefinition of genre boundaries took place.[6] New conceptions of painting had first to lay claim to the surfaces of large panels, and this meant that they had to contend with the resistance posed by the conventions of the altarpiece. The series of works studied in this book offer a textbook case of this process, but parallel developments may be noted elsewhere in Italy at this time, with or without Albertian motivation: Altarpiece conventions were everywhere being tested and revised under the pressure of new artistic developments, particularly in narrative painting. This situation produced, in Jacopo Bellini for example, highly sensitive and conscientious efforts to preserve altarpiece traditions even while incorporating a new array of narrative and descriptive devices. The same situation produced in some of Vittore Carpaccio's works a breakdown of altarpiece conventions altogether. Not surprisingly, this generic instability also provoked backlashes, efforts to "reinstate" a traditional conception of altar painting in the face of the new developments.[7]

As is well known, Raphael arrived at the final solution for his altarpiece only after an extended process of preparation and self-revision. This process can be substantially reconstructed from the unusually large number of surviving drawings for this project. The scholarship on these much-studied drawings has tended to see them as documents of a process of free and exploratory artistic creation. I interpret them, instead, as documents of generic tension and rupture. They reveal, I believe, the powerful resistance of altarpiece conventions to a new conception of painting, and the process by which that resistance was overcome. Several scholars have viewed the essential change in composition and theme, from a lamentation to an entombment, as the result of a pivotal encounter, at a certain point in the preparation process, with Mantegna's *Entombment* engraving, Albertian theory, or with an ancient Meleager sarcophagus of the kind mentioned by Alberti.[8] This view is, I believe, contradicted by the very gradual nature of the change documented by the drawings themselves. I propose, instead, that even the earliest drawings show a knowledge of the Mantegna print and the Meleager model. This reference was, indeed, a quite appropriate and natural response given its relevance to the client, Atalanta Baglioni, whose name and whose family's literary patronage gave her good reason to be acquainted with the myth. I argue that Atalanta fashioned her appeal for divine mercy on the basis of thematic resonances among the three registers of pagan myth, Passion narrative, and personal history – a highly novel strategy in altarpiece painting of the period. Raphael's compositional studies were, I believe, efforts to meet these devotional purposes by incorporating features of the Meleager model into a traditional altarpiece scheme. This process of integration was uneasy, and sharply illuminates the generic controls and institutional imperatives governing easel painting at this time. In the end, a persistent pushing forward of the preparation process provoked a disruption of altarpiece conventions altogether, to which painters of the following decades were compelled to respond.

It is well known that this process was marked, especially in its later stages, by a critical dialogue with works by Michelangelo, such as the *Pietà* (see Figure 59), the *St. Matthew* (see Figure 74), and the *Battle of Cascina*. In this chapter, I attempt to show that the final step was a direct response to Michelangelo's own effort to adapt this subject to the demands of altarpiece painting, in the London *Entombment*. Michelangelo's singular solution is, I believe, the key to understanding the primary difference that separates Raphael's final conception from the Mantegna and Meleager models: The reorganization of the subject as a drama of separation, in which Christ is shown being carried away from the lamenting group. Rupture at the level of genre corresponded to rupture at the level of theme. Michelangelo's work is thus essential to understanding the process that led to Raphael's final solution, and Raphael's is a strong early interpretation of the significance of Michelangelo's work in the history of the altarpiece.

Raphael's altarpiece, dated 1507, was commissioned by Atalanta Baglioni for her family chapel in the church of San Francesco al Prato in Perugia. Although the exact date of the commission is not known, it has often been seen in relation to the events that had recently occurred in Perugia and that had resulted in the death of Atalanta's son in 1500. Already Vasari, in a highly "familial" reading of the work, assumed that the painting was shaped by reference to the events that preceded the commission: "In composing this work Raphael imagined the grief felt by the closest and most loving relatives in carrying to burial the body of their dearest, on whom all the welfare, honor and advantage of the entire family depended."[9] This reading of the painting became standard after the publication, in 1851, of the chronicles attributed to the Perugian humanist Francesco Matarazzo, which tell the story of the Perugian wars in great detail. Jacob Burckhardt's famous passage on the painting set the stage for innumerable speculations on the correspondence of the depicted figures to the personages involved in the Perugian events of 1500.[10] Based loosely on a belief in the artwork as a mirror of its time, these accounts often assume that the picture's dramatic qualities were at least in part inspired by these extraordinarily dramatic events.[11] While not denying the relevance of these events for the intentions of the patron, the following argument insists instead on the mediating factors – thematic transpositions among the historical, mythological, and biblical registers, as well as structural and generic considerations – that complicate this model of the relationship between art and the circumstances in which it is made. Let us begin, then, with the chronicle, our primary source. Although it is presented as a chronicle, it contains a strong dramatic structure, which in turn makes it susceptible to thematic transposition. It is thus necessary, for the purposes of thematic analysis if not of historical "background," to give it a close reading.

Atalanta Baglioni, herself a descendant of a branch of the Baglioni family, was the young widow of Grifone Baglioni, by whom she had had a son named Grifonetto. Grifonetto, universally admired for his beauty – *"de bellezza fu un altro Ganimede,"* said Matarazzo – was the youngest among the youthful cohort of the ruling Baglioni clan.[12] He was also the richest, and he lived in a house built by his grandfather Braccio that had been decorated in high style; in it was a room of *"uomini illustri,"* like those that decorated the palaces of other humanist princes.[13] The other members of this cohort, although close in age to Grifonetto, were in fact the cousins of Grifonetto's father. Matarazzo implies that these cousins, the most prominent of whom were Astorre, Sigismondo, Simonetto, and Giovan Paolo, were closer among themselves than they were to Grifonetto, whom he describes as their *"pronipote."* Grifonetto's somewhat marginal status thus became a contributing factor in the events surrounding the celebration of the wedding of Astorre in July of 1500. Two other *pronipoti* pressed him to join them in a plot against their uncles, promising greater power over the city, but Grifonetto managed to resist their inducements, at least initially. Matarazzo, who remains sympathetic to the youth throughout the narrative, suggests that he might have resisted completely had he not been left unguided by the absence of a father. He finally succumbed, Matarazzo says, when the plotters managed to arouse in him suspicions of illicit relations between his wife and Giovan Paolo. On the night of the wedding he participated in a synchronized raid on the bedrooms of the principal men of the Baglioni clan. Astorre, Sigismondo, their father Guido, and their cousin Simonetto were all killed in their nightclothes. The formidable Giovan Paolo managed to escape and leave town; quickly gathering forces outside the city, on the following day he mounted a counteroffensive.

Amidst these events Matarazzo introduces Grifonetto's mother, Atalanta, Raphael's future patron: "Atalanta was her name, a widow she was, young and beautiful, and was left a widow when not yet twenty years old, and ever lived in widowhood for the love she bore her son Grifone." With the violent turn of events, Atalanta's love for her son quickly turned into scorn. Matarazzo notes with approval that she lost no time in sending for the children of Giovan Paolo, her son's enemy, to protect them from the insurgents. She then abandoned her son's house, with nothing but the shawl on her back, swearing that she would never return. Together with Grifonetto's wife, Zenobia, their children, and the children of Giovan Paolo, she retreated to the house of her father. Grifonetto came to her several times that day to plead forgiveness, but Atalanta refused him entry and cursed him repeatedly:

> And he, not once, nor twice, but again and again returned to speak to his sweet mother, and she, for the wrath and scorn that was in her, would not listen to her son; nay, rather cursed him and the place where she bare him and the hour of his birth. For the noble Grifonetto had repented him of the great betrayal, but they sufficed not.

Finally giving up, Grifonetto utters the pathetic final words: "Never again will I come to you, and the time shall be when you shall wish to speak to me and shall not be able, you that are a harsh mother to your unhappy son Grifone."[14]

Meanwhile, Giovan Paolo was successfully leading the *revanche.* Matarazzo hints that Grifonetto, defeated by his mother's rejection, virtually gave himself up. He was brought to Giovan Paolo, who, declining to follow Grifonetto's example in staining his hands with family blood, left him in the hands of his men. Grifonetto was immediately put to the sword and left to die in the piazza, his body lacerated with wounds. When word of this reached Atalanta, she came running with his wife Zenobia to his side. At this point Matarazzo slows down the pace of his narrative and gives an extended, poignant description of the scene. At the approach of the mother and wife, Giovan Paolo's men scattered for fear of being recognized. Atalanta, finding Grifonetto lying on the ground but not yet dead, came to his side and, finding him unable to speak, acknowledged the prophetic truth of his warning: "'Son, behold the mother that was wrath with you! and now I would speak to you, but you cannot, even as you said it would be.'" Overcoming the initial maternal impulse to dissolve in lament, however, she recovers her original purpose and exhorts him to forgive by some sign all those who had helped to kill him: "And thereupon the noble youth stretched out his right hand to her that was herself so young, and clasped his mother's white hand in his. Then at once the soul left that beautiful body and departed comforted with the infinite blessings of his mother in requital for those former curses."[15]

Under the ministrations of Atalanta, Grifonetto's death is transformed into a scene of Christian forgiveness and redemption – or so, at least, Matarazzo chose to represent it. (Did it also become the stuff of popular legend?) Matarazzo has, indeed, interpreted the entire story as a series of moral exchanges and compensations, almost as if it were a morality tale. In retribution for her son's murderous act, Atalanta refused him succor and effectively gave him up to execution. At the moment of dying, however, he forgives his killers, communicating the very act of forgiveness directly to his mother through the pressure of the hand. This act of forgiveness is itself sealed by his expiration, thus transforming his death into a sort of sacrifice. He dies with his mother's benedictions, in exchange (*"in cambio"*) for the curses she had hurled at him earlier. Finally, Matarazzo records that Grifonetto's body was taken to the main square, where it replaced the body of the assassinated Astorre, which had been put there exactly twenty-four hours before – a final exchange that he notes as a sign of "how God's justice works."[16]

Matarazzo did not rely solely on these internal correspondences to structure his narrative. He also draws parallels, throughout the story, to the events of Christ's Passion. For example, he describes how, in the days before the fateful coup, those involved in the plot continued to greet their enemies with "caresses feigned and false, even as Judas Iscariot did Christ."[17] After the coup, the friends of the Baglioni were abused by the people "just as the disciples of Christ were by the Jews when their master was taken."[18] These parallels clearly reveal Matarazzo's partisan leanings toward the Baglioni, who were his patrons. When it came to Grifonetto, of course, his loyalties were divided, as were Atalanta's and accordingly he uses subtler rhetorical devices in treating the scene of reconciliation played out between them. Matarazzo transformed the scene of the guilty Grifonetto's death into a drama of Christian atonement and reconciliation by, again, drawing parallels to Christ's Passion, but he did so by means of delicate resonances rather than by explicit declaration. For example, he enhanced the pathos of the mutilation of Grifonetto's body by emphasizing Grifonetto's physical beauty, a device commonly employed in the devotional literature of the life of Christ. Likewise, Atalanta is described as a pure and virtuous mother: She has white hands and has preserved her youthful beauty, Matarazzo hints, through her chastity ("she . . . ever lived in widowhood for the love she bore her son"). She was, like the Virgin, a mother without being a wife. Above all, she was "sage and prudent;" she understood that her son's life must be sacrificed and her own motherly affections set aside for the purposes of a higher redemption. After his death, she is described as a *"dolorosa matre."* Her lamentation, together with that of

Zenobia, echoes many familiar representations of the Virgin and the Magdalene at the lamentation of Christ: "The tears that his woeful mother shed and the wife that so dearly loved him when they saw the street drenched with that noble blood, and how sad was the wailing of his wife when she saw herself bereft of her husband, whom she loved deeply, who shall tell?"[19] Grifonetto's body is then left at the hospital, and Atalanta, covered in his blood, proceeds through the main piazza, exposing herself to the potential hostility of the crowd; instead of receiving abuse, however, "she was reverenced by all men."[20] To anyone familiar with the rhetoric of Umbrian *laude drammatiche* in the period, the parallels to Christ's Passion are unmistakeable.

Raphael's first conception for his altarpiece progressed as far as a highly finished squared *modello,* now in the Louvre[21] (Figure 66). This conception effectively realizes the parallel to the Christ story only intimated by Matarazzo: It represents a *Lamentation of Christ* that almost exactly matches the scene of Grifonetto's death as it was described by the chronicler. Christ lies on the ground, his legs supported by the Magdalene and his head by the Virgin. Special attention is given to the Virgin, who swoons in grief. The drawing, elaborately finished in pen over a stylus and black-chalk underdrawing, was itself the result of an extensive preparation process. It is, in fact, comparable in finish to the squared composition study for the final version in the Uffizi. At

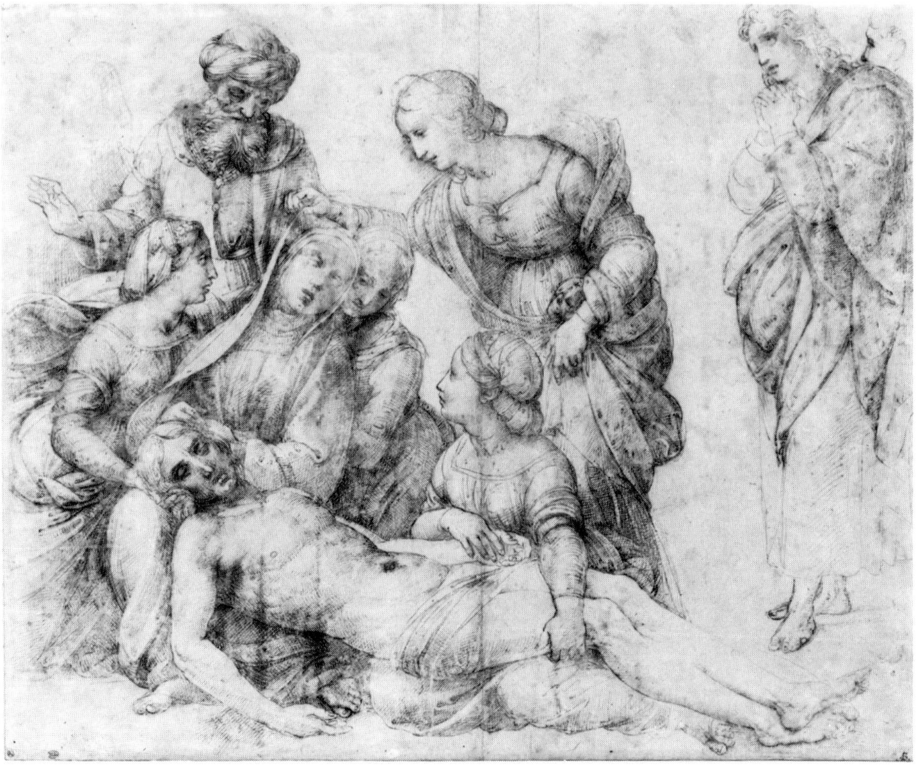

66. Raphael, *Lamentation.* Drawing. Louvre, Paris, France. © Réunion des Musées Nationaux.

one point it was thus considered a "terminus," and it was probably intended for presentation to the patron.

Even without precise knowledge of the terms of the commission, it is important to attempt to understand how such a conception for the altarpiece would have served Atalanta's primary devotional concerns. The altarpiece was intended to serve in the Baglioni family burial chapel in the church of San Francesco al Prato. Astorre, Gismondo, and their father Guido, killed in the revolt of 1500, were buried in this chapel, as was, probably, Grifonetto himself.[22] Masses for their souls, and later for the soul of Atalanta, were celebrated at this altar. The tragic events of 1500 thus do not simply constitute a potentially relevant historical circumstance for the painting; they placed a direct liturgical burden on its chapel and its altar. It is likely that Atalanta's primary concern was for her own soul and for that of her traitorous son. The strategy she adopted in her altarpiece is not unrelated to the dramatic role she plays in Matarazzo's chronicle, where she functions as a crucial intermediary in helping her son die a virtuous and Christian death. Her altarpiece was also designed to refer to that episode and to make a parallel to the lamentation of Christ the basis of an appeal to divine mercy on behalf of both their souls.

This is an uncommon strategy for recommending oneself to divine mercy in an altarpiece. A more conventional device would have been to represent herself or her son in worshipful supplication before the Virgin, and presented by their patron saints. A strategy somewhat closer to that adopted by Atalanta was employed by Francesco Sassetti in his chapel in the Florentine church of Santa Trinità. The chapel comports a double dedication to Francesco's name saint Francis and to the Nativity. Warburg first suggested that the second dedication was prompted by the death in the preceding year of Francesco's eldest son Theodoro, and the birth shortly thereafter of a new son, whom he named Theodoro II.[23] Ghirlandaio's altarpiece of the *Nativity* offered a thematic parallel to Sassetti's story, a parallel then reinforced on the level of the Francis legend through the scene of the *Resurrection of the French Notary's Son*. The altarpiece puts the birth of the new son under the sign of divine intervention and also celebrates the birth of the Savior who will bring eternal life to the dead Theodoro I, as well as to Francesco and the rest of his kin. Both Francesco Sassetti and Atalanta Baglioni showed great resourcefulness in building an appeal for divine mercy on the basis of a thematic parallel between their family histories and episodes from sacred history.

What about Atalanta's role in the episode of her son's treason and murder warranted such an exalted parallel? At the time of the coup, Atalanta was unwavering in her loyalty to family and state, even though this demanded the condemnation of her beloved son. She resolutely refused to acknowledge his appeals to her motherly sentiment, but when he received the punishment that was due him, she finally came, in the spirit of Christian mercy, to minister to him in his final hour. The events had placed her in an impossible predicament, pulled in opposite directions by the two most powerful imaginable demands on her loyalty. But that intermediary status also allowed her to perform a special mission of reconciliation. Her strict adherence, until this point, to moral right and family loyalty over the appeals to her motherly affection gave a special efficacy to the noble act by which, she could hope, her son died redeemed.

This fundamental appeal was concretely connected to the liturgical apparatus of the Mass and the altar through the other elements of the altarpiece structure. The altarpiece was designed to be surmounted by a panel, now in the Galleria Nazionale dell'Umbria, which represents God the Father acknowledging and blessing the sacrifice of the Son below. This image figures the desired response to the opening prayer of the canon of the Mass: *"Te igitur, clementissime Pater, per Iesum Christum Filium tuum, Dominum nostrum supplices rogamus ac petimus, uti accepta habeas et benedicas haec dona. . ."* God the Father's mercy is shown to be moved in response to the scene represented below. By implication, Atalanta might have hoped, his mercy would also be aroused by the story of her and her son, modeled as it was on this scene of sacrifice. Indeed, God the Father's gesture is an explicit double blessing, addressed both to Christ and to the Virgin, as if to facilitate the wished-for extension to Atalanta and Grifonetto.[24] The frieze originally separating the panel above the main field was, moreover, decorated with putti and griffons, the Baglioni emblem but also a direct reference to Grifonetto.[25] Representations of the three theological virtues in the predella, finally, were designed to sustain the appeal made in the main field. Faith holds the chalice of the Mass, the institutionally sanctioned means of invoking divine mercy. Hope makes a more direct plea, gazing up into the main field of the altarpiece. Charity, in the center, protects and nurses the children – perhaps a reference to Atalanta's protection of the Baglioni children and her commitment to the preservation of the family line, as well as to her ultimate compassion for her son, by which he died a redeeming death.[26]

HISTORY, MYTH, AND PASSION NARRATIVE

The scheme for the Louvre composition, as has often been pointed out, was adapted from that used by Perugino in the Pitti *Lamentation* of 1495, formerly in the church of Santa Chiara in Florence (see Figure 15). If the Louvre composition had been put into execution, however, it already would have constituted a significant departure from the Peruginesque schema. As I observed in chapter 1, Perugino's *Lamentation* represents a scene of meditative attention on the body of Christ. As observed in chapter 1, active, "momentary" gesture is softened or entirely absent, making it possible to imagine an indefinite suspension of the narrative sequence. Dramatic relationships among the figures are kept to a minimum, and instead the figures engage in independent meditation on the dead Christ, who is shown propped up on a square, altarlike block. In these ways, the attitudes represented in the painting are "dehistoricized" and assimilated to the activity of the worshipper before the altar and the painting. Raphael's Louvre composition (see Figure 66), by contrast, while preserving some Peruginesque poses, particularly in the two standing men, animates the figures and brings them into more active relation to one another. It places greater emphasis, in other words, on the historical and narrative coherence of the scene, as something that occurred "back then," rather than primarily as a framework for worship in the here and now. Perugino's blocklike step is replaced by active figural support: Christ's legs rest on the Magdalene's thighs and his head rests on the lap of the Virgin. An intermediary moment is represented by a composition study at Oxford, which I believe to be preparatory to the Louvre *modello*: The Virgin is shown seated on a block, and Christ's upper body is propped up in a manner more closely resembling his pose in Perugino's painting (Figure 67).[27] In the Louvre sheet the Virgin is brought closer to the ground; her left leg is pushed down by the weight of Christ's torso, and she faints more dramatically. She now clearly constitutes a second focus of dramatic attention, apart from the figure of Christ.

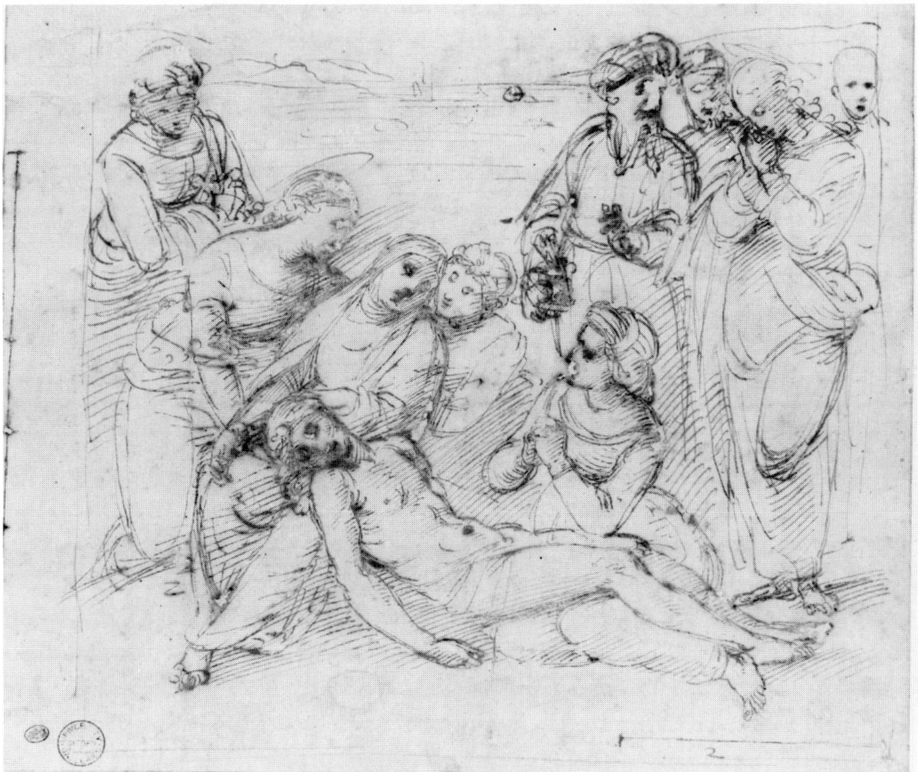

67. Raphael, *Lamentation*. Drawing. Ashmolean Museum, Oxford, England.

All of these developments toward a more dramatic conception are clearly intelligible in light of the special nature of Atalanta's appeal, which involved a strong "historical" component. In making them, Raphael relied, already at this early stage, on elements of Mantegna's famous *Entombment* engraving. Although it is often thought that Raphael became aware of this print at a later stage, when the subject was recast into that of the carrying of the body, an awareness of Mantegna is noticeable, already here, in a number of features: in the figure of St. John, in the arm of the Magdalene, reaching across Christ's thighs (a gesture often found on Meleager or Meleager-inspired compositions), and in the group of the swooning Virgin, who is supported by one Mary while being attended to by a third.[28]

Although Raphael's awareness of Mantegna's print at this early stage has been observed by several scholars, the implications of this observation need further examination. Raphael knew the print and was clearly interested in incorporating aspects of its composition, yet he did not adapt the narrative of the carrying of the body, instead making adjustments within a more traditional lamentation composition. I have suggested that one reason for this decision is that the lamentation over the body more closely matches the story of Atalanta and Grifone as transmitted by Matarazzo (and perhaps as it was generally known and recounted). A further and related consideration is that of altarpiece decorum: The lamentation, which in the immobile body of Christ offers a stable focus of devotional attention, was better suited to the implicit functions of altar painting. At the very least it was a subject with an established tradition in altar painting; the subject of the carrying of the body was, by contrast, quite unheard of, and rather uncommon even in other categories of religious art.

This is not the only time that the Mantegna print, and the Meleager model, were adapted in this restricted fashion. For example, a Foppa school panel in Pavia (see Figure 18) makes precise quotations from Mantegna's print but likewise adapts them to a composition more closely resembling a lamentation – and perhaps for similar reasons of altarpiece decorum. Even in other categories of painting we see evidence of such a conventional resistance. The most famous case in Luca Signorelli's fresco in the chapel of San Faustino and San Pietro Parenzo in the Cappella Nuova in the Cathedral of Orvieto, which clearly alludes both to the relief composition of the *Carrying of Meleager* and to Mantegna's print in the grisaille *Carrying of Christ* shown on Christ's sarcophagus but depicts in front of it a scene of the lamentation (Figure 68). Signorelli's work is especially important in this context, as we have clear evidence of Raphael's contact with Signorelli, and with his Orvieto frescoes, in exactly these years.[29] The most poignant and innovative gesture in Raphael's Louvre *modello,* that of the standing Mary who carefully lifts the veil from the fallen head of the Virgin, is quite close to the gesture of one of the Maries in the *Crucifixion* banner that Signorelli had recently painted (ca. 1505) for the

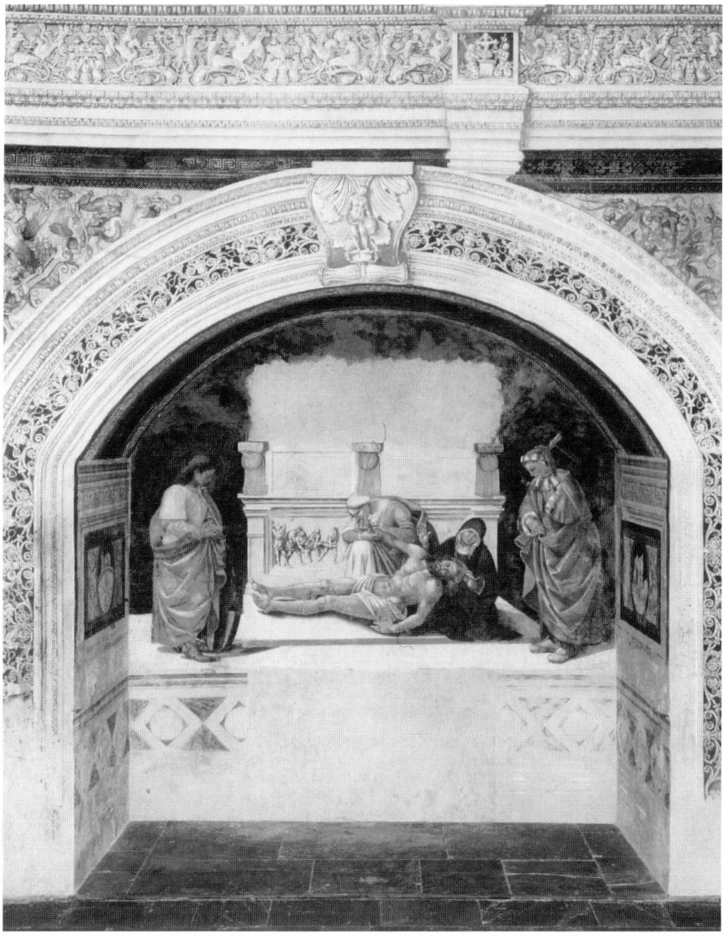

68. Luca Signorelli, *Lamentation.* Fresco. Cathedral, Orvieto, Italy.

Confraternità dei Battuti di Sant'Antonio of Borgo San Sepolcro.[30] This painting shows in the background, again, a scene of the carrying of the dead Christ to the tomb – a clear adaptation of the Meleager composition Signorelli "quoted" a couple of years earlier in the fresco at Orvieto. This and the Orvieto fresco indicate that by this time the reference to the Meleager model in scenes of Christ's Passion had become virtually de rigueur among informed and ambitious painters. They show, specifically, a great interest in this model on the part of a painter who exerted a significant influence on Raphael in these very years. The connections to Signorelli thus reinforce the hypothesis that Raphael was aware of the Meleager model specifically at the stage of the Louvre *modello.* They suggest that, like Signorelli, Raphael knew the model but did not see fit to make it the main subject of his painting.

In the context of Raphael's commission from Atalanta Baglioni the myth of Meleager was more than an artistic model. Atalanta's very name, as has been noted, involves a reference to the Meleager story.[31] But it is more than merely her name and the fact of her son's death that suggest a relation to the myth; the entire account of the events of 1500, and especially her complex role within it, unfold in astonishing similarity to the story of Meleager, especially as it is told in the post-Homeric tradition transmitted by Ovid in *Metamorphoses* 8:260–546. In these years Ovid's text was undergoing something of a revival in Italy generally, and specifically in Perugia. Giovanni Bonsignori's translation of Ovid's text into Italian, complete with woodcuts, was first published in Venice in 1497. At the same time the Latin text, with commentary by Raffaele Regio of Padua, achieved great popularity and went into numberless editions.[32] In Perugia, the humanist Lorenzo Spirito, an associate of Matarazzo's, made his own translation from the Latin, a part of which was eventually published in 1519 with a dedication to Giulia Baglioni.[33]

Ovid recounts that when Meleager was seven days old the Fates appeared, threw a piece of wood on the hearth, and announced that the boy would die as soon as the burning billet was consumed. Althaea, his mother, thereupon took the wood from the fire and guarded it in a secret place, thus preserving her son's life. Meleager himself became invincible and already as a young man was renowned for his courage and valor. After his success in the boar hunt, he gave his prize, the boar's skin, to his beloved Atalanta, the huntress nymph. This caused disgruntlement among the other hunters, among whom were the sons of Thestius, brothers to Meleager's mother, who took the prize away from Atalanta. Enraged at this offense, Meleager killed them both. Althaea, as she was in the temple offering thanks for her son's victory, saw the corpses of her brothers carried in. When she discovered who was their murderer, her grief was transformed into a conflicted wrath. In her rage, she took the billet of wood from its hiding place and had a large pyre lit.

In an extended and virtuosic passage, Ovid describes the conflicting passions that fought within her as she stood before the flames with the fateful billet in her hand. It is probable, given her name, that Atalanta Baglioni was aware of the story of Meleager and knew this passage in particular. Nowhere could she have found a more penetrating description of the conflict she herself had suffered. Like her son, Meleager had been moved to commit a rash act of familial murder by the passions aroused for the love of a woman, and he had as a consequence put his mother in an impossible predicament of conflicting loyalties: "Mother and sister strove in her/and the two names tore one heart this way and that" (8.463–64).[34] Ovid gives a vivid description of her ambivalent jerking between these opposing passions. As she approaches the fire, Althaea gathers resolve: "I avenge and I do a wicked deed; death must be atoned by death;/to crime must crime be added, death to death./Through woes on woes heaped up let this house go on to ruin!" (8.483–5).

Ovid explores the moral complexity of her situation and gives the paradoxical rationale for her solution, described as an uncommon form of ritual sacrifice: She must "appease with blood the shades of her blood kin" (8.476).

But because this blood is that of her own son, it is a sacrifice of an ambiguous kind: She is pious in impiety (*"impietate pia est"*) (8.497). The foremost Renaissance commentator of the Latin text, Raffaele Regio, acknowledged the seeming contradiction of this line but defended its aptness to the situation: "This line appears senseless. For how indeed can someone be pious in impiety? Yet Althaea was pious in avenging her brothers' murder, impious in killing her son."[35] Further on, Althaea compares her son's blood to the costliest of sacrifices and describes it as "the baleful tribute of my womb" (8.490).

If we turn to the medieval allegorical tradition of the *Ovide Moralisé* and Pierre Bersuire, we will not find this passage interpreted "figurally" in reference to the Virgin and Christ. Meleager is certainly taken as a figure of Christ: His death by the internal consuming fire is, for example, likened to the burning love of the Lord for humankind, for whom he was willing to suffer mortally.[36] But these Christian interpretations do not touch specifically on the drama and excruciating ambivalence of Althaea's situation, which gives a peculiar character to her "sacrifice." These elements acquire Christian relevance, apparently uniquely, within the peculiar constellation of references brought together in Atalanta's altarpiece. The three thematic levels – the Perugian history, the Passion narrative, and the ancient myth – all acquire meaning by being brought together in this work. The myth, so to speak, provides the thematic mortar that joins Atalanta's story and the Passion narrative. After articulating the complexities of Althaea's predicament, Ovid interprets her final gesture as a form of sacrifice, by which a paradoxical appeasement is achieved. It is an extraordinary sacrifice, with her own son as the victim. Interpreted through the lens of the myth, Grifonetto's death claims a stronger parallel to the sacrifice of Christ and thus offers a more effective appeal to divine mercy. It is difficult to overestimate the novelty of such a thematically complex, multilayered strategy in altarpieces of the period. For Aby Warburg, the Sassetti chapel was an effort to marry Christian traditions and a humanist culture nurtured on the study of the antique and thus offered special insight into the social and cultural tensions of late fifteenth-century Florence.[37] Here, too, we see traditional institutions and structures of Christian piety radically reinterpreted within a humanist setting.

Radical reinterpretations can push conventions to the breaking point. Viewed in terms of the requirements of the commission, there was no reason for Raphael to proceed beyond the carefully worked up Louvre composition (see Figure 66). He nonetheless did, despite the fact that he had brought the initial composition to the level of a finished *modello.* We can only speculate as to what induced Raphael to dismantle the composition and to begin in a new direction after having brought it to this point. But we can be certain of two things that have remained unclear in previous analyses of the drawings: (1) The drawings to which we will now turn are, indeed, subsequent to the Louvre *modello,* and (2) they were not the result of the discovery of

Mantegna's print or of a Meleager sarcophagus. We know these two things because the drawings show a *gradual* dismantling of the first conception, in the direction of the more mobile carrying conception: Raphael introduced the Meleager-like conception only through a slow breakdown of the earlier model, with the result that his final solution presents significant differences both from Mantegna and from the ancient sarcophagi.

A crucial document of the transition is a drawing in Oxford that shows two figures bent close to the ground with the body in their arms (Figure 69).[38] The head studies at the top of the sheet, clearly drawn *after* the group sketched below, show Raphael still thinking through, however, the poses of the Louvre composition. Christ's legs also preserve the crossed position of the Louvre composition, as if Raphael were thinking, almost cinematically, of that same figure now taken into the arms of the carrying figures. So far from embodying an abrupt change in idea, this sheet thus shows a gradual and tentative effort to introduce a dynamic element within the structure of the initial scheme. The fact that it is a departure from the Louvre composition but does not resemble at all the Meleager composition demonstrates that Raphael was attempting to introduce the idea of the conveyance of the body "organically," from within his initial composition.

The attempt to integrate the Meleager and Mantegna model within the traditional scheme reached its limit point in another drawing, in the British Museum (Figure 70).[39] The body is shown lifted entirely off the ground, carried by one figure at either end. Mantegna's print is now explicitly invoked but its influence extends only so far as the two figures physically involved in

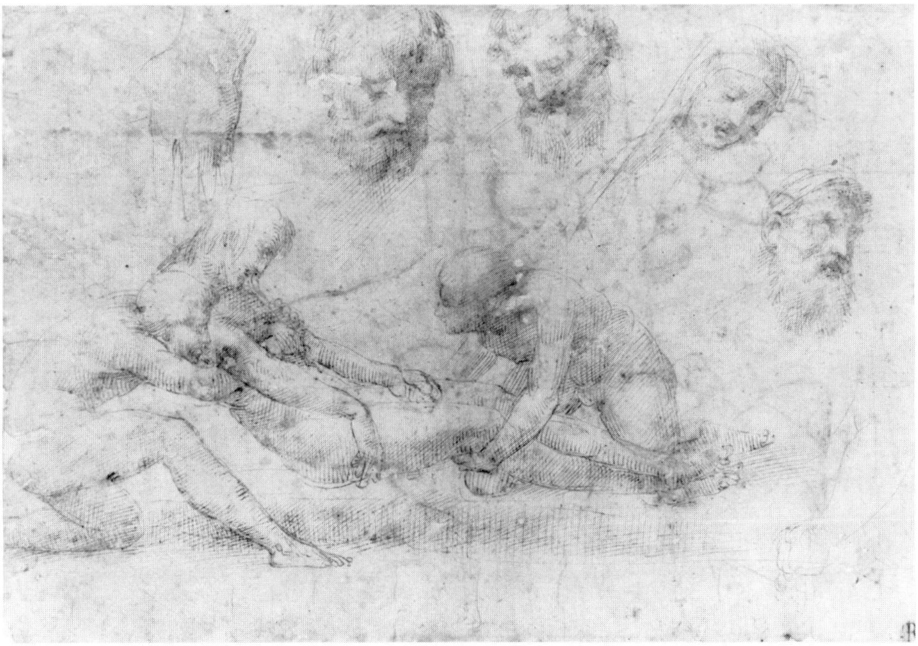

69. Raphael, *Male Figure in the Arms of Two Carriers.* Drawing. Ashmolean Museum, Oxford, England.

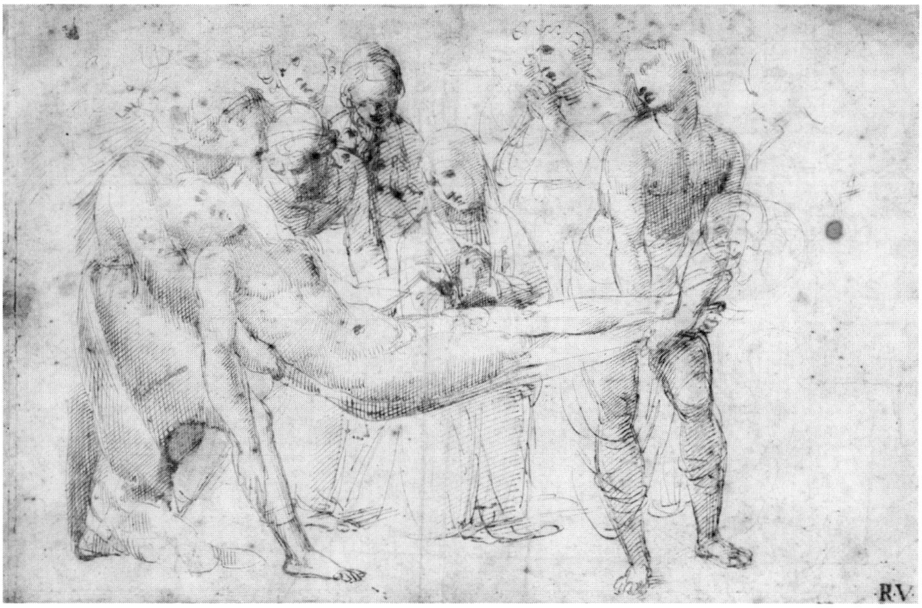

70. Raphael, *Christ Held Before the Virgin*. Drawing. British Museum, London, England. © The British Museum.

the carrying, whose leg movements almost exactly repeat those found in the print.[40] Their postures also closely resemble the carrying figures in a contemporaneous drawing by Raphael himself after a Meleager-like composition, showing that he understood them in these terms.[41]

This drawing demonstrates that Raphael knew and studied the print and yet was determined to preserve the more static scheme for his altarpiece. Indeed, apart from the carriers, the composition preserves many of the features of the earlier drawings. There is no clear indication of lateral movement: The Virgin, rather than walking with the body, kneels behind it and takes Christ's hand; Mary Magdalene, sketched in at the right, kneels at Christ's feet; the other figures remain, for the most part, in the poses of quiet meditation that characterize the Louvre composition. The composition is, in fact, still closer to a composition such as the *Pietà* by Perugino in the Uffizi (Figure 71) than to Mantegna's half-invoked model.[42] In Perugino's panel, Christ's horizontal body is similarly raised off the ground, supported in the middle on the lap of the Virgin Mary and on either end by St. John and Mary Magdalene. Even as he attempted to incorporate the motifs learned from Mantegna and the Meleager model, therefore, Raphael accommodated them to the dominant paradigm of the lamentation and *pietà*. The result was an uncomfortable and nearly incoherent compromise between the two. This drawing thus documents the point of greatest tension reached by Raphael in the effort to accommodate the theme to the implicit demands of altarpiece painting.

After this point Raphael broke with those demands altogether, by making the scene of carrying, involving ideas of conveyance and trajectory, the main subject of the altarpiece. The new idea is studied in a sheet at Oxford and

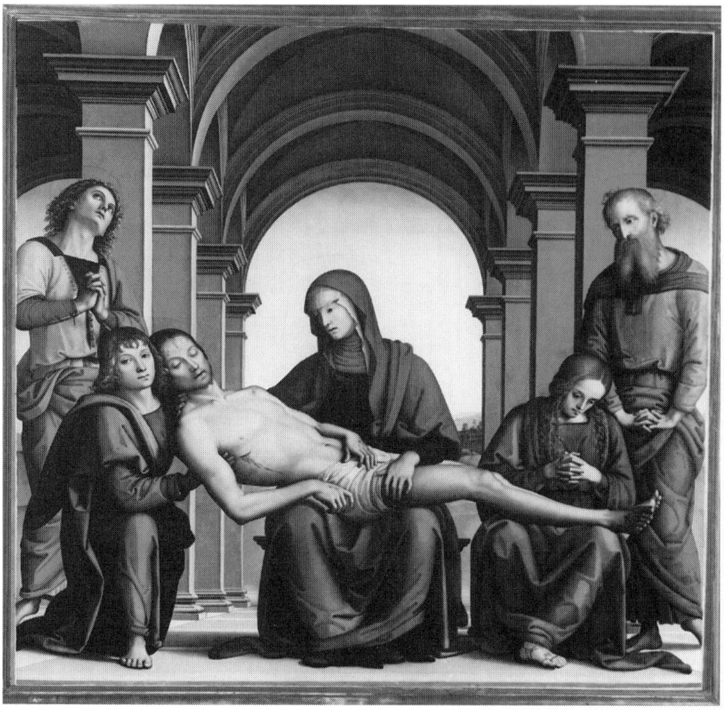

71. Pietro Perugino, *Pietà*. Panel. Uffizi, Florence, Italy. Alinari/Art Resource, NY.

worked up into a composition study in a sheet at the British Museum.[43] In the Oxford sheet (Figure 72), Raphael restudied the mechanism of carrying with the group now set in motion. He concentrated on the carriers, who are finished in pen, whereas the figure of Christ is lightly drawn in red chalk (it is almost invisible in black-and-white photographs). The figures carry Christ head first from right to left and the two foremost figures climb up a step. This is an innovation with regard to the Meleager model, and its derivations such as the Mantegna print, where the dead body is shown (to my knowledge without exception) carried feet first from left to right, and on level ground. In most of the sarcophagi the subject represented is the carrying of Meleager feet forward, *toward* his mother Althaea, who is sometimes represented on the right edge of the relief.

In the sheet in the British Museum, the new conception is elaborated into a full composition (Figure 73). The setting of the carrying group in motion has initiated a separation from the Virgin and the lamenting women, who are shown following behind. This change in conception cannot, as we have seen, be attributed to the intervention at this point of the Mantegna print or the Meleager sarcophagi. If we are to adduce an influence at this stage, it is overwhelmingly that of Michelangelo. The figure of Christ, for example, now shows a striking resemblance to the Christ in Michelangelo's Roman *Pietà* (see Figure 59).[44]

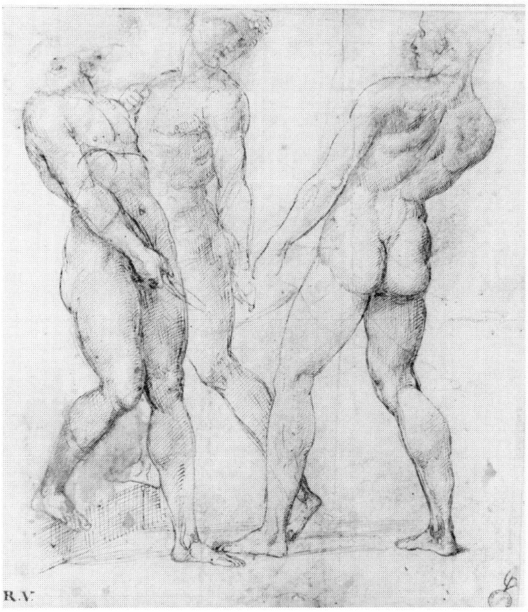

72. Raphael, *A Male Figure in the Arms of Three Carriers.* Drawing. Ashmolean Museum, Oxford, England.

The Oxford study showing the three carriers (see Figure 72) is a crucial document in the evolution of the new conception offered in the British Museum sheet (see Figure 73). Raphael drew the Christ, modeled on that of Michelangelo's *Pietà,* in red chalk. He then drew, in pen, the group of carriers around it. The carrying figures show substantial differences from those of the

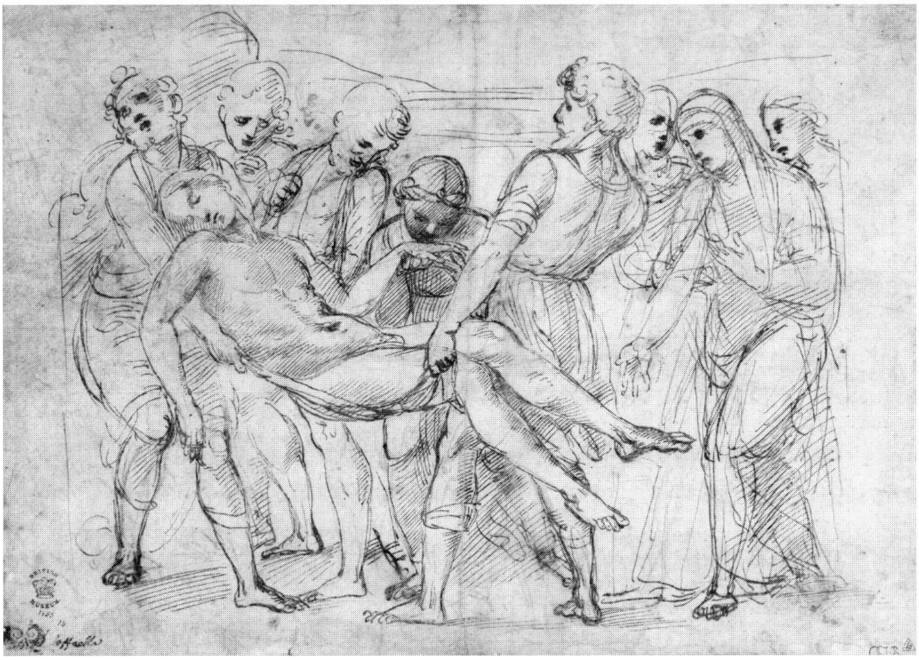

73. Raphael, *The Carrying of Christ to the Tomb.* Drawing. British Museum, London, England. © The British Museum.

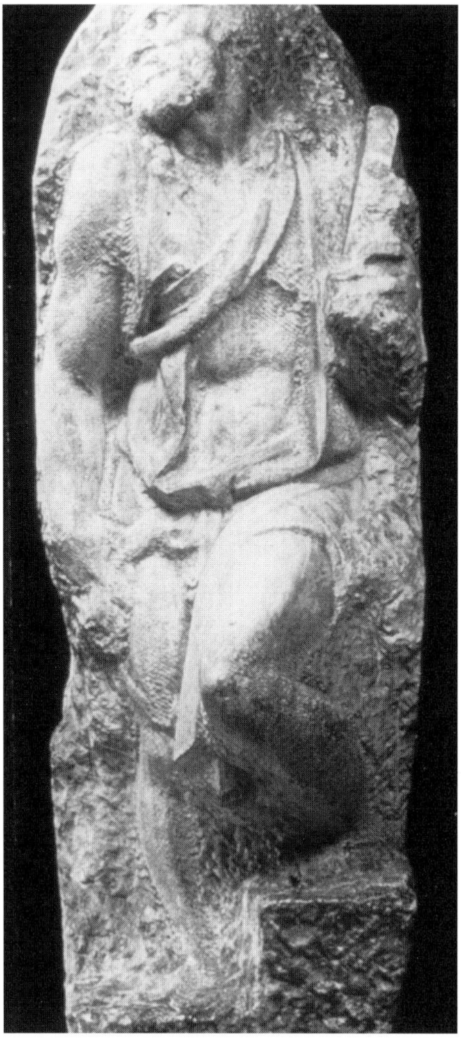

74. Michelangelo, *St. Matthew.* Marble. Accademia,

earlier drawings: There are three of them, they are very close together, and they are shown in motion, with the two foremost carriers climbing up a step. If the new Christ figure is modeled on the *Pietà,* the new carrying figures show striking similarities to their counterparts in the London *Entombment* (see Figure 6), which was then also probably in Rome.[45] Indeed, in its general composition, the sheet shows a striking similarity to the figural arrangement of the London panel.[46] The similarity is especially remarkable given the fact that in Raphael's drawing the group is shown moving in a different direction.

The drawing is, I believe, an attempt to adapt the carrying motifs of the London painting back to the lateral conception of the theme. As in the London painting, the two principal carriers in the Oxford study form a tight Y-shaped structure. The figure on the left in both compositions is shown moving backward, with his right foot raised onto a step and his left leg planted firmly on the ground.[47] The figure on the viewer's right, likewise, resembles the corresponding figure in the London painting, especially from the waist up: His left arm is stretched taut, his head is in tense profile, and his shoulders and back are turned towards the viewer. The carrier in between is an amalgam of the same two carriers in the London painting. His legs, the left pushing off the ground in an arched profile, the right raised onto a step, follow the posture of the figure to the viewer's right in the London painting; his head, however, which looks down at the Christ figure, is adapted from Michelangelo's St. John on the other side.[48]

The Oxford sheet (Figure 72) thus shows the young Raphael sparing no effort to incorporate the impressions of Michelangelo's early Roman works. In Michelangelo's Roman *Pietà* Raphael recognized a new and more powerful conception of the dead body of Christ; in the *Entombment,* an innovative, and ultimately frustrated, attempt to make the carrying of the body to the

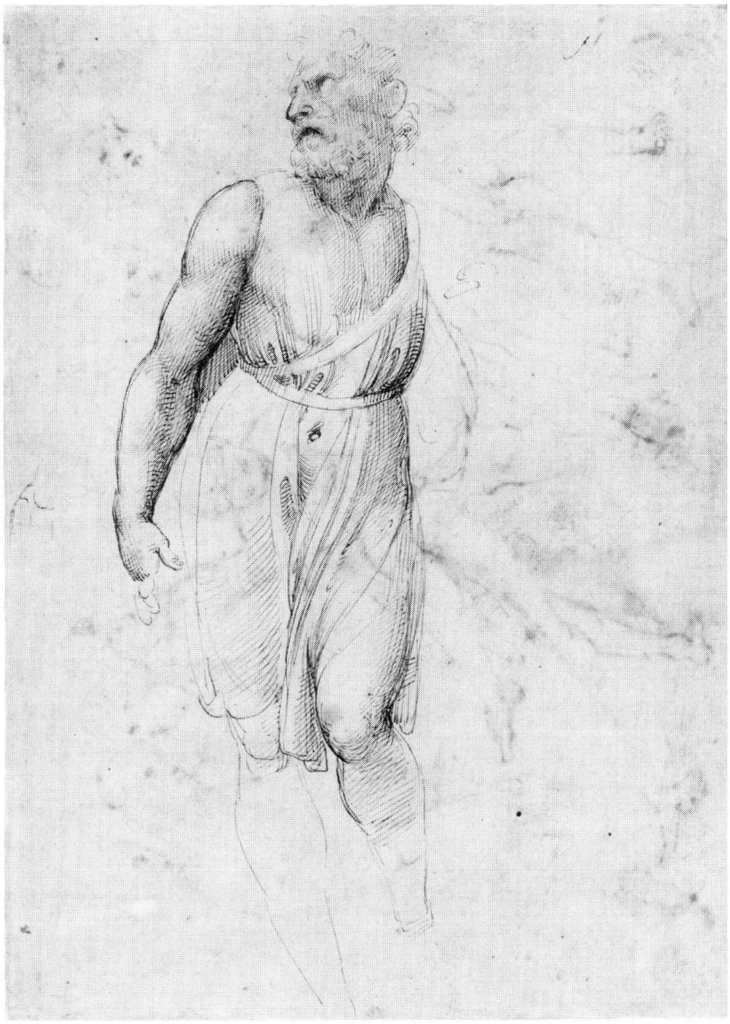

75. Raphael, *Study after Michelangelo's St. Matthew* (verso of 73). Drawing. British Museum, London, England. © The British Museum.

tomb the principal subject of a large altarpiece panel. The more elaborate composition study for the new conception in the British Museum (Figure 73), was, by contrast, probably worked out in Florence, as indicated by the drawing after Michelangelo's *St. Matthew* on the verso (see Figure 75). In it Raphael introduced his new carrying group and began to work out its consequences for the entire composition. The Virgin is now shown being left behind by the progression of the carriers, and she extends her arm in a pathetic gesture of farewell. Her outstretched hand, which just meets the profile of the right-hand carrier, is still another feature that shows close similarities to Michelangelo's *Entombment*.[49]

This sheet shows yet further study of Michelangelo, whose *St. Matthew* is copied on the verso (Figure 74 and 75). The ecstatic pose of Michelangelo's sculpture has been interpreted by Raphael in more rational terms; St. Matthew seems, in Raphael's interpretation, to be purposefully engaged in a specific activity. For this reason, and because the figure appears on the verso of this sheet, it has been reasonably suggested that Raphael was considering adapting the figure for one of his carriers. Significantly, the left arm, which in Michelangelo's sculpture is curled around a book, is not drawn at all, as if to leave it open to new uses. Indeed, after one sees Raphael's drawing, the idea of adapting the pose in this manner seems quite plausible; when one is confronted directly with the sculpture it is not so obvious.

It is my belief that Raphael's ability to see in the *St. Matthew* a potential carrier for his panel was facilitated by the fact that the sculpture is itself an adaptation, in reverse, of the left-hand carrier in Michelangelo's *Entombment* (see Figure 6). This similarity was remarked upon long ago by Bernard Berenson. "Reverse the figure [in the London painting]," he said, "and in all essentials of movement, and even of drapery, he is the Matthew and nothing but the Matthew, with the difference, however – much in the [former's] favor – that his action has a purpose."[50] Raphael's drawing, as it were, anticipated (and perhaps subliminally facilitated?) Berenson's observation.

Raphael did not limit himself to adapting individual motifs; rather, he absorbed the central idea of Michelangelo's conception, which was to make the drama of separation between the carrying group and the lamenting women the core of the picture's theme.[51] This is, indeed, what most clearly distinguishes Raphael's composition from the Meleager reliefs, which show the dead Meleager being carried, feet first, *toward* his mother and sisters. In his *Entombment* engraving, Mantegna adapted the sarcophagus relief to the scene of Christ being carried to the tomb, which is located within the image itself. The tomb is placed endwise in the center, and the figures are shown carrying the body, again feet first, from left to right – that is, again *toward* the group clustered around the Virgin. Thus, although there are two main groups of figures, the scene is not structured by a narrative of separation.

It was Michelangelo who, in his effort to adapt the subject to a frontal composition, elaborated a conception organized by the drama of separation (see Figure 6). Indeed, he made it the very basis of the transaction between viewer and picture. Raphael grasped Michelangelo's innovation and reincorporated the new conception back into the classical lateral composition. In the final painting, Raphael accentuated the separation by showing the Virgin falling away and by introducing the figure of the Magdalene rushing forward to take Christ's hand. This compositionally unlikely detour through Michelangelo's experiment with the subject is a measure of the importance of structural and generic controls in the making of artworks in this period:

Michelangelo's work was of crucial importance because it provided a rare example of the subject within the category of altar painting. The episode embodied in these two works thus offers strong evidence that the conventions controlling altar painting, though never explicitly stipulated by church authority, were powerful and real.

THE PARTING OF THE GENRES

The process leading to Raphael's final solution was, we have seen, marked by the breakdown of successive altarpiece paradigms and a critical, ongoing dialogue with Michelangelo. What we see in the final painting is informed at a deep thematic level by this process of resistance and rupture. Before this time large-format easel painting was dominated by the altarpiece. By the end of the sixteenth century, the altarpiece had lost its near-exclusive nights to the format, and large easel pictures had found a stable home in the picture gallery. One might even argue that by that time altarpieces were following in the footsteps of the gallery picture. In short, altarpiece painting ceased to function as a generic "dominant": by the end of the century this role had been taken over by a now-familiar conception of history painting – a conception whose fundamental rules and ideals pertained to painting understood as an art and applied whether the depicted subject was sacred or secular. Raphael's painting is one early, and highly revealing, moment in this transformation: it was shaped by a break with the altarpiece tradition, but it cannot simply be called a gallery picture *avant la lettre.*

This process of generic rupture was, as we have seen, directly correlated to the representation of rupture at the thematic level:The introduction of a transitory conception involving the carrying of the body of Christ broke open traditional altarpiece paradigms, resulting in a reinterpretation of the thematic model – the sarcophagus reliefs as well as Mantegna's print – as a drama of separation. Altarpieces, even when depicting biblical subjects, generally kept the focus of the scene stable, a convention that tacitly respects their function as a focus of liturgical attention. Even in scenes of the Assumption, the Virgin is most often shown as a static focus of attention at the top of the composition; where she is shown in movement a depiction of the heavens and of God the Father usually contains this movement within the limits of the altarpiece. In Raphael's more mature years, he found a means of meeting the demands of dynamic narrative without severing the link to the liturgical setting. As John Shearman demonstrated, the planned altarpiece of the *Assumption* for the Chigi chapel in Santa Maria del Popolo in Rome was intended to show swift movement out of the picture, but this implied movement was to be taken up, across the space of the chapel, in the cupola, where God the Father appears in the oculus in the act of drawing the Virgin toward him.[52] Through an ingenious dialogue of elements across the space of the chapel, dramatic movement out of the picture was given meaning and function in a liturgical setting.

The problem of depicting movement in an altarpiece, as we have seen in chapter 1, provoked Michelangelo to fashion a quite novel solution in his London *Entombment*. By bringing the narrative in line with altarpiece conventions of frontal display he produced a composition that is "motivated" by the relation between subject and viewer. The figure of Christ is shown being withdrawn from the lamentation group, to which the viewer is understood to belong. Raphael's *Entombment* returned to a lateral conception, and as a result the conveyance of the body threatened an implicit dislodging of the Christ figure from the field of representation altogether: To attend to the painting's cues is to become aware that the center of the picture is about to be left empty and that the body is about to disappear into the black depths of the cave depicted at the picture's edge.

This conception challenges the long-accepted convention according to which altarpieces were meant to provide a stable object of prayer and worship. This convention was strong enough that even narrative subjects were commonly rendered static and made into vehicles of devotional attention – that is, coordinated with the structures of Christian prayer and worship.[53] Raphael's final painting has in important respects lost this overt coordination with the liturgical environment. To imagine the figures in a painting moving out of the picture is to embrace a new form of pictorial attention altogether, one that accepts the painting as a fiction, independent of its surroundings. This more removed gaze is in several respects different from the sort of gaze that, say, looked to altarpieces to find an addressee for prayer. This is not to say that the exploration of narrative and spatial devices had not already produced effects of "removal" in earlier altarpieces or that such an exploration necessarily and always violates the codes of altarpiece painting. It is only to point out that in this work, as the sequence of preparatory drawings makes clear, the new devices did indeed test and disrupt the limits of the genre.

The reception of Raphael's work suggests that contemporary painters recognized it as a watershed. Titian's *Entombment* of the early 1520s in the Louvre, for example, carried Raphael's innovations firmly into the world of the gallery picture (Figure 76). Nothing is known for certain concerning the circumstances of the commission, but the painting, on canvas, bears little affinity to any known altarpiece conventions. Even if by an unlikely circumstance it was in fact used on an altar, it would have been an altarpiece only in name. In form and structure it in every way belongs to the early history of the gallery picture, to which Titian himself had already made significant contributions by this time. This is not to deny that the painting has religious meaning. It is only to claim that here the communication of religious meaning has very little to do with the devotional and liturgical functions traditionally served by altarpieces. The painting is addressed to a thoughtful and sensitive viewer, one who

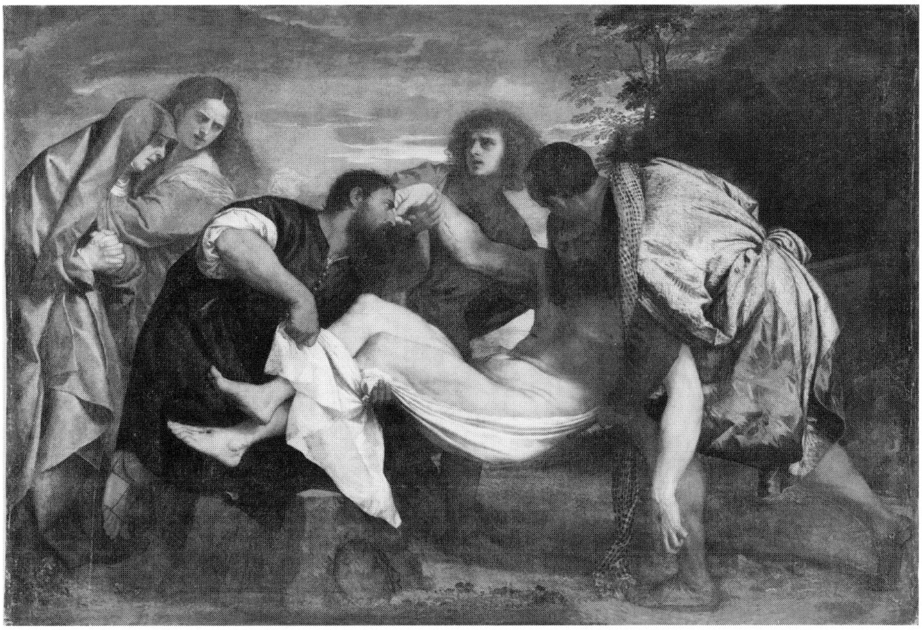

76. Titian, *The Carrying of Christ to the Tomb.* Canvas. Louvre, Paris, France. © Réunion des Musées Nationaux.

could also be expected to be moved and edified by a painting from Roman history.

Titian's interpretation of Raphael's altarpiece was part of a larger trend in the history of painting and collecting that would in time retroactively absorb Raphael's painting itself within the new category. A century after Raphael's panel was installed on its altar, it was forcibly removed and placed in the private gallery of Cardinal Scipione Borghese, where it became a prize possession. Even when it was still in the church of San Francesco al Prato in Perugia, it had become an attraction for tourists, dignitaries, and cognoscenti visiting the city.[54] The removal of the altarpiece to the picture gallery was the extreme consequence of a history of response that goes back to the years immediately following the work's initial installation – and that begins with the fact that Raphael's painting had loudly declared itself to be a departure from tradition.[55]

Such a process frustrates conventional art historical procedures. As stated earlier, to study this work simply according to the "normal" requirements of altarpieces in the period is to obscure its own claims to historical novelty and thus to fail fully to address the historical problems it raises. But to study it simply as a gallery picture is retrospectively to impose upon it a category whose very formation is part of the historical problem that demands to be studied. The work thus brings into focus the more general hermeneutic difficulty raised by the fact that the history of easel painting between 1500 and 1600 unfolded on undecided terrain. No systematic attempt has yet been made to write a history of sixteenth-century painting along these lines.[56] Such a study would entail rigorous analysis of the rhetorical devices used in the different genres and special attention to moments of cross-fertilization. It would also attend to such concrete issues as the introduction of canvas in altarpiece painting, where it was resisted well after it had come into common use in other forms of painting. It would attempt a systematic study of the period uses of such terms as *tavola, tavola d'altare, pala,* and *quadro.* It would assemble instances in which altarpieces were removed from church altars and placed in galleries. It would tell the story, ultimately, of how the altarpiece ceased to play the crucial and leading role in the development of painting that it had done until the end of the fifteenth century.

It is, however, one thing to be sensitive to this history of generic rupture and contamination and quite another to dispense with the categories altogether. Paul Hills, for example, pointing to the many difficulties in distinguishing between altarpieces and nonaltarpieces in the period, has suggested that the category of the altarpiece is itself a construction of art historians whose validity should be thrown into question.[57] I believe it is less useful to question the validity of the categories per se than to submit them to more carefully historicized analysis, as Hills also suggests. As genres develop they undergo redefinition and are brought into active contact with other genres and traditions.[58] A history of volatile generic change produces a good deal of runoff and many historically revealing *unica.* In dealing with the history of the altarpiece, therefore, it is a good idea to take into account works or traditions that the altarpiece influences, responds to, or absorbs through the course of its development. An account of the altarpiece in the early fifteenth century in Florence that excludes consideration of Masaccio's *Trinity* on strict categorical grounds would, for example, be fatally ignoring the active dialogue among chapel architecture, tomb design, fresco painting, and altarpieces that marks this period.

Flexibility and a sensitivity to limit-cases need not, therefore, lead to a complete denial of the existence of categories; that would amount to an abandonment of the very effort to understand these processes historically. In the sixteenth century, the distinction between altarpieces and other forms of easel painting became increasingly blurred, but this blurring has a history and thus carries cultural implications that deserve careful study. The lack of appreciable differences between a Tintoretto canvas made for an altar and one that was not is not the result of an absolute categorial "fuzziness" (in Hill's words) but rather of the fact that things had become fuzzy by midcentury, especially in Venice. This state of affairs was one of the consequences of the changes in painting that occurred in the late fifteenth century, changes that were structurally and thematically confronted in Michelangelo's, Raphael's, and Titian's *Entombments*. Historians may question at will the validity of the category of the altarpiece, but Raphael, in 1507, was responding to the fact that he was tampering with its limits.

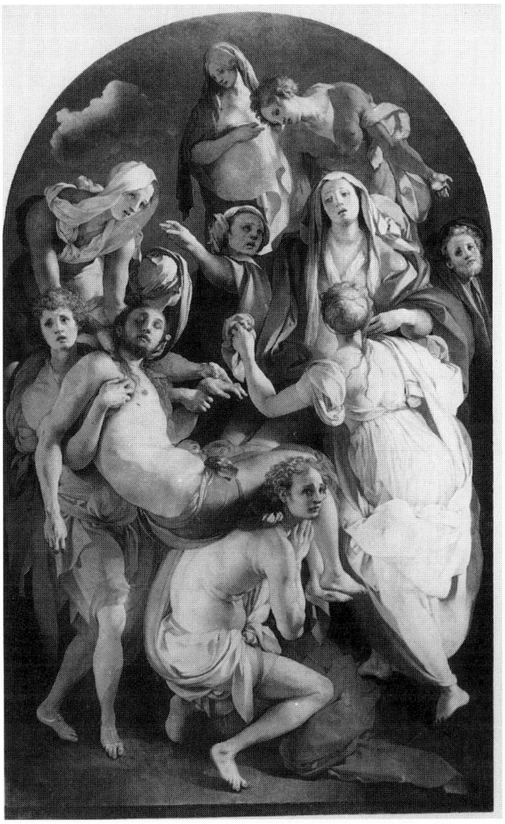

77. Jacopo da Pontormo, *The Carrying of Christ to the Tomb.* Panel. Santa Felicita, Florence, Italy.

The point is confirmed, again, by the work's reception. The departure from the altarpiece tradition, celebrated by Titian, was in turn tellingly resisted by Jacopo Pontormo: His altarpiece of 1525–28 in Santa Felicita in Florence was a deliberate effort to put this theme, and the conception of history painting it embodied, once again into meaningful interaction with a liturgical environment (Figure 77). It offered, in other words, an extreme defence of the altarpiece – an eloquent counterpoint to Titian, polemically in the tradition of Michelangelo. Michelangelo had depicted a movement into the picture, away from the viewer, and thus had "motivated" the relation between worshiper and subject through a drama of distanciation. On the far side of Raphael's painting, Jacopo da Pontormo was more specifically concerned with reestablishing the connection to the physical chapel setting – a connection that he may well have felt Raphael's lateral composition had lost. If Michelangelo had concentrated almost exclusively on the relation between viewer and picture, Pontormo was concerned to offer a thoroughgoing reinterpretation of the entire relation between the altarpiece and its ritual space. He thus produced yet another refashioning of the theme, this time conceived through a diagonal, spiraling movement leading out of the picture. It is not necessary for the purposes of this chapter to enter into the debate over where this movement is understood to lead. However one interprets it, the movement out of the picture involves – in contrast to Raphael's conception in the Baglioni *Entombment* and in closer affinity to Raphael's conception in the Chigi chapel – a mobilization of the elements of the chapel setting and thus active claims on the altarpiece's liturgical environment.[59]

The acrobatics of Michelangelo and Pontormo were not simply exercises in artistic virtuosity. They were extremely resourceful attempts to reaffirm the purpose of altar painting in an era when pictorial developments had threatened the integrity and dominance of the institution. Both incorporated the antique-inspired modes of figural movement and the greater narrative complexity embodied in a new conception of history painting, but both forcibly reoriented the classical, lateral orientation of their models. In both, the narrative elements are thus employed to reinterpret, on a new and more spectacular level, the function of the altarpiece and its connection to its liturgical setting. Both were, in other words, strenuous assertions of the conviction that painting, even in its modern form, still derived its deepest meaning and purpose from its position above an altar. But the future of painting lay with the gallery picture, not with the altarpiece, and these experiments remain, together with those of Rosso and Parmigianino, a brief and strange episode in the history of Western art.

PART TWO

PRESENTATION AND WITHDRAWAL: MICHELANGELO'S LATE *PIETÀS*

CHAPTER FIVE

Passionate Withdrawal

ART AND REFORM

The first part of this book studied efforts by Michelangelo and others to preserve traditions of religious imagery at a time when artistic developments threatened their integrity and dominance. These efforts were not merely formal experiments but reinterpretations of the nature and function of religious images, and they deserve to be understood in the light of debates over religious reform that mark the period as a whole. They constitute one aspect of the early sixteenth-century "crisis of the image" that has been observed by Hans Belting, among many others. Crisis is a convenient abstraction invoked by historians when attempting to describe historical change, but it is very difficult to point to objective correlatives to such a description, as one can when one talks of a change in the weather. We do gain historical purchase on the idea, however, if crisis is understood as a function of criticism.[1] The perception of change and the framing of critical attitudes presuppose a reflective distance, an awareness of cultural disjunction, and thus are themselves instances of crisis. In the works under study we see a consciousness of artistic tradition that anticipates the critical approach to the history of art developed later in the sixteenth century.

Acute art historical awareness often accompanied a concern for reform. The prevailing mode of reform thought in Rome in the early part of the sixteenth century mingled an interest in early Christianity with a general interest in ur-religions and traditions of archaic wisdom.[2] Such an orientation encouraged a special openness to nonalphabetic symbolic languages considered to be primordial, such as hieroglyphs, which many believed to contain direct insight into religious and cosmic truth. Such an attitude, in turn, encouraged a strong belief in the capacity of the visual arts and architecture to serve as instruments and symbols of spiritual renewal. This highly open-minded intellectual culture remained predominant only for a few decades, and the more regulatory and restrictive culture that succeeded it did not sustain its belief in the wide scope and license to be accorded to the visual arts.[3]

The strange experiments of Michelangelo, Jacopo da Pontormo, Rosso, and Parmigianino, among others, can be understood as artistic parallels to these investigations. To see them in this way in turn releases them, and thus our understanding of significant aspects of High Renaissance and Mannerist art, from some familiar and unuseful historical models. If understood as part of a general advance away from medieval Christianity and toward the era of modern secular art, the religious aspects of these works can be understood only negatively, as concessions to a continuing and waning tradition, as little more than a pretext upon which the artists could express "modern" artistic values. If they are understood within the humanist and reform-minded culture that dominated the intellectual life of the period – the culture of Giovanni Pico della Mirandola, Jacopo Sadoleto, Giles of Viterbo, Johannes Goritz, Giovan Matteo Giberti, Paolo Giovio, Pietro Bembo, and Pierio Valeriano – then the "innovative" qualities of these works need not be understood in contradiction to their religious purpose, and their archaism need not be understood in contradiction to their modernism.

This is not to say that the situation was stable or that it produced lasting solutions. Efforts to reform religious art could produce highly eccentric works in traditional categories, such as the *Entombments* of Michelangelo and Pontormo (see Figures 6 and 77) and the *Dead Christ* of Rosso (see Figure 84), and they could also lead to a departure from the traditional categories altogether. Michelangelo, for example, never again returned to altar painting after the London *Entombment,* although he continued to be preoccupied by the theme of the Man of Sorrows until the end of his life. It is logical to assume that this was the result of circumstantial factors, such as the absence of such commissions, but what we know about his attitudes on the matter suggest a more motivated avoidance. It is well known that in his later years Michelangelo developed a disdain for "normal" artistic work and for the entire practice of making works of art on commission – a disdain closely bound up with the aristocratic claims, familial and otherwise, that preoccupied him later in life. In a letter of 1548 to his nephew, Michelangelo irritably expresses this disdain, betraying regret even at having had to work for popes:

Tell the priest not to address me any more "to Michelangelo, sculptor," because I am known in no way but as Michelangelo Buonarroti, and if a Florentine citizen wants an altarpiece painted he must find a painter, for I was never a painter or sculptor like the ones who keep a shop. I have always avoided that for the honor of my father and brothers, although I have served three popes, which has been perforce.[4]

The reference to altarpieces was made in response to a specific request and thus cannot be taken as a programmatic statement on the issue. Nonetheless, Michelangelo does categorically associate the making of altarpieces with the inferior, workaday artist. He does not simply decline the commission; he says that this *sort* of commission is beneath him, and always has been. Do not come to me for an altarpiece, he says, "for I was never a painter or sculptor like the ones who keep a shop." Of course, he had in fact accepted quite standard commissions for church art, such as the tomb/altar of St. Dominic in Bologna and the Piccolomini altar in Siena. The important point is that toward the end of his life he preferred to think he never had.

The late *Pietà*s are the strongest expression of this neo-aristocratic ethos. They continued to engage the Man of Sorrows tradition, but in contrast to the London *Entombment* they abandoned the realm of traditional church art altogether. It is a historically revealing irony that Michelangelo's efforts to preserve a tradition of religious cult imagery appreciated precisely for its associations with past forms of public, "communal" religious life, should have been undertaken in a highly rarefied atmosphere of private investigations, new conceptions of art, unprecedented claims to artistic originality, and exquisite protocols of aristocratic courtesy. The deliberate withdrawal from the economy and institutions of traditional church art coincided with a time of increasingly heated debate over the question of reform, and with the emergence of an increasingly defined reform faction within the Church – a faction whose acknowledged leaders were Gasparo Contarini and Reginald Pole. With the support of Pope Paul III, this reform-minded group reached a peak of influence and activity in the late 1530s, only to have circumstances turn decisively against them in the 1540s. Any implicit affinities Michelangelo might have felt for reforming ideas early in life – affinities I explored in the first part of this book – developed in these years into an active engagement with some of the most illustrious members of this group, such as Vittoria Colonna and Cardinal Pole himself. These friendships placed Michelangelo in direct contact with the circle that produced that most important document of Italian reform thought before the Council of Trent, the *Beneficio di Cristo*.[5]

In a study of the *Beneficio,* Carlo Ginzburg and Adriano Prosperi noted how far the culture presupposed by this best-seller of 1543 had come from the culture of civic religion so forcefully in evidence in the late Quattrocento. The public processions and liturgies, the miraculous relics and the venerated saints that were held up as symbols of the city, the pomp of private and confraternity chapels – in short, the "ritual setting" studied by, among others, Richard Trexler – stands in stark contrast to the direct relation between believer and God celebrated in the *Beneficio,* a relation mediated only by the figure of Christ crucified. Public rituals, of course, continued to be celebrated in the Cinquecento, but the enormous success of the *Beneficio* – a contemporary estimated that between 1543 and 1549 40,000 copies had been sold in Venice alone[6] – indicates the emergence of deep-seated spiritual needs that were no longer satisfied by these traditional ritual forms.[7]

This transformation is sharply illuminated by developments in the nature and status of religious images in the period. Michelangelo's engagements with the tradition of the Man of Sorrows not only implicitly reveal such a transformation at work but also directly confront and interpret its implications. My purpose is not simply to show in which ways Michelangelo's later works reveal the influence of reforming thought. I am more interested in pointing out where developments in the claims of works of art became relevant to the concerns of reform-minded thinkers. The drawing of the *Pietà* that Michelangelo made for Vittoria Colonna about 1540, for example, belonged to a new category of artwork altogether: It was a drawing made as a finished work in its own right and offered as a gift (see Figure 93). The development runs roughly parallel to the religious developments noted above: The direct and private experience offered by the new category of artwork marks a deliberate retreat from the traditional forms of religious art, such as altarpieces, and from the entire economy of piety – the system of endowments, paid Masses, vows, and indulgences – that such forms served and symbolized.

This chapter studies the process by which Michelangelo arrived at the new conception, through a literal "withdrawing" from the traditional institutions and repertoire of religious art. Part of the inchoate, preparatory phase of the making of a work of art, the realm of drawing became for Michelangelo a fertile subsoil in which to continue experiments with the figure of the dead Christ free from the restrictions governing more formal artistic arenas, such as church art. In this sense there are affinities between Michelangelo's mode of investigation and the subject that obsessed him. After death Christ descended into the tomb and into the depths of Limbo. For Michelangelo, the interval between Christ's death and resurrection was not simply a time of darkness and absence but a time of withdrawal and gathering, a time of stripping and release that is also a preparation for regeneration. In a state of suspended animation between death and life, a state that Michelangelo interpreted alternatively as a sleep, an ecstasy or a transport, Christ becomes an especially volatile and susceptible conduit of spiritual energy. He is taken out of himself, and thus newly connected with his divine nature, yet his body is still there, vibrant and palpable, communicating as it were directly, on this side of overt language and gesture.

Michelangelo's drawings were, similarly, a withdrawal into a more obscure and ambiguous realm, on this side of the finished work of art. In the scrawl of drawn lines figures are not quite embodied: Their boundaries are ambiguous and their forms are volatile and susceptible to change. Registering the stroke of the artist's hand, the figures flicker with an animation that in part belongs to them as actors in the story, but everywhere passes through them as a force of energy that belongs to the drawing as a whole. Their semantic status is unstable: Sometimes they are full-fledged, identifiable characters attached to the story, but often they are nameless nude figures, deprived of identity, raw figural matter on this side of denotative clarity. It was not just that sketches allowed for freedom in the composition of a subject; for Michelangelo they offered freedom from the very limits of subject matter. Not yet bound by the declarative exigencies of the subject, drawings participate in exchanges at the level of motif, exploring affinities at the level of posture and gesture, and thus elaborating figures that might be used not only for different subjects but in entirely different iconographic spheres. In other words, drawings encouraged Michelangelo to move one level down, from the depiction of subjects to the exploration of themes: Not the *Entombment* in particular, but in general the problem of death, interment, and a return to the earth. This figure lying on the earth in a composition for a lamentation does not only resemble a river god; in the "pre-semantic" realm of drawing it is quite literally a version of a river god, even as it also is a version of the dead Christ. The same goes for wailing figures and bacchic maenads. For Michelangelo similar bodily states were not merely formally similar motifs but the sign of deep thematic affinities. The river god combines almost inanimate torpor with a closeness to the earth's deeply generated fertility, and so was not far, in Michelangelo's mind, from the figure of the dead Christ, brought to earth, entombed, and (thus) the source of new life.

Little wonder, therefore, that this shift downward from subject to theme should itself involve the theme of going down. Just as Christ gives up and goes down, releasing new spiritual energies in his ecstatic death, so the drawings abdicate finished art and go down, releasing a fertile creative process that breaks down the boundaries between separate realms of subject matter, even between separate religious systems. The basic idea, that it is necessary to undergo a death, a dismantling, a breaking down in order to undergo renewal, was of course a favorite topos of reform rhetoric. This sequence of investigations, however, did not surface again in a painting, a new public statement, but in a drawing of the *Pietà* offered to Vittoria Colonna, studied in chapter 6. In effecting a generic extension of the category of the drawing Michelangelo was perhaps asserting that these experiments, even in their most formal mode, still belonged on this side of the conventional categories of religious art. Michelangelo thus reinvented the traditional cult image as a work of art, offering an exquisite aesthetic experience to suit the rarefied – and ultimately ineffectual – reform sensibility of the spiritual circle to which Colonna belonged. This chastened and refined proposal came, significantly, just as the *Last Judgment* was making the issue of public religious art into a matter of raging cultural and political debate. The late *Pietà* sculptures, studied in chapter 7, belong to a later phase, when the delicate hopes of Colonna's spiritual circle had been dashed and it had become harder to believe in the marriage of art and religion, of elegance and piety, dreamed of since the days of Pico della Mirandola and Giles of Viterbo.

CHRIST IN ECSTASY

The connection between Michelangelo's experiments in the London *Entombment* and the late *Pietà*s is more than a matter of shared subject. Scholars have noted that a drawing in Vienna of the dead Christ in the arms of the Virgin shows similarities with the London painting (Figure 78).[8] The similarity is so strong that Henry Thode actually took the drawing as a study for the painting.[9] No one now would seriously doubt that the drawing should be dated later, probably circa 1530, and that it shows affinities to the presentation drawings produced at that time. It thus documents the reception of the London *Entombment* in the context of the investigations that led directly to the Colonna *Pietà*. The Christ figure in the drawing is not only strikingly similar to that depicted in the London painting; it is directly copied from it. This is evident above all in the legs and left arm. The torso as well was carefully drawn after the painting: The original guiding lines in black chalk, still visible along Christ's proper right profile (but entirely invisible in a black-and-white photograph), are virtually a tracing of the profile of the figure in the painting. Another feature confirms the direct dependence of the drawing on the painting: The genitalia, missing from the painting, are dutifully omitted in the drawing.

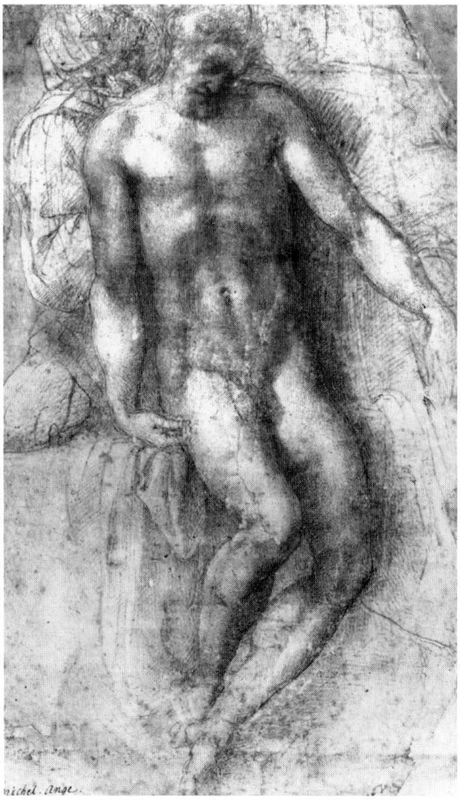

78. Michelangelo (?), *Dead Christ Supported by the Virgin*. Drawing. Graphische Sammlung Albertina, Vienna, Austria.

All of these points strongly suggest that the drawing was made from direct study of the painting rather than having been elaborated freely from memory.[10] And yet the pose has been altered. In the London painting the body of Christ is a gentle helix turned upon the abdomen. The turning of the body – the upper torso toward the left, the legs toward the right –

is delicately suggested rather than fully realized: Shoulders are still squarely above legs, and all movement is contained within a blocklike rectangle and a primarily frontal presentation of the body. This invites the use of foreshortening, which in turn preserves the ambiguity between a sitting posture and a standing one. In the first part of this book, I interpreted this ambiguity as an inheritance from the Man of Sorrows tradition, where it served as a sign of the ambiguous status of the dead Christ, who is both pathetic victim and redeeming Lord. In the drawing, the delicate balance between sitting and standing has been lost.[11] The figure is placed on the edge of the tomb, but the pose is not reconceived for a seated figure; rather, the drawing maintains many of the outward features of the pose from the painting and attempts somewhat awkwardly to force them into a seated posture. The legs are turned to the viewer's right, the left leg now being shown more nearly in profile and resting passively on the ground. The torso, however, is now rigidly upright and front facing.[12]

Connoisseurs might point to these features as evidence of the drawing's "weakness," and they may well be right, but they are fault lines in a more significant sense. They speak to the difficulty of adapting the delicate and ambiguous pose of the London Christ figure to a reduced composition involving only Christ and the Virgin. The figure must be more firmly seated because, in a very practical sense, the Virgin cannot be expected to hold the Christ figure in an upright posture all by herself. The only way the Virgin can fully support Christ is to lay him across her lap as she did when he was a child – that is, to assume the posture of the *Vesperbild*. This is what we see in a closely contemporary and perhaps related drawing in the British Museum, where Christ is supported laterally across the Virgin's legs.[13] Another solution, offered in the earlier *Pietà* that Michelangelo designed for Sebastiano del Piombo in Viterbo, was to leave Christ entirely alone on the ground. Rather than opt for a lateral, supine Christ, the Vienna drawing maintained the frontal presentation of the figure of Christ that attaches it to the tradition of the *imago pietatis.* It recognized, so to speak, the figure of the Man of Sorrows within the London painting's elaborate narrative, and extracted it once again, producing a composition similar to the Man of Sorrows images of Giovanni Bellini and Antonello da Messina, with the difference that here we have the figure in full length. But it is not simply a return to a traditional Man of Sorrows scheme. The drawing preserves the historically embedded form in which the London painting had left it, and thus had to find a new accord between the dictates of naturalism and the traditional cult image. Quite practically, it meant finding a seated posture for the frontal and full-length figure of Christ drawn from the painting, and the result was the somewhat awkward arrangement that we see.

The difficulties encountered in this drawing signal a set of problems confronted in all of the late *Pietà*s. Rather than simply return to the traditional Man of Sorrows, they investigate the mystery of the sacramental Christ within the compass of a modern conception of narrative art. Whereas the traditional Man of Sorrows was detached from the Passion narrative, Michelangelo's experiments focus on the precise interval between crucifixion and entombment – that is, between the end of Christ's earthly life and the triumph of his divine nature within the tomb. Michelangelo – and, as we shall see, Vittoria Colonna – looked for the key to the mystery of Christ's sacrifice in the intimate and animating contact of the dead body with his mourners, and above all with the Virgin. As in the London *Entombment,* the actors are thus not simply conceived as actors in a historical drama of lamentation but instead as participants in a form of cult to the dead Christ. Such a cultic interpretation of the subject was, for Michelangelo, closely bound up with the motif of the front-facing body of Christ – that is, with the tradition of the Eucharistic Man of Sorrows. The entire series of works, from the London *Entombment* through to the Rondanini *Pietà,* can be understood as a search for a Christocentric alternative to the "other" *pietà* type, the *Vesperbild,* represented by Michelangelo's early group in St. Peter's (see Figure 59) – a search that was marked throughout by a distinctly archaizing sensibility.[14] The *Vesperbild* tradition served a strain of piety that was primarily Marian in orientation: It was a form of the devotion to the Virgin, structured by a parallel to the Virgin and Child image. Just as the Virgin and Child image often incorporated a proleptic reference to the Passion, the image of the *pietà* in the form of the *Vesperbild* is charged with an emotional reminiscence of the image of the Mother and Child.[15] Not surprisingly, Michelangelo had also adapted the theme of the Virgin and Child in this more Christological direction – in the *Bruges Madonna,* for example, where he placed a forward-facing, standing Christ Child between the Virgin's legs. In readapting these themes toward a Christocentric focus, Michelangelo was acting in accordance with the reformist tendencies of his day.[16]

To propose a sacramental interpretation of the figure of Christ while remaining within the historical interval between crucifixion and entombment demanded an intensive reevaluation of the nature and status of the dead body. If traditionally the Man of Sorrows image asserted the redemptive efficacy of the sacrifice by presenting a dead body that was miraculously self-supporting and self-offering – a dead Christ with half-open eyes, capable of willful gestures – in a narrative situation, this efficacy had to be expressed by subtler means. Michelangelo's response was to qualify the depiction of the dead weight of the body and of the attendant efforts to give it support – to suggest agency and radiance in the body, and a corresponding responsive and participatory animation in the surrounding figures. These difficulties of physical description were not generally ones that writers faced. The life of Christ literature surely abounded in meditations on theological mysteries, but these usually took the form of digressions into doctrine. Very few writers expounded on the life-giving power of the Eucharist by describing the "behavior" of Christ's body after the crucifixion and before the resurrection. In chapter 3 I quoted one exceptional passage from a Passion tract by the preacher Pietro da Lucca, where he affirmed that through contact with the Virgin and the other mourners the dead and mutilated body of Christ "was made once again healthy, pure, and white, as if he had never received a wound or a blow."[17] A very similar interpretation was offered, not surprisingly, by Michelangelo's soul mate Vittoria Colonna, and will be studied in the next chapter.

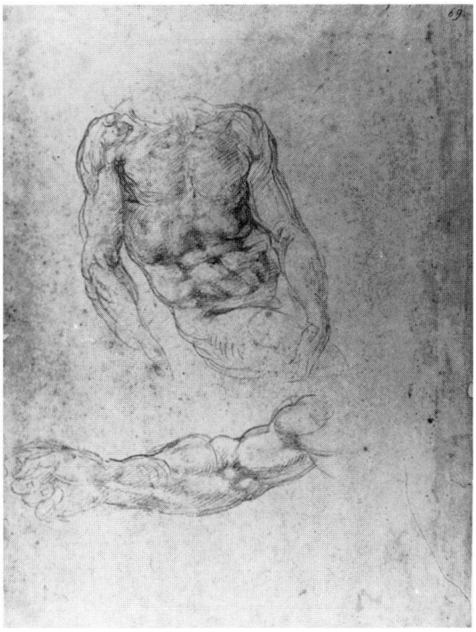

79. Michelangelo, *Male Figure Study.* Drawing. Casa Buonarroti, Florence, Italy.

The solution to the problem of combining a Virgin with a front-facing Christ – of finding, as it were, a Man of Sorrows–based alternative to the *Vesperbild* – came in a drawing by Michelangelo now in the Casa Buonarroti (Figure 79).[18] The drawing served as the basis for Sebastiano del Piombo's Úbeda *Pietà* now in the Prado, commmissioned in the summer of 1533 by Ferrante Gonzaga as a gift for the imperial minister Francisco de los Cobos (Figure 80).[19] The sheet also bears studies for the *Last Judgment* and probably dates from the beginning of Michelangelo's work on the composition for the fresco – that is, shortly after his arrival in Rome in November of 1533. The drawing shows a seated figure in a pose adapted from a famous antique relief known at the time as the *Bed of Polycleitus,* which shows a semi-reclined, sleeping male figure attended to by a female figure (Figure 81). A version of the relief was owned by Lorenzo Ghiberti and was at this time still in the possession of his grandson, Vittore, a close friend of Michelangelo's.[20]

The torso on the Casa Buonarroti sheet was expanded nearly to a full figure, and brought to a very high level of finish, in a sheet in the Louvre (Figure 82).[21] The Casa Buonarroti study is a drawing after the nude model and, although it was certainly used as a model for the Louvre sheet, it is not certain that it was made "for" this commission. It shows an unambiguously vibrant, active body[22] and thus had to be adapted for the body of the dead Christ. This caused problems, above all in the treatment of the right arm, as the two marginal efforts to correct it reveal. If in the Casa Buonarroti drawing we do not ask what supports that arm, in this drawing it appears odd: The head falls on an upraised right shoulder, yet that shoulder receives no support from the arm, which falls limp. The Vienna drawing discussed above (see Figure 78) offered a better explanation for the loosely hanging arm: It showed the Virgin

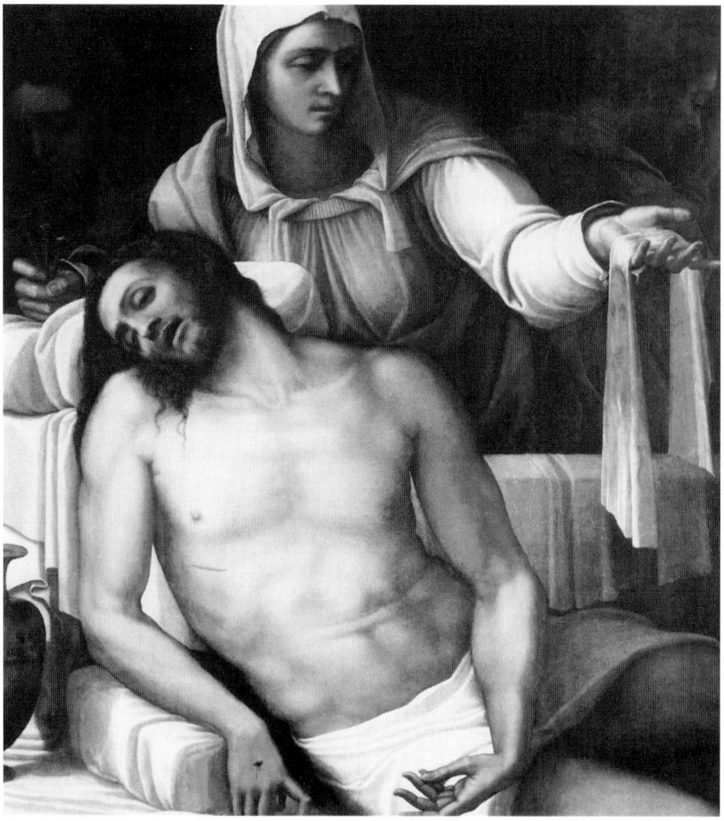

80. Sebastiano del Piombo, *Pietà*. Slate. Museo del Prado, Madrid, Spain. Fundación Casa Ducal de Medinaceli.

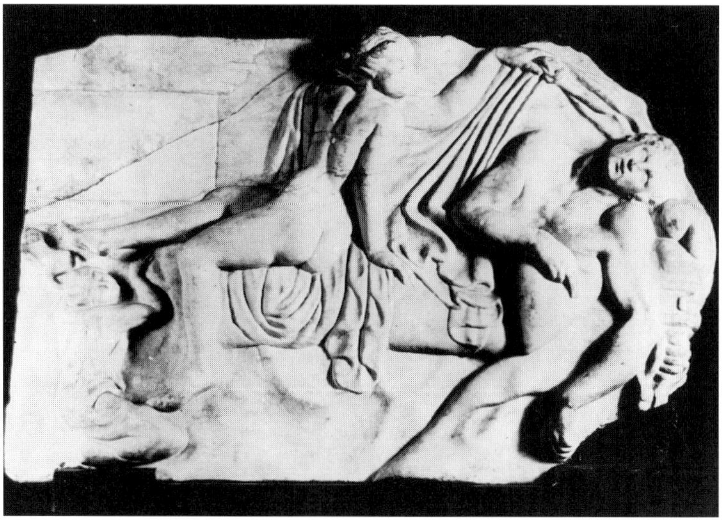

81. *Bed of Polycleitus.* Marble. Renaissance copy of Roman relief, location unknown. Courtesy of the Institute of Fine Arts, New York University.

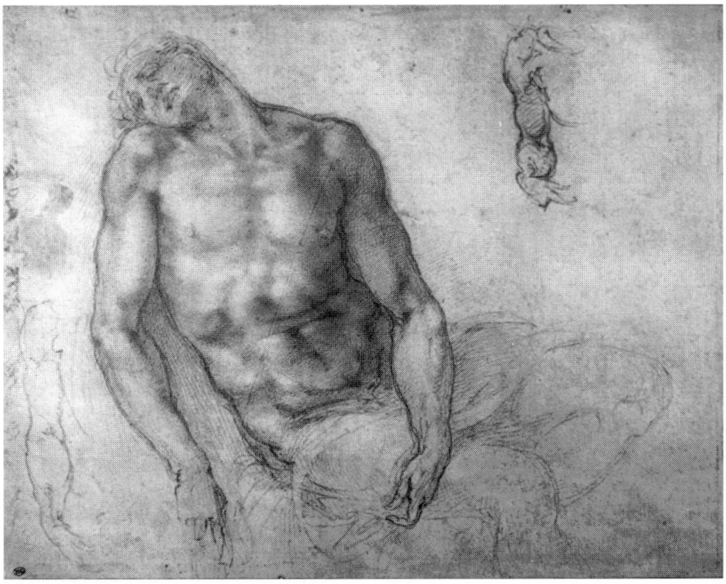

82. Michelangelo (?), *Study for the Úbeda Pietà.* Drawing. Louvre, Paris, France. © Réunion des Musées Nationaux.

supporting Christ from the underarm – a motif taken over from the London painting, on which the drawing is based – thus allowing the arm to fall straight down to the tomb seat. In the Louvre sheet, just to the left of the problematic arm, an alternative is sketched that follows quite precisely the arm motif found in the Vienna sheet. The similarity is so strong, in fact, as to suggest the possibility that the Vienna sheet was an earlier idea for the Úbeda *Pietà,* with which it shares several features, such as the blocklike seat shrouded in drapery.[23]

In the upper right-hand corner of the Louvre sheet another solution is proposed for this arm, showing it supported on an arm rest, a solution more or less taken over in the final painting. This is in a sense the opposite solution to the loosely hanging arm offered in the first alternative sketch to the left. If there the arm shows utter dependency, here the arm is actively supporting the body, and this in turn carries significant implications that are best understood through comparison. It is very close, in fact, to the right arm of Adam in the *Creation of Adam* on the Sistine Chapel ceiling (Figure 83). The legs of the Christ figure also resemble those of Adam, a motif also adopted for the figure of Lazarus in the painting of the *Resurrection of Lazarus,* now in the London National Gallery, that Michelangelo designed for Sebastiano del Piombo fifteen years earlier. These are not simply formal borrowings but thematically related investigations, for all of these works are at bottom investigations into the process by which an inanimate body comes (again) into life. As has been eloquently observed on many occasions, the figure of Adam is an exquisite balance between agency and dependency. He is not simply a passive body lifted up from the ground by God, as, say, Lorenzo Ghiberti showed him in

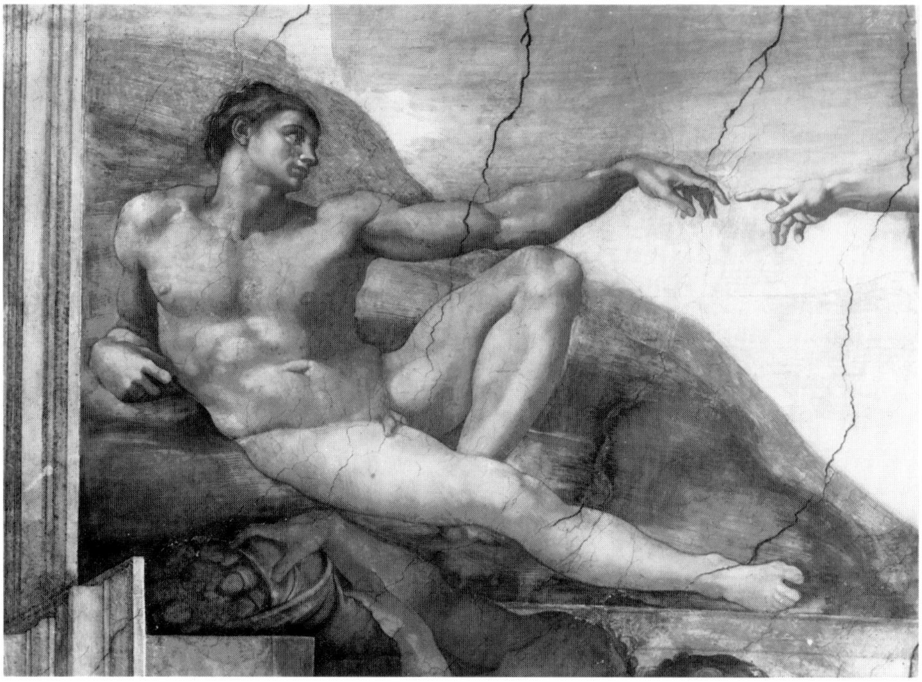

83. Michelangelo, *Creation of Adam, detail of Adam.* Fresco. Sistine Chapel, Vatican City.

the doors of the Florence Baptistery. Instead Adam is shown receiving and yet reaching, languid and yet instinct with an incipient autonomy. His upraised knee, like that of Lazarus, is a primary indicator of his stirring into life.

The main source for the composition of the Úbeda *Pietà,* the antique relief of the *Bed of Polycleitus* (see Figure 81), was also more than a formal model. The subject of the relief was not known at the time, but its immanent thematic qualities – a powerless male figure receiving the attentions of a supple female attendant – exerted a fascination over the artists of the day.[24] Michelangelo evidently found in the figure of sleep and in the activity of unveiling and awakening a number of thematic associations that were relevant to his interpretation of the dead Christ. For Michelangelo, as we have seen, the body of the dead Christ was not merely an inert corpse but was endowed with a mysterious and quasi-animate energy. In part 1 I argued that in the London *Entombment* the ambiguous figure of the upright dead Christ was based on the swaying figure of the drunken Bacchus supported by attendants, a figure well known from antique reliefs and adapted in Andrea Mantegna's famous bacchic prints. I argued that this conception of the scene as a kind of bacchic procession, a form of animated rite, was part of an overall strategy to lift the narrative out of history and to set it into a more "present" relation with its ritual context. Here, in a less dramatic scene focused on the intimate relation between Christ and the Virgin, Michelangelo turned to a more quiet and lyrical source, but one with distinct affinities to the bacchic subjects. For Michelangelo the sleeping figure in the *Bed of Polycleitus* was in a state not far from a bacchic swoon – he even adapted it in a drawing of a bacchic subject discussed below (see Figure 87) – and as such it served him as a model in his ecstatic reinterpretation of the dead Christ. In the end, of course, the figure of Christ as finally painted by Sebastiano in the Úbeda *Pietà* – a stiff corpse, inviting pity perhaps, but nothing in the way of these more mysterious associations – fell far short of these ambitions.[25]

Michelangelo was not the only artist in these years to adopt the *Bed of Polycleitus* model for an image of the dead Christ. As John Shearman noted, Rosso Fiorentino adopted the model in his panel, now in Boston (Figure 84), and to very similar ends.[26] Shearman convincingly proposed that Rosso's panel represents the highly novel subject of Christ inside the tomb, where the angels are holding a sort of vigil over the body of Christ before the resurrection. The subject is quite unique, and unlike anything Michelangelo attempted, but it is a response to a similarly perceived problem. Like Michelangelo, Rosso was also interested in penetrating the mysterious properties of the dead Christ. Neither Rosso nor Michelangelo, however, wished

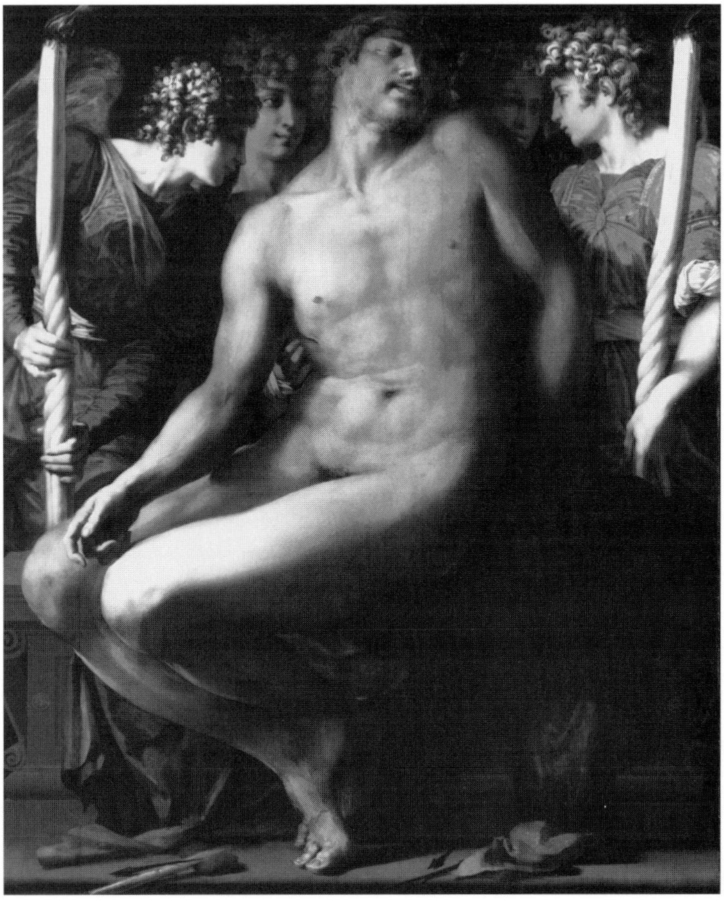

84. Rosso Fiorentino, *Dead Christ with Angels.* Panel. Museum of Fine Arts, Boston, U.S. Charles Potter Kling Fund.

entirely to abandon the narrative framework of the historical life of Christ – the conditions, as it were, of modern history painting. They both approached the problem by focusing intense attention on the "status" of Christ's body in the interval after the death but before the resurrection, and by finding there a quasi-animate quality, an incipient stirring of a life force.[27] The difference is that Rosso pushed this investigation closer to the *outre-tombe.* Indeed, he pushed it closer than has been recognized. The torch-candles have just blown out, and light enters from the left, reflecting like blades against Christ's shins. The smoke from the just extinguished candles indicates that a gust has also come from this direction. A moment before the dark, enclosed tomb was lit only by the candles of the angels' vigil. But now, as Christ writhes into wakefulness, the stone gives way and a new day breaks.

As in the case of Michelangelo, Rosso's mystery-oriented approach to the dead Christ went hand in hand with a conscious return to the tradition of the *imago pietatis.* In Rosso's case the figure appears in the truly archaic type of the Man of Sorrows with angels, or *Engelpietà* – a type that he now "explains" as part of a historical episode. As innovative as his painting was, Rosso consciously connected it to the Man of Sorrows tradition, for he once described it specifically as a Christ "in forma Pietatis."[28] Once again, extreme experimentation went hand in hand with deliberate archaism.

The affinity between Rosso's panel and the works by Michelangelo and Sebastiano studied here is not merely a matter of general approach but of specific features: The upturned head and ecstatic, almost smiling expression in Rosso's Christ – a poignant expression of "animatedness" – also appears in the Louvre drawing (see Figure 82), perhaps with distinct knowledge of Rosso's panel.[29] Both Michelangelo and Rosso reshaped the traditional Man of Sorrows on the model of antique sculpture. The body of Christ is no longer pitiful but beautiful, pristine, and radiant, and death has been reconceived as a languid, ecstatic swoon. These interpretations stand at the opposite extreme to Hans Holbein's *Dead Christ* (Figure 85) in Basel, which is perhaps the most exacting and relentless depiction of a dead corpse produced in the period. Where the Christs of Michelangelo and Rosso close their eyes in ecstasy, Holbein's Christ remains open eyed, the gaze dead and empty. As Julia Kristeva put it, "(T)he empty stare,

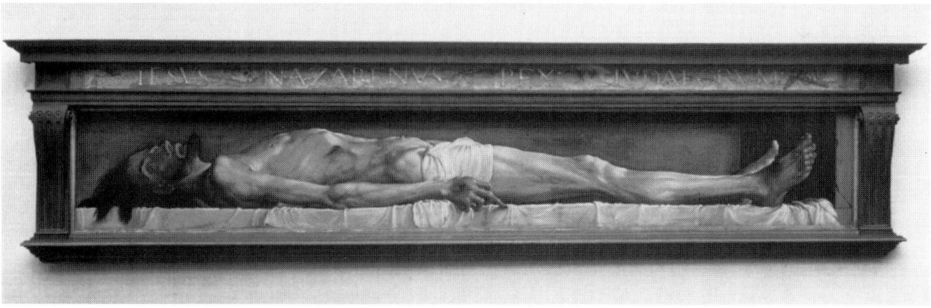

85. Hans Holbein the Younger, *Dead Christ.* Panel. Kunstmuseum, Basel, Switzerland. Giraudon/ Art Resource, NY.

the sharp-lined profile, the dull blue-green complexion are those of a man who is truly dead, of Christ forsaken by the Father ('My God, my God, why have you deserted me?') and without promise of Resurrection."[30] The unrelenting realism of the depiction extends even to the scale of the painting, which shows the body at exactly life-size. To set these works against one another is to appreciate the extremes to which art could be pulled in a period of open-ended artistic exploration and volatile religious uncertainty.

The important point is that neither extreme stands as the viable, "truly Christian" solution. Holbein's panel famously horrified and haunted Dostoyevsky; it appears several times in *The Idiot,* where it provokes loss of faith by encouraging doubts about Christ's resurrection.[31] Historians have cautioned against projecting Dostoyevsky's response back into the Renaissance and have rightly connected Holbein's panel to late-medieval devotions that concentrated on the gruesome details of Christ's suffering and death.[32] And yet Dostoyevsky also had his precursors. His horrified response echoes those of medieval clerics, such as Humbert of Silva Candida, to the first images of the dead Christ on the cross, discussed in chapter 1. The criticisms of Girolamo Savonarola, discussed in chapter 1, and the passage from Pietro da Lucca, discussed in chapter 3, suggest that there were also those in this period who would have seen such a depiction, and even such devotions, as a threat to Christian belief. I have tried to show that Michelangelo was partisan to this view and that he consciously offered an alternative to what he perceived as a predominant tendency in the art and piety of his time. And yet his proposals, too, had both defenders and detractors.

In this case as in others, we must wait until the latter part of the century for an extensive critical commentary on the issue as it concerned the visual arts. One of the most perceptive art critics of the sixteenth century, Francesco Bocchi, addressed the issue in the context of a discussion of Baccio Bandinelli's *Pietà* in the church of Santissima Annunziata in Florence:

> The *disposizione* given to this figure [of Christ] is most beautiful, and graceful beyond belief. Above all, it is difficult to express beauty and majesty in the head of a dead body, since this is very contrary to death. As soon as death harshly affects a body it takes away all that splendour which generates reverence. Nevertheless, not only the body is most beautiful, but also the head displays unique beauty. . . Beyond the unique artifice it thus seems to be more than human, and to inspire reverence by its appearance.[33]

The sentiment is directly in line with a more general theological interpretation offered by Vittoria Colonna several decades earlier:

> Besides having the divinity which never left him, I believe [the dead Christ] had the usual great Majesty, indeed even greater, because whereas in others death is an act of violence and deals them an offence [*et perhò rimangono come persone offese*], in Christ who had called for it and desired it with such sweetness, I believe it was an

act so soft, sweet, and pious that it softened all hard hearts, and inflamed all cold minds, the ugliness of death being not only beautiful in this most beautiful face but the brutality becoming a great sweetness.[34]

In a period of articulate art critics and art-sensitive theologians, it is not surprising also to find an opposing voice. The most articulate defender of the late medieval tradition of the afflicted dead Christ was Giovanni Andrea Gilio, whose *Degli errori dei pittori* appeared in 1564. His tirade is of special interest in that it comes as a reaction against Michelangelo, whose wide influence Gilio saw as a disaster for religious art. Pointing to the figure of Christ (designed by Michelangelo) in Sebastiano's San Pietro in Montorio *Flagellation,* Gilio criticized the painters under Michelangelo's influence "who do not know or do not want to know how to express the deformity evident in [Christ] at the time of the Passion," for "it would be a stronger inducement to devotion to see him bloody and misshapen, than to see him beautiful and delicate." Let the glorious Christ be shown in the scene of the transfiguration, resurrection, or ascension, but "in the flagellation, Ecce Homo, crucifixion, deposition, and entombment let him be shown bloody, ugly, misshapen, afflicted, ravaged, and dead," so that the pious may see the extreme humility and charity displayed by Christ in sacrificing himself for humanity. "Many times I have discussed this with painters, and all with one voice they responded: 'Painting doesn't allow it; it would go against the decorum of art.'"[35] Contemporaries of Michelangelo were able to see his antique-inspired conception of the beautiful dead Christ not simply as a stylistic choice but as a theologically consequential departure from tradition, and, more portentously, as the sign of a conflict between the ideals of modern art and the purposes of religion.

LAMENTATION AS BACCHANAL

If Rosso moved into uncharted iconographic territory by presenting an image of Christ within the tomb, Michelangelo's experiments remained within the more traditional sphere of the deposition, lamentation, and entombment – the open realm of Friday, rather than the darker reaches of Saturday. Only through these investigations did he arrive at a formula more detached from a historical context, *his* proposal for a modern *Engelpietà,* in the Colonna *Pietà*. The help he gave Sebastiano for the Úbeda *Pietà* in 1533 appears to have prompted renewed experiments of his own into the Passion narrative, which are preserved in an understudied drawing in Bayonne (Figure 86). We would suspect a connection between this drawing and the Úbeda *Pietà* on the basis of the similarities between the figures of Christ, but there is harder evidence to connect the two. The *verso* of the Bayonne sheet

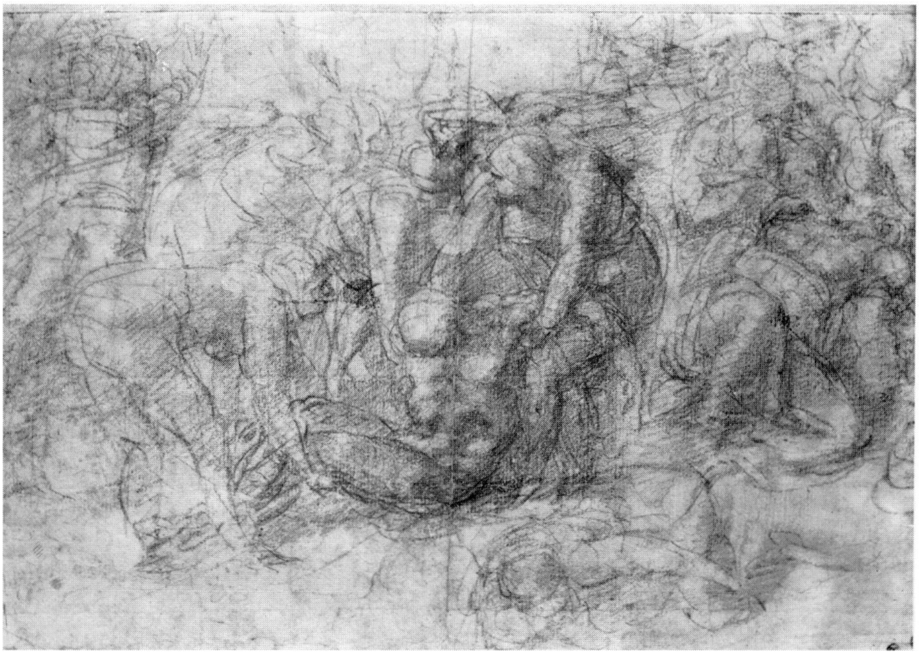

86. Michelangelo, *Lamentation*. Drawing. Musée Bonnat, Bayonne, France. Arch. Phot. Paris/ CNMHS.

(Figure 87) contains drawings for the *Children's Bacchanal* (Figure 88), thus dating the sheet to 1533–34.[36] It is thus made almost exactly contemporary with the drawings for the Úbeda *Pietà* (see Figure 80).

In the Bayonne drawing Michelangelo has left behind the focused three-quarter-length formula of the Úbeda *Pietà* (see Figure 80) and returned to

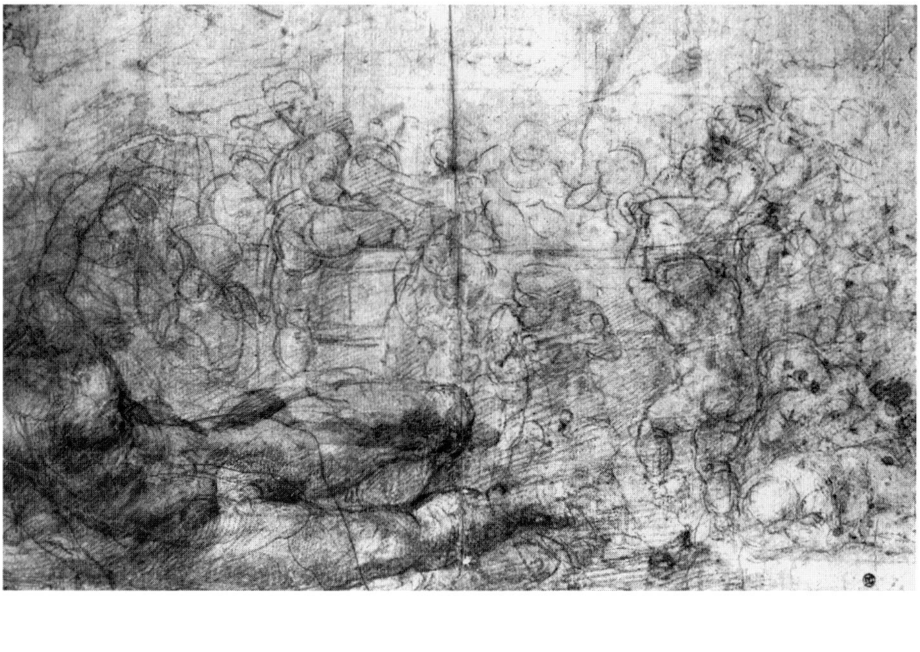

87. Michelangelo, *Putti around a Wine Vat* (verso of 86). Drawing. Musée Bonnat, Bayonne. Arch. Phot. Paris/ CNMHS.

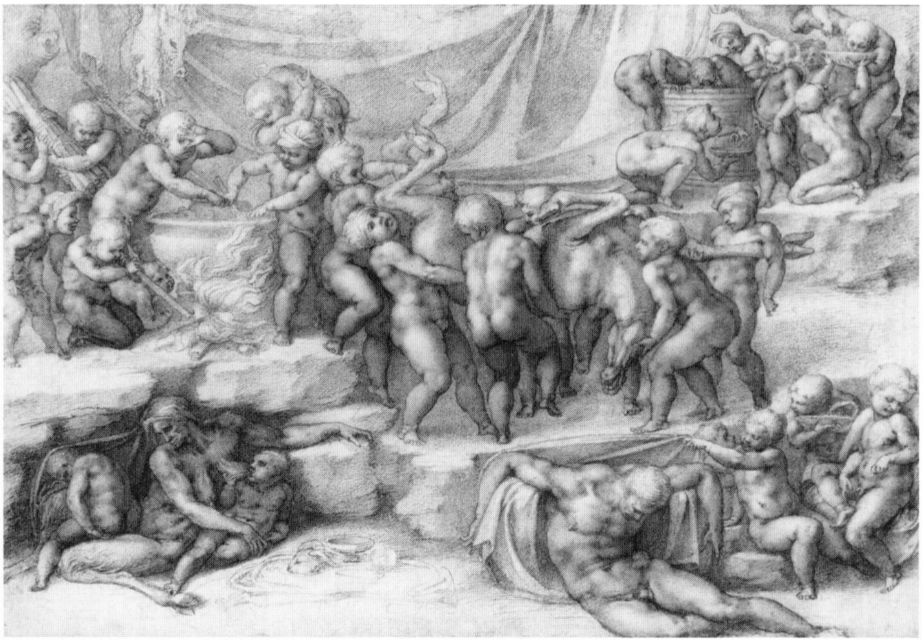

88. Michelangelo, *Children's Bacchanal.* Drawing. Windsor Castle, England. The Royal Collection © 1999 Her Majesty the Queen.

the more elaborate narrative preoccupations of the London *Entombment* (see Figure 6). He also returned to the full figure conception of the dead Christ, a conception that was to remain a part of his treatment of the *Pietà* theme until the end of his life.[37] In fact, the subject of the drawing is very close to the London painting. In the center, Christ is being lifted from the ground by several figures. On the right edge of the drawing, a figure – certainly the Virgin – is shown swooning and attended to by other figures. The conception and arrangement immediately bring to mind Raphael's Baglioni *Entombment* (see Figure 65) where the Virgin swoons at the right as Christ is being carried off to the tomb at the left. Indeed, the figure at the extreme right supporting the Virgin, shown turning her head away from the viewer, is virtually a direct quotation from Raphael's painting. That Michelangelo was specifically remembering Raphael's painting is also suggested by the fact – as I show below – that he quoted it in the *Children's Bacchanal* (see Figure 88), for which the Bayonne sheet contains a preparatory drawing. The difference from Raphael's painting lies in the fact that Christ is shown still seated on the ground rather than in the process of being carried. It is in this position that his torso can remain in the crucial front-facing orientation – that is, in the Man of Sorrows–like arrangement that Michelangelo had recently adapted from the *Bed of Polycleitus.* It would have been impossible to show Christ's body frontally while he was being carried – that is, not without returning wholesale to the strange solution of the London *Entombment.* So instead, we have a somewhat awkward compromise between Raphael's composition and Michelangelo's most recent adaptation of the Man of Sorrows.[38]

If we needed proof of the fact that the Christ on the *recto* of the Bayonne sheet (see Figure 86) is informed by the *Bed of Polycleitus* composition (see Figure 81), we need look no further than the bottom right-hand corner of the verso (see Figure 87) where we see one of the children in a drunken sleep, having adopted, in reverse, precisely the pose from the ancient relief. These are more than formal associations, and encourage us to open our eyes to the inspired dialogue between the bacchic scene on the verso and the Passion scene on the recto. In the Passion scene, the figure of the swooning Virgin shows distinctly bacchic qualities, and in fact bears close similarities to the wallowing, wine-producing river god in the background of Titian's *Bacchanal of the Andrians,* which Michelangelo had certainly seen during his visit with Alfonso d'Este in Ferrara only a few years earlier in 1529. Michael Hirst has made the parallel observation that the *Children's Bacchanal* is generally informed by Titian's *Worship of Venus,* also painted for Alfonso's *camerino.*[39] That Michelangelo should interpret the Virgin's swoon as something close to a state of bacchic drunkenness is not a frivolous association but a part of Michelangelo's interpretation of the Passion. If Christ's body is more than a mere corpse, if his state is closer to the ecstatic sleep represented in the *Bed of Polycleitus,* then it is only logical that this should affect the activity of the attendant figures, and above all of the Virgin. The Virgin traditionally bears the closest affective ties to Christ, and thus her traditional *compassio* becomes, in Michelangelo's interpretation, a passionate *co-ebrietas.*

The parallels do not end there. If Michelangelo's Passion subjects are something more than historical scenes of lament, his bacchic subjects are something more than playful scenes of revelry. They investigate the darker side of the bacchic mysteries, connected to the cycles of death and regeneration, and at this level they approach the concerns of his Passion subjects.[40] As already noted, the Bayonne sheet figured strongly in the gestation of the *Children's Bacchanal* (see Figure 88) and it is therefore no surprise to find that the latter should contain a wealth of motifs drawn from Michelangelo's experiments with Passion subjects. The "sleeping" river god–like figure at the bottom of the scene adapts the Man of Sorrows–like dead Christ from the Bayonne sheet (see Figure 86); the shared source in the *Bed of Polycleitus* is explicitly declared in the child who lifts the veil from him. The affiliation was clearly appreciated by Michelangelo's contemporaries: In a *Lamentation* by the Michelangelo epigone Battista Franco the river god from the *Children's Bacchanal* is readapted as a dead Christ (Figure 89). In the upper register of the *Children's Bacchanal,* we see some children around a wine vat and others around a cauldron. In the center a deer is being carried with great effort toward the cauldron. Panofsky, among others, noted that the arrangement of

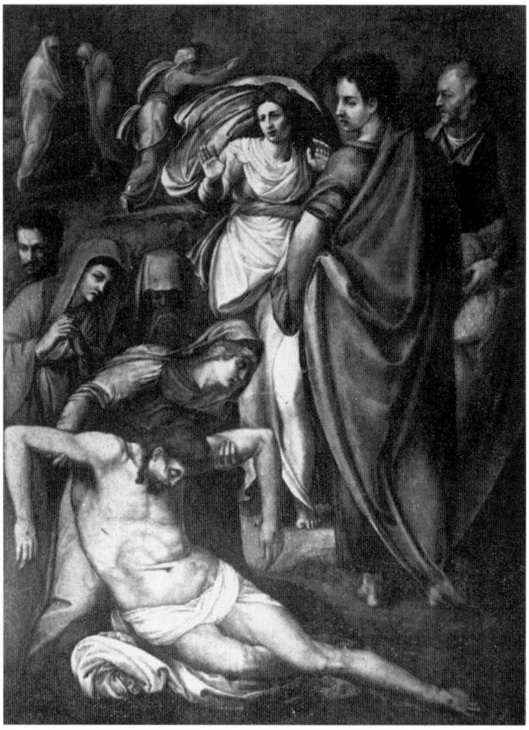

89. Battista Franco, *Lamentation*. Panel. Pinacoteca, Lucca, Italy.

this middle carrying group is highly reminiscent of Raphael's Baglioni *Entombment*.[41]

In other words, several parts of the *Children's Bacchanal* recapitulate, in a bacchic context, motifs that recur over and over in Michelangelo's experiments with the Man of Sorrows and entombment. The iconography of the *Children's Bacchanal* remains elusive, and Hirst rightly noted that the development from the sketch on the verso of the Bayonne sheet (see Figure 87) argues against the idea that Michelangelo set out to illustrate a given textual source.[42] If the sheet was the artist's own invention, then what matters is not the subject per se but the development of ideas at the level of motif and theme. The drawing retreats from specific subject matter and instead explores a thematic subsoil that is deeply relevant to his Passion subjects. Whatever else the drawing is about, it is concerned with the ritual of sacrifice, and the relation between death and the larger cycles of regeneration. It goes down into a "lower zone," a place of sacrifice and dark stirring, a deathly realm that feeds and makes possible the regions of light – a place, that is, not so far from those Christ reaches in his ecstatic withdrawal and entombment. Michelangelo had spent the previous fourteen years exploring closely related ideas in the Medici chapel in San Lorenzo, a distinctly Christian setting, proving that in his view this was a common ground where pagan and Christian subjects met.

Although the sacramental orientation of Michelangelo's *Pietàs* loosens their links to the historical circumstances of the Passion story, the dramatic narrative remains an important and necessary part of Michelangelo's reinterpretation of the subject. The Passion story is, as it were, the motor that generates the figural energy around Christ. Apart from the special case of the Úbeda *Pietà,* made to satisfy relatively conventional requirements for a half-length devotional image, Michelangelo's later investigations into the theme generally start not with the reduced configuration of an *Andachtsbild* but rather with a fairly elaborate narrative episode, from which they then draw out a dense, animated essence concentrated in the dead Christ. The Bayonne drawing, as we saw, returned to the narrative of the entombment that Michelangelo had first investigated in his early London panel. In the drawings closer to the conception of the *Pietà* for Vittoria Colonna (see Figure 93), we see an effort to extract tighter formulas from the Passion narrative. In these drawings Christ is placed in the most intimate contact with the Virgin. Her *compassio* is not alluded to through analogy of physical state but is realized through passionate physical contact. Michelangelo continued these investigations in his later sculpted *Pietàs* (see chapter 7), in which the conditions of marble statuary as it were materially enforced the tendency to condense.

The new, more intimate conception was the result of exchanging the narrative of the entombment, which Michelangelo understood essentially as a drama of departure, with the narrative of the deposition, which a long-standing devotional tradition had understood as an allegory of approximation.[43] An elaborate drawing of the *Deposition* now in Haarlem (Figure 90)[44] fueled a series of investigations into more condensed formulas that led directly to the *Pietà* for Vittoria Colonna (see Figure 93) and culminated in the *Pietà* now in the Museo dell'Opera del Duomo in Florence (see Figure 98).[45] He left the realization of the more narrative conception of the *Deposition* to his followers: The artist of the relief copy in the Casa Buonarroti and, most famously, Daniele da Volterra in Santa Trinità dei Monti. This was not, as we shall see, the last time that Michelangelo's followers took up and developed the more elaborate narrative conceptions that Michelangelo discarded on his way to more condensed figural formulas.

A recently discovered drawing in the Louvre (Figure 91) allows us to see very clearly the process by which Michelangelo extracted a *Pietà* formula from the Haarlem *Deposition* (see Figure 90).[46] The shift occurred in a significantly circuitous way. At the bottom of the Haarlem drawing, the Virgin is shown fainting into the arms of her attendants. In another sketch at the upper right of the sheet, Michelangelo redrew the group, paying closer attention to the means by which the figure is supported. But now it has begun distinctly to resemble a lamentation group around Christ, not the Virgin, an impression that is especially strong when the sketch is viewed with a knowledge of the

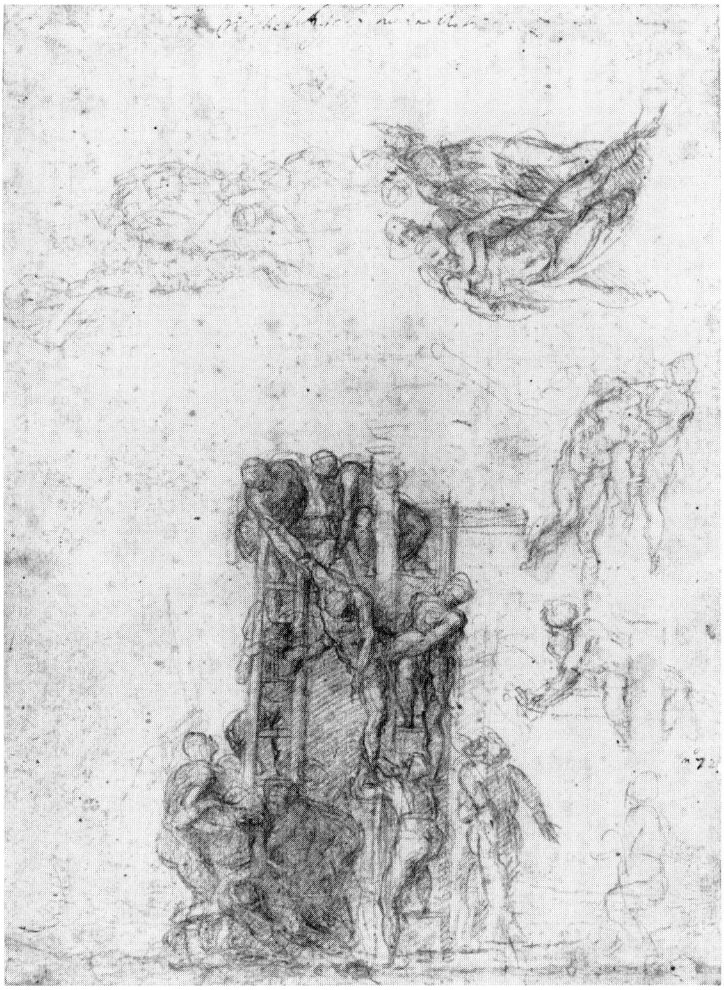

90. Michelangelo, *Deposition*. Drawing. Haarlem, Teylers Museum.

later studies. That it is still, however, a sketch for the group around the Virgin is indicated by the fact that the figure to the right is still shown looking up towards the cross. The Louvre sheet derives directly from this sketch – we can almost feel Michelangelo reaching for another sheet of paper – but now it is Christ who occupies the central position, and it is the Virgin who holds him.

This act of figural substitution is, implicitly, a powerful assertion of the fundamental similarity of their bodily states. It is, in fact, not so much a substitution as a kind of nesting and incorporation: Christ has, as it were, been introduced into the Virgin's body, and she spreads her legs to receive him. The attendants now work to support both of them. The Virgin and Christ are no longer in "parallel" states but rather in an intimate and animating bond, sealed by expressions of both erotic and filial love. Christ is both spouse and son: Christ's body is turned to receive a violently amorous kiss,

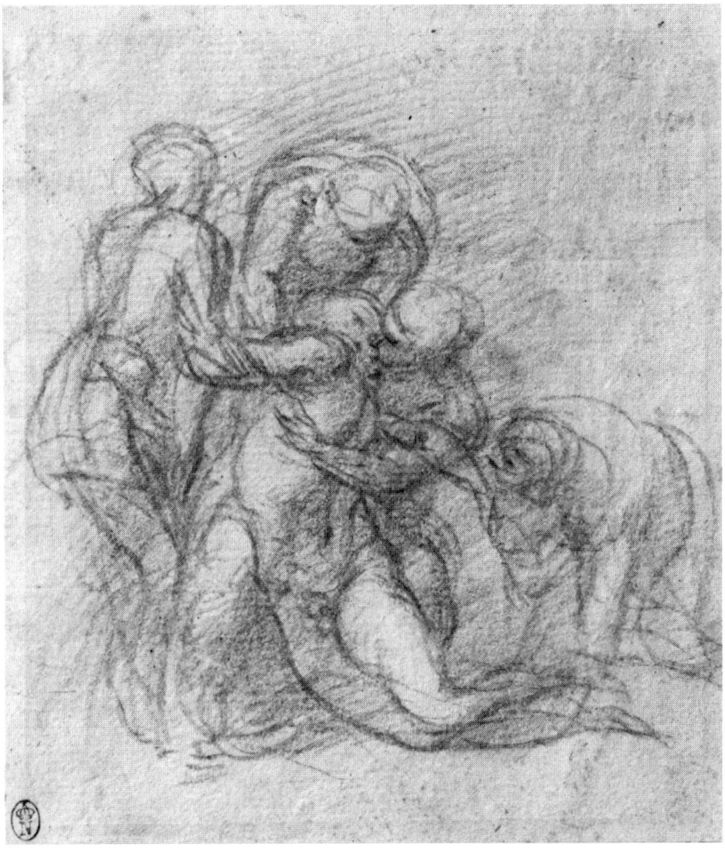

91. Michelangelo, *Lamentation*. Drawing. Paris, Louvre. © Réunion des Musées Nationaux.

all the while ensconced between the Virgin's legs, a motif that Leo Steinberg has convincingly interpreted as a symbol of filial "issuance."[47] The fact that this motif also serves to maintain Christ's torso facing forward – that is, to preserve the link to the Man of Sorrows tradition – is a key to its significance. As I showed in chapter 2, the Man of Sorrows image was an emblem of the life-giving efficacy of the dead Christ, and thus of the redemptive power inherent in the sacrifice, making it especially common in Eucharistic contexts. The very front-facing posture, which effectuates the idea of an offering and a benefit made to the faithful, epitomizes this sacramental emphasis. Michelangelo refashioned this life-giving emphasis by recourse to themes of fertility and regeneration, embodied in the motifs of amorous and maternal love that bond Christ to the Virgin – a reinterpretation that, as we will see, was very much in line with Vittoria Colonna's interpretation of the subject. Below, Christ issues from between the Virgin's legs; above, he is turned to receive an embrace of rapturous love. This combination of filial and spousal motifs produces a strange, almost untenable configuration that is not to be understood merely as an uncomfortable transitional moment in

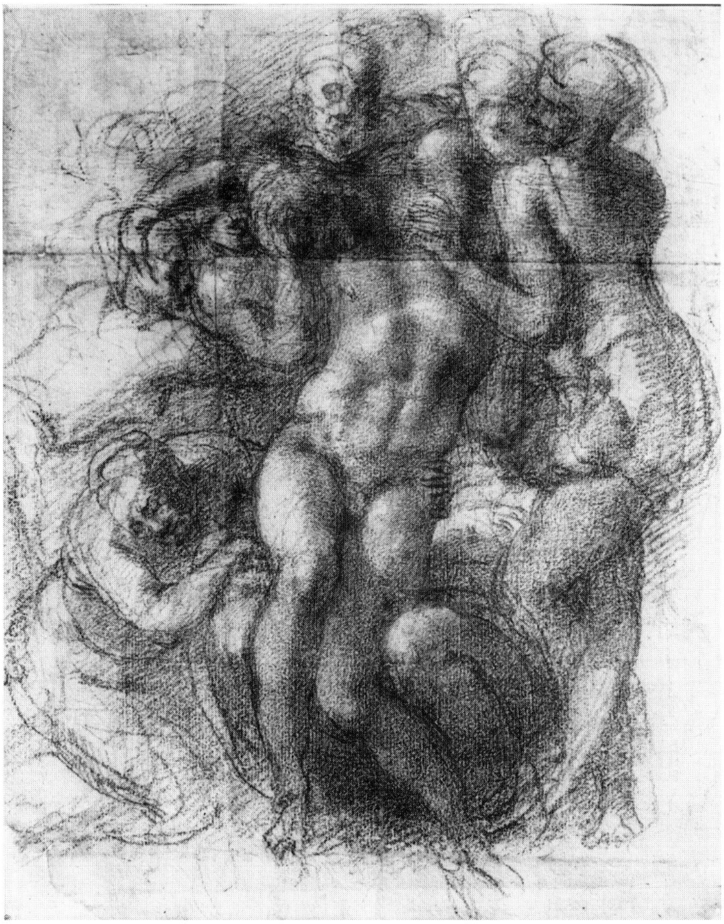

92. Michelangelo, *Lamentation*. Drawing. Graphische Sammlung Albertina, Vienna, Austria.

the narrative. Rather than working to move Christ to the next stage in the story, the figure above attempts to hold Christ and the Virgin together in their twisted but efficacious union. In this sense the drawing represents a movement away from the episodic concerns of the London *Entombment* (see Figure 6) and the Bayonne drawing (see Figure 86), exploring instead an expressive and "invested" bodily configuration.

These ideas are elaborated in a drawing in Vienna (Figure 92), which I believe closely follows the tiny Louvre sketch.[48] Christ's body is still in a twisted pose, but now he is upright. The Virgin, still seated, continues to hold Christ between her knees, but now at the level of his legs. The full extension of Christ's body puts it into active contact with a larger number of figures, who almost trample the Virgin below. What is this surging mass of figures doing? Their frantic activity is far in excess of the actual physical effort required to sustain a body upright, suggesting that in this contact we are seeing something more than a simple "mechanical" moment in the narrative. The activity has moved beyond the purposeful, beyond even the sphere of lamentation, and into the realm of the ecstatic. These are certainly genuine expressions of lament, but lament has broken through to catharsis, where grief becomes a paradoxical euphoria, a form of quasi-erotic participation and release. Christ's body radiates light and seems almost to dance. The bodies of the attendants writhe, as if participating in an exchange of energy flowing to and from the body. As in the Louvre drawing, the figures are not engaged in an activity that has a clear "before" and "after." Rather than working to move Christ to the next "station" in the narrative, they participate in a form of animated cult to the dead Christ.[49] The figure to Christ's left pushes his torso up, while the figure to Christ's right props up his drooping head, as if their function was none other than to keep him upright, to preserve and celebrate his majesty in death. This understanding of the attendance on the body as a mysterious rite was one shared by Vittoria Colonna, as I show at length in the next chapter. Here it will suffice to quote one of her sonnets on the Passion:

> *Con la piagata man dolce e soave*
> *Giogo m'ha posto al collo, e lieve il peso*
> *Sembrar mi face col suo lume chiaro.*
>
> [With his wounded hand, soft and sweet,
> he placed a yoke on my neck, and his weight
> Seemed to me to become light to me with his clear radiance.][50]

Like the poem, Michelangelo's drawing works within the framework of the Passion narrative but moves beyond the mechanics of carrying and the drama of lamentation. The "yoke" of Christ's weight, rather than being a burden, becomes a source of light, sweetness and beauty. This mysterious inversion was something that Michelangelo associated specifically with the figure of the Man of Sorrows.

All of the drawings in this group contain highly awkward moments. The Bayonne study (see Figure 86) adapted the seated pose from the studies for the Úbeda *Pietà* but, in showing the whole body, produced an awkward and partially obscured figure. The Louvre sketch (see Figure 91) attempted to put Christ in direct relation to the Virgin but produced a twisted and untenable configuration. In the multifigure Vienna drawing (see Figure 92) Christ is held upright, but the Virgin is nearly trampled below. The near absurdity of aspects of these drawings is no argument against their "quality" or autograph status. It instead testifies to the extreme nature of the project, which was an effort to preserve and reinterpret the central mystery of the Christian faith under changing artistic and cultural conditions.

The Colonna *Pietà* (Figure 93) was, in one sense, a highly effective and elegant solution to these problems. The crucial move was to introduce a difference in ground level, a feature adapted directly from the *Children's Bacchanal* (see Figure 88). The ground drops away under the Virgin's feet and the lower

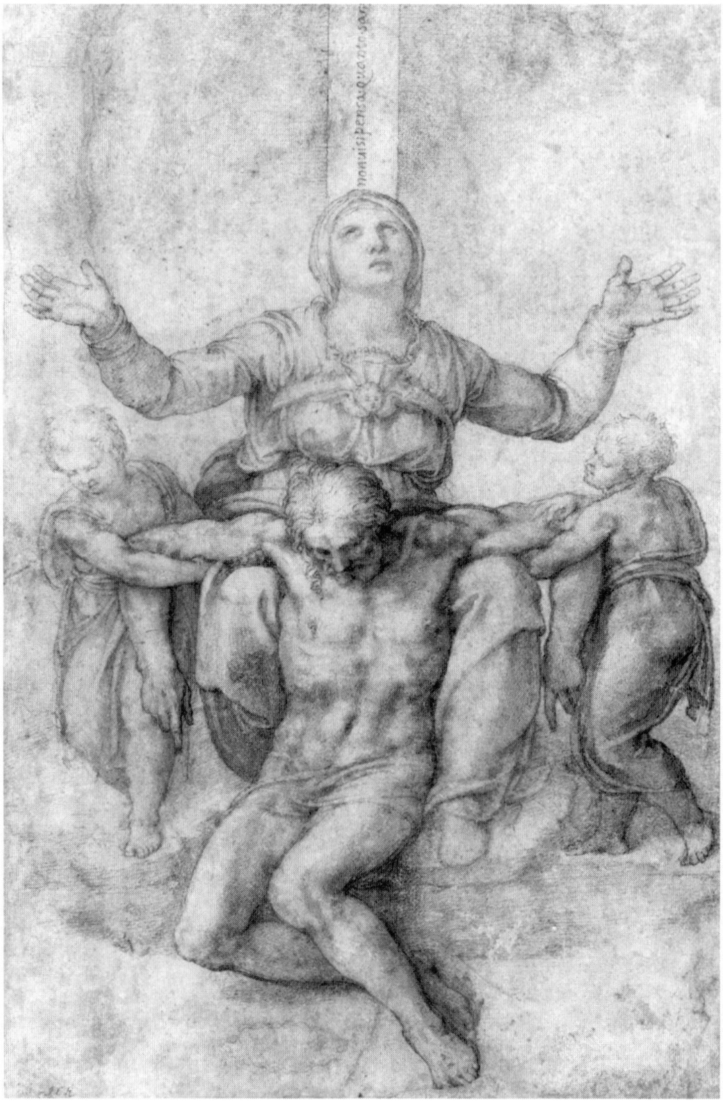

93. Michelangelo, *Pietà for Vittoria Colonna.* Drawing. Isabella Stewart Gardner Museum, Boston, U.S.

part of Christ's body falls neatly into the lower region. The yokelike posture of Christ's arms now fits, almost architectonically, into the lower part of the Virgin's body.[51] The drawing is thus a reduced concentrate of the various physical relations explored in the previous sheets, powerfully focused on the relation between the Virgin and Christ. It also makes explicit the dehistoricizing tendencies of these drawings, and their lingering attachment to the tradition of the *imago pietatis,* by placing Christ's arms in the care of angels. An overtly archaizing image realized in the most modern of formats, the presentation drawing was very much an experiment of its time, and deserves closer analysis within its specific cultural context.

CHAPTER SIX

Artwork and Cult Image

THE ART OF THE GIFT

Michelangelo's *Pietà* drawing for Vittoria Colonna (see Figure 93) was the result of unprecedented investigations, essays at the limits of Christian iconography. It was a searching effort to interpret the meaning and efficacy of Christ's sacrifice at a time when this question had become a matter of volatile controversy – the center, in fact, of the contemporary debate over the role of works and grace in the scheme of Christian redemption. This circumstance in turn reinforced Michelangelo's inclination to pursue these explorations in a private sphere, outside of the conventional categories of religious art. The new category of the presentation drawing that Michelangelo adopted for the purpose had initially – in the work of Leonardo da Vinci, Rosso Fiorentino, and Michelangelo himself – served as a venue for secular and pagan subjects, that is, as an alternative to religious art per se.[1] Here it was adopted as a means of reforming the religious image itself. In the London *Entombment,* Michelangelo had made a strenuous effort to reform the altarpiece from within. The Colonna *Pietà* pursued the effort of reform, marked by a continuing dialogue with the Man of Sorrows tradition, but now outside of the traditional categories altogether. Instead, it based its claims in a new conception of art.

Crucial to these claims was the notion of the gift, a notion inherent not only in the drawing's subject, the sacrifice of Christ, but also in the circumstances of its making and presentation. As a gift, the presentation drawing was deliberately exempt from the normal economy of art production in the period. Traditional religious art came, by definition, with a brief, and thus with at least basic requirements about iconography, such as the inclusion of certain patron saints, that were determined by the role it played within a devotional economy.[2] The stipulations that made up the painter's contract were, in other words, a function of the higher system of "contracts" – the economy of vows, dedications, and endowments – within which religious art worked generally. It was the excessive reliance on this contractual system that reformers, from Girolamo Savonarola to Erasmus to Martin Luther, most consistently deplored.

The conception of art as a gift elaborated by Michelangelo and Vittoria Colonna was, among other things, an effort to remove it from this economy. The new category of the presentation drawing they adopted for the purpose was special in several ways. It was unlike a preparatory study in that it expressly claimed to be a work of art in its own right. As a drawing, on the other hand, it retained an experimental quality, a freedom from the conventions that controlled finished panel painting in the period – a freedom that in turn reinforced the exemption from the conventional practice of making works of art on commission. The claim to freedom of invention, and the corollary demand for sensitive appreciation, was integral to the conception of art as a gift. In this chapter I attempt to show that for Michelangelo and Colonna a "liberal" conception of art served as a model in their efforts to fashion a new conception of faith along reformed lines. I argue that the new conception of art, the idea that it is an unbidden gift and as such makes special claims on its viewer, epitomized and gave interpretative scope to some of the most significant aspects of reforming thought at this time – in particular its "subjective" orientation and its preoccupation with the role of the believer's conscience in acknowledging and receiving divine grace. The relationship was, I hope to show, mutual: The form of hermeneutic engagement demanded by the one activity provided a privileged arena for the development of the other. These ideas were very well suited to the ideals and concerns of the highly cultivated group of reform-minded thinkers with whom Michelangelo, and especially Colonna, were associated.

These reform-minded thinkers shared a sympathy for the doctrine of justification by faith expressed, most canonically, by St. Paul (Ephesians 2:8): "For by grace are ye saved through faith; and that not of yourselves: it is the gift of God." They also shared a distaste for the notion that salvation could be "earned" through works, insisting on the individual's faith in the redemption freely offered to humankind through the sacrifice of Christ. They were, however, unable to translate their sympathies into a coherent program of Church reform and failed to achieve the hoped-for reconciliation with the Protestants at Regensburg in 1541.

One of the primary documents to come out of this milieu, the *Beneficio di Cristo,* appeared in these very years: Circulated in manuscript form at least from 1542, the edition of 1543 enjoyed enormous popularity until 1549, when the book was placed on the Inquisition's Index of prohibited books and, to judge from the number of remaining copies, very effectively suppressed. Written in a first version by the Benedictine monk Benedetto Fontanini and revised, possibly twice, by the humanist and poet Marcantonio Flaminio, the tract represented the mingled strains of reforming thought in Italy, including the northern Italian Benedictine reforming movement and the Naples circle congregated around Juan de Valdés, to which Flaminio belonged until his relocation in the fall of 1541 to the community gathered around Cardinal Reginald Pole in Viterbo. In Viterbo Flaminio completed his revisions of the manuscript of the *Beneficio.* Vittoria Colonna, also heavily influenced by Valdés, moved to Viterbo in the same year, placing herself under Pole's spiritual guidance.[3]

The connections between Michelangelo, the Viterbo circle, and the *Beneficio di Cristo* are somewhat more than a matter of inference; they are reinforced by the circumstances described in Francisco de Hollanda's *Four Dialogues,* in which discussion with Michelangelo and Colonna take place at the church of San Silvestro al Quirinale, after sermons on St. Paul by "Fra Ambrogio" – Fra Ambrogio Catarino Politi, the author of an extended critique of the *Beneficio,* in response to which Flaminio made his revisions to the text in Viterbo in 1542.[4] The most revealing portrait of Vittoria's religious life in these years was offered by Flaminio's friend, Pietro Carnesecchi, during his later heresy trial. He remembered that he, Alvise Priuli (also a close associate of Pole's at Viterbo), and Flaminio would visit Colonna often, and that on matters of dogma they would speak almost exclusively of justification by faith:

> . . .and on this question as well I wouldn't be able to say exactly to what terms she held, but suffice it to say that she attributed a good deal to grace and faith in her conversations. And on the other hand in her actions she demonstrated a great regard for works, giving alms generously, and always practising charity with everyone, in which actions she was observing and following the advice that had been given her by the Cardinal [Pole], whom she believed in like an oracle, and that is that it was necessary to believe as if salvation depended only on faith, and to do good as if salvation depended on works.[5]

Cardinal Pole was directly connected to the focus of gift giving studied here, for he owned a version of Michelangelo's *Pietà* for Colonna (see Figure 93), which he offered up as a gift in his turn.[6]

The very title of the treatise that came out of this milieu, the *Beneficio di Cristo,* gives some indication of the central role that it accords to the concept of the gift. In the concluding paragraphs we read a passage that succinctly connects this concept to the tract's main arguments and that can stand as a fair representation of the attitudes that prevailed in the Viterbo circle:

> You will say to me: "I really believe in the remission of sins and I know that God is truthful, but I doubt that I am worthy of such a great gift." I reply to you that

> the remission of sins would not be a gift and a grace but a payment, if God granted it to you because of the worth of your works. But I repeat that God accepts you as just and does not impute your sins to you through the merits of Christ, which are given to you and become yours through faith. Therefore, following St. Bernard's saintly advice, do not believe only in general of the remission of sins, but apply this belief to your own case, and believe without doubt that through Christ all your iniquities are pardoned.[7]

Preoccupations with the operations of divine grace were a pervasive part of the culture of the Viterbo circle, so pervasive that even the exchange of courtesies and the practice of gift giving were, semiplayfully, couched in the terms of the debate over grace.[8] The correspondence between Michelangelo and Vittoria Colonna, which draws witty and serious parallels between divine grace and the giving of gifts, specifically the giving of artistic and literary gifts, is one instance of this practice that deserves closer study.

There are many unanswered questions surrounding these letters, beginning with the matter of their precise date: They are usually dated between 1538 and 1541, but they have also been dated as late as 1545–46. Nor has it been possible to identify with certainty the works to which they refer. My goal in this chapter is not to resolve these matters – I do not believe it is possible without further empirical evidence – but to pay closer attention to the rhetoric of the letters themselves. The letters may be unclear as to which works are being discussed, but they are extremely eloquent on the question of what makes art a gift and what this has to do with art's religious vocation – questions that are, in turn, basic to understanding works such as the *Pietà* drawing (see Figure 93). To come to a fuller understanding of the conception and reception of the *Pietà* drawing in particular it is necessary to look beyond these letters. The second section of this chapter accordingly studies Colonna's own writings on the Passion, which allow us to read the drawing through her eyes.

As we do not know the sequence of the letters, it is best to proceed topically, beginning with a letter of Michelangelo's that offers a brief but cogent statement on the nature and ethics of gift giving. The fact that this meditation is framed in the language of the theological debate over grace has not been sufficiently recognized, and this oversight has led to misreadings of an important passage in the letter.[9] Having been offered some items (most likely poems) by Colonna, Michelangelo confessed that his initial impulse was to make something to give her in return, so as to receive her gift less unworthily. He then recognized, he says, that to introduce a gift into an economy of exchange violates the very principle of the gift, which he goes on to describe in terms of the operations of divine grace: "Then, having recognized and seen that the grace of God cannot be bought, and that to have it with discomfort [*tenerla a disagio*] is a grave sin, I say the fault is mine and willingly I accept these things." The letter, incidentally, confirms an observation of Vasari's, that the artist was loath to accept presents "because it seemed to him, when someone gave him something, that he was put under a permanent obligation."[10]

The point of Michelangelo's letter, however, was to announce that he was able to overcome this resistance by "having recognized and seen that the grace of God cannot be bought" – that is, by invoking the model of divine grace. Through this parallel he understood that Colonna's gift, like divine grace, is already given; it cannot be earned or paid for. To attempt to do so is to deny its unsolicited, gratuitous nature, and thus to resist it as a gift [*"tenerla a disagio"*]. The idea is not far from ideas developed in more elaborately theological terms by Marcantonio Flaminio, coauthor of the *Beneficio* and associate of Vittoria Colonna's. According to Flaminio, divine grace is already there, like the light of the sun. It is not up to the recipient to call it down; instead, it is a matter of not acting to reject it, not putting up an obstacle to the light. And it is faith that allows one to enact this double negative, to abstain from resisting the gift.[11] In not accepting the gifts, in attempting to "buy time" in order first to make something so as to be worthy of them [*"per riceverle manco indegniamente ch'i' potevo, fare prima qualche cosa a quella di mia mano"*], Michelangelo was in this sense putting up an obstacle to grace, resisting the prevenient claim of the gift. His enlightenment came in realizing that he could not actively take possession of them, because he was already possessed by them. He expressed this reversal in an elegant transposition: "And I am sure, when I will have them, I will think myself in paradise, not because they are in my house but because I am in theirs."

We are, apparently, far from the conception of the gift proposed in Marcel Mauss's classic study of "archaic" societies, where the gift serves as a token of exchange and an inducement to reciprocity.[12] It is interesting for our purposes that Jacques Derrida's critique of Mauss marks exactly this divide. Derrida argued that even within the terms of Mauss's argument the gift resists a system of exchange by always passing "beyond measure," by being in excess of the possibility of repayment – a tendency that Mauss half avowed at key points in his argument.[13] The gift, according to Derrida, is "beyond recompense or retribution, beyond economy," effecting a sort of sacrifice of economy itself.[14] Derrida's notion of "the gift" is conceived in abstract terms, independent of a given historical and cultural context. It is not my purpose to espouse or contest his conception of the gift, or to make the letters under discussion an illustration of his theory. Instead, our letters allow us to historicize and contextualize Derrida's theory itself, for in elaborating his extra-economic conception of the gift Derrida draws explicitly on a tradition of Christian thought – for him embodied above all in Søren Kierkegaard – that is in line with the tradition of reform thought here under study.[15] His critique of Mauss restaged a historical debate over reciprocity and gratuitousness in gift giving whose terms were clearly established in the sixteenth century.[16] The rigorous, antireciprocal, Augustinian conception of the gift upheld by

Protestant reformers, and elaborated by Derrida, itself had stoical roots, and this relation was in turn reinforced by the popularity of Seneca's *De Beneficiis* in the sixteenth century. According to Seneca, "The logic of gifts is simple: so much is given out. If something is returned it is called gain; if not, there is no loss. I made the gift for the sake of giving."[17] The gift goes in one direction and is not to be understood as a payment for a service or a loan to be repaid. The idea became a commonplace in sixteenth-century debates over divine grace and found clear expression in the *Beneficio di Cristo*:

And what can man do in order to merit such a great gift and treasure as Christ? This treasure is given only through the grace, favor and mercy of God, and it is faith alone that receives such a gift and allows us to enjoy the remission of sins. . . . These things cannot be accomplished or done by all the works of all humankind put together.[18]

It is the distinction of the cultivated milieu that produced the *Beneficio* and that constituted its first readership to have reintroduced this theologically exalted conception of the gift into the human sphere of courtesies and of gift giving – that is, back into the secular world of Seneca's *De Beneficiis.* Michelangelo's letter is one example of this tendency and is of special interest in that it applies these ideas to the making and receiving of art.[19] The sonnet included in the letter develops this association in even more explicit terms.[20] His efforts to repay Colonna's *"immensa cortesia"* by his own works [*"'l mie basso ingegno"*] are compared to the errors of those who believe mortal works can equal or somehow earn the immensity of divine grace. In the last three verses the analogy is fully "crossed" in a general statement on the inability of human works, specifically works of culture [*"l'ingegnio e l'arte e la memoria"*], to repay a divine gift:

l'ingegnio e l'arte e la memoria cede:
c'un don celeste mai con mille pruoue
pagar può sol del suo chi è mortale.
[Talent and art and memory give way:
for a heavenly gift cannot, even with a thousand attempts,
be paid by the sole efforts of one who is mortal.]

In another sonnet, also dedicated to Vittoria and probably written in close succession to this one, he made explicit the theological point. What is there to repay a great benefit, he asked, so that the debtor is let free? Nothing, for such a payment would take away or deny the infinity of the gift, its absolute sovereignty over the one served, and thus deny that one the chance of receiving it in the appropriate spirit and thus of serving in return. Therefore, one must risk ingratitude if one is to acknowledge the true power of the giver; one must submit as to a lord, for there is no compensation, no possibility of adequation.[21] As Emerson was later to put it, "There is no commensurability between a man and any gift."[22] The immense claims of the gift demand an attitude of submission and trust. This is why for Michelangelo – as for many members of the Viterbo circle – the capacity for faith in divine grace was itself the "gift of gifts" [*"il don de' doni"*].[23]

Despite its pessimism, Michelangelo's letter does implicitly leave room for a conception of art that would conform to this higher principle of grace: It is a challenge to make works of art that would, so to speak, cease to be "works" and would aspire instead to the status of gifts. What, according to Michelangelo, does it take to make a work of art a gift? One criterion, a further letter suggested, is that it be made without or beyond any expectations on the part of the recipient.[24] In this case it was Colonna, not Michelangelo, who had violated the delicate code of the gift. He scolded her for having left a *"Crocifisso"* – an unfinished drawing or some form of *modello* – with Tommaso de' Cavalieri so as to prompt him, Michelangelo, to complete the finished work for her. Not only does true love not have need of intermediaries, he tells her, but it consists of a faith that does not need reminders and that operates in secret: "And although it may have seemed that I had forgotten, I was doing what I wasn't saying, in order to follow through with something unexpected [*io facevo quello che non dicevo, per giungiere con cosa non aspectata*]." Unlike a work made under commission for a client, Michelangelo's gift for Colonna, actuated by love, is not subject to the usual surveillance: It is meant to be done in silence and to exceed her every expectation.[25]

It is this claim to a secret contract between donor and recipient that most closely associates the drawings to the sonnets that often accompanied them.[26] This is not to say that the drawings and sonnets were not available to a wider public but only that on those occasions the public was given access to something understood to be private and secret. As Leonard Barkan put it: "As genres, presentation drawings and sonnets are quite parallel: both are acts of introspection transferred into privacy *à deux,* but beyond that often circulated within a larger, but still private, coterie."[27] By introducing an intermediary and by attempting to intervene in the gift's silent gestation – in what Lewis Hyde calls the "stirring" of the gift[28] – Colonna violated the gift's condition of secrecy, a violation whose ruinous consequences are summed up by Michelangelo in a deft and bitter pun: "My design [*disegno*: drawing *or* plan] has been spoilt [*È stato guasto el mio d[i]segnio*]."

Michelangelo concluded the letter by referring the whole matter to the question of faith, through the quotation of part of a verse from Petrarch: *"Mal fa chi tanta fè [sì tosto oblia]:"* one does wrong so soon to forget so much faith.[29] Petrarch was scolding Laura for doubting his faithful love. In that case, too, the beloved's doubts stemmed from having permitted the intervention of an intermediary, and thus having broken the secret contract between donor and recipient. (Laura had been made to believe that Petrarch was writing to another woman under her name.) It is characteristic of Michelangelo to have appropriated the Petrarchan *topos* within the apposite context of an amorous relation and simultaneously to have expanded its semantic scope to apply both to religious faith and to his work as an artist. The adaptation of the verse implicitly asserts that in the context of gift giving the discourses of love, art, and divine grace mingle inextricably.

Elizabeth Cropper has argued for a correlation between the emergence of an affective, gendered, subjectivized beholder in High Renaissance painting and a predominantly Petrarchan culture of poetic desire.[30] She argued that new conceptions of picture making in this period, Michelangelo's presentation drawings an eminent case among them, invoked relations to the beholder whose closest parallel and cultural model is the relation between lover and beloved, between *io* and *tu,* found in the tradition of the Petrarchan love lyric. The crucial element that connects the two is the invocation of an unattainable object of desire, and the corresponding exploration of the themes of possession, loss, and excess. In thematizing a relation to something that exceeds the possibility of possession (that resists being treated as "property"), the lyrical mode, whether artistic or literary, engages in the dynamic of the gift – a point Michelangelo made explicitly in the letter discussed above, by invoking Petrarch in the context of the claims of his own artistic gifts.

For Michelangelo, this nexus of aesthetic and amorous claims was also connected to an explicitly religious discourse of divine grace and faith. It is my contention that besides the language of the Petrarchan love lyric, the language of religious devotion – which, at least since St. Bernard's highly influential *Sermons on the Song of Songs,* itself often made use of the rhetoric of amorous love – also served as a means by which the claims of such works were conceived and experienced. These traditions were, indeed, so deep-seated that they informed the experience even of nonreligious painting – a fact that is not surprising given that many of the new secular venues for art after 1500 emerged from within the traditional religious categories.[31] To take an example close to our period, the Dominican preacher Savonarola explicitly drew the parallel between the beholder's experience of beauty in painting and the believer's experience of Christ's love:

> Love is like a painter. The works of a good painter so charm men that, in contemplating them, they remain suspended, and sometimes to such an extent that it seems that they have been put in ecstasy and have been taken outside of themselves, and seem to forget themselves. This what the love of Jesus Christ does when it is in the soul.

In the same passage, he explicitly associated both the effects of painting and the effects of the divine with the beloved's effect on the lover. The experience of lover, believer, and viewer are thus assimilated to one another:

> Ask a man who is in love with a woman what love paints in the chamber of his imagination. He will respond, "her face, her eyes, her movements, her clothes," and other such things. And love paints them so well that all his powers remain suspended before these pictures [*tali pitture*] and he is not interested in thinking of anything else, or of contemplating anything other than those pictures. . . . If carnal love produces such effects, spiritual love, that is love of Jesus Christ, produces even more powerful ones.[32]

As we have seen, Michelangelo and Colonna understood the claims of art specifically in relation to the question of divine grace, the crux of religious debate at the time. I suggested above that the association was bound up with the relatively novel practice of presenting drawings as gifts. In Colonna's eyes, the quality that most powerfully elevated such works to the status of gifts was their claim to a kind of infinity or inexhaustibility, a claim that, she realized, places a special burden on the viewer as interpreter. Their exemption from the normal economy of works made on commission involved a semantic opening: They were not to be explicated by recourse to traditional iconographic conventions, and this meant that they required special hermeneutic receptivity on the part of the viewer.

Upon receiving a drawing of the "*Crucifixo*", perhaps the work mentioned in the last-cited letter, Colonna confesses to Michelangelo that she could never fully comprehend its miraculous qualities: "Certainly I could never explain how subtly and admirably it is done." The point was of sufficient importance for her to demand to know if the copy intended for her was to be done by Michelangelo or by his assistant, "because knowing the difficulty of imitating it, I would prefer that he [the assistant] do something other than this."[33] The drawing cannot be reduced to its "invention" or "content"; it must be visually realized by the inimitable and unfathomable grace of the master.[34] The corollary of this claim is that it demands to be appreciated by an especially sensitive viewer.

A further letter, acknowledging the receipt of a finished drawing, revealed that these claims go beyond matters of technique. In an effort to describe its effects on her, she immediately turned to the language of divine grace and faith. As the wording is crucial, I quote the uninterrupted Italian text of the relevant passage first: *"Li effetti vostri excitano a forza il giuditio di chi li guarda et per vederne piu exsperientia parlai di accrescer bontà alle cose perfette. Et ho visto che omnia possibilia sunt credenti. Io ebbi grandissima fede in Dio, che vi dessi una gratia sopranatural a far questo Christo."*[35] In an untranslatable phrase, she states in the opening line that his works urge the viewer to new efforts of understanding: *"Li effetti vostri excitano a forza il giuditio di chi li guarda."* The implications of this aesthetic judgment – that his works stretch the limits of human understanding – moved her in the following sentence to make a fully theological pronouncement, a renewed declaration of the very principle of Christian faith: "And I have seen that all things are possible to those who believe." She underscored the shift in discourse by switching into biblical Latin in midsentence: *"Et ho visto che **omnia possibilia sunt credenti*** [sic]." The words, quoted from Mark 9:23, are addressed by Christ to the father of the possessed boy, enjoining him to believe in God's capacity to heal his Son. The healing, crucially, happens only after the Father squarely faces the trial of faith: "Lord, I believe; help Thou mine unbelief" (Mark 9:24). Given what we know about Colonna's religious concerns, it is not surprising that she would quote a biblical passage that placed an emphasis not on God's capacity to perform a miracle but on humankind's capacity to believe in its possibility.[36] The truly novel thing about this letter is that Vittoria invoked this trial of faith in describing the hermeneutic challenges of Michelangelo's drawing, which also tests the viewer's capacity to believe and understand. Fittingly, the analogy was completed by the according of a divine grace to the work of the artist: "I had the greatest faith in God, that he would grant you a supernatural grace in making this Christ."

That special claims should be made on the individual's personal capacity for belief and understanding is a direct consequence of the workings of grace, because a gift in the sense elaborated by Michelangelo and Colonna is never general but singular, exclusive, and secret. As William West has put it, in a recent analysis of the theme of the gift in Derrida and Shakespeare, "when something *means for* someone, it is *meant for* someone."[37] Or, to return to the passage in the *Beneficio di Cristo* quoted above: "Do not believe only in general of the remission of sins, but apply this belief to your own case." This belief is possible only when the individual hears the word of God and the promise of redemption addressed to her or him personally and directly. No external assurances from authorities or institutional structures can replace this personal experience of having one's conscience addressed. The true gift, therefore, what Michelangelo called *il don de' doni,* is to feel this capacity to believe stir within oneself. At moments like this, the *Beneficio* is closest in spirit to the thinking of Juan de Valdés, Flaminio's spiritual advisor and an important influence on Colonna. In the prefatory letter Valdés's *Commentary on Romans,* a copy of which was sent to the community at Viterbo by Giulia Gonzaga, Valdés's primary pupil and the book's dedicatee,[38] Valdés termed this inner certainty "knowledge," which he opposes to mere "opinion":

It is very true indeed, that the knowledge which they have that Christ is the son of God, who feel not themselves reconciled to God, cannot properly be termed knowledge [*conozimiento*]: for were it knowledge it would work in them the same effect that it does in others, making them certain of their reconciliation with God, and giving them peace in their consciences [*zertificándoles de su reconziliazion con Dios, i dándoles paz en sus conszienzias*].[39]

Elsewhere, Valdés describes this inner conviction and intensity of feeling as "experience":

The first and principal intent which we who accept the Gospel ought to have, believing that in Christ God has chastised all our sins, is to get the experience of this, to the end that with our faith thus confirmed no man may be able to separate us from it, or make us doubt or stumble in it, as they are able while our faith is not confirmed with experience.[40]

Faith as experience is not a matter of understanding the doctrine propounded by preachers. Still less does it consist in a superstitious belief in the objective power of the sacraments or the virtues of miracle-working images or relics. Nor is it a matter of believing in the objective truth of what is related in the Bible. This is merely "historical faith."[41] Real faith results from the work of the Spirit in making the Word of God speak directly to one's individual conscience.[42] This fundamental belief lies at the basis of the highly private orientation of this group of reformers: They formed exclusive circles in secluded places and used highly intimate and "secret" means of communication, not primarily for fear of persecution but because such practices suited their religious orientation.[43] Theirs was not a doctrine easily adapted to the traditional modes of public dissemination: As several members of the reforming group noted with dismay, it tended to suffer a notable coarsening when it left their privileged circles and was spread to the larger public.[44]

Parallels to issues in religious art come immediately to mind. People with these tastes and this religious orientation, one imagines, would not be inclined to see the commissioning and veneration of religious art as a sort of good work or as an effective means of propitiating God's mercy through heavenly advocates or patron saints. Nor would one expect them to be interested in images laden with highly doctrinal iconographical content, such as became common in the Counter Reformation. It is also likely that they would have had objections to works that represented Christ's life merely as a historical drama. They would be interested, instead, in Christocentric works that directly addressed the movements of the viewer's conscience, works that inculcated in the viewer the experience of being personally implicated by the immensity of Christ's sacrifice. They would be interested, in other words, in works that made the sorts of claims described by Vittoria Colonna in her letters to Michelangelo.

THE PASSION ACCORDING TO VITTORIA COLONNA

Until now, I have described only in general terms the status of the artistic gifts exchanged between Michelangelo and Colonna, and the spirit in which they were given and received. In the previous chapter I described the means by which Michelangelo arrived at his solution in the Colonna *Pietà*. But we have yet to see how Colonna might have interpreted the specific features of this drawing, and to do so it is necessary to turn to Colonna's own writings on the Passion. The most significant work in this context is her *Pianto sopra la Passione di Cristo.*[45] An extraordinarily personal and innovative attempt to penetrate the significance of the image of the Virgin holding the dead Christ, the *Pianto* presents an approach strikingly close to the approach taken visually by Michelangelo – so close as to arouse the suspicion of a relation between the two. This need not be the case; the text is valuable above all for what it tells us about how Colonna would have viewed and understood Michelangelo's drawing. The *Pianto* is one of the most powerful and moving expressions of the conviction that most clearly binds Michelangelo to Vittoria Colonna and to the religious thinkers of her circle: that the language of Christian faith needs to be reformed and rediscovered, that it is, indeed, the primary challenge to faith to seek the direct and dependent relation that binds it to the promise of redemption embodied in the Passion of Christ.

Colonna began with a physical and affective description of the image of the dead Christ in the lap of the Virgin. Through close attention to its intimate details she drew her own inferences concerning the properties of Christ's body, the nature of the Virgin's relation to it, and, ultimately, the means by which this relation realizes the transmission of divine grace to humankind. This searching investigation, and the theologically innovative ideas to which it leads, are of exactly the kind that characterize Michelangelo's drawings. As in the drawings, highly intimate relations are described not merely to express pathetic emotion. We are offered something different from a historical scene of lamentation over a dead hero. Physical and affective relations serve, instead, as the path into the heart of the mystery: The effort to sustain the dead Christ in majesty celebrates the efficacy of his sacrifice and the claims made on the believer's faith. This arrival at religious understanding through affective "experience," in turn, parallels the forms of response elicited from the viewer and reader. The *Pianto* provides a language ideally suited to understanding the nature of the *Pietà* and thus warrants an especially careful reading.

Although the title given to the printed text was *Pianto sopra la Passione di Christo,* Colonna concentrates on only one "episode" of the Passion, the lamentation of the Virgin over the body of Christ. She begins by proposing to describe the "pious effect of seeing the dead Christ in the arms of his Mother."[46] She emphasizes above all the closeness of their union; Christ lies not only upon her but virtually within her, as in a tomb: She has made "of her nearly dead body a sepulchre in that hour."[47] She gives special emphasis to the means by which the affective relation between the two transforms them reciprocally. The Virgin's love and pain, which she had until this moment modestly held within, are now, at the touch of the sacred body, allowed to flow forth:

That fire of love and torment that consumed and penetrated the intimate reaches of her soul . . . now at the touch of the sacred body of Christ spread through her to its maximum extent, and was released through her eyes in more bitter tears, and through her mouth in more burning sighs.[48]

These effluences have, in turn, an animating effect on the body of Christ, making him appear alive rather than dead: "She washed and warmed him such as to make him appear truly alive."[49] Colonna is thus led to explain why it is that Christ's body, unlike the bodies of regular mortals, retained its dignity and majesty in death:

Besides having the divinity which never left him, I believe he had the usual great Majesty, indeed even greater, because whereas in others death is an act of violence and deals them an offence, in Christ who had called for it and desired it with such sweetness, I believe it was an act so soft, sweet and pious that it softened all hard hearts, and inflamed all cold minds, the ugliness of death being not only beautiful in this most beautiful face but the fierceness becoming a great sweetness.[50]

She goes on to explain how the divine qualities that had animated his features while alive left their *"vestigij"* on his dead form, even though they had departed with his soul upon his death. These qualities were, she argues, still present on the body itself and palpable to those who attended to his body, above all to the Virgin.[51] The Virgin's response is thus more than a mere expression of anecdotal grief. She understands the great benefits that proceed from the sacrifice and is thus filled with a paradoxical combination of joy and pain. We see her *"dilettar in questa pena,"* for she is aware that she holds in her arms the source of all grace. Indeed, Colonna imagines her wishing the whole world to be present to participate in its direct transmission: "with what sincerity, I believe, did she desire that all the world were there to see what she saw so that they may enjoy such immense grace."[52] She thinks above all of those for whom it was possible, historically, to assist at the event but did not. She calls all the apostles, all those who had come into contact with Christ while he was alive and, one by one, describes how they could have benefited from direct contact with the body. She specifically states that their absence was compensated for by the presence of angels, who assumed in their place the task of attending to the body: "and if not for the angels who compensated for the ingratitude of man, those who could have been there but were not would feel great sorrow and regret."[53] Thus she includes the attendance of the angels upon the body of Christ – an idea that if not directly adapted from Michelangelo's drawing might well have been adapted generally from images of the Man of Sorrows supported by angels (the *Engelpietà*) – and explains their presence as the result of a *historical* circumstance.

It is remarkable how strictly this meditative text adheres to what might be called the conditions of historical possibility. The guiding principle of the meditation is that the very transmission of grace to humankind hinges on the virtues of physical contact with Christ in the precise interval postmortem and *ante resurrectionem,* and this is what brings her close to Michelangelo's understanding of the subject. A significant portion of the text consists of Colonna's urging those to whom it was possible to come and attend to the body of Christ: "And if you do not all come now it will be impossible again to see him, adore him and thank him. That time is finished that he has deigned to inhabit the earth."[54] She explains that this is the most propitious moment of all, for never was he more full of humility and grace: "And even if you have seen him alive in no other act has he displayed more his humility, indeed all of his excessive graces put together."[55] She describes the privilege enjoyed by the Magdalene, Joseph of Arimathea, and Nicodemus to have been present at the event but gives them clearly secondary roles. The Magdalene laments Christ and accompanies the Virgin, and Joseph offers his winding cloth and consoles the Virgin.

Nothing, however, mitigates the Virgin's solitude, and the greatness and exclusiveness of her burden; she is the one "who alone sustained the faith alive in her holy breast."[56] For this reason, the Virgin gives infinite thanks to the angels "who were there to make up for the absence of man."[57] Then, in a curious conclusion, Colonna affirms that in the absence of Christ's soul it was left up to the Virgin to preserve the honor and majesty of Christ before God:

> Thus the Madonna, seeing the absence of the holy soul of Christ, which alone was sufficient to honor the immense grandeur of divinity, saw that it was up to her to supply such a great debt, and would have wanted to liquefy herself, consume herself to the very limit in the fire of love and in the tears of compassion in order to rid the world and herself of such ingratitude, and to render to God the obsequy and the cult that were due him.[58]

She searches in all of Christ's limbs for a place inhabited by his soul, even though she knows that it is nowhere to be found. All of her greatest virtues, charity, humility, patience, and obedience, are exhausted and overcome in the search. In the end, it is only faith that preserves her: *"solo la fede la sostenne in vita."* That act of faith in turn plays a crucial role in sustaining the faith at a time when it was entirely missing in the world. Through her the world is reinvested with that faith "which if not for her would have been extinguished."[59]

In very naturalistic terms, Vittoria's text found in the contact with Christ's dead body the means by which divine grace is transmitted to humankind. She implicitly argued that it is transmitted by means of the faith sustained at the death of Christ, and initially and crucially by that of the Virgin.[60] Christian faith is thus drawn to its origins in the Passion and is specifically forged in relation to the dead body of Christ. This direct link between the Passion of Christ and the dissemination of the faith sheds new light on the inscription of the verse from Dante on the cross in the drawing: *"Non vi si pensa quanto sangue costa."* In the original context, this verse alludes to the spread of the Gospel; it occurs in a passage condemning the obfuscation of the original Gospel message by the later inventions of preachers (*Paradiso,* 29:91–6):

Non vi si pensa quanto sangue costa
Seminarla nel mondo, e quanto piace
Chi umilmente con essa s'accosta.
Per apparer ciascun s'ingegna, e face
Sue invenzioni, e quelle son trascorse
Dai predicanti, e il vangelio si tace.

[They think not there how much blood it costs to sow it in the world, nor how much he pleases who humbly keeps close to it. Each one strives for display and makes his own inventions, and those are treated of by the preachers, and the Gospel is silent.][61]

By appropriating the verse in the context of the Passion, Michelangelo radicalized its message in a manner that could not fail to be appreciated by a reform-minded audience: If in Dante the blood refers to the effort expended by preachers and martyrs in the spreading of the Gospel, here the blood springs directly from its source in Christ's sacrifice.

But it is the reference to the "cost" of Christ's blood that most clearly links the verse to the reformist context studied here, for it directly contrasts payment and gift. The reference is not made in the calculating spirit that prevailed in late-medieval devotions, where it was common to count and measure Christ's blood in exact quantities. In a late fifteenth-century prayerbook, for example, we find the legend of a nun who wanted to know exactly how much blood Christ spilled and who received a vision from Christ that gave her a precise answer: "Whosoever should say 100 Pater Nosters and Ave Marias every day will at the end of fifteen years have prayed a Paternoster to every drop (of my blood). This many drops have I spilled for you and all men."[62] The passage clearly reveals the relationship between this calculating mentality and a numbers-oriented approach to the saying of prayers. This link, of course, also played a role in the system of indulgences, which had a direct bearing on the image of the Man of Sorrows, one of the most heavily indulgenced images of the late Middle Ages.[63]

This entire array of practices was highly distasteful to humanist reformers.[64] Michelangelo's drawing in every sense offers an alternative. In Michelangelo's drawing the cost and quantity of Christ's blood are invoked in a spirit of grandiose irony, to stress the giftlike *in*calculability of Christ's sacrifice. The "cost" of redemption is beyond reckoning (*"non vi si pensa"*). There is no way to render it or account for it, as the nun from Colmar cited above was able to do through the counting up of prayers. The antinumerical irony is offered in the same spirit as that voiced by Christ when asked by Peter,

"'Lord, how many times must I forgive my brother when he has sinned against me? Seven times?' Jesus said to him, 'Not seven times, seventy-seven times'" (Matthew 18:21–22). In stark contrast to the number-crunching Christ that appeared in the nun's vision, the Christ of the Bible compounds the digit seven not to correct Peter's calculations but to explode Peter's quantitative reasoning altogether and to point him to infinite, unaccountable forgiveness, like that offered by divine grace. Christ goes on to illustrate the point (in the explicit language of money and gifts) through the parable of the king who frees the indebted servant of all payment (Matthew 18:23–35).[65]

Like Colonna's text, and a host of other writings produced in her circle, the drawing was an effort to establish a direct relation to the source of grace in Christ's Passion. The *Pietà* and the *Pianto* have several motifs in common: the centrality of the body of Christ, its enfoldment within the lap of the Virgin, the presence of the angels "who wished to assume the human weight," and finally the special role given to the Virgin. What binds them above all is the emphasis they both place on engendering and amorous motifs, a tendency already signaled in Dante's use of the verbs *seminare* and *accostarsi* to describe the spreading and reception of the Gospel. In both Colonna's and Michelangelo's works, these metaphors assumed a physical immediacy in direct relation to the body of Christ. The series of studies that prepared Michelangelo's drawing for Colonna are the closest imaginable visual analogue to Colonna's passionate and highly erotic rhetoric: "That fire of love and torment . . . that had consumed and penetrated the intimate reaches of her soul . . . was released through her eyes in more bitter tears, and through her mouth in more burning sighs."

The compact solution offered in the final drawing replaces the overt rhetoric of physical intimacy with more abstract metaphors of generation and fertility. Christ is nestled deep down between the Virgin's legs, and the lower half of his body is submerged below ground. At a concrete and literal level, such an arrangement effectively displays the heaviness of the dead body and suggests its imminent interment.[66] At a "figural" level, however, Christ's simultaneous embeddedness in the Virgin's body and in the earth combines a metaphor of birthing with a metaphor of horticultural growth. There is, in fact, very little emphasis placed on Christ's wounds or the deadness of the body. Instead, the drawing throughout suggests an incipient stirring, a life-giving energy that contrasts the deathward tendency.[67] The two "senses" in the drawing, deathward and lifeward, are simultaneous, inseparable, and mutually reinforcing. The womb, as Leo Steinberg has put it, is conjoined with the tomb, an idea clearly expressed by Colonna when she said that the Virgin had made "of her nearly dead body a sepulchre in that hour."[68] Because Christ's death is itself the source of regeneration, the process of entombment, the gift of death, is inseparable from the renewing of life, the giving of birth. His death is a birth, and his dead body ambiguously flickers with signs of life. As

Colonna explained, Christ is dead, but because he "had called for it and desired it with such sweetness" – in the drawing Christ is shown semiwillfully pointing downward[69] – his body does not show the violence of death but rather a radiant beauty that suggests life. As we have seen, Colonna was careful to point out that the animated *"vestigij"* of life that were discernible in the dead body (even before it was "glorified in a better life" in the resurrection) were not quite objective features: They shine for those who see them, and above all for the Virgin who was closest to him. They shine, that is, for those who see the life in the death, the redemption in the sacrifice. As Colonna put it in another place, *"il vero Christo qual nudo e puro, ex fide vivit"* – the true Christ, nude and pure, lives from faith.[70]

We are far, here, from the emphasis on Mary's grief found in so many late medieval Passion dramas, and in general we are far from the entire Marian orientation of late medieval piety.[71] The reference to birthing, for example, is not simply a version of the sentimental tradition associated with *pietà* imagery, according to which the Virgin remembers having the Child in her lap. The motif insists, instead, on the more profoundly theological point of Christ's death as a source of regeneration. The drawing, like Colonna's text, is concentrated on the mystery of redemption through Christ's sacrifice and locates it in the stirring of a life force within the dead body. The implied descent tombward simultaneously releases a lifeward energy. Christ's downward-pointing arms are answered by the Virgin's upward gesture, a movement that would have continued, before the drawing was cropped, up the arms of the Y-shaped cross. This combination of downward and upward movement is Michelangelo's most consistent "figure" for the paradox of Christ's sacrifice: Where the historical blood of Christ's mortal body ran down the cross, the "verse of blood" – the ever-flowing wellspring of grace – runs up the cross.

Colonna's letters to Michelangelo, studied above, reveal that for her such a drawing does not merely depict the mystery of the gift: It embodies and enacts it, both through its unfathomable technique and through its figural inexhaustibility. Its meaning is not reducible to an objective doctrinal content but arises through the viewer's experience of the configuration and energy of the drawing. And the viewer's receptivity to the drawing's delicate ambiguities, so far from merely being a path to understanding a mystery, is itself an instance of the mystery at work. When Colonna asserted that Michelangelo's works move the viewer to new efforts of understanding (*"li effetti vostri excitano a forza il giuditio di chi li guarda"*), she was not only making an aesthetic judgment. Rather, she was making an aesthetic judgment that, in her mind, carried theological implications. For Colonna, to be receptive to the hermeneutic challenge of this kind of art – an art, that is, conceived as a gift – is to engage in the very movements of faith, to open oneself as one does in receiving divine grace. It is to see that "all things are possible to those who believe."

CULT AND CULTURE

In an illuminating study on books as gifts in the sixteenth century, Natalie Zemon Davis studied the effect of the early modern book market on the medieval tradition that conceived of knowledge as a gift that cannot be sold. "Could such a cultural ideal," she asked, "survive the desacralising technology of the printer's shop?"[72] The problem was, for her, an instance of the larger problem, raised by Mauss, of the decline of a premodern culture of gift exchange with the rise of modern conceptions of private property. Davis showed that although it succumbed to various pressures, the tradition of knowledge as a gift was powerful enough to ensure that the book continued to be treated, in various ways, as "a privileged object that resisted permanent appropriation." The book's status as a gift was reaffirmed especially forcefully, she noted, in Protestant circles.

Michelangelo's and Vittoria Colonna's preoccupation with the ethics and aesthetics of the gift was part of a similar reaction. They, too, sought an alternative to the latter-day "economization" of religious devotion, to the prevailing system of works, indulgences, and "endowments" in which art production had become so centrally implicated. And their rejection of these "modern" abuses likewise led to an emphasis on gift giving as a means of restoring originary and thus purer religious values, a project of restoration and reformation bound up with a distinct reassertion of aristocratic ideals. Their insight was to see that an emerging conception of liberal art served their enterprise very well. In a form of art that was free from the economy of works made on commission they saw the possibility for a reformed religious image, and a privileged model for the type of personalized religious experience they espoused. This circumstance helps to explain why a work made to satisfy the most sophisticated artistic tastes should be marked throughout by a conscious archaism.

The archaism is present in the adoption of the strictly frontal Christ (stricter than in any of the preceding drawings), in the return to the *Engelpietà,* and in the quote from Dante on the cross. It is there also in the Y-shaped form of the cross, as it appeared before the drawing was cropped. The medieval associations of this form would be plain from the visual evidence alone, but in this case Condivi explicitly states that the cross in the drawing was based on the cross "which was carried in procession by the Bianchi at the time of the plague of 1348, and afterwards placed in the church of Santa Croce, at Florence."[73] As it happens, Condivi's (and perhaps Michelangelo's) historical knowledge was not entirely accurate: The Bianchi arose in the year 1399, and their crosses were not Y-shaped.[74] The important point, however, is that the reference to the medieval past was a considered one: The cross in the drawing was adopted in imitation of a cross in Santa Croce (Michelangelo's parish church), which Michelangelo associated with the history and penitential movements of the Tuscan Trecento.

The overtness of the archaism is one signal of the fragility of the enterprise, which was as short-lived as the culture for which it was made. Michelangelo's drawing for Vittoria Colonna is one very clear instance of the optimism and hopes for reconciliation that mark this earlier, more fluid phase of reform in Italy – and it is, by the same token, also an expression of its conflicts. These reformers proposed their brand of thoughtful piety as an antidote to the abuses and superstitions that plagued the church, and as the basis of their hope to heal the Protestant schism. The proposition was full of weaknesses, as the history of their efforts, especially after the failed colloquy at Regensburg in 1541, was to show. A major weakness was that their attitudes were in the end that of a sophisticated elite, and were not clearly adaptable to a true program of reform – a point repeatedly made by Delio Cantimori.[75] As a group, they were united as much by their aesthetic and cultural tastes as by their religious convictions, and this combination was the source of acute internal conflicts.

CHAPTER SEVEN

Sculpture as Relic

THE CONTROVERSY OVER IMAGES AND THE *PARAGONE*

Holy Father, the College of Cardinals has no need of men who know how to write sonnets."[1] This was, reportedly, the reaction of Gian Pietro Carafa, the future Pope Paul IV, to Pietro Bembo's assumption to the cardinalate in 1539. In this one dry remark we have the lit fuse of a culture war. The marriage of elegance and piety celebrated by Giles of Viterbo, the consciously antique-inspired atmosphere whipped up by Johannes Goritz around Sansovino's *St. Anne* – in short, the festive convergence of religious authority and humanist refinement that dominated papal culture in the early part of the century – was no longer an obvious cultural mode after the Sack of Rome and the hardening of the Protestant Schism. By the 1550s Ludovico Beccadelli, a survivor of the earlier era who spent his last years avoiding the wrath of Pope Paul IV, had transformed those early days into an object of intense nostalgia, and even of formal artistic and literary commemoration.[2] In the 1530s and 1540s Pope Paul III, himself a product of the earlier culture, attempted to adapt the earlier ideals to the new conditions by supporting the strain of humanist culture most closely allied with the spirit of religious reform. Several people affiliated with the Viterbo circle – people such as Jacopo Sadoleto, Pietro Bembo, Marccantonio Flaminio, and Ludovico Beccadelli – were children of the earlier culture who, with the support of Paul III, attempted to adapt humanist ideals to more sharply reform-minded ends. The result was a highly refined spirituality that made literary and artistic communication a model for religious experience – a spirituality well suited to the claims of Michelangelo's *Pietà* drawing (see Figure 93). The work's status as a near *unicum* is the clearest mark of its tenuous and revealing historical position.

This period produced other short-lived cultural experiments. Amedeo Quondam has studied the efforts made at this time to found a new poetic typology that would adapt the form and language of lyric poetry to "spiritual" subjects. These efforts, which include Girolamo Malipiero's *Petrarca spirituale* (1536), Vittoria Colonna's *Rime spirituali* (1546), and Luca Contile's *Rime cristiane* (ready for the press in 1546, but never printed), attempted to coordinate two axes that one might see as vertical and horizontal: The vertical axis of the Petrarchan tradition (*"il codice lirico petrarchistico"*) and the horizontal axis of the contemporary religious context (*"la questione religiosa del primo Cinquecento"*).[3] We saw a similar effort of coordination in the Colonna *Pietà*, although there the axes are reversed: The dominant artistic tradition (vertical axis) was the Christian cult image, which was here adapted to the aesthetic tastes of humanist culture (horizontal axis).

These experiments in poetic typology did not survive the Council of Trent. Contile's own comments on his poems, written in 1560, reveal the somewhat tortured effort required to explain them in a radically changed religious and cultural environment.[4] The open condemnations were, in turn, not slow in coming. A text dating from the 1570s, entitled *Avertimento sopra le rime dell'Ariosto, del Bembo et del Sannazaro,* offered a ruthless assault on the poetic culture of the early part of the century. Most objectionable, in the author's view, was the mingling of the sacred and profane – the "deification" of the Petrarchan *Donna* and the dubious introduction of Christian themes in the context of courtly love.[5]

Already in the earlier period, tensions were palpably high. In the midst of the Viterbo circle no one felt the conflict more acutely than did Giberti's former secretary Marcantanio Flaminio, who was a poet before he was a religious author. A letter of 1540 from Francesco della Torre to Donato Rullo, both friends of Flaminio and Reginald Pole, casts a sharp light on the repercussions of this conflict among Flaminio's readers:

> I have received from him [Cardinal Pole] verses by Messer Marcantonio [Flaminio], and when I have collected some others I will send you those as well, which in my judgment will satisfy you much more, since they are that much more lovely [*vaghi*] and more beautiful [*venusti*] when they treat of matters that are more capable of loveliness [*più capaci di vaghezza*], for in truth in trying to treat these matters of religion in a lovely manner [*vagamente*] more often than not one merely makes the sacred profane: and I believe it is a difficult thing to do it well, and with dignity. These others are of pastoral and amorous subjects, but be careful not to show them to certain Stoics who are scandalized by everything.[6]

The incompatibility appears to have become axiomatic also in the arena of the visual arts by this time. This is the clear impression given by a letter of 1541 by Nino Sernini, an agent of the Gonzaga, reporting on the initial recep-

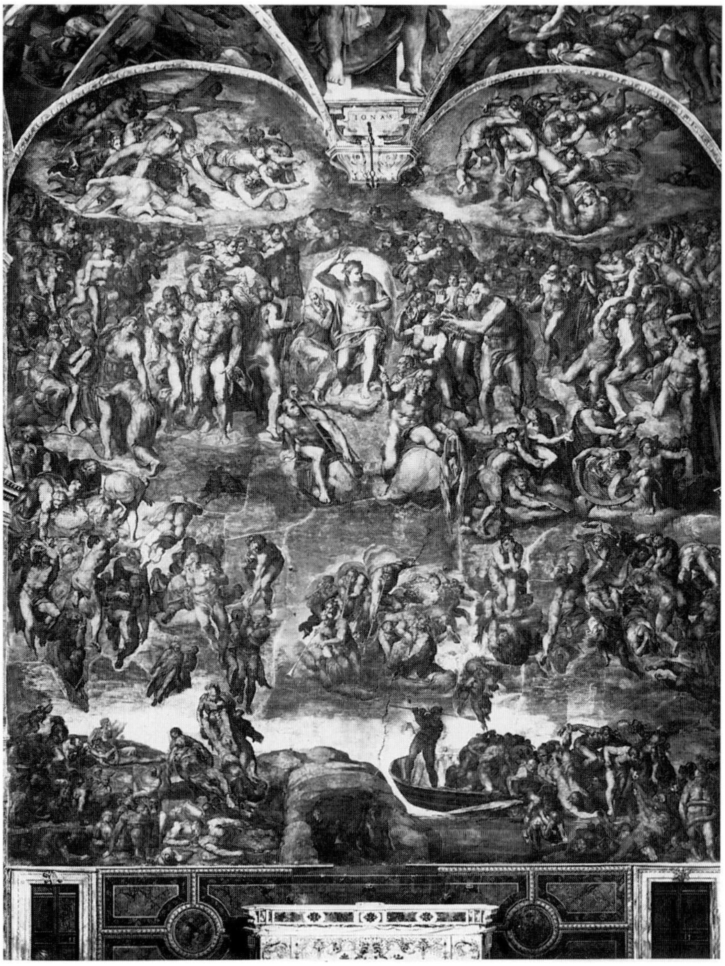

94. Michelangelo, *Last Judgment.* Fresco. Sistine Chapel, Vatican City. Alinari/ Art Resource.

tion of Michelangelo's *Last Judgment* (Figure 94): "The work is of such beauty that your excellency can imagine that there is no lack of those who condemn it." For Sernini, as for most *intendenti* of the period, "beauty" in visual art was embodied above all in the nude, and "(t)he very reverend Theatines are the first to say that the nudes do not belong in such a place."[7] In just two decades we have come a significant distance from the optimistic pronouncements on the unity of beauty and religion, of elegance and piety, that pervaded the writings of Giles of Viterbo and the poems of the *Coryciana.*

The parting of the ways between art and religion acknowledged here was already clearly recognized in the north, owing to the earlier and more violent impact of the Reformation. In 1522, for example, Martin Luther's protector Franz von Sickingen acknowledged that church images were all too often appreciated for their "art and beauty" rather than for their religious significance and suggested that they should be used instead as "ornaments in fine rooms" – that is, in a secular environment – so that the effort and expense would not be in vain.[8] Sickingen's cultivated and accommodating sense of decorum was, of course, to become a point of doctrine for Calvin, for whom images were inherently in contradiction to the tenets of the Christian religion. As a man of learning, Calvin did not condemn image making per se but instead believed that it should be cultivated as an art, which he considered a gift from God. The only "pure and legitimate use" of art, for Calvin, was thus as a secular pursuit.[9]

The separation was never so sharply drawn in Italy, but as the letter of Francesco della Torre quoted above clearly shows, there was a clear consciousness of an emerging incompatibility, an uneasy awareness that "matters of religion" did not so easily, or appropriately, lend themselves to elegant expression. When Federico Gonzaga, in 1524, asked Baldassare Castiglione to acquire a work by Sebastiano del Piombo, of any kind "so long as it is not about Saints, but some picture that is lovely and beautiful to look at [*non siano cose di sancti, ma qualche picture vaghe et belle da vedere*]," he was not merely stating an iconographical preference.[10] The phrasing (*"ma"*) implies, quite clearly, that religious images tend not to belong to the category of pictures that are lovely and beautiful to look at. Without leaning too heavily on the phrasing, the main thrust of Gonzaga's comment is clearly that secular subjects offer better opportunities for the display of artistic excellence – that they are, in della Torre's neat phrasing, *"più capaci di vaghezza."*

By Vasari's time the question had become a matter of open debate. In a passage that introduces his 1550 Life of Fra Angelico, Vasari clearly identified the problem, referring to paintings made by "men of little belief," which "excite dishonorable appetites and lascivious desires, so that the work is blamed for what is disreputable, while praise is accorded to its artistic excellence." Nonetheless, he held out the possibility that modern aesthetic ideals – embodied above all in the beautiful human figure – could still serve the purposes of religion. People should not, he said, be fooled into thinking that only an awkward, clumsy thing – *"goffo et inetto,"* terms he uses repeatedly to describe medieval art – can be devout, and that modern paintings with more beautiful figures must be more lascivious.

By the second edition of 1568 circumstances had changed. The decree on images was issued by the Council of Trent in its closing session of 1563, and censorious interventions were undertaken on Michelangelo's *Last Judgment* in 1565. Vasari's optimism, accordingly, grew more cautious, and in the second edition he surrounded his earlier plea for the unity of beauty and religion with carefully worded caveats. In the same passage from the Life of Fra Angelico Vasari now explained that he did not want anyone to believe that he approved of "those figures in the churches that are painted practically nude, because in them one sees that the painter has not had the appropriate respect for the place." Fra Angelico was thus given a more motivated role within

Vasari's historical scheme, representing a pinnacle of Christian art between the artistic clumsiness of the "devout" Middle Ages and the religious indecorousness of the nudes of Vasari's own day, fine and good work though it may be on artistic grounds.[11]

In incorporating a condemnation of the depiction of "practically nude" figures in a church setting in the 1568 edition, Vasari was implicitly agreeing with the critics of Michelangelo's *Last Judgment,* even if his description of the fresco itself remained unchanged. He had indeed come around to a position close to that which Pietro Aretino had adopted two decades earlier in his attack on Michelangelo's fresco. In his public letter of 1545, Aretino questioned not Michelangelo's artistic genius but his judgment. His nude figures were, Aretino claimed, more appropriate to a loggia than to the central chapel of Christendom. Beyond condemning the display of nudity, Aretino also condemned the obscurity and intellectual difficulty of Michelangelo's art, which he also felt to be inappropriate to a religious work. With an opportunist's unerring sense for the shifting ideological winds, Aretino already in 1545 set out the fundamental points to be developed in the Counter-Reformation polemic on images: that what is good for art (the depiction of the nude, the pursuit of *difficultà*) is not necessarily good for religion and thus that it is necessary to observe a sense of appropriateness to place, or decorum.[12]

Michelangelo also had things to say about art and religion, and some of the most significant comments attributed to him date from the period of the *Last Judgment.* The most famous appear in Francisco de Hollanda's *Dialogues on Painting,* which was purportedly based on conversations that took place in 1538.[13] In a famous passage, Michelangelo condemned Flemish painting for appealing to women, "especially very old ones, or very young ones," and also to "friars and nuns and also some noble persons who have no ear for true harmony."[14] These comments are not just part of an aesthetic debate. The *Dialogues* take place at the church of San Silvestro al Quirinale, after sermons by "Fra Ambrogio" (Ambrogio Catarino Politi, the author of an extended critique of the *Beneficio di Cristo,* later a harsh critic of the *Last Judgment*), and in the company of Vittoria Colonna. These circumstances strongly encourage us to read them in the context of the concerns over reform that mark the period.[15] The absence of an intellectual basis in Flemish painting is directly linked to a form of sentimental piety that Michelangelo particularly disdained. This was the piety of the women who, in the words of Girolamo Savonarola (discussed in chapter 1), "want to cry with the Virgin" and who in their sentimentalism reveal their blindness to a proper theological understanding of the necessity of Christ's sacrifice within the Christian scheme of redemption.[16] It is a form of piety that leads to superstition and gullibility, and, in the humanist tradition from Lorenzo Valla to Erasmus, was associated with the corrupt and hypocritical practices of the "religiosi," the "friars and nuns" derided by de Hollanda's Michelangelo.[17] One did not have to be a closet Protestant to espouse this kind of anticlericalism: It had become fairly common by the mid-sixteenth century, affording among other things a rich mine of material for jokes.[18] A few of Michelangelo's jibes were, in fact, recorded by Vasari.[19]

In de Hollanda's dialogue, Michelangelo's antidote to the sensual and emotional appeal of Flemish art was an intellectual art that arouses a noble, high-minded piety. There is nothing more "noble and devout" than Italian painting at its best, he said, "for with wise persons (*nos discretos*) nothing causes devotion to be remembered, or to arise, more than the difficulty of the perfection which unites itself with and joins God."[20] The dispersiveness of Flemish painting, in this view, bespeaks a narrow, subjective bias, for its effects invite the viewer's curious, roaming gaze and excite her or his emotions. Such an individualist orientation was most eloquently described by Aby Warburg, for whom it was epitomized in the donor portraits so often found in this form of painting, and it was those same donor portraits that Michelangelo, from what we can gather, particularly disdained.[21] The more high-minded art, by contrast, puts the viewer in touch with noble, suprapersonal ideas, which "intellect only can appreciate, and with great difficulty."[22]

Other sources corroborate the ascription of these views to Michelangelo and indicate further that for him the difference between the two kinds of painting was not so much a difference of nationality as of mode and technique, a difference embodied in the difference between oil painting and fresco painting. Michelangelo had occasion to express his opinions on the matter with characteristic harshness, for it was at the heart of his break with Sebastiano del Piombo at the beginning of work on the *Last Judgment*. Vasari wrote that Sebastiano had wanted Michelangelo to paint the fresco in oil and had prepared the altar wall of the Sistine Chapel accordingly. This incensed Michelangelo, who removed Sebastiano's preparations, applied a proper *arriccio,* and proceeded to pour abuse on Sebastiano, calling oil painting a "woman's art" (*arte da donna*).[23] Michelangelo's criticisms of Flemish painting were in fact part of a disdain for oil painting in general – quite logically, as oil painting encourages and allows for the description of "the grass of the fields, the shadows of trees, and bridges and rivers"[24] in a way that *buon fresco* does not. Indeed, there was a good deal of this kind of oil painting being produced on Italian soil by the 1530s. Michelangelo very likely got to see some prime examples of it – by Giovanni Bellini and Titian, among others – in 1529 during his visits with Alfonso d'Este in Ferrara.

Within panel painting, Michelangelo might well have exempted tempera painting from censure, and for related reasons. For this the evidence comes, as it were, intrapictorially in the *Doni Tondo,* where it is no surprise to find an implicit polemic given that it was, among other things, a conscious response to Leonardo da Vinci (Figure 95). Recent analysis has shown that in this panel Michelangelo used the oil technique but applied it in a tempera-like way.[25]

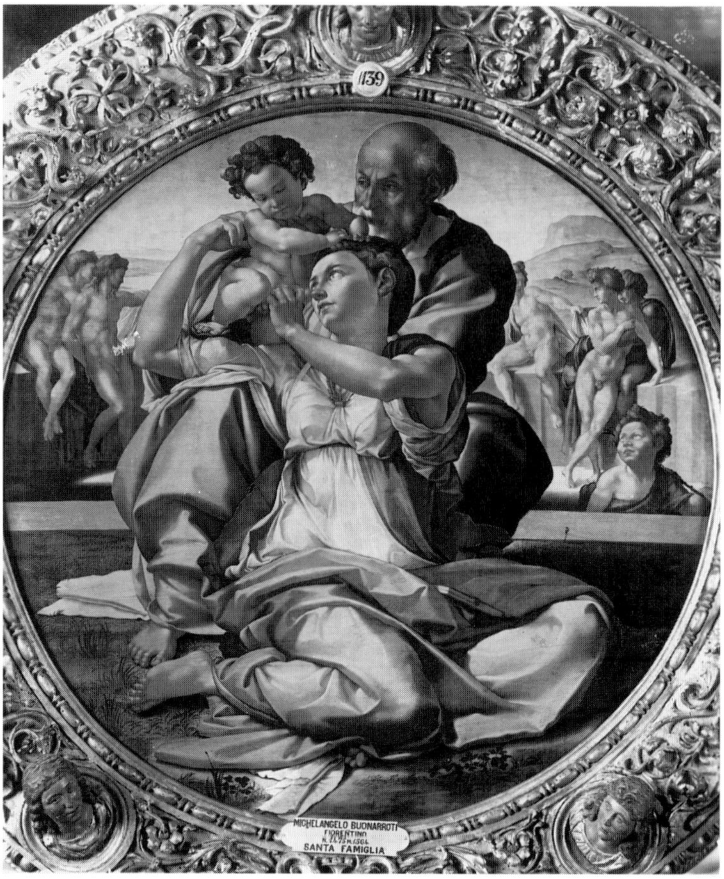

95. Michelangelo, *Doni Madonna.* Panel. Uffizi, Florence, Italy. Alinari/Art Resource.

The result is a highly sculptural treatment of the figures, amounting to a pictorial manifesto of a *parti pris.* All of these indications suggest that Michelangelo's true enemy was not Flemish art per se but the mode of oil painting that was developed there and that was so enthusiastically received in late fifteenth-century Italy. In Florence, this taste was satisfied above all by the workshop of Andrea del Verrocchio, which produced Leonardo and Pietro Perugino,[26] and in northern Italy by the circle of Francesco Francia and Lorenzo Costa, and later the circle of Giorgione, which of course produced Sebastiano.

We perhaps get a direct whiff of this disdain, shortly after the painting of the *Doni Tondo,* in Michelangelo's extraordinarily abusive treatment of Francia in Bologna in 1506, as recounted by Vasari in the first edition: "You and Costa can go fuck off, because you are both royal fools in art. [*Va a bordello tu e'l Cossa* [sic], *che siete due solennissimi goffi nell'arte*]."[27] By 1530, however, Michelangelo had to concede that the soft and pleasant oil painting manner, whether of the Giorgione–Titian persuasion or of the Leonardo–Raphael variety, had won the day in the arena of the easel picture, and this meant that he was forced into a wholesale retreat to the art of fresco, from whose scaffoldings he could shout *"il colorire a olio è arte da donna!"* The blandishments of the easel painters, associated with a soft and woolly-headed feminine piety, now stood in the starkest contrast to the masculine and high-minded *virtù* of *buon fresco,* whose consummate example he was about to offer in his depiction of the end of the world.

It is not my intention here to give a comprehensive account of the *Last Judgment.* I only want to make the point that, as an effort to prove that modern artistic excellence was (still) congruent with art's Christian purpose, it was a colossal failure. Rather than being unveiled to universal celebration in 1541, the fresco immediately became a matter of debate. As noted above, one of the very first eyewitness reports of the unveiling noted that "[t]he work is of such beauty that . . . there is no lack of those who condemn it." What should have been a timeless vision of the end of human history became instead a touchstone of early modern debates on the question of cultural contingency.

The idea that the *Last Judgment* not only depicts but itself marks an "epochal" turning point informs the earliest written responses to the fresco. For Vasari, it was a *summa* of Michelangelo's art and thus served as a consummation of the entire historical scheme of the *Lives* – a role that was especially clear in the first edition of 1550, which concluded with the description of the fresco. Aretino had also acknowledged its consummate artistic excellence but added the damning and fateful caveat that these artistic ambitions were not necessarily appropriate to a Christian chapel.[28] Aretino's distinction became the keynote of a wave of Counter-Reformation criticism. The Dominican Ambrogio Catarino (who makes an appearance in Hollanda's *Dialogues*) declared: "I commend the art used in the matter, but I vehemently vituperate and detest the matter itself. For this nudity of limbs appears most indecent on altars and in the most important of God's chapels."[29] For Giovanni Andrea Gilio, Michelangelo was at the head of those modern painters who "twist the purity of the subject to satisfy the charms of art." Gilio perceived this as a cultural crisis and put it in clear historical perspective. He saw these excesses as modern abuses that needed to be stripped away in order to restore religious art to its "first purity." He was among the first to offer a sustained modern appreciation of medieval art, to which he was drawn by his conviction that "the painters before Michelangelo attended more closely to truth and to devotion than to pomp."[30] By the end of the century, not even Michelangelo's supporters could discuss the fresco without qualification, defensiveness, or outright irony.[31]

In sum, Aretino's criticism prevailed, a victory sealed by the irreversible addition of patches of clothing to the figures, carried out in the 1560s by Daniele da Volterra. Less often noticed is that Michelangelo anticipated his defeat. It has been shown that Michelangelo included a rather gruesome self-portrait in the skin of St. Bartholomew, and it is also generally agreed that the saint bears the features of Aretino (Figure 96). It is reasonable to assume that

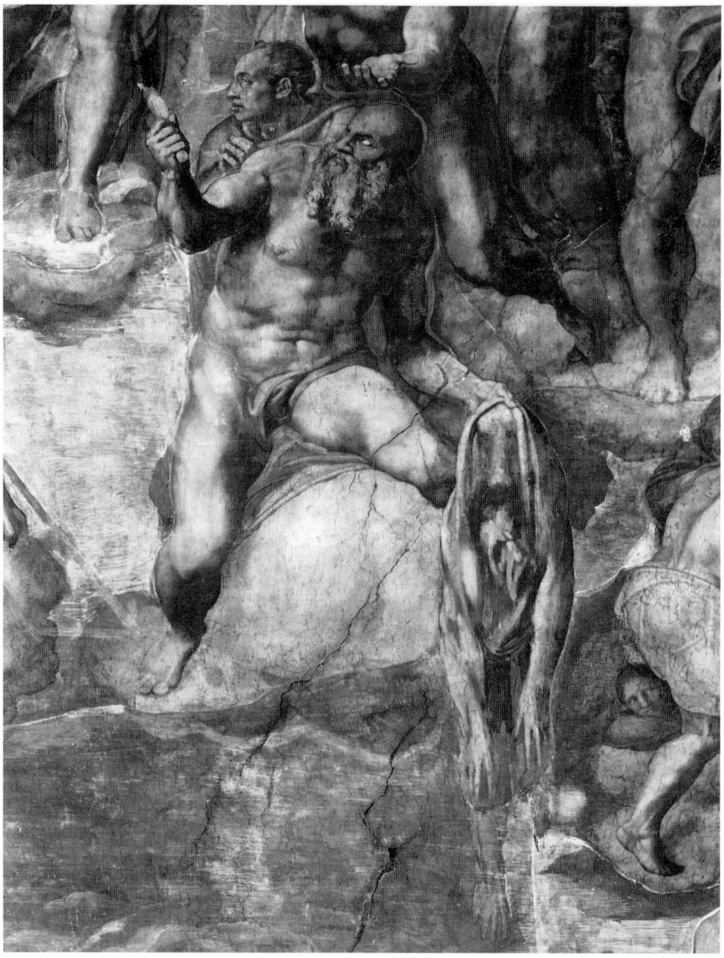

96. Michelangelo, *Last Judgment, detail of self-portrait.* Sistine Chapel, Vatican City. Alinari/ Art Resource.

Michelangelo, even before finishing the fresco, had advance notice that he was going to be flayed alive by Aretino. He thus shows Aretino/Bartholomew holding the knife in one hand and in the other, the skinned self-portrait, precariously hanging over the boat of Caron. The fact that it is Aretino who holds the skin has not been sufficiently incorporated into readings of the self-portrait. In my view, it strongly encourages us to understand the self-portrait in relation to the polemic brewing around the fresco and as a kind of anticipated response to Aretino's critiques. But what kind of response is it?

Michelangelo's skin is the antithesis of all the other figures in the painting. The other figures, endowed with strong, athletic bodies, twist and turn in complex contrapposti. Michelangelo's figure, by contrast, is emphatically flat and frontal: the front limbs hang directly in front of the "hind" limbs. The other figures are nude, whereas Michelangelo's figure is, as it were, only clothing. The other figures in the fresco embody the highest achievements of art, as was often proclaimed at the time. This flat, hanging skin represents, instead, an abnegation, quite literally a deflation of the ideal body. In many ways the figure seems a conscious reversion to what, from the point of view of the period, would have been considered medieval artlessness. As we have seen, Giovanni Andrea Gilio admitted that "to modern eyes" medieval cult images "look vile, awkward, lowly, old, humble, without skill or art" and that they are characterized by a rude frontality or *prosopopea* – all qualities that, in his view, bespoke their authentic piety.[32]

Michelangelo's self-portrait, indeed, bears comparison with certain earlier Man of Sorrows images. As we have seen, Michelangelo was fascinated with the figure of the Man of Sorrows throughout his life and perceived it as a vital link to the tradition of the Christian cult image. Like Michelangelo's self-portrait, Meister Francke's *Man of Sorrows* (Figure 97) is thin and fragile, a pathetic victim of physical mortification. It is difficult to imagine a starker contrast to Michelangelo's normative style of heroic figures than the invertebrate form of this weak and vulnerable Christ. Michelangelo's self-portrait, however, is the obvious, glaring exception.

But there is a crucial difference even between Michelangelo's self-portrait and Meister Francke's *Man of Sorrows.* One affirms and the other denies. One belongs to tradition and the other howls over the loss of tradition. Meister Francke's *Man of Sorrows* is pathetic but also beautiful and triumphant. We see his wounded, mortal flesh already clothed with the new, pristine skin of divinity, figured as a white mantle. Here Christ's suffering is paradoxically the source of his efficacy, and he himself displays his wounds, which are the guarantors of his redemptive virtue. In Michelangelo's work, the paradoxical unity of the Christian cult image is lost: We have, in the rest of the fresco, beautiful figures that contemporaries deemed to be of dubious Christian relevance, and, in the self-portrait, a Christian and penitential gesture that takes the form of the wretched abnegation of all beauty and artistry. In contrast to the careful contours of the other figures, this figure is made up of violent, slashing, formless strokes that clearly leave the mark of the brush: It is, paradoxically, an act of iconoclasm assuming figural form.[33]

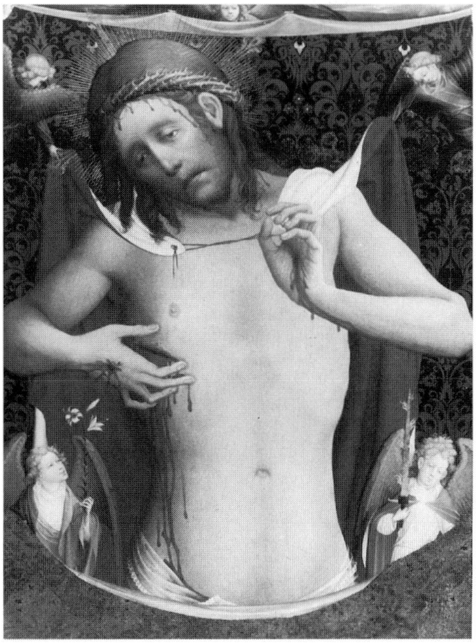

97. Meister Francke, *Man of Sorrows.* Kunsthalle, Hamburg, Germany.

Embedded in the triumphant claims of the work as a whole, therefore, is a brooding admission of failure. In the abject self-portrait we have a moment of ironic admission, an acknowledgment that perhaps Aretino (and other like-minded critics) would be right to condemn his work, that in the end real piety might indeed mean abandoning high artistic ambition. It was a theme that was to crop up quite regularly in Michelangelo's late poems, most famously, perhaps, in one written in the 1550s:

Onde l'affettüosa fantasia
che l'arte mi fece idol e monarca
conosco or ben com'era d'error carca
e quel c'a mal suo grado ogn'uom desia.

[So the affectionate fantasy
that made art an idol and sovereign to me
I now clearly see was laden with error,
like all things men want in spite of their best interests.][34]

Whether or not the *Pietà* for Vittoria Colonna (see Figure 93) was made before the *Last Judgment* was fully completed (the conventional date of 1540–42 would put it just at the end of work on the fresco), it can be understood as an effort to respond to some of these conflicts. It was a stripped down, less hubristic effort to salvage the union between aesthetic and religious ideals. Rather than attempting to join modern aesthetic ideals with a tradition of monumental public art, the *Pietà* for Vittoria Colonna worked more comfortably within a new, more private category – the presentation drawing – that was in line with contemporary developments both in religious and aesthetic attitudes. Michelangelo had initially used the presentation drawing for the exploration of sometimes obscure, largely pagan subjects, often with strongly erotic associations. In the Colonna *Pietà* he attempted to make this most modern of artistic arenas the site of a new kind of religious image, to forge a new link between artistic and divine *grazia* – "a difficult thing to do . . . well, and with dignity," as della Torre said. The old cult image was thus in a sense preserved, but in a rarefied and attenuated form, one that offered an introversion of the image's traditional public function and address. The Man of Sorrows, one of the most heavily indulgenced cult images of the Middle Ages, was reinvented as a work of art and thus accommodated to the tastes and religious inclinations of Vittoria Colonna and her circle. The drawing can be understood, in this sense, as a tradition of religious art reduced to a purified and refined form. It is as if only in this vestigial form – where the monochrome and inherent economy of drawing constitute an ascetic virtue – could the two-dimensional image be "safe" from the secularizing/paganizing tendencies of modern painting and could continue to serve as a viable purveyor of religious values.[35]

This, too, was a dead end. The conception of the drawing as a work of art was inherited by the modern collector, not the religious reformer. The artistic claims that Michelangelo and Colonna upheld and made into a model for their conception of faith – the idea that art is made "liberally" and not plied as a trade, that it results from a process of free invention, that it presents as yet unrealized ideas and thus makes special hermeneutic demands on its viewer – these were to become the basis of a secular conception of art whose primary locus was to be the cabinet and the picture gallery. Likewise, the notion of art as a gift, so far from providing the basis for a reformation and preservation of religious ideals, became the basis for an even more radical marketing of art as a commodity: The claim of the art work's autonomy and disinterestedness was in effect the cornerstone of a truly free art market, one no longer grounded in the premodern system of art made on commission. The idea that this conception of art could form the basis of a "reformed" religious image was a short-lived dream.

After the retreat from panel painting to fresco, and from painting to drawing, in the final phase of Michelangelo's engagement with the theme of the Man of Sorrows we see a full retreat into sculpture. If the economy of drawing was a means of chastening the religious image, the structural laws of marble statuary provided an even stronger built-in ascetic principle. The turn to sculpture was also an archaizing gesture, since it represented a return to a mode of cult statuary that historically preceded the ascendancy of easel painting. According to Vasari, Lorenzo de' Medici's regret over the decline of sculpture in relation to painting was his main motivation in establishing his sculpture garden/academy.[36] If this is true, then Michelangelo's very training in the San Marco garden unfolded within an archaizing cultural program designed to revive sculpture's former dominance. By the end of his life Michelangelo associated this former dominance explicitly with an earlier period of a purer and more pious Christian art. Free-standing marble statuary had become for him the last outpost of the Christian image.

The idea that sculpture has more "integrity," in every sense of the word, and the idea that it bears a stronger relationship to tradition were leitmotifs of the debate on the comparison of the arts, known as the *paragone,* a debate to which Michelangelo contributed in his response to the forum on the subject organized by Benedetto Varchi in 1547. Michelangelo's late sculptures demand that we set the *paragone* dispute, which has most often been treated as an aesthetic and academic question, into the wider context of the concerns over reform that mark the period as a whole – an approach that seems especially justified given the fact that Benedetto Varchi himself was associated with "spiritual" circles at this time.[37] The characteristics routinely attributed to sculpture – that it lasts longer, that it has greater public utility, that it is ontologically more "grounded," even that it requires harder work – all have special resonance in the midst of the debates surrounding religious art at this time.

Perhaps the most-often repeated argument in favor of sculpture was that it stands the test of time better than painting. Whereas few paintings survive from antiquity, many works of sculpture have come down through history.

This is an inherent virtue but also a question of utility, for, in Baldassare Castiglione's words, "being made to preserve memory, sculptures fulfill this function better than painting."[38] The relation between endurance and utility also comes up in the letter of Agnolo Bronzino to Varchi, where he reports the sculptors' argument that sculpture is a magnificent adornment for cities, "because it serves to make colossi and statues . . . that honor illustrious men, and adorn the land." Sculptures also play an architectural function, "since one can use its figures for architectural support instead of columns or corbels, or for water spouts on fountains, for tombs, or for an infinite number of other things one comes across all the time." With painting, on the other hand, "one can only make fictitious things of no utility other than pleasure."[39] Sculpture's durability, on the other hand, gives it a civic function and makes it an appropriate ornament for enduring institutions, such as buildings and tombs.

The point about sculpture's utility is in fact connected to the more abstract point, also often repeated, concerning sculpture's objecthood. Leonardo da Vinci was the first clearly to articulate the point that painting includes more "competences" than sculpture. Where nature "aids" the work of the sculptor, supplying the conditions of lighting and color, painters must supply these and all other conditions, such as viewing distance, through their own artifice.[40] Bronzino followed Leonardo in rejecting the sculptor's claim to a more faithful imitation of nature: Because they "take over the object that was already made three-dimensional" their achievement is attributable to nature, whereas painters' achievements are due entirely to their art.[41] By the same token, however, sculpture's existence in the world makes it more suitable to public functions: Completed by the world around it, it is part of the city fabric and participates in the arena of public life.

The greater self-sufficiency and universality of painting, which "includes within itself all things," was instead an inducement to private delectation. This was a favorite theme of the defenders of painting, and is developed in the sections devoted to the *paragone* in Castiglione's *Courtier* as well as in Paolo Pino's *Dialogue on Painting*.[42] And yet, as David Summers has stressed, these Renaissance celebrations in fact overturned a long-standing tradition, reaching back through Alain de Lille, Isidore of Seville, and St. Augustine to Plato, that associated the fictitious nature of painting with sophistry and deceptiveness. The licence of the painter, which produces delectation in the viewer, is an unreliable guide to truth and is downright dangerous in the illustration of scripture.[43] Bronzino himself declared, as we saw above, that painters "can only make fictitious things of no utility other than pleasure." The association of painting with pleasure bears a relation to another major *paragone* theme, also first developed at length by Leonardo, that compares the hard labor of sculpture with the ease of painting. Leonardo famously contrasted the dirty, sweaty sculptor with the well-dressed, gentlemanly painter "at great ease in front of his work," a contrast that remained standard even in comparisons that were less hostile to sculpture.[44]

For many Renaissance commentators all of this was to the greater glory of painting, but in a Counter-Reformation climate it was also cause for suspicion. Did not Aretino make the point – to be frequently repeated in subsequent decades – that Michelangelo had put art and beauty before religion in his *Last Judgment*? The theologian Giovanni Andrea Gilio wrote an entire treatise, published in 1564, devoted to exposing the breach between trends in modern painting and the purposes and traditions of religious art. He did not doubt that modern painters, following the example of Michelangelo, were pursuing the highest goals of art. He merely questioned whether the *"vaghezza dell'arte"* cultivated in his day was appropriate to the purposes of religious images. The "simple truth" of a wooden cross, he argued, is more conducive to religious devotion than the "richness and ornament, the nobility of the matter, and the excellence of the artist" that ask to be appreciated in a work of modern art.[45] His quite modern solution was to opt for a *"regolata mescolanza,"* a conscious and regulated compromise between the unreligious beauties of modern painting and the pious rudeness of earlier art. Such a reform of art, he realized, cannot be carried out without subjecting art to rules and controls, and he recognized that this would be a novelty in itself, for "we do not have any rule or law, except what the custom of painters (*la consuetudine de' pittori*) before Michelangelo has demonstrated."[46]

People with similar concerns could have different views about Michelangelo. Writing in 1571, the Florentine Francesco Bocchi criticized the excessive affectation of painters, whose works reveal *"troppa diligenza"* and *"i troppi isquisiti ornamenti."* Unlike Gilio, however, he found a great alternative in the works of Michelangelo, which are not "involved in ornaments" but rather display "gravity of design, profound intelligence, and sage awareness [*gravità di disegno, profonda intelligenza, e savio avviso*]."[47] His primary counterexample to the decadence of modern art, however, was Donatello, on whose *St. George* he lavished the longest single-work analysis so far written by any art critic. There he found *"semplice ragione, senza ornamento"* as inevitable as Brunelleschi's "simple and natural" solution for the cupola of the Duomo, about which it is impossible to say whether one admires the strength or the beauty, because they are so inextricably conjoined. The criticism of contemporary painting was once again bound up with a distinctly retrospective sensibility, here combined with a developed appreciation of the enduring nature and public function of sculpture. Bocchi's concern was not with the reform of religious art per se – his concerns were primarily moral and civic – but his criticisms and his tastes were in line with a reform-minded sensibility. Given the implications of the *paragone* debate in the context of Counter-Reformation critiques of painting, it was but a short step to see in sculpture the path to a reformed religious art.

THE FLORENCE *PIETÀ* AND THE INTEGRITY OF SCULPTURE

So far from simply ignoring or rejecting the lessons of painting, the very project of the late sculptures was determined by an effort to address the challenges set by painting to sculpture. Henry Thode once made the observation that even the effect of the unfinished in the late sculptures, like the unclear outlines of the late drawings, showed a final opening of the plastic realm to the world of pictorial effects.[48] But it was above all the pictorial preoccupation with narrative that affected the nature of the late *Pietà*s. In the London *Entombment* Michelangelo had adapted some of the most sophisticated devices of pictorial storytelling to the demands of altar painting. It was precisely the elaboration of such devices that, in Italy, had spelled the victory of painting over sculpture on the Christian altar. The late *Pietà* sculptures, like the drawings studied in chapter 5, incorporate many of these ambitions: They were shaped and conceived by a continual and searching dialogue with the episodes of the Passion. In the drawings we saw Michelangelo intensively exploring the physical relationships "motivated" by the events of Christ's deposition, lamentation, and entombment and from these, attempting to draw a figural formula concentrated on the front-facing figure of Christ – an investigation whose theological motivations are clearly expressed in Vittoria Colonna's writings on the Passion. From the London *Entombment* (see Figure 6), or the highly narrative conception for the *Deposition* in the Haarlem drawing (see Figure 90), Michelangelo developed ideas for more condensed groups. The process tended, inevitably, to lead away from scenic narrative description, yielding, for example, the concentrated solution of the *Pietà* for Vittoria Colonna. The narrative composition, once surpassed, was left to his followers to study, copy, and develop. The Colonna *Pietà,* for example, had a more elaborate narrative cousin, preserved in a miniature by Giulio Clovio in the Pitti Gallery that was engraved by Diana Scultori.[49]

From the Florence *Pietà* (Figure 98) forward, these investigations became efforts to extract figural formulas that could, as it were, be submitted to the conditions of sculpture. It is as if for Michelangelo the laws of sculpture provided an inherent test of the image's efficacity and viability – a test of integrity in every sense. Sculpture stipulated the reduction of movement and pathos to an essential meaningful form. As Irving Lavin has pointed out, the Florence *Pietà* was to be the first multifigure group carved from a single stone and was thus conceived as a direct challenge to Pliny's claims for the *Laocoön.* The *Laocoön,* as Michelangelo knew, was in fact carved from various pieces, and in making good on the claim to integrity, Michelangelo's *Pietà* was to surpass the antique, providing a Christian response to the ideals of antique sculpture. The dramatic language of pathos formulas inherited from the antique and developed in Renaissance art was to be castigated, reduced to lasting form, given religious efficacity. In the end, the effort broke down under the strain: The Florence *Pietà* ended in a violent act of destruction, the Rondanini *Pietà* in a terminal process of consumption. For

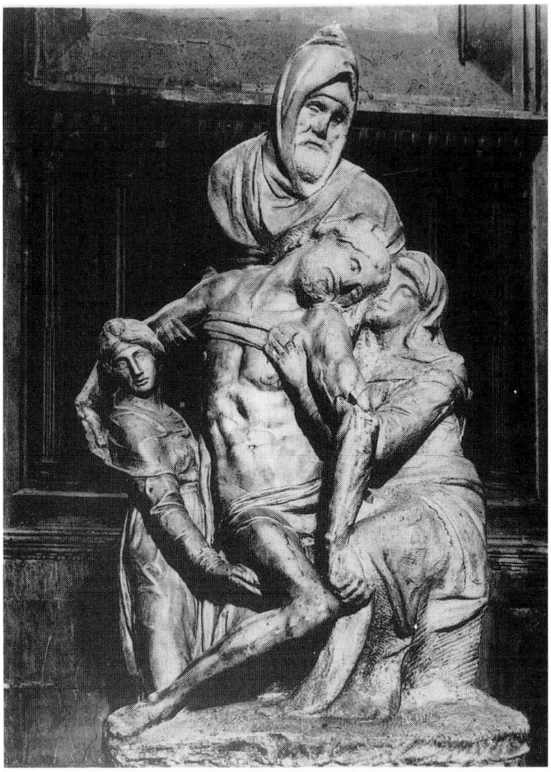

98. Michelangelo, *Pietà*. Marble. Museo del Opera del Duomo, Florence, Italy.

Henry Thode, this was not just a failure of Michelangelo's art but instead the swan song of Christian sculpture at the beginning of the modern age. "The art of Michelangelo," he said, "is the last act in the tragedy of Christian sculpture."[50] It is not my purpose in this study to pronounce objectively on epochal endings. I am more interested in showing that the sense of an ending itself shaped the conception and making of the late *Pietà*s.

To view them in this way is to acknowledge their strangeness, beginning with the fundamental irony that these are the most private of works carried out in the most public of media, monumental marble sculpture. These works occupy an even more private realm than the drawing for Colonna, whose function as a gift at least contained an interpersonal dimension. But whereas the personal address of the Colonna *Pietà* was suited to the nature and claims of the new category of the presentation drawing, here an even more private statement is made in the language of public art, and that extreme mismatching is the root cause of the conflict that critics have so often recognized in these works. This sense of conflict is not very profitably studied psychobiographically as an expression of Michelangelo's inner anxiety – not because he did not have any but because such an inquiry is a fruitless speculative enterprise. It is, however, possible to point to a structural, objective tension, a conflict between a work and its genre, that can be studied in historical terms.

The Florence *Pietà* (see Figure 98) was begun circa 1547–1548 and was, according to Vasari, intended for Michelangelo's tomb in Santa Maria Maggiore.[51] The conception is significantly more dynamic than that of the Colonna *Pietà,* made not long before. The strict symmetry of the latter is replaced by an oblique arrangement, articulated by a dramatic crossing of limbs. A somewhat perplexing sheet in Oxford, showing Christ being lowered to the ground with great effort by at least six figures (Figure 99), documents the transition (or return) to the more narrative conception.[52] It reveals that this shift involved a return, once again, to the Haarlem drawing of the *Deposition* (see Figure 90), produced roughly twenty years earlier. The Oxford sheet develops the two marginal sketches on the Haarlem sheet, themselves alternative solutions to the central composition: Christ's contorted pose on the Oxford sheet, especially the upper body, corresponds quite closely, in reverse, to that of the Christ sketched just to the right of the arm of the cross on the Haarlem sheet,[53] the lower part of the figure, in particular the motif of

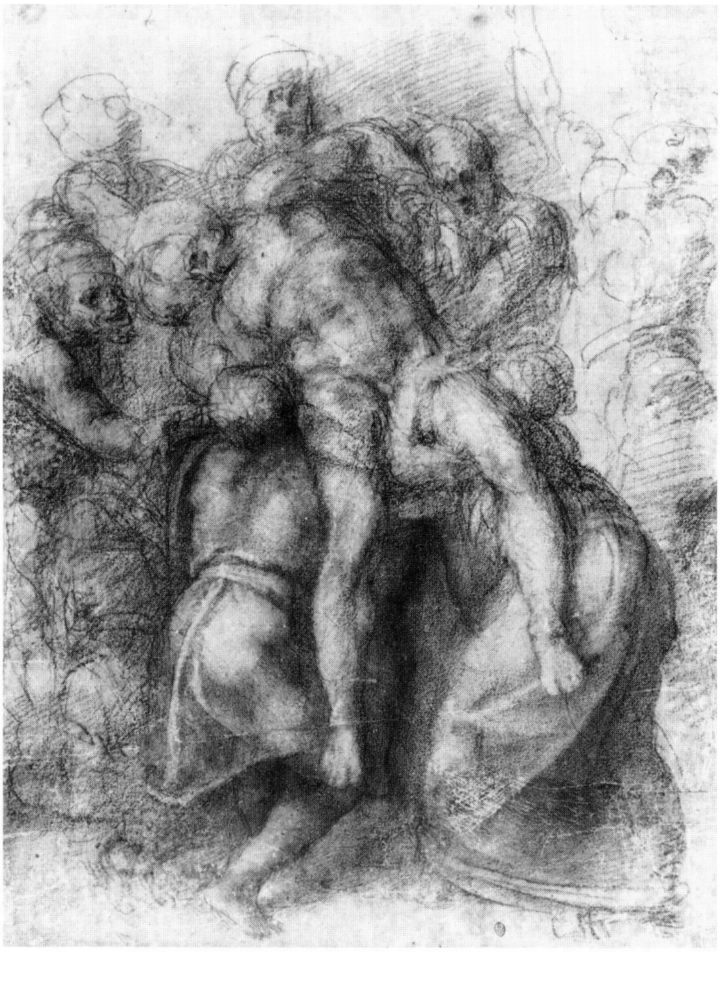

99. Michelangelo, *Deposition.* Drawing. Oxford, Ashmolean Museum.

the leg resting on the shoulder of the figure below, derives from the group sketched at the upper left of the Haarlem sheet.

I have argued elsewhere that the extreme scholarly uncertainty over the dating of the Oxford sheet (see Figure 99) – proposals range from the 1510s to the 1550s – derives in part from the fact that the drawing is physically a palimpsest, drawn not only in different techniques but at different times.[54] The central three figures, as Parker affirmed, have been worked over in a darker red chalk and with a technique of denser modeling. Robinson remarked that the execution is unequal, and Frey noted *"ein fremdartiges Element in der Behandlung."*[55] The parts of the drawing that were not worked over, the more lightly sketched marginal figures, show the drawing's original state. If one isolates those figures, it becomes clear that they are drawn in exactly the mode of the drawings made in the early 1530s in the wake of the Haarlem sheet (studied in chapter 5). They resemble in their frenetic energy above all the figures of the Vienna sheet (see Figure 92). If the Vienna and Louvre sheets (see Figure 91) discussed above developed the ground-based group around the dead Christ (derived originally from the group around the fainting Virgin in the Haarlem *Deposition,* Figure 90), this sheet explored the motifs of the deposition proper, bringing together precisely those sketches thrown off at the margins of the Haarlem sheet. The figures that have been worked over are, by contrast, in the figural style of the Pauline chapel frescoes of the 1540s. The drawing thus shows Michelangelo, in the aftermath of the Colonna *Pietà,* going back into his file of narrative drawings deriving from the Haarlem *Deposition*. This dramatic energy was then, once again, reduced to a sculptural formula in the Florence *Pietà.*

In the Oxford sheet (see Figure 99) Christ is still off the ground and thus requires the attentions of many figures. As in the Vienna sheet discussed earlier (see Figure 92), the figure of Christ appears animated in the contact with the figures, and the figures press against Christ with a passionate, even erotic energy that exceeds the merely mechanical act of lowering Christ from the cross. In strictly narrative terms it is in fact unclear what they are doing with the body, other than tenderly and passionately propping it into a quasi-standing posture – a posture not unlike that shown in the Vienna drawing (see Figure 92). Christ's right foot is about to touch ground and his upper body is being pushed into an upright posture. Again, the activity produced by the narrative situation is transformed into an enthusiastic and cultic participation, focused on preserving and celebrating the majesty of the dead Christ. In adapting this idea to a freestanding sculptural group in the Florence *Pietà* (see Figure 98), Michelangelo brought the figure to the ground and reduced the number of figures. In the process, the raging temper of the drawing has been modulated to a slow-burning intensity.

In the *Pietà* for Vittoria Colonna, we saw the twisted configuration of the Louvre sheet (see Figure 91) resolved into almost geometric regularity, and the passionate rhetoric of amorous and maternal love transformed into more abstract metaphors of fertility and birthing. I argued in the last chapter that

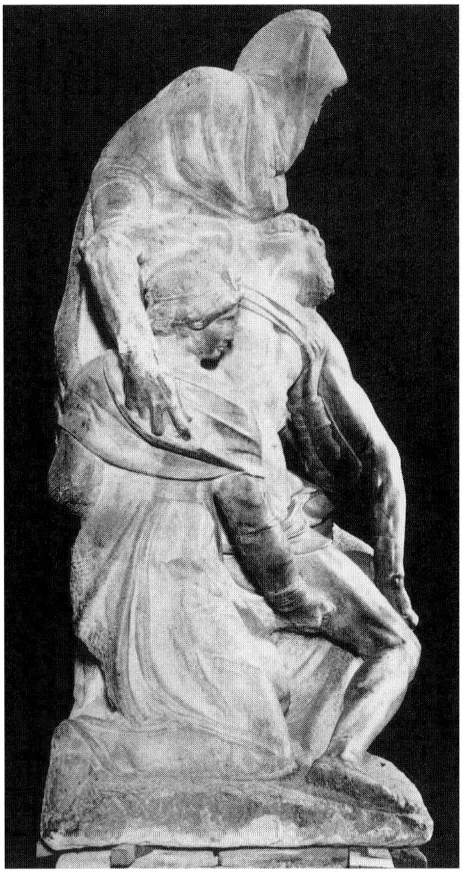

100. Michelangelo, *Pietà,* side view. Marble. Museo del Opera del Duomo, Florence, Italy.

these severe restrictions, together with the use of the monochrome and abbreviated medium of drawing, produced a chastened and reformed cult image in a highly modern form. Sculpture, however, came with its own inherent restrictions, and this meant that the restraints did not need to be self-imposed. Michelangelo could reintroduce the pathos formulas and then push them to the very limits that sculpture would organically allow. Rather than placing Christ entirely between the knees of the Virgin, a strictly frontal orientation that recapitulates the conditions of the two-dimensional image, Michelangelo attempted a more dynamic and oblique conception that articulates the possibilities of sculpture in the round.

In the Florence *Pietà* (Figure 98), the Virgin supports Christ's torso from behind and yet he is seated on her lap, and this means that Christ's shoulders turn in one direction and his hips in the other – a helix formation continued in the zigzag of the right leg. The center line does not run down the valley in the middle of Christ's torso, as it does in the strictly frontal arrangement of the Colonna *Pietà,* but is instead a protruberance, a sharp ridge formed by the meeting of the two "edges" of the helix, the pronated left arm and the inward bent right knee. The twisted posture multiplies the points of contact with the Virgin, allowing Christ to sit on her lap and at the same time to join his head to hers. This is not merely a piece of formal virtuosity but rather an effort at semantic and theological enfoldment: The pose allows Christ to be both on her and next to her, both son and spouse. The two roles are expressed emblematically in the two legs: One falls between the Virgin's knees, and the other (now missing) was slung over the Virgin's thigh. Leo Steinberg has shown that the one position carries associations with birthing or "issuance" and the other with erotic love.[56]

To have both of these associations in one work reinforces the essential theological argument of the work, which is still grounded in the understanding of the Passion promoted by Vittoria Colonna: that it is through the intimate and animating contact of the dead body of Christ with his mourners, and above all with

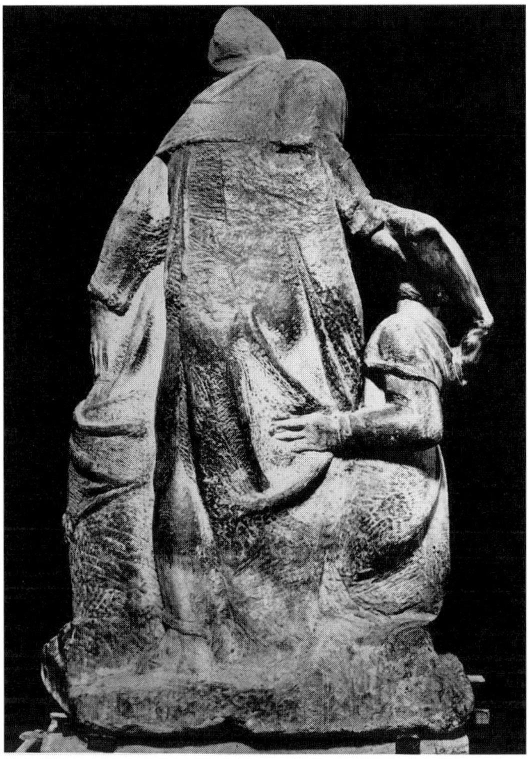

101. Michelangelo, *Pietà,* back view. Marble. Museo del Opera del Duomo, Florence, Italy.

the Virgin, that divine grace is transmitted to humankind. The gift of redemption made possible by Christ's incarnation reaches humankind through the passionate love released in his sacrifice. As we saw in Colonna's account, the figure most directly consumed in this passionate fire is the Virgin. Like Christ, she closes her eyes and, with an ecstatic expression on her face, joins her head to his. The "benefits" of this union, its transmission to larger humanity, are manifested on the other side of the group, where Christ semiwillfully embraces the figure of the Magdalene, the symbol of human love, as she looks out at us.[57]

The multisided communication of love has forced Christ's body into a contorted and splayed posture and, as a result, into a three-dimensional testing of the limits of the sculptural block. The view from the side (Figure 100) shows that the protruding arm and knee extend to the very front limit of the original marble block. Likewise the right arm and leg test the left edge, and the left leg originally met the right edge. The containing power of the block is, as it were, embodied in the figure of Nicodemus, who towers above and behind the figures. Seen from behind the figure is a sheer face of marble; there is no differentiating the figure and the monolithic mass of the stone (Figure 101). The figure, as it were, translates the material integrity of the block into the rhetoric of dramatic action: With one hand he holds Christ's right arm, the arm that embraces the Magdalene, and with the other he presses the Virgin against Christ, his entire massive form leaning forward in an effort to sustain and preserve their union. Nicodemus' role in the group is at once humble and privileged: He labors at one remove from the central action and yet he helps to consummate the ecstatic, grace-giving contact between Christ and the Virgin, and he aids in its communication to larger humanity by supporting Christ's embrace of the Magdalene.

As has long been recognized, the figure is a self-portrait, a natural identification given the legend that Nicodemus himself was a sculptor.[58] Other Renaissance sculptors had, for similar reasons, portrayed themselves as Nicodemus in their works.[59] But Michelangelo was doing more than applying his features to a patron Saint. The very work that this figure is doing in the group symbolizes the labor of the sculptor and embodies the material virtue of the stone. The mountainous figure of Nicodemus–Michelangelo physically holds the group together, epitomizing the efforts of the artist to craft and sustain a meaningful union among his figures – a union that, in Michelangelo's understanding of the subject, held the key to the mystery of Christian redemption. His work *in* the group, symbolizing his work *on* the group, is the expression of a piety that belongs specifically to the sculptor.

The intense rhetorical emphasis placed on the effort to hold the group together, of course, implies the looming threat of disintegration. Michelangelo often expressed frustration with the group and, at some point before the end of 1555, attacked it with a hammer. The struggle for integration, symbolized by Michelangelo's figure within the group, yielded to the destructive impulse of the hammer-wielding artist before the group. He seems to have approached it from in front, breaking the left arm into pieces and, presumably, also the now-missing left leg. He then also broke the right arm. Vasari said that Michelangelo intended to destroy the group entirely but was stopped by his servant Antonio del Franzese, who asked Michelangelo to give it to him as it was and to allow it be repaired and finished by Tiberio Calcagni.[60] That the now-missing leg was a prime source of difficulty is suggested by Vasari's anecdote of a nocturnal visit before 1553 to Michelangelo's studio:

At one o'clock one night Vasari was sent by Julius III to Michelangelo's house for a drawing. He found the master engaged upon the marble Pietà which he broke. Recognizing the knock, Michelangelo rose from his work and took a lantern. When Vasari had explained his errand, he sent Urbino upstairs for the design and began to speak of other things. Vasari's eyes wandered to a leg of Christ on which he was working and attempting to alter, and in order that Vasari might not see it he let the lantern fall, and so they were in the dark.61

Even if Michelangelo had not broken the group, we would know from Vasari's account that the leg caused particular difficulty. And this difficulty was, as I have attempted to show, part of the larger difficulty of reinterpreting the Man of Sorrows tradition by incorporating new motifs of physical and amorous contact – that is, by introducing the pathos formulas inherited from the antique and developed in Renaissance art. In a very straightforward sense, the frontal orientation of the Man of Sorrows was in inherent conflict with the bodily contact demanded by these gestures of "passionate" love. The frontal orientation mattered a great deal to him, as is evident from his persistent efforts to preserve it in the face of the enormous awkwardness and difficulty it caused him. The twisted, splayed, and yet beautiful figure of Christ in the Florence *Pietà* – testing and prodding the very limits of the block – was Michelangelo's virtuosic and ultimately frustrated effort to resolve the problem. The work was intended for his own tomb and was clearly intended as a final testament to the unity of his art and his piety. But it was a unity strenuously achieved, and after eight years of struggling with it Michelangelo concluded that a crude iconoclasm was preferable to – and spiritually less dangerous than – a strained and artistically pretentious integration.

An alternative was simplification, as it were a modulated iconoclasm. Already while Michelangelo was working on the Florence *Pietà* he was exploring simpler, more strictly frontal solutions. The germ of the new conception is preserved in a famous sheet in Oxford, probably dating to the years 1552–53 (Figure 102).[62] In all of the sketches on this sheet, Michelangelo had abandoned the motif that had caused him such trouble up to this point: The frontally presented Christ in the lap or between the legs of the Virgin. Instead, we see once again a return to the fully upright posture, where Christ is supported by standing figures. Three of the sketches show Christ supported by a single figure and are related to the first version of the Rondanini *Pietà* in the Castello Sforzesco in Milan (see Figure 105). The large right arm and the legs on the present sculpture are remnants of this first version of the group.[63] The configuration is now very close to northern Man of Sorrows/Trinity images in the tradition of Robert Campin (see Figure 38), with the significant difference that in Campin Christ is supported by a male figure and in Michelangelo he is supported by a female figure. Such an arrangement challenged a rational understanding of bodily support.

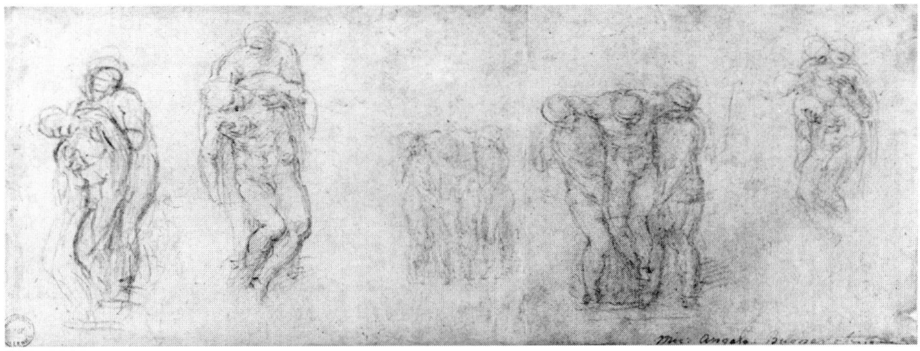

102. Michelangelo, *Studies for a Pietà sculpture.* Drawing. Ashmolean Museum, Oxford, England.

The other two drawings are, as it were, a more reasonable alternative to this conception, showing Christ carried by two male figures to either side. This idea evidently held Michelangelo's attention, as he elaborated it in several studies, some of which are known only through copies. One copy, formerly in the Gathorne–Hardy collection, contains the essential carrying conception of the three-figure groups on the Oxford sheet and develops them in the direction of an entombment scene: It shows the figure of Christ supported at shoulder height and led forward by two figures who support him at the thighs (see Figure 103).[64] The important novelty of the "two-carrier" conception is that the Virgin is no longer part of the group, and there is, accordingly, a reduction in the expression of passionate love. The investigation of the motif of carrying leads to a composition remarkably close to that of the London *Entombment* of fifty years earlier (see Figure 6), where the Virgin was placed at some distance from the body.[65] As in the London painting, Christ's feet graze the ground, thus alluding to a paradoxical self-supporting efficacy within the dead body. But if in the London painting Michelangelo proposed the novel conception of Christ's being carried away from the viewer into the picture, here the figures are shown proceeding forward, as if out of the block. The "presentation" gesture of the Magdalene in the Florence *Pietà* has now become a more purposeful element in a narrative of conveyance, possibly now understood as a carrying of Christ *toward* the Virgin after the deposition. In

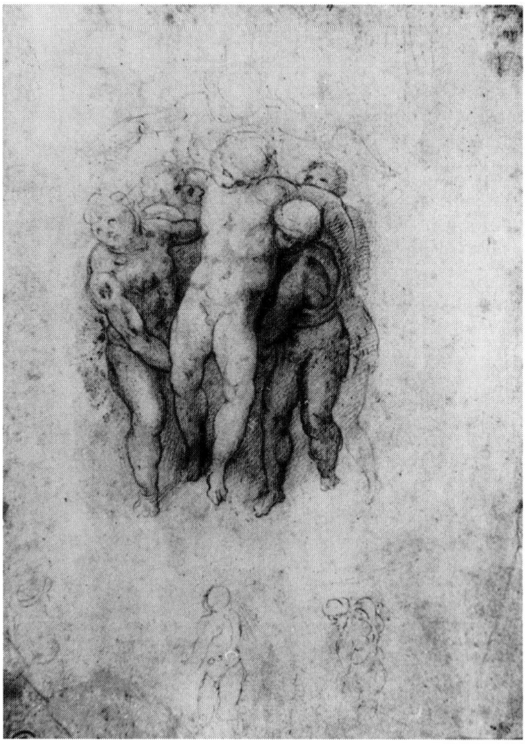

103. Copy after Michelangelo, *The Carrying of Christ to the Tomb.* Drawing. Formerly Gathorne-Hardy Collection.

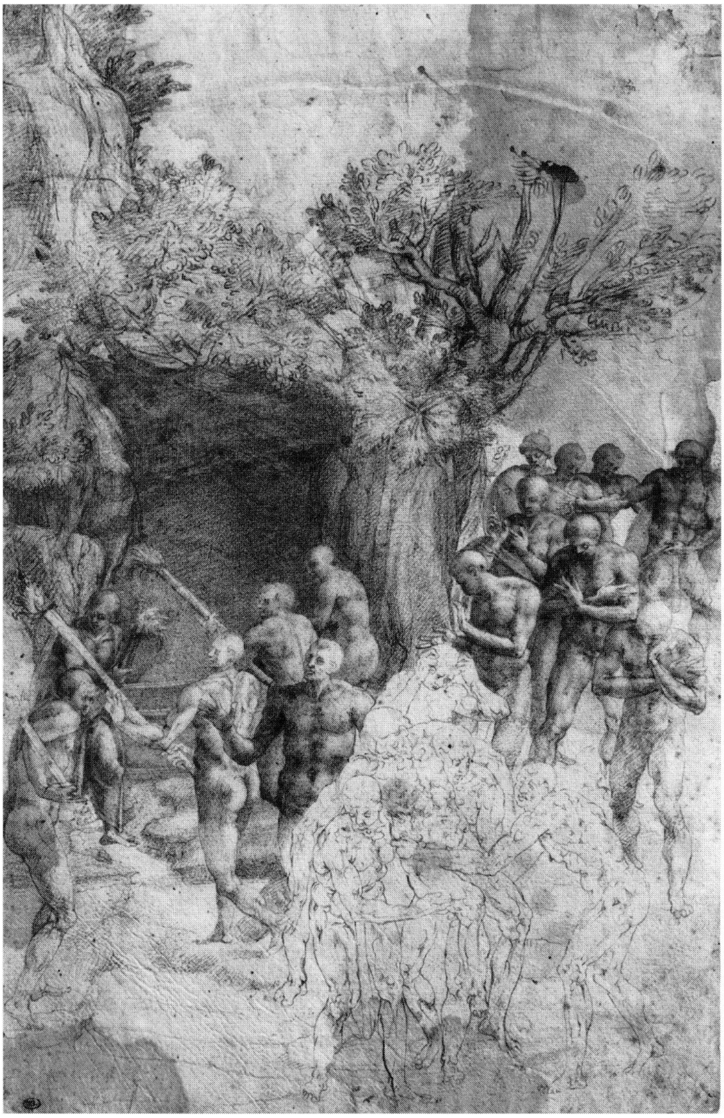

104. Giulio Clovio, *The Carrying of Christ to the Tomb.* Drawing. Louvre, Paris, France. © Réunion des Musées Nationaux.

either case, the relation between the dead Christ and the viewer is once again made a part of the subject and supplants the immediate physical contact between Christ and the Virgin.

A roughly contemporary Michelangelesque drawing in the Louvre (Figure 104), recently attributed to Giulio Clovio, adapted the conception explored in these studies once again in the direction of a more elaborate "pictorial" representation of the Entombment scene.[66] Yet another narrative "spinoff" elaborated by a pupil from a conception explored by Michelangelo on the way to a *Pietà* composition,[67] the drawing clinches the connection between these "carrying" studies and the ideas explored in

Michelangelo's early London panel. Indeed, in expanding the conception back into a fully scenic narrative, the drawing reverses the forward-striding direction of the "carrying" studies into a backward movement towards a tomb depicted in the distance – that is, it returns full circle to the conception of the London *Entombment*.[68]

THE SENSE OF AN ENDING

This return speaks of a consistent process of investigation over a fifty-year period. From the London *Entombment* through these late studies, Michelangelo had experimented with every stage between crucifixion and entombment in an effort to give expression to the mystery of Christ's sacrifice within the compass of "earthly" historical conditions and "natural" bodily relations. Michelangelo's experiments continually put him at a crossroads, and his twisted solutions were his efforts to negotiate it. Throughout this book I have argued that the front-facing figure of Christ, and the motif of frontal orientation generally, served as a link to a Christian tradition of cult imagery. This link was not merely formal but inherently functional, for the frontality of the image articulated and effectuated the relation between image and believer, between sacred history and ritual observance, a relation underwritten by an enduring socioreligious consensus. To give oneself over entirely to the virtuosic exploration of expressive gesture would be to lose contact with this tradition, whereas abandoning that figural language altogether would be to fall into wholesale archaism and thus to abandon contemporary relevance. We have seen several instances of Michelangelo's acute sense of decorum in applying an antique-inspired figural language in a Christian context, a tact that matches that of the most sensitive humanist stylists of the period. Michelangelo attempted, over and over again, to find in the animating physical contact between the dead body of Christ and his mourners a new path into the theological significance traditionally embodied in the traditional Man of Sorrows image. After several earlier efforts in painting and drawing, sculpture became for Michelangelo the privileged arena of this enterprise, and the ultimate test of its feasibility.

This lifelong project was abandoned in the second version of the Rondanini *Pietà,* which was probably begun shortly after 1560 (Figure 105).[69] The state in which Michelangelo left the block emphasizes the radical nature of the rupture: The powerfully sculpted right arm of the first version stands juxtaposed to the withered form of the new Christ. The arm is no longer necessary to the block and could easily have been removed – work on the new group would certainly have been made easier as a result – but Michelangelo chose to keep it there, standing free in the air and connected to the block by a thin bridge of marble. For Dagobert Frey, this was a form of *vanitas,* left there by Michelangelo to remind himself of what he had left behind.[70] Without speculating about the artist's intentions, it is certainly true that having the old arm there could only emphasize the contrast between the old and the new conception.

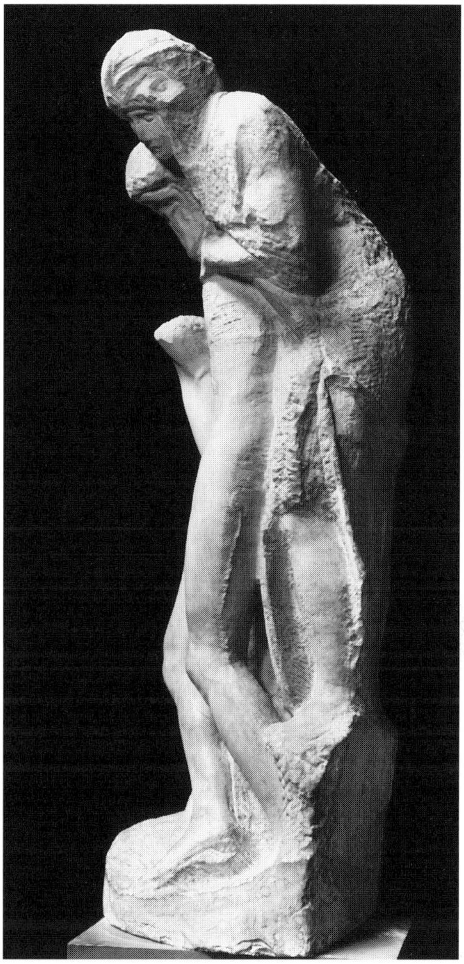

105. Michelangelo, *Rondanini Pietà.* Marble. Castello Sforzesco, Milan, Italy. Alinari/Art Resource, NY.

The contrast is not simply the result of an effort to conceive the theme afresh. The second version was almost passively determined by what was left of the block, and this in itself was a different approach to sculptural conception. The thin, arching piece of stone that remained after the elimination of the first group allowed no more room for the pathos formulas of hanging heads and intertwined limbs "motivated" by the narrative of support and carrying. Michelangelo knew this. In deciding to continue with what was left of the block, he effectively renounced the rhetoric of physical movement upon which his art had hitherto been based. The resulting union between Christ and the Virgin is not the product of dramatic gesture but is imposed on them by the conditions of the sculpture. It transcends the laws of physical weight and support, and even of human drama. The figure of Christ is literally sculpted out of the figure of the Virgin: His head, carved out of her shoulder, is thus joined to her chin; his arms, carved out of her body, are pressed against her hips and thighs. The Virgin no longer actively supports him – for example from under the arm, as in the first version – but simply presses his shoulder against her chest.

At first her head, and to a lesser degree that of Christ, were turned upward. This last vestige of a dramatic conception then disappeared in the very final state, which shows them both looking down. The passionate gestures of struggle and desire are gone, the laws of physical support are overcome, and the figures stand there, one pressed against the other. The result is something that has always reminded critics of Romanesque sculpture. But this is not a mere instance of archaizing quotation. It resulted from the whittling away of the stone, as if the stripping away of Renaissance gestural language was also a form of archeological digging, a means of excavating an earlier conception of sculpture.

Throughout his career, Michelangelo's works had been forged on the basis of a negotiation with the laws that here are finally suspended. He had made it his life's work to make the expressive resources of figural art a carrier of "figural" theological meaning. He reformulated Christian mysteries within a conception of figural movement and expression inherited from the antique and developed in Renaissance art, a conception of art whose cultural implications were most eloquently described by Aby Warburg. This effort of reconciliation, which finds parallels in the writings of contemporary humanists, is clearly at work in the London *Entombment,* as it is in his later revisions of the theme of the *Pietà*. It was a tortuous task that often involved an extreme warping of that figural language, and at times even the incorporation of pre-Renaissance, medieval forms, or elements of the art of the north. Here the effort itself reaches an end. As Wilhelm Worringer put it, the greatest exponent of Renaissance art was the one most significantly to come up against its limitations, and it is this encounter that constitutes, at a metathematic level, the "tragedy" of the Rondanini *Pietà*.[71]

Michelangelo's lifelong preoccupation with the theme of the *Pietà,* and specifically with the cult image tradition of the *imago pietatis,* constitutes a sustained meditation on the fate of the religious image at the beginning of the modern era. It reveals Michelangelo's efforts to put a humanist conception of art in the service of the traditional functions of religious images, and in the process to reinterpret and reform those traditional functions. It is one revealing example of the way that humanist culture and reform concerns informed historical attitudes in sixteenth-century Italy. It also casts a sharp light on some of the period's central cultural conflicts. Michelangelo's last work is notable for acknowledging that these conflicts admitted of no solution. In its unfinished state, surrounded by the ruins of the earlier conception, it stands, indeed, as no more than an acknowledgment.

As we have seen, there were those in the sixteenth century who saw a relationship between unfinished works and archaic works. The crude and rough images of the earliest times, it was believed, were slowly brought to refinement by history, just as the artist brings a sketch (*abbozzo*) to perfection in the finished work.[72] When Vittoria Colonna looked at a "St. Luke" Madonna, she saw a work without finish, a work that stopped at the basic outlines and was as yet innocent of the refinements of color and shade that were to come in later times. The remnant of a process of artistic stripping, the Rondanini *Pietà* stages a reversal of history's refining process, rendering moot the question of whether it was meant to be finished. The work would have an unfinished quality – the quality of something stripped down, something that is both a kernel and a vestige – whether or not it had been brought to technical completion. The Rondanini *Pietà* abandons the idea of the image as complete work and instead strives for Christian significance in a slow iconoclasm that is at once a form of historical meditation. Stripping away the present without restoring the past, it does not effectuate reform so much as it stages the predicament of reform. It offers the figmentary result of the present's digging, marked by the uncanny fragmentariness that past things have in the eyes of the present. It engages an unending effort of recovery that is also a path to historical self-awareness. Dismantling the image, it subsumes Christian piety in the art historical imagination.

Notes

INTRODUCTION: MICHELANGELO'S WORK AS AN ART HISTORIAN

1 Vasari, VI, 411.

2 Vasari, VI, 11, Condivi, 1911, 12. On the relationship between Poliziano and Michelangelo, with reference to Michelangelo's early imitations, see Summers, 1981, 242–9. See also Giovanni Agosti's entry on Michelangelo's *Battle of the Centaurs* in Agosti and Farinella, 1987, 25–7. On Poliziano's philological methods, see Anthony Grafton, *Defenders of the Text: The Traditions of Scholarship in an Age of Science, 1450–1800,* Cambridge, MA: Harvard University Press, 1991, 47–75. On the extension of Poliziano's philological interests to the field of artistic monuments, see Michael Koortbojian, "Poliziano's Role in the History of Antiquarianism and the Rise of Archeological Methods," in *Poliziano nel suo Tempo,* ed. L. Secchi Tarugi, Florence: Cesati, 1996, 265–73.

3 Vasari, VI, 8–9. See also Condivi, 1911, 8.

4 Cennini, 1960, sec. 1, part 17, 15.

5 Kris and Kurz, 1970, 97–98.

6 Anthony Grafton, *Forgers and Critics: Creativity and Duplicity in Western Scholarship,* Princeton: Princeton University Press, 1990.

7 The drawing after Giotto, Paris, Louve, 706*r.*, Corpus 3*r.*, pen and ink on paper. The drawing after Masaccio, Munich, Graphische Sammlung, 2191, Corpus 4*r.*, pen and ink on paper.

8 See Tolnay, 1947, 65–6 and 176–8; Wilde, 1978, 22–3; and Hirst, 1988, 59.

9 Berenson, 1938, I, 186.

10 The drawing is reproduced in Tolnay, 1947, pl. 70.

11 See, for example, Paul F. Gehl, *A Moral Art: Grammar, Society, and Culture in Trecento Florence,* Ithaca, NY: Cornell University Press, 1993.

12 Roger Ascham, *The Schoolmaster* (1570), ed. Lawrence V. Ryan, Ithaca, NY: Cornell University Press, 1967, 119.

13 Nelson Goodman, "Art and Authenticity," in *The Forger's Art,* ed. Denis Dutton, Berkeley: University of California Press, 1983, 93–114. This is not to disregard the

important role that the physical and visual aspects of texts have played in processes of textual imitation and interpretation, a subject that has received much attention in recent times. See, among many other studies, John Sparrow, *Visible Words: A Study of Inscriptions in and as Books and Works of Art,* Cambridge: Cambridge University Press, 1969; Armando Petrucci, "La concezione cristiana del libro," *Studi Medievali,* 3rd ser., 14, 1973, 961–84, and "Aspetti simbolici delle testimonianze scritte," in *Simboli e simbologia nell'alto medioevo,* Spoleto: Centro italiano di studi sull'alto medioevo, 1976, 813–44, both of which appear in English in idem, *Writers and Readers in Medieval Italy: Studies in the History of Written Culture,* ed. and trans. Charles M. Radding, New Haven: Yale University Press, 1995, chs. 2 and 6, respectively; Linda Nix, "Manuscript Layout and Re-Production of the Text in Anglo-Saxon England: A Preliminary Examination," *Gazette du livre médiéval,* 25, 1994, 17–23; Paul Saenger, "Word Separation and its Implications for Manuscript Production," in *Die Rationalisierung der Buchherstellung im Mittelalter und in der frühen Neuzeit,* eds. Peter Ruch and Martin Boghardt, Marburg an der Lahn: Institut für Historische Hilfswissenschaften, 1994, 41–50, and, more broadly, idem, *Space between Words: The Origins of Silent Reading,* Stanford, CA: Stanford University Press, 1997; and Christopher Wood, "Layout, Lettering, and Illustration in the Earliest Archeological Publications," *Word and Image,* forthcoming.

14 We encounter an awareness of the same historical divide in other areas of Michelangelo's youthful work. The tomb/altar of St. Dominic in Bologna, which was begun in the late thirteenth century and received additions in the fifteenth century, is virtually a laboratory for Michelangelo's response to the art of the past. In the two saints above, the nineteen-year-old Michelangelo was clearly vying with his immediate predecessor on the tomb, Niccolò dell'Arca, as well as with his recent predecessor in Bologna, Jacopo della Quercia, whereas in the angel below Michelangelo adopted an archaizing mode, in imitation of the original work on the tomb, which then as now was attributed to the late thirteenth-century sculptor Nicola Pisano. According to Alison Luchs, "Michelangelo's Bologna Angel: 'Counterfeiting' the Tuscan Duecento," *Burlington Magazine,* CXX, 1978, 222–5, Michelangelo's angel was the result of a deliberate effort to counterfeit the earlier style by imitating not only physiognomic idiosyncracies but also the generally rounded and abstract appearance of the forms, which require an elaborate technique of finishing. As noted by Luchs, the distinction in style between angel and saints had been observed by Tolnay, 1947, 141 (who dubiously took it as grounds for a slightly earlier dating of the angel) and Frederick Hartt, *Michelangelo: The Complete Sculpture,* New York: Abrams, 1968, 65. The documentary evidence indicates that the angel was originally meant to be placed directly next to the Pisano reliefs, leading Luchs to suggest that Michelangelo might have wanted this figure to be perceived as an integral part of the "original" work on the tomb. It is also possible that Michelangelo felt this archaizing mode, characterized by a generalization of features, was appropriate to the ethereal qualities of an angel, in contrast to the saints above. Whatever the explanation, the fact that Michelangelo adopted this mode for the angel but not for the saints reveals that his archaism was a matter of choice, that it was the result of reflection. It is little surprise that this considered appreciation of the art of the late thirteenth century should have occurred at the same time that the young artist was being introduced to the reading of Dante Alighieri by his Bolognese host, the *letterato* Giovan Francesco Aldovrandi.

15 Vasari's primary statements concerning his historical schema occur in his three prefaces. On Vasari's historicism, see Panofsky, 1970. See also C. A. Isermeyer, "Il Vasari e il restauro delle chiese medievali," in *Studi vasariani; atti del Convegno internazionale per il IV. centenario della prima edizione delle "Vite" del Vasari, Firenze, Palazzo Strozzi, 16–19 settembre 1950,* Florence: Sansoni, 1952, 228–36; Paul Frankl, *The Gothic: Literary Sources and Interpretations through Eight Centuries,* Princeton: Princeton University Press, 1960, 284–315; Giovanni Previtali, *La Fortuna dei Primitivi: Dal Vasari ai Neoclassici,* Turin: Einaudi, 1989, 3–21; and Antonio Thiery, "Il Medioevo nell' Introduzione e nel Proemio delle *Vite,*" in *Il Vasari Storiografo e Artista: Atti del Congresso Internazionale nel* IV *Centenario della Morte,* Florence: Istituto Nazionale di Studi sul Rinascimento, 1974, 351–81.

16 Vasari, V, 125–8.

17 Girolamo Mancini, "Vite d' Artisti di Giovanni Battista Gelli," *Archivio Storico Italiano,* 5th series, XVII, 1896, 41, 42.

18 Cennini, 1960, sec. 1, part 1, 2: "I was trained in this profession for twelve years by my master, Agnolo di Taddeo [Gaddi] of Florence; he learned his profession from Taddeo [Gaddi], his father; and his father was christened under Giotto, and was his follower for four-and-twenty years; and that Giotto changed the profession of painting from Greek back into Latin, and brought it up to date; and he had more finished craftsmanship than anyone has had since."

19 See Pierre Nora, "Between Memory and History: Les lieux de Mémoire," *Representations,* 26, 1989, 7–25.

20 My comments here are informed primarily by Felix Gilbert, *Machiavelli and Guicciardini: Politics and History in Sixteenth Century Florence* (1965), New York: Norton, 1984, esp. 153–200 and 236–70, and by Pocock, 1975, especially 3–113. On the *questione della lingua,* see Bruno Migliorini, *Storia della lingua italiana,* 2nd ed., Florence: Sansoni, 1960, ch. 8; Carlo Dionisotti, *Gli umanisti e il volgare fra Quattro e Cinquecento,* Florence: Le Monnier, 1968; Maurizio Vitale, *La questione della lingua,* 9th ed., Palermo: Palumbo, 1978; and the period texts collected in Pozzi, 1988. On developments in political thought in early sixteenth-century Florence and Venice, see Felix Gilbert, "Bernardo Rucellai and the Orti Oricellari: A Study on the Origins of Modern Political Thought," *Journal of the Warburg and Courtauld Institutes,* XII, 1949, 101–31; idem, "The Venetian Constitution in Florentine Political Thought," in *Florentine Studies,* ed. Nicolai Rubinstein, London: Faber and Faber, 1968, 463–500 (these two articles republished in idem, *History: Choice and Commitment,* Cambridge, MA: Belknap Press, 1977, chapters 9 and 8, respectively); Nicolai Rubinstein, "Politics and Constitution in Florence at the End of the Fifteenth Century," in *Italian Renaissance Studies,* ed. Ernest Fraser Jacob, London: Faber and Faber, 1960, 140–83; and now Patricia Fortini Brown, *Venice and Antiquity: the Venetian Sense of the Past,* New Haven, CT: Yale University Press, 1996. On the relation of political thought to reform concerns, see Felix Gilbert, "Religion and Politics in the Thought of Gasparo Contarini," in *Action and Conviction in Early Modern Europe,* ed. Theodore K. Rabb and Jerrold E. Seigel, Princeton: Princeton University Press, 1969, 90–116 (republished in idem, *History: choice and commitment,* supra, chap. 10). On reform concerns in the early sixteenth century, see Delio Cantimori, *Eretici italiani del Cinquecento* [1939] *e altri scritti,* ed. Adriano Prosperi, Turin: Einaudi, 1992; Hubert Jedin, *A History of the Council of Trent,* trans. Ernest Graf, St. Louis: Herder, 2 vols., 1957–61; Adriano Prosperi, *Tra Evangelismo e*

Controriforma: G.M. Giberti (1495–1543), Roma: Edizioni di storia e letteratura 1969; Carlo Ginzburg and Adriano Prosperi, *Giochi di pazienza: un seminario sul Beneficio di Cristo,* Turin: Einaudi, 1975; Elisabeth Gleason, "On the Nature of Sixteenth-Century Italian Evangelism: Scholarship, 1953–1978," *Sixteenth Century Journal,* 9, 1978, 3–25; Paolo Simoncelli, *Evangelismo italiano del Cinquecento: questione religiosa e nicodemismo politico,* Roma: Istituto storico italiano per l'età moderna e contemporanea, 1979; Barry Collett, *Italian Benedictine scholars and the Reformation: the Congregation of Santa Giustina of Padua,* Oxford [Oxfordshire]: Clarendon Press; New York: Oxford University Press, 1985; Elisabeth Gleason, "Italy in the Reformation," in *Reformation Europe: A Guide to Research II,* ed. William S. Maltby, St. Louis: Center for Reformation Research, 1992, idem, *Gasparo Contarini: Venice, Rome, and Reform,* Berkeley, Los Angeles: University of California Press, 1993; Massimo Firpo, *Riforma Protestante ed Eresie nell'Italia del Cinquecento: Un Profilo Storico,* Roma: Laterza, 1993. On the rise of art-history attitudes, see above all the sources cited in n. 15.

21 See Hans Georg Gadamer, *Truth and Method,* trans. Joel Weinsheimer and Donald G. Marshall, 2nd rev. ed., New York: Crossroad, 1992, especially 291–300: "The Hermeneutic Significance of Temporal Distance," and Hans Robert Jauss, "Literary History as a Challenge to Literary Theory," in Jauss, 1982, 3–45.

22 Vasari, III, 13–14;VI, 410. Panofsky, 1970, has provided an excellent analysis of these and other passages.

23 Pietro Bembo, *Prose della volgar lingua,* in *Prose e rime di Pietro Bembo,* ed. Carlo Dionisotti, Turin: Unione Tipografico, 1966, 131: *"Vedesi tuttavolta che il grande crescere della lingua a questi due, al Petrarca e al Boccaccio, solamente pervenne; da indi innanzi, non che passar più oltre, ma pure a questi termini giugnere ancora niuno s'è veduto. Il che, senza dubbio a vergogna del nostro secolo si trarrà."*

24 Gelli, 1549, 15–17.

25 Gelli, 1549, 34: "*Et maestro Simone da Siena, non ci e memoria alcuna, che fussi di tanta fama* [as Polycleitus, just discussed]; *& oltre a di questo, non si vede ancora molta arte, in quelle opere che si truovano a i tempi nostri di suo, che ne sono alcune in santo Spirito & quella facciata del capitol di Santa Maria Novella. . .*"

26 Giovanni della Casa, *Galateo ovvero de' Costumi,* in *Opere di Baldassare Castiglione, Giovanni della Casa, Benvenuto Cellini,* ed. Carlo Cordié, Milan: Ricciardi, 390.

27 Vasari,V, 152–3. On this and other restoration efforts in the early modern period, see Alessandro Conti, *Storia del restauro e della conservazione delle opere d'arte,* Milan: Electa, 1988, 7–60.

28 See Belting, 1981, 281–8.

29 *Religio Medici,* I, 28.

30 Vasari,VI, 410: *"Oltre che in questo secolo, il quale è nel colmo della perfezzione, non sarebbono nel grado che sono, se quelli non fussero prima stati tali e quel che furono innanzi a noi."*

31 Sheryl E. Reiss, "A Medieval Source for Michelangelo's Medici Madonna," *Zeitschrift für Kunstgeschichte,* L, 1987, 394–400. See also the discussion in chapter 3 of this book.

32 Condivi, 1911, 73, and see the full discussion in chapters 6 and 7 of this book. Michelangelo also used the Y-shaped cross in several late crucifixion drawings, which are among several examples of Michelangelo's archaism studied by Paul Joannides, "'Primitivism' in the Late Drawings of Michelangelo," in *Michelangelo Drawings,* eds. Craig Hugh Smyth and Ann Gilkerson, Washington, D.C.: National Gallery of Art, 1992, 145–61.

33 Hollanda, 1911, 274. Confirmation of Colonna's – and Michelangelo's – interest in archaic images has been presented by William Wallace, "Friends and Relics at San Silvestro in Capite, Rome," *Sixteenth Century Journal,* 30, 1999, 419–39, who has shown that the "testa di Cristo che Sua Gratia disse mostràmi" referred to in a letter from Michelangelo to Vittoria Colonna (*Carteggio,* IV, 122) was the miraculous "Veronica" cloth held at San Silvestro in Capite in Rome.

34 Colonna, 1982, S2 23, 188: *"Mentre che quanto dentro avea concetto/ dei misteri di Dio ne facea degno/ la vergin Luca oprava egli ogni ingegno/ per formar vero il bel divino aspetto,/ ma de l'immensa idea sì colmo il petto/ avea che, come un vaso d'acqua pregno/ che salir non può, fuor l'alto dissegno/ a poco a poco uscì manco e imperfetto./ In parte finse l'aer dolce e grave;/ quel vivo no l'mostrò, forse sdegnando/ de l'arte i gravi lumi e la fiera ombra;/ basta che l'modo umil, l'atto soave,/ a Dio rivolge, accende, move, e quando/ si mira il cor d'ogni altra nebbia sgombra."* Both the Hollanda passage and the Colonna poems have been discussed by Deswarte-Rosa, 1997, 363. The archaizing aesthetic became a programmatic concern of the Capuchins, which benefited from the early patronage of Colonna; on this, see Stuart Lingo, "The Capuchins and the Art of History: Retrospection and Reform of the Arts in Late Renaissance Italy," doctoral dissertation, Harvard University, 1998.

35 *A Reformation Debate: Karlstadt, Emser, and Eck on Sacred Images*, ed. and trans. Bryan D. Mahgrum and Giuseppe Scavizzi, Ottawa: Dovehouse Editions, 1991, 86.

36 Gilio, 1961, 110–11.

37 Gilio, 1961, 55–6.

38 On the associations between contrapposto and the rhetorical traditions of ornament and license, see David, Summers, "Contrapposto: Style and Meaning in Renaissane Art," *Art Bulletin,* 59, 1977, 336–61.

39 Gilio, 1961, 56: "*Se quelli* [the medieval artists] *erravano nel poco, e questi* [the modern artists] *errano nel molto; però sarebbe bene di quel poco e di questo molto fare una regolata mescolanza e cavare un mezzo che suplisse al difetto degli uni e degli altri, acciò l'opere abbino le debite proporzioni.*" Zeri, 1957, is still the most concerted effort to study stylistic trends in sixteenth-century Italy that are consonant with Gilio's ideas.

40 Vasari, III, 273–4. The passage is discussed at further length in chapter 7 of this book. Perhaps views similar to Vasari's were at the basis of Pius V's 1571 commission to Bartholomeus Spranger to make a copy of Fra Angelico's *Last Judgment* in San Marco. So much is suggested, at least, by the analysis of the episode offered by Zeri, 1957, 52. For Spranger's picture, see Michael Henning, *Die Tafelbilder Bartholomäus Sprangers (1540–1611): Höfische Malerei zwischen "Manierismus" und "Barock,"* Essen: Die Blaue Eule, 1987, 18–20, cat. A3. Spranger had been a guest in the house of Cardinal Alessandro Farnese, to whom Gilio dedicated his treatise.

41 See Gilbert, "The Venetian Constitution in Florentine Political Thought," and Rubinstein, "Politics and Constitution in Florence at the End of the Fifteenth Century," as in n. 20.

42 See Donald Weinstein, *Savonarola and Florence: Prophecy and Patriotism in the Renaissance,* Princeton: Princeton University Press, 1970. For Machiavelli, see *The Discourses on Livy,* ed. Bernard Crick, Harmondsworth: Penguin, 1983, I.12–13, 142–8, but see also II.2, 277–8, and III.1, 385–90. Machiavelli's quasi-anthropological approach to the study of religion has been studied by J. Samuel Preus, "Machiavelli's Functional Analysis of Religion: Context and Object," *Journal of the History of Ideas,* XL, 1979, 171–90. On the relation between the two, see J. H. Whitefield, "Savonarola and the Purpose of *The Prince,*" in *Discourses on*

Machiavelli, Cambridge: Heffer, 1969, 87–110 and Donald Weinstein, "Savonarola and Machiavelli," in *Studies on Machiavelli,* ed. Myron P. Gilmore, Florence: Sansoni, 1972, 253–64; and Pocock, 1975, 103–113. Certain affinities were recognized in the period: Ideas from both Machiavelli and Savonarola can be found, for example, in the writings of the Florentine republican, reformer, and exile Antonio Brucioli, whose *Dialoghi della morale filosofia* was published in 1526, see Delio Cantimori, "Rhetoric and Politics in Italian Humanism," *Journal of the Warburg Institute,* I, 1937/38, 83–102. Brucioli was a friend of Michelangelo's; a letter of 1529 from Giambattista della Palla to Michelangelo in Venice (*Carteggio,* III, 285) asked the artist to recommend him to Brucioli. Condivi, 1911, 67, informed us that, later, when the Venetian Signoria attempted to persuade Michelangelo to reside in their city on a permanent basis, their emissary to the artist in Rome was none other than Brucioli. The other major thinker close to Michelangelo who mingled Savonarolan and Machiavellian strains was of course Donato Giannotti.

43 The association of older art with strong outlines and later art with refined shading and coloring is an ancient one. A locus classicus is the account of the origin of painting in Pliny, *Historia Naturalis,* XXXV, 16. The idea is elaborated by Dionysius of Halicarnassus, *Isaeus,* 4, in *The Critical Essays,* trans. Stephen Usher, I, Cambridge, MA: Harvard University Press, 1974, 180–8: "There are some old paintings which are worked in simple colours without any subtle blending of tints but clear in outline, and thereby possessing charm; whereas the later paintings are less well-drawn but contain greater detail and a subtle interplay of light and shade, and are effective because of the many nuances of colour which they contain." This passage is cited and discussed by Philip Sohm, *Style in the Art Theory of Early Modern Italy,* forthcoming, Cambridge University Press, to whom I am grateful to him for giving me an advanced viewing of the manscript and for several discussions on these and related matters.

44 Vincenzo Borghini, *Modo di salvare il Bembo,* in Pozzi, 1988, 742: *". . .che le lingue ne' lor principii, come le altre opere della natura, sono imperfette, rozze, acerbe, ecc. e che il tempo le dirozza, matura e affinisce."*

45 Paolo Cortesi, *De Hominibus Doctis Dialogus,* ed. Maria Teresa Graziosi, Rome: Bonacci, 1973, 16.

46 Quoted and translated by Kenneth Gouwens, *Remembering the renaissance: Humanist narratives of the Sack of Rome,* Leiden: Brill, 1998, 132. On the association of reform concerns and historical thought during this period, see John O'Malley, "Historical Thought and the Reform Crisis of the Early Sixteenth Century," *Theological Studies,* 28, 1967, 531–48, esp. 537. (Reprinted in O'Malley, 1981 essay II.) See also Minnich, 1969, esp. 233*ff.* for the "basic orientation backward" found in the proposals for reform presented at the Fifth Lateran Council (1512–17).

47 See Gerhard B. Ladner, "The Concept of the Image in the Greek Fathers and the Byzantine Iconoclastic Controversy," *Dumbarton Oaks Papers,* 7, 1953, 1*ff.*

48 St. Augustine, Sermon XLIII, 3, 4, in *PL,* XXXVIII, 255: "We, therefore, . . . must after a fashion resculpt [the image] and reform it. But who would be able to do this, except if he were the artist who shaped it? We could deform the image of God in us, but we cannot reform it." Quoted in Gerhart B. Ladner, *The Idea of Reform: Its Impact on Christian Thought and Action in the Age of the Fathers,* Cambridge, MA: Harvard University Press, 1969, 194.

49 Girolamo Savonarola, *Prediche Italiane ai Fiorentini,* I, *Novembre-Dicembre del 1494,* ed. Francesco Cognasso, Perugia: La Nuova Italia, 1930, 108 (December 7, 1494):

"Dio li beati ed el cielo non invecchiano, che non sono sottoposti al tempo, ma le cose temporali e composte di elementi mancano ed invecchiano e però hanno bisogno di rinnovazione. Similmente la Chiesa di Dio che fu costrutta ed edificata della unione de' fedeli e delle loro buone opere operazioni, quando quelle mancano, si chiama invecchiata ed ha bisogno di rinnovarsi. . ." It is significant that he should have made this point at the same time that he was fervently advocating the building of the new Great Council Hall as a symbol of the reformed Christian republic.

50 Minnich, 1969, 170.

51 I have not had access to the original source for this information, G. della Corte, *Dell'istorie della città di Verona,* Verona, 1592, which is cited by Antonio Fasani, "Verona durante l'episcopato di Gian Matteo Giberti," in *Riforma Pretridentina della Diocesi di Verona: Visite pastorali del vescovo G. M. Giberti 1525–1542,* ed. Antonio Fasani, Vicenza: Istituto per le ricerche di storia sociale e di storia religiosa, 1989, CXXX.

52 Writing ca. 1420 Symeon, Bishop of Thessalonica declared: "What other innovation have they [the Latins] introduced contrary to the tradition of the Church? Whereas the holy icons have been piously established in honor of their divine prototypes and for their relative worship by the faithful . . . these men, who subvert everything, as has been said, often confect holy images in a different manner and one that is contrary to custom." The passage is excerpted and translated in Cyril Mango, *The Art of the Byzantine Empire, 312–1453,* Englewood Cliffs: Prentice-Hall, 1972, 253–4.

53 The early fifteenth-century reformer Giovanni Dominici, for example, couched his critique of images specifically in terms of an appeal to earlier religious art: he believed images that were "old, smoky" [*vecchie affumate*] to be closer to "the figures, or to the truth represented by those figures" than the highly ornamented pictures of his day. See Giovanni Dominici, *Regola del governo di cura familiare,* ed. Donato Salvi, Florence: Garinei, 1860, 133. For an English translation of the passage, see Gilbert, 1980, 146. Ernst Kitzinger, "The Cult of Images in the Age before Iconoclasm" (1954), in 1976, 91–156, argued that the eighth-century iconoclastic controversy resulted from the largely unregulated development of new kinds of images and image cults in the preceding centuries. For the intermittent critique of images in the medieval West, see William R. Jones, "Art and Christian Piety: Iconoclasm in Medieval Europe," in Joseph Gutmann, ed., *The Image and the Word: Confrontations in Judaism, Christianity and Islam,* Missoula, MT: Scholars Press for the American Academy of Religion and the Society of Biblical Literature, 1977, 75–105, and Horst Bredekamp, *Kunst als Medium sozialer Konflikte: Bilderkämpfe von der Spätantike bis zur Hussitenrevolution,* Frankfurt: Suhrkamp, 1975. The proliferation of cults and images in the later Middle Ages produced, inevitably, more varied criticism; see, for example, William R. Jones, "Lollards and Images: The Defence of Religious Art in Later Medieval England," *Journal of the History of Ideas,* 34, 1973, 27–50. The question of independence from theological authority in the making and use of images has been directly addressed by Berliner, 1945, and, more recently, by Belting, 1994, especially 11–19.

54 Belting, 1994, esp. chap. 20: "Art and Religion: The Crisis of the Image at the Beginning of the Modern Age."

55 Paul de Man, "Criticism and Crisis," in De Man, 1983, 3–19.

56 For the principal literature and provenance see Cecil Gould, *The Sixteenth Century Italian Schools,* London: National Gallery, 1975, 147. The oldest documentation of

the work's provenance, a Farnese inventory of 1649, was presented by Hirst, 1981a, 584.

57 These scholars' views are discussed over the course of this book. The principal arguments against the attribution were made by J. C. Robinson in *The Times,* September 1, 1881, and by Heinrich Wölfflin, *Die Jugendwerke des Michelangelo,* Munich, 1891, 82, and were answered in their time by Jean-Paul Richter, *Italian Art in the National Gallery,* London, 1883, 81–84, and Berenson, 1938, I, 179–82, respectively. Hirst, 1981a and Nagel, 1994, presented documents that suggest a link between the London panel and a documented altarpiece commission to Michelangelo for the church of Sant' Agostino in Rome in 1500. Many parts of Wölfflin's and Robinson's arguments have been recently revived by James Beck, "Is Michelangelo's Entombment really Michelangelo's?" *Gazette des Beaux-Arts,* ser. 6, 127, 1996, 181–98, and by Michael Daley, "How to make a Michelangelo," *Art-Review,* 46, 1994, 28–33, who remain opposed to the Michelangelo attribution. The most sustained treatment of the panel, and the strongest argument so far made in its favor, are offered by Dunkerton and Hirst, 1994.

58 Tolnay, 1975, 233.

CHAPTER ONE. TRANSPORT AND *TRANSITUS*

1 The best account of medieval figural thought is still Auerbach, 1984.

2 Savonarola, 1971, 75: *"[Dio] ha fatto scrivere quelle scritture e quelle istorie con quelli nomi e con quelli loci (come abbiamo dichiarato di sopra) non solo per dimostrare che così elle fussino, ma per significare altro. Non è così delle altre scritture: vedi Livio che non scrisse perché quella scrittura significassi cose future, ma solo le passate; non lo può fare ancora nessuno questo. . . . Però nessuna altra scrittura, se non la Sacra, ha allegoria: non la poesia, come dicono alcuni, perchè tre cose si richiedono alla allegoria: prima, la istoria; secondo, la significazione di altre cose; terzio, che quella istoria sia statta fatta per significare quello. Dunque le favole de' poeti non hanno senso allegorico, perchè in esse non è verità di storia. Similiter, non lo hanno le istorie de' pagani, perchè non furono fatte nè scritte per significare altro, ma se qualche volta pare che si allegorizzino, è quella allegoria senso litterale. . . . Dunque dobbiamo credere che la Scrittura Sacra solo ha la allegoria, e bisognati, quando tu vuoi cavare allegoria della Scrittura, intendere bene prima la istoria, e la verità di quella servare immobile, e sopra quella fondare el senso morale o allegorico, el qual senso è vago e puossi pigliare in più modi, ita che non sta fermo come la istoria."* The point that poetry is unlike sacred scripture because it lacks the literal, historical level was made already by Dante in his introduction to the *Convivio,* where he recapitulates the fourfold system of biblical exegesis precisely to make this polemical point. It is discussed in relation to late-medieval Christian narrative painting by Nagel, 1993, 93–5. It is likely that Dante's polemic was fashioned in response to thirteenth-century efforts (for example, by Guillaume de Lorris) to claim this system of textual exegesis for poetry. On the question of the uses of typology in medieval secular literature, see Hans Robert Jauss, *Genèse de la poésie allégorique française,* Heidelberg: Winter, 1962, and Robert Hollander, "Typology and Secular Literature: Some Medieval Problems and Examples," in *Literary Uses of Typology from the Late Middle Ages to the Present,* ed. E. Miner, Princeton: Princeton University Press, 1977, 3–19.

3 Paulus de Middelburgo, *De recta Paschae celebratione et de die passionis Domini nostri jesu christi,* Fossombrone, 1513, f. 79: *"Nullum autem mysterium vel sacramentum per diem nativitatis domini significatur, sed solum denotatur quod eo die natus fuit Christus. Paschae vero habet in se mysterium et sacramentum, quia transitum significat, est enim*

phase transitus domini. Et praefiguravit transitum Christi de morte ad vitam et liberationem nostram a diabolo devastante." Cf. f. 8: "*In hoc namque festa quae lunae motum consequuntur, et quae mobilia vocantur, differunt a festis fixis, quia fixa festa nullam habent in se figuram vel sacramentum, sed solum significant rem gestam. Festa vero mobilia habent in se mysterium aliquod, et ultra rem gestam aliquid aliud praefigurant. Exempli gratia dies natalis domini nihil futur demonstrat, sed solum significat, Christum eo die natum fuisse. Pascha vero a deo institutum habet in se mysterium, quia non solum significat rem eo die gestam vel agni immaculati immolatione, sed fuit etiam figurativum rei futurae et rememorativum rei praeteritae. Praefigurabat namque Christum tanquam agnum immaculatum eodem die in cruce immolandum, per cuius sanguinem in ara crucis effusum humanum genus liberaretur a diabolo insidiante, sicut filii Israel per sanguinem agni postibus illitum liberati sunt ab angelo devastante.*" On Paul of Middelburg, who is buried in the church of Santa Maria dell' Anima in Rome, see D. J. Struik, "Paulus van Middelburg (1445–1533)," *Mededeelingen van het Nederlandsch Historisch Instituut te Rome,* 5, 1927, 79–118, and Lynn Thorndike, *A History of Magic and Experimental Science,* New York: Columbia University Press, IV, 1934, 560–1, and V, 1941, passim. He makes several appearances in Aby Warburg's study, "Heidnisch-antike Weissagung im Wort und Bild zu Luthers Zeiten (1920)," in Warburg, 1932, 487–558, 647–56.

4 At issue here is the important distinction between the presupposed story – the "fabula" or "diegesis" – and the level of representation, the particular structure of the work – the "discourse." See Jean Genette, *Narrative Discourse: An Essay in Method,* trans. Jane E. Lewin, Ithaca, NY: Cornell University Press, 1980; Seymour Chatman, *Story and Discourse: Narrative Structure in Fiction and Film,* Ithaca, NY: Cornell University Press, 1978; Jonathan Culler, *The Pursuit of Signs: Semiotics, Literature, Deconstruction,* Ithaca, NY: Cornell University Press, 1981, ch. 9: "Story and Discourse in the Analysis of Narrative"; and Mieke Bal, *Narratology: Introduction to the Theory of Narrative,* trans. Christine Van Boheemen, Toronto: Toronto University Press, 1985.

5 Jill Dunkerton, paintings conservator at the National Gallery, has informed me that she believes the feet are hovering above the ground. In the painting's present condition, this point cannot, I believe, be conclusively determined. Nonetheless, even if Dunkerton's view is correct, the essential ambiguity I am describing in the figure of Christ – between sitting and upright, between heavy and weightless, between inanimate and animate – remains an important aspect of the figure's conception and a crucial link to the Man of Sorrows tradition, as is argued below.

6 The motif may well have been adapted from Filippino Lippi's fresco of the *Crucifixion of St. Peter* in the Brancacci chapel: There the figure pulls downward on a rope that is part of a pulley mechanism used to hoist Peter up. Michelangelo, indeed, seems to have studied this group quite carefully: As Hirst, 1988, 43, has observed, a few years later Michelangelo derived from it his group of two figures holding up a third for the *Battle of Cascina* fresco; see the drawings in the Louvre (*Corpus* 47*r.*) and in the British Museum (*Corpus* 46 *r.* and *v.*).

7 A word about the gender and identification of the figures, which has been the subject of some debate. Although there is certainly an ambiguity in these figures, there is just as certainly an emphasis, in each figure, on one gender over the other. Thus, the figure in red to Christ's right, despite its ambiguity, falls predominantly into a long and established tradition of long-haired St. Johns clad in red in Passion scenes. See Hirst, 1981a, 589. The figure on the other side, as I argue in ch. 3, is

drawn from a female tradition of bacchic maenad figures. Furthermore, she wears a headdress of a type worn only by women in the Sistine Chapel lunettes. A very close example occurs in the lunette of Ezekias, Manasses, and Amon.

8 Leo Steinberg suggested to me the possibility of an allusion to the Magdalene's devotion to Christ's feet, as recounted in the story of the supper with Simon the Pharisee (Luke 7:36–50). If this is true, then Michelangelo was adapting, within the conditions of his unusual frontally oriented conception, a long-standing tradition of Passion scenes in which the Magdalene's special affective relation to Christ is expressed through an attachment to his feet. Two examples among many: the panel by the Master of the Fogg *Pietà* in the Fogg Museum, and Fra Angelico's Santa Trinita *Deposition* in the San Marco Museum in Florence.

9 Paris, Louvre, inv. 689*r*.; *Corpus* 23*r*. Black chalk, pen and ink, and white heightening, on pink paper; 27 × 15 cm.

10 The drawing was published by Cecil Gould, "Some Addenda to Michelangelo Studies," *Burlington Magazine,* XCIII, 1951, 279–83. The drawing should be used with caution: It is an effort to interpret this unfinished and confusing work, rather than merely a simple record of its appearance at a time when it was less damaged than it is now. It is doubtful, for example, that the painting ever showed the Magdalene's left arm around the Virgin's shoulder, as the drawing has it – the two figures occupy positions too far apart in space to make this possible. The draftsman most likely introduced this feature in an effort to interpret and explain this obscure passage.

11 The "impassivity" of the figures in this painting was observed by Hirst, 1981a, 588, who also discussed it in Dunkerton and Hirst, 1994, 64.

12 The moment represented in this painting was correctly identified by Shearman, 1971, and more extensively analyzed in relation to other representations of the subject by Shearman, 1992, 79–94.

13 Shearman, 1992, 85.

14 The analogy of lateral images with third-person accounts and frontal images with first person accounts addressing an implied "you," was suggested by Schapiro, 1996, 73.

15 Alberti, 1991, paragraph 37.

16 Ibid.

17 Auerbach, 1984.

18 *Republic,* 392A–B. Nussbaum, 1986, 382 and, generally, 378–94.

19 *Poetics,* 1453a5 and *Rhetoric* 1385b10–15, cited and discussed by Nussbaum, 1986, loc. cit.

20 *Poetics,* 1451b4–11, cited and discussed by Nussbaum, 386.

21 See Auerbach (1946), 1968, ch. 7, "Adam and Eve," especially 157–8.

22 On this and related controversies, see Grondijs, 1941, especially ch. VII; John Martin, "The Dead Christ on the Cross in Byzantine Art," in *Late Classical and Medieval Studies in Honor of Albert Mathias Friend,* Princeton: Princeton University Press, 1955, 189–96; Hans Belting and Christa Belting-Ihm, "Das Kreuzbild im 'Hodegos' des Anastasios Sinaites: Ein Beitrag zur Frage nach der ältesten Darstellung des toten Crucifixus," in *Tortulae: Studien zu altchristlichen und byzantinischen Monumenten,* ed. Walter Nikolaus Schumacher, Freiburg: Herder, 1966, 30–39; and Belting, 1994, 120–21 and 269–71.

23 See Introduction, n. 51.

24 The most comprehensive collection of medieval texts on the question is Georg Zappert, "Über den Ausdruck des geistigen Schmerzes in Mittelalter,"

Denkschriften der Kaiserlichen Akademie der Wissenschaften, Philosophisch-Historische Klasse, 5, 1854, 73–136. Ernesto de Martino, *Morte e pianto rituale: Dal lamento funebre antico al pianto di Maria,* Turin: Boringhieri, 1975, 322–59, discussed the early Christian polemic against pagan forms of lamentation and the rise of a specifically Christian ethos of measured lament, conceived in accordance with the belief in Christ's resurrection and the doctrine of redemption. Nonetheless, as de Martino shows, dramatic lamentation never disappeared, a fact demonstrated by the later history of the *Planctus Mariae* and the late-medieval Passion plays, as well as by works of art such as Niccolò dell'Arca's group. Mosche Barasch, *Gestures of Despair in Late Medieval and Early Renaissance Art,* New York: New York University Press, 1976, 92–3, correctly noted that a decorum of restraint was still observed even in relatively late examples of devotional literature, such as the famous late thirteenth-century *Meditationes Vitae Christi* by Pseudo-Bonaventure, where the Virgin's grief does not involve violent wailing and frantic movement. Diane Owen Hughes, "Mourning Rites, Memory, and Civilization in Premodern Italy," in *Riti e rituali nelle società medievali,* ed. Jacques Chiffoleau, Lauro Martines, and Agostino Paravicini Bagliani, Spoleto, 1994, 23–38, studied the means by which public and violent forms of lamentation – which, as Savonarola suggested, were enacted above all by women – were subject to legal controls and enforced "domestication" in late-medieval Italy. See also Sharon Strocchia, "Funerals and the Politics of Gender in Early Renaissance Florence," in *Refiguring Woman: Perspectives on Gender and the Italian Renaissance,* ed. Marilyn Migiel and Juliana Schiesari, Ithaca: Cornell University Press, 1991, 155–68. For the modes and social functions of lament in the later Middle Ages, with some very useful comments on their adaptation in Passion images, see Bernhard Jussen, "*Dolor* und *Memoria.* Trauerriten, gemalte Trauer und soziale Ordnungen im späten Mittelalter," in *Memoria als Kultur,* ed. Otto Gerhard Oexle, Göttingen: Vandenhoeck & Ruprecht, 1995, 207–52. The question of the Virgin's role in Passion images has been studied in relation to Reformation and Counter-Reformation debates by Harvey E. Hamburgh, "The Problem of *Lo Spasimo* of the Virgin in *Cinquecento* Paintings of the *Descent from the Cross,*" *Sixteenth Century Journal,* XII, 4, 1981, 45–75.

25 Savonarola, 1971, 263–6: *"Queste donne vorrebbono piangere con la Vergine. Ma non pensate che piangesse come si dice. . . . E non pensare che ella andassi per le strade gridando, non scapigliata, nè con modo indecente, perchè poteva comandare alla parte sensitiva che non si dolessi. Andava bene drieto al Figliuolo, ma con mansuetudine e con grande modestia, gittando qualche lacrima; non era fuora tutta triste, ma lieta e triste, in modo che gli uomini se ne maravigliavano, perché lei non faceva come sogliono fare le altre donne. Nè anche è vero che da Maria Maddalena fussi consolata, ma lei consolava bene Maddalena. Non aveva bisogno di essere consolata dalle altre donne, essa che confortava quelle nella fede e diceva: – State salde, lasciatelo patire: questo è quello che è stato profetato."*

26 Pietro da Lucca, 1527, 3 *v.*–4*r.*

27 See Braun, 1924, vol. 2, 282; Hope, 1989; and Nagel, 1996b.

28 Belting, 1981, 28–30.

29 Ferdinand de Saussure, *Cours de Linguistique Générale,* Paris: Payot, 1972, part 2, chs. V and VI, 170–80. And see also Roland Barthes, *The Elements of Semiology,* trans. Annette Lavers and Colin Smith, New York: Hill and Wang, 1967, 58–88.

30 Roman Jakobson, "Deux aspects du langage et deux types d'aphasies," in *Essais de Linguistique Générale,* I, Paris: Editions de Minuit, 1963, 43–67.

31 Schapiro, 1996, 11–67, offered a sustained analysis of the relation and relative priority of the two modes in Christian narrative art, arguing that the literal or historical mode became increasingly prevalent toward the end of the Middle Ages.

32 The structures of reading are clearly described by James Stubblebine in his introductory essay, in *Giotto: The Arena Chapel Frescoes,* ed. James Stubblebine, New York: Norton, 1969, 71–100.

33 The problem has been addressed by Julian Gardner, "The Louvre 'Stigmatization' and the Problem of the Narrative Altarpiece," *Zeitschrift für Kunstgeschichte,* 24, 1982, 217–47.

34 A. M. Birkmeyer, "The Pietà from San Remigio," *Gazette des Beaux-Arts* ser.6, 60, 1962, 464.

35 Büttner, 1983. I do not mean to argue that only altarpieces perform such a figural function. Büttner's book, indeed, offers abundant examples in many other categories of image. Giotto's frescoes in the Arena chapel, as is well know, are themselves connected to one another, and thus to the Christian scheme of redemption, through figural and specifically typological correlations. The difference in the case of the single-scene altarpiece is that there is no recourse to a serial structure in order to multiply meanings: The representation of the event and of its figural dimension occur in the same picture and thus are more densely folded into one another.

36 See Henri de Lubac, *Exégèse médiévale: Les quatre sens de l'Ecriture,* Paris: Aubier, 1959–64, II, 549–620.

37 See F. W. Kent, "Lorenzo di Credi, his patron Iacopo Bongianni and Savonarola," *Burlington Magazine,* CXXV, 1983, 539–41.

38 See Aby Warburg, "Dürer und die italienische Antike," in Warburg, II, 1932, 443–9, and "L'Ingresso dello Stile Ideale Anticheggiante nella Pittura del primo Rinascimento," in Warburg, 1966, 285–307.

39 Alberti, 1991, paragraph 42. The Homeric association was pointed out by Shearman, 1992, 89, who also suggests that Botticelli's altarpiece is probably to be identified with that seen by Vasari in the Florentine church of Santa Maria Maggiore; see Vasari, III, 513.

40 One exception is a lost altarpiece that shows the transport of Christ by Rogier van der Weyden, whose composition is preserved in drawings in Paris and Leipzig (see Figure 2.40) and in a painted copy in the Getty. To judge by these copies, Rogier framed the scene in a shrinelike box like the one depicted in the Prado *Deposition,* which can be understood as a form of restraint imposed on the narrative. The work is discussed at greater length in chapter 2 of this book.

41 Jakobson, 1971, 82–7.

42 The best single source of information on the range of formats and genres in which a very conventional and busy painter's shop of the mid-fifteenth century worked is Neri di Bicci's *Ricordanze.* The greater part of his commissions are for *tavole,* which are almost always designated as *tavole d'altare*; see, for example, Neri di Bicci, 1976, 12 (n. 23), 25 (n. 50), 33 (n. 64), 48 (n. 95), 56 (n. 111), 60 (n. 121), etc.

43 The link between the modern easel picture and this form of altarpiece was first explicitly hypothesized by Burckhardt, 1988, 64: "As is well known, the modern Italian word *quadro* signifies any type of picture, irrespective of its shape, size or subject. But the fact that the most numerous and important Italian altarpieces

were painted on a square (or near-square) picture field prompts the suspicion that it was in the context of the church altar that the term *quadro* first originated."

44 Max Ernst, *"Au-delà de la peinture,"* in idem, *Ecritures,* Paris: Gallimard, 1970, 256. My thanks to Elizabeth Legge for giving me the exact reference of this proverbial remark.

45 The concrete circumstances of the rise of the new format have been analyzed by Gilbert, 1977, and Gardner von Teuffel, 1982 and 1983. The fact, stressed by Gardner von Teuffel, that in these early experiments elements within the painting throw fictional bridges to the picture frame, and to the painting's physical architectural surroundings, does not contradict the principle of a notional disjunction between picture and frame. It presupposes this principle.

46 For this reason, I am in disagreement with the claim made by Anne B. Barriault, *Spalliera Paintings of Renaissance Tuscany: Fables of Poets for Patrician Homes,* University Park, PA: Pennsylvania State University Press, 1994, that spalliera painting is the ancestor of the modern easel picture.

47 Sarah Lawrence, *"Conversazioni profane:* In dialogue with the Pagan Gods," doctoral dissertation, Columbia University, 1994.

48 The role played by the altarpiece in the rise of the modern easel picture is a recurring concern in the work of Hans Belting; see, most succinctly, Belting, 1987.

49 The passage concludes *Giotto and the Orators: Humanist Observers of Painting in Italy and the Discovery of Pictorial Composition 1350–1450,* Oxford: Oxford University Press, 1986, 139: "Seen through *compositio* the replacement of a Pisanello by a Mantegna, or indeed of the triptych form by the form of the Sacra Conversazione, is part of the same movement as the replacement of Guarino's prose by that of the generation of George of Trebizond: the *dissolutum* was becoming *compositum*."

50 Hirst, 1988, 64.

51 We find such a composition in an ancient sarcophagus of the *Carrying of Silenus,* Matz, 1969, n. 119. The reception of the composition, which was well known to Renaissance artists, is discussed in ch. 5 of this book.

52 See Alois Riegl, *Das Holländische Gruppenporträt,* Vienna: Österreichische Staatsdruckerei, 1934.

53 Hirst, 1981a, 589, was the first to note that one consequence of Michelangelo's unusual composition was to attach it to the tradition of the Man of Sorrows.

CHAPTER TWO. MAN OF SORROWS AND ENTOMBMENT

1 This part of my dicussion relies fundamentally on Hans Belting, "An Image and its function in the liturgy: The Man of Sorrows in Byzantium," *Dumbarton Oaks Papers,* 34–5, 1980–81, 1–16; and idem, 1981, ch. 5.

2 Panofsky, 1927, 261.

3 Vetter, 1963, 218, showed that one of the earliest Western examples of the subject, a miniature of the *Man of Sorrows* from a Roman Missal of 1254 in the Museo Archeologico of Cividale (Cod. LXXXVI, f. 167), decorates the Canon of the Mass.

4 Quoted in Belting, 1981, 112–13: ". . .*apparuit mihi effigies illius benedicti Dei et hominis crucifixi, quasi tunc noviter de cruce depositi: cujus sanguis apparebat sic recens . . . et per vulnera effluens."* Further examples quoted by Vetter, 1963, 218 and 224. The eucharistic associations of the image have been stressed above all by Bauerreis, 1931, 3–14 and passim.

5 Belting, 1981, 281–8.
6 The image's freedom from specific theological prescription has been stressed above all by Berliner, 1956, 97–117. For a more general statement of the principle, see Berliner, 1945.
7 See Belting, 1981, ch. 4: "Realismus und Bildrhetorik."
8 Gilio, 1961, 110: *"Dite bene, rispose M. Francesco; or dunque dite voi, M. Ruggiero, come vogliono essere dipinte le sacre immagini." Rispose M. Ruggiero: "Difficil cosa è a volerne rendere vera e indubitata ragione che così sia e che altramente esser non possa, perché di questo non abbiamo legge alcuna né regola, se non quanto che la consuetudine de' pittori, innanzi che Michelagnolo fusse, n'ha dimostrato (la quale però, come voi signori leggisti sapete, è legge), e quanto che Guglielmo Durante nel Razionale de' divini offizii ne scrive."*
9 Belting, 1981, 253: *"die Imago Pietatis ist nicht aus einer theologischen Konzeption 'geboren', wie manchen einschlägigen Studien glauben machen, sondern als östliches Tafelbild in den Westen gelangt. . ."*
10 See Ferdinand Cabrol, *The Mass of the Western Rites,* London: Sands, 1934, 43. For an account of Gregory's involvement in the writing of the earliest liturgical books, see Jungmann, 1986, 61–6.
11 See Carlo Bertelli, "The Image of Pity in S. Croce in Gerusalemme," *Essays in the History of Art Presented to Rudolf Wittkower,* London: Phaidon, 1967, 40–55.
12 See Mâle, 1908, 93. An intermediate stage in this inflationary process is represented by a highly informative mid-fifteenth-century Umbrian indulgence panel of the *Man of Sorrows – Gregory Mass* in the Wallraf-Richartz Museum in Cologne (reproduced in Belting, 1981, 285, Fig. 108), whose inscription reads that the 14,000 years of true pardon traditionally accorded to worshippers who say the prayers before this image has since been increased to 27,036 years: *"Sancto Gregorio essendo papa et dicendo la messa gl'aparve el nostro signore yhu xpo in forma de piatate onde vedendolo sancto gregorio fo mosso apiatate et devotione et si fece questa oratione a sua reverentia. Et si a concesso ad omne persona confessa et contrita che le dira inançe ala piatate cum cinque pater nostri et cinque ave maria avera [?] quatordece milia anni di vera indulgentia. Et molti altri pape anno agionto intanto che suma in tucto vintasette milia anni et trenta sei de vera indulgentia."*
13 Jacobus de Voragine, *The Golden Legend,* trans. Granger Ryan and Helmut Ripperger, London: Longmans, Green, 1941, 185: "Then Gregory prostrated himself and prayed to God for the woman's unbelief; and when he arose the Host which lay upon the altar had been changed into a piece of flesh in the form of a finger. He showed this flesh to the incredulous woman, who immediately came back to the faith." The source of the story transmitted by the *Golden Legend* is the Life of Gregory written by Paulus Diakonus (Migne, P.L. LXXV, 52); it is quoted and discussed in J. A. Endres, "Die Darstellung der Gregoriusmesse im Mittelalter," *Zeitschrift für Christliche Kunst,* 30, 1917, 147*ff.*
14 Mâle, 1908, 92.
15 Cf. Millard Meiss, *Painting in Florence and Siena after the Black Death,* New York, 1964, 124, n. 75.
16 This fact, together with some exceptions, was noted by Braun, 1924, II, 451.
17 By the fifteenth century it had become standard practice to include the image, often called a *pietà,* in one or the other position. The demand comes up regularly, for instance, in Neri di Bicci's records of altarpiece commissions. See, for example, Neri di Bicci, 1976, 60 (f. 26.r.): *". . .e nella predella la Piatà e quattro meze fighure da lato, da ogni lato dua."*

18 See Henk van Os, "The Discovery of an Early Man of Sorrows on a Dominican Triptych," *Journal of the Warburg and Courtauld Institutes,* 41, 1975, 65 *ff.*
19 See Millet, 1916, 483 *ff.*
20 See the excursus in Panofsky, 1953, 273–4, and Belting, 1981, 229.
21 See Berliner, 1956, 107.
22 The tabernacle-altarpiece is ascribed to Bartolomeo Giolfino by Ulrich Middeldorf, "Three Sculptors of the Veneto Represented at Fenway Court," in *Fenway Court 1973,* Boston: Isabella Stewart Gardner Museum, 1974, 6–8.
23 See, for example, Guillaume Durand, *Pontificale Romanum,* ed. Michel Andrieu (*Studi e Testi* 88, vol. III), Vatican City: Biblioteca Apostolica Vaticana, 1937–41, lib. 2, cap. 3, no. 30: *". . .foraminis seu sepulcri in quo reliquie debent recludi",* and no. 38: *". . .foramen seu sepulcrum fit in medio are seu altaris in parte superiori. . ."*
24 See Durandus, 1937–41, lib. 2, cap. 2, no. 3: ". . .vel, deficientibus reliquiis, ponat ibi corpus domini." On the question in general, see G.J.C. Snoek, *Medieval Piety from Relics to the Eucharist: A Process of Mutual Interaction,* Leiden: Brill, 1995, 175–202.
25 See Gaetano Moroni, *Dizionario di Erudizione Storico-Ecclesiastica,* Venice, 1851, vol. LIII, s.v. "Pietra."
26 The panel is close to one in the Cherbourg Museum, where the narrative elements are strengthened. The Cherbourg panel has recently been reattributed to the young Filippino Lippi by Patrizia Zambrano, "The 'Dead Christ' in Cherbourg: A New Attribution to the Young Filippino Lippi," *Burlington Magazine,* CXXXVIII, 1118, 1996, 321–4.
27 See Belting, 1986, 48–56. Humfrey, 1993, 167–8, has pointed out a parallel discrepancy between the innovative altarpiece designs found in his drawing books and the more conventional formats and designs he adopted, or was forced to adopt, in his panel paintings.
28 Robert Suckale, "Arma Christi: Überlegungen zur zeichenhaftigkeit mittelalterlicher Andachtsbilder," *Städel Jahrbuch,* n.s. 6, 1977, 190, 196 and passim. Although I find his description of the process illuminating, I take issue with Suckale's terminology. In my view, the more "pictorial" treatments that emerge in the fifteenth century are *more* signlike than the earlier images.
29 Cf. Gertrud Simon, *Die Ikonographie der Grablegung Christi,* Rostock: Hinstorff, 1926, 51: *"Das Bild des Fra Angelico trägt mehr noch den Charakter einer Schmerzensmannes-Darstellung als einer Grablegung."*
30 On the use of cloths and veils in Christian ritual see, Joseph Braun, *Die liturgische Gewandung im Occident und Orient,* Freiburg: Herder, 1907, 515–61, and idem, *Die liturgischen Paramente in Gegenwart and Vergangen,* 2nd ed., Freiburg: Herder, 1924, 228–31. The Eucharistic associations of the depiction of veils, above all in Epiphany imagery, are discussed by Rab Hatfield, *Botticelli's Uffizi 'Adoration': A Study in Pictorial Content,* Princeton, 1976, 38, n. 11.
31 I am grateful to John Shearman for first opening my eyes to this feature of the fresco.
32 Georges Didi-Huberman, *Fra Angelico: Dissemblance and Figuration,* trans. Jane Marie Todd, Chicago, 1995. See also my review in *Art Bulletin,* 78, 1996, 559–65.
33 Hood, 1993, ch. 2, discussed the innovative stamp given to the San Marco complex under Medici patronage. He also specifically suggested (45) that the modern Renaissance *pala* was a form that Cosimo might have wanted to associate specifically with his patronage. The argument receives support from the program of chapels projected for San Lorenzo in 1434, where the new altarpiece format is

stipulated for all the altars, and the Medici chapel in the church transept was held up as the model to follow; see Jeffrey Ruda, "A 1434 Building Programme for San Lorenzo in Florence," *Burlington Magazine,* CXX, 1978, 361. Hood, 1993, 104–7, argued plausibly if not conclusively that Fra Angelico's Annalena altarpiece stood on the altar of the Medici transept chapel at the time. Howard Saalman, "The 1434 Chapel Project," *Burlington Magazine,* CXX, 1978, 363, saw the document as part of an anti-Medici project, proposing that the new nave chapels planned in the 1434 document were intended for people "outside the Medici circle" who saw an opportunity to gain rights at San Lorenzo during the Medici exile. Caroline Elam, "Cosimo de' Medici at San Lorenzo," in *Cosimo 'il Vecchio' de' Medici, 1389–1464,* ed. Francis Ames-Lewis, Oxford: Clarendon, 1992, 175, convincingly rejected this view, contending that "the chapter and canons of San Lorenzo continued to be firmly associated with the Medici during 1433–34 . . . and that Cosimo was informed of its affairs."

34 Although Fra Angelico's panel enjoyed a rich history of reception later in the century, the earliest known response to Fra Angelico's panel, a drawing in the Uffizi formerly attributed to Andrea del Castagno, Florence, Gabinetto dei Disegni e delle Stampe, 252E; pen, 22.1 × 18.7 cm, shows how uneasily its innovations were assimilated into the Florentine tradition. The drawing was mentioned in general relation to Fra Angelico's panel by von Einem, 1940, 91, n. 2. Once attributed to Andrea del Castagno, the drawing is now attributed tentatively to Francesco Pesellino. The drawing concentrates on the quite new motif of the full-length Christ supported from behind; Fra Angelico's experiment with narrative consistency was, however, evidently of little importance to him. Christ stands supported by a figure adapted directly from the figure of Joseph of Arimathea in Fra Angelico's panel; St. John and the Virgin, however, have returned to seated positions on either side, an arrangement familiar from more conventional Man of Sorrows compositions. The figure behind Christ has, evidently without knowledge of the drawing's dependence on Fra Angelico, often been taken as a figure of God the Father. This identification is presumably due to its similarity to northern European images of this kind, but this similarity is probably coincidental. The drawing is more reasonably read as a natural readaptation of Fra Angelico's full-length motif back into the traditional Man of Sorrows scheme. The drawing shows, indeed, just how strong the pull of this tradition remained for contemporary viewers. The panel did eventually provoke less hesitant responses, which are discussed below.

35 More conclusive arguments than those proposed by Ernst Kantorowicz, "The Este Portrait by Rogier van der Weyden," *Journal of the Warburg and Courtauld Institutes,* 3, 1939–40, 165–80, need to be put forward before the occurrence of this trip can be called into question. Michael Hirst (Dunkerton and Hirst, 1994, 62) has said he believes the panel to have been made "in the orbit of Rogier" rather than by him. Again, until arguments are produced to sustain such scepticism there is, it seems to me, no compelling reason to change the traditional attribution. Although the analysis of the panel's relation to the Fra Angelico predella proposed here will, in fact, serve to support the attribution to Rogier himself, the attribution question is of minor importance to my larger arguments. The important matter remains the panel's fifteenth-century provenance from Florence, which is attested by evidence adduced by Hirst (see especially Dunkerton and Hirst, 1994, 80, n. 35), and abundantly confirmed by the Florentine reception of the panel studied in this chapter.

36 Jähnig, 1918, 171–6.
37 Goldschmidt, 1903, 56–7: "*. . .der obere Teil der Komposition – etwa bis zu den Häften der Figuren – größte Verwandschaft aufweist mit jener symbolischen Darstellung der 'Pietà,' deren in Oberitalien besonders beliebten Typus Carlo Crivelli ofters gemalt hat.*"
38 For exceptions in the north, see the Man of Sorrows standing in the sarcophagus with St. John and the Virgin on the back of the Imhof altar in Nuremberg (illustration in Carl von Gebhardt, *Die Anfänge der Tafelmalerei in Nürnberg,* Strasbourg, 1908, pl. III, cited by Jähnig, 1918); or, interestingly, the Man of Sorrows placed *behind* the sarcophagus and supported by angels in the lower central register of the small Mosan altarpiece of ca. 1415, in the van Beuningen collection in Vierhouten (Panofsky, 1953, Fig. 107). By the end of the century, perhaps as a result of greater contact with Italy, the composition became more common: See, for example, the print by Martin Schongauer (B. 69) and the copy of the Santa Croce in Gerusalemme icon by Israel van Meckenem (B. 135). It also existed, of course, in half-length versions of the deposition deriving from Rogier's lost panel; for these, see Ringbom, 1965, 117–41, and the remarks below.
39 For some initial steps toward a comparative analysis, see Penny H. Jolly, "Rogier van der Weyden's Escorial and Philadelphia Crucifixions and Their Relations to Fra Angelico at San Marco," *Oud-Holland,* 95, 1981, 113–26.
40 Panofsky, 1953, 168 and 258.
41 One wonders, as a matter of purely biographical interest, whether Rogier ever had the opportunity to examine Fra Angelico's panel and make the comparison for himself. It is probable that at least Gentile da Fabriano's *Adoration of the Magi,* originally on the adjacent altar in the Strozzi sacristy in SS. Trinita, would have been high on the list of any artistic visitor to Florence.
42 For the tradition deriving from this lost panel, see Ringbom, 1965, 117–41.
43 Rogier's panel is almost certainly to be identified with the chapel altarpiece described, with great precision, in the 1492 inventory of the villa at Careggi; Müntz, 1888, 88: "*Una tavola d'altare chon cornicie dorato atorno, dipintovi drento el sepolcro del nostro Signore schonfitto di crocie e cinque altre figure.*" Its nonidentity with the panel recorded by Fazio and Ciriaco d'Ancona in Ferrara was argued in 1903 by Aby Warburg in dialogue with Adolph Goldschmidt (Warburg, 1903, 58, reprinted in Warburg, 1932, 215–16). It is very likely that Michelangelo had had occasion to make the comparison for himself during his years in the Medici household.
44 Panofsky, 1927, 276–8.
45 The resilience of the half-length format in Italy is demonstrated by a moment in the reception history of Giovanni da Milano's panel: In Masolino da Panicale's fresco in the Baptistery at Empoli, for example, the posture of the Christ figure is taken over almost verbatim from Giovanni da Milano, and yet it is reinserted into the still dominant half-length format.
46 For the role of this and other Italian Trecento elements in late fourteenth-century French art see Erwin Panofsky, *Renaissance and Renascences in Western Art* (1960), New York: Harper & Row, 1972, 159–160.
47 See Georg Swarzenski, "Insinuationes divinae pietatis," in *Festschrift Heinrich Wölfflin; Beiträge zur Kunst – und Geistesgeschichte zum 21. Juni 1924 überreicht von Freunden und Schülern,* München: Schmidt, 1924, 65–74. The idea of the Man of Sorrows presented by angels had already been developed in Italy in the fourteenth century, usually in a specifically Eucharistic context. The composition, however, conformed to the typical

Italian flanking-figure scheme with the half-length, self-supporting Man of Sorrows in between. See, for example, the predella of the stone altarpiece by Tommaso Pisano in San Francesco at Pisa (illustration in Belting, 1981, Fig. 35). The composition survived in later works, such as the predella of Matteo di Giovanni's St. Matthew altarpiece in the Cathedral of Pienza (illustration in van Os, 1990, Fig. 208).

48 Otto Pächt, *Van Eyck and the Founders of Early Netherlandish Painting,* trans. David Britt, London: Miller, 1994, 39–40.

49 For an account of the development and meaning of the prayer, see Jungmann, II, 1986, 226–37.

50 The relation of this prayer to the Man of Sorrows–based images is discussed, unfortunately with too rigid a concern for whether or not it is a "source," by Gert von der Osten, "Engelpietà," in *Reallexikon zur Deutschen Kunstgeschichte,* vol. 5, Stuttgart, 1960, 603, and Hubert Schrade, "Beitrag zur Erklärung des Schmerzensmannbildes," in *Deutschkundliches – Friedrich Panzer zum 60. Geburtstag überreicht,* Heidelberg: winter 1930, 178–9.

51 Goldschmidt, 1903, passim. The discussion transpired largely between Goldschmidt and Aby Warburg.

52 Ibid., 56: "*. . .in beiden fällt eine gewisse Unmotiviertheit der Situation, ein zum Schaustellen des in ganzer Vertikale aufrecht gehaltenen, nicht horizontal getragenen Leichnams ins Auge.*"

53 See the more sustained reading of the work offered in the opening of ch. 1, above.

54 The clearest description and justification of the practice was offered by Ludolph of Saxony (1300–77 or ' 78) in the "Proemium" to his widely read Life of Christ (*Vita Jesu Christi ex Evangelio et approbatis ab Ecclesia Catholica doctoribus sedule collecta,* ed. Louis-Marie Rigollot, Paris: Palmé, Brussels: Lebrocquy, I, 1878, 1–10). Much of Ludolph's prologue was taken over, almost verbatim, from the *Meditationes Vitae Christi,* especially from the prologue and the theoretical ch. 50, "On the three kinds of contemplation."

55 *Meditations,* 1961, 342–5. In this account, the Virgin accompanies the body to the tomb.

56 Thomas à Kempis, *Meditations on the Life of Christ,* ed. and trans. Henry P. Wright and Samuel S. Kettlewell, New York: Dutton, 1892, 222.

57 This panel might correspond to one recorded in the 1492 Medici inventory; Müntz, 1888, 64: *"Una tavoletta dipintovi il nostro Signore morto chon molti santi che lo portano al sepolcro, di mano di fra Giovanni."*

58 See Millet, II, 1916, 489–516, and Kurt Weitzmann, "The Origin of the Threnos," in *De Artibus Opuscula XL: Essays in Honor of Erwin Panofsky,* New York: New York University Press, 1961, I, 476–90.

59 The altarpiece recorded in these drawings has been hypothetically identified with that described by Ciriaco d'Ancona in 1449 in the collection of Lionello d'Este in Ferrara. For the text of Ciriaco's description, see Friedrich Winkler, *Der Meister von Flémalle und Rogier van der Weyden,* Strasbourg: Heitz, 1913, 181*ff.*; it is reprinted, with some emendations, by Panofsky, 1953, 361. For the most emphatic argument in favor of the identification, see W. Houben, "Raphael and Rogier van der Weyden," *Burlington Magazine,* 91, 1949, 312–15, who argues that Rogier's composition influenced Raphael's Borghese *Entombment.* Warburg, 1903, 58, in refuting the admittedly less believable suggestion that the work be identified with the Uffizi *Entombment,* asserted that the text can only be understood to describe a deposition, but the text does not seem to support such a definitive reading: *"tabel-*

lam nobis ostendit . . . e supplicio humanati Jovis depositi pientissimo agalmate circum et plerumque virum [virorum] imaginibus mulierumque moetissime deploratum [deplorantium] imaginibus. . ." Perhaps the strongest evidence against the identification of the altarpiece recorded in the drawings with that recorded by Ciriaco is the latter's enthusiastic description of the landscape elements in the painting ["*. . .virentiaque prata, flores, arbores et frondiferos atque umbrosos colles. . .*"], which are not represented in the shrinelike conception of the altarpiece as shown in the drawings. On the other hand, the painted copy by the Master of St. Bartholomew in the J. Paul Getty Museum, although maintaining the shrinelike box, does show a ground covered with foliage. Did he add this feature? If the work recorded in the Paris and Leipzig drawings is to be identified with the altarpiece seen by Ciriaco d'Ancona, then the question of its relation to Mantegna's print of the *Entombment* also arises: Mantegna's work would become, in part, an "Italian" classicizing response to Rogier's altarpiece.

60 Cf., for example, Koch, 1975, n. 98.

61 The classic statement is by Schapiro, 1996, especially ch. 4, "Frontal and Profile as Symbolic Forms," 69–95, 107–12.

62 See, for example, Klaus Wessel, "Frontalität," in *Reallexicon zur Byzantinischen Kunst,* ed. Klaus Wessel, II, Stuttgart: Hierseman, 1971, ca. 586–93.

63 Meyer Schapiro, "The Frescoes of Castelseprio" (1952), in *Late Antique, Early Christian, and Mediaeval Art: Selected Papers.* New York: Braziller, 1979, 85. The increased emphasis on portrait-icons, and its relationship to the "intensification" of the cult of images in the era before the iconoclastic controversy, was observed by Kitzinger, "On Some Icons of the Seventh Century" (1955), in 1976, 233–55, especially 244–5. See, also, idem, "The Cult of Images in the Age before Iconoclasm" (1954), in 1976, 91–156, and "Byzantine Art in the Period between Justinian and Iconoclasm" (1958), in 1976, 157–232, especially 199–202.

64 See Hans von Campenhausen, "Die Bilderfrage in der Reformation," *Zeitschrift für Kirchengeschichte,* LXVIII, 1957, 96–128.

65 Schapiro, 1996, 81–2. Túy's polemic is also discussed by Berliner, 1945, 278–9, 282.

66 Both passages are excerpted and translated in Mango, 1972, 253–4.

67 Ringbom, 1965.

68 Hollanda, 1911, 274.

69 Colonna, 1982, S2 23, 188. This and the passage from Hollanda are cited and discussed by Deswarte-Rosa, 1997, 363. See also the Introduction of this book.

70 Gilio, 1961, 55–6. Zeri, 1957, studied several examples of this archaizing sensibility in Italian painting of the middle and later sixteenth century.

71 Angelo Poliziano, *Prose Volgari inedite Poesie Latine e Greche edite e inedite,* ed. Isidoro del Lungo, Florence: Barbèra, 1867, 7: "*Lui disposto giù di croce, colle braccia distese, col capo chino, col cuore aperto, vi chiama, Padri miei, v'invita a pianger seco il suo acerbissimo dolore; far compagnia a la sua santa sposa, vedova sconsolata. . .; a inginocchiarvi a inchinarvi e prosternervi dinanzi a' suoi santissimi piedi.*" Presentational devices were also a common feature of epideictic oratory, which O'Malley, 1979, showed was applied with great frequency in the sermons delivered at the papal court in this period. Some examples of this form of oratory are studied in relation to Michelangelo's experiments in ch. 3.

72 This panel is an innovative adaptation of the more conventional composition represented by a panel in the Museum Boymans-van Beuningen in Rotterdam; Henk van Os and Marian Prakhen, *The Florentine Paintings in Holland,* Maarssen:

Schwartz, 1974, no. 27. Berenson, 1963, vol. 1, 145–7, attributed both to the Master of San Miniato. Van Os and Prakhen attributed the Rotterdam panel to a different hand. The Rotterdam panel shows a strictly frontal composition more closely related to the Fra Angelico predella, although the cave has been replaced by a simple sarcophagus at the foot of the cross. Christ is supported by St. John and Joseph from his underarms, whereas the Virgin and the Magdalene sit on the ground at Christ's feet; the group is further amplified by St. Jerome and St. Bernardino, who touch Christ's outstretched hands. This arrangement and certain details, such as Christ's legs and the pose of the Magdalene, perhaps show that Fra Angelico's model was enriched by an acquaintance with Rogier's panel. The near-*Rückenfigur* of the Virgin shows some similarities to that projected by Michelangelo. As far as the thematic conception is concerned, however, the Master of San Miniato's Avignon panel (Figure. 41) is a clearer precedent for the attempt to reconcile a narrative scene, involving transitional movement, with the frontal composition. I believe this painter is also the painter of a panel in Sta. Felicita in Florence (given the unlikely attribution of Francesco d' Antonio by Berenson, 1963, 63), which proposes a similarly ingenious but awkward experiment with the theme of the adoration of the Magi.

73 Ugo Procacci, *La Reale Galleria dell'Accademia di Firenze,* Roma: Libreria dello Stato, 1936, no. 8628. It was originally flanked by predella panels of *St. Jerome* and of the *Stigmatization of St. Francis,* nos. 8627 and 8629, respectively. For the provenance, see Walter and Elizabeth Paatz, *Die Kirchen von Florenz,* III, Frankfurt: Klostermann, 1952, 48, who record the altarpiece in San Marco "an unbestimmten Ort." The theme is taken in a similar direction in a predella panel by Jacopo del Sellaio also in the Accademia (no. 8655), which is closer to the Fra Angelico predella. Christ, still upright and frontal, is being dragged toward the tomb at the right while the Virgin faints into the arms of the holy women at the left. As they fall away from each other, their limp arms cross – a trace of the traditional Man of Sorrows composition now poignantly treated as an "accident" of the scene.

74 These works were adduced in relation to the panels of Fra Angelico and Michelangelo by Hirst, 1994, 62. A similar effort to preserve the frontality of the dead Christ within a narrative subject can be found in Ghirlandaio's *Lamentation* over the altar of the Vespucci chapel in Ognissanti. Michael Rohlmann, "Ein flämisches Vorbild für Ghirlandaio's 'prime pitture,'" *Mitteilungen des Kunsthistorischen Institutes in Florenz,* XXXVI, 1992, 388–96, set this work in relation to Rogier's Uffizi *Entombment.* The trend to "historicize" Man of Sorrows images was not confined to the tradition stemming from Fra Angelico and Rogier. By the late fifteenth century the traditional Man of Sorrows image was distinctly old-fashioned for most painters, and increasingly we find the image contextualized in a scene of entombment or lamentation. Two fairly typical examples, north and south of the Alps: The Dürer-school *Lamentation* in the Ca' d'Oro in Venice, and the *Lamentation* by Giovanni Agostino da Lodi, also in the Ca' d'Oro, where the effort to maintain Christ's frontal orientation in a narrative context produces a solution similar to Ghirlandaio's Vespucci chapel fresco discussed above.

75 Although the *Great Passion* was not published in complete form until 1511, it is generally agreed that the seven woodcuts made before 1500 originally circulated as single prints. See Erwin Panofsky, *Albrecht Dürer,* Princeton: Princeton University Press, 1945, 45.

76 Beyond the moment chosen, certain further particulars are close to Michelangelo's conception. In both scenes, Dürer has been careful to show Christ entirely nude; the bodies and drapery of the other figures "accidentally" cover his genitalia. Michelangelo shared this conception of Christ, and in his panel showed him, quite remarkably, frontally and completely uncovered. Also, the highly expressive figure sitting on the left in the *Lamentation,* her body facing away from the scene but her head turned against her shoulders to cast a teary gaze back, was, I believe, adapted by Michelangelo for the figure at the right of his panel; he has even preserved her particular kind of cloak and fastening device.

77 See Büttner, 1983.

78 On the rise of narrative themes in fifteenth-century altarpieces, see Eva Friederike Werner, *Das italienische Altarbild vom Trecento bis zum Cinquecento: Untersuchungen zur Thematik italienischer Altargemälde,* Munich: Inaugural-Dissertation, Ludwig-Maximilians-Universität, 1971. On the increasing incidence of Deposition altarpieces during the period, see Harvey E. Hamburgh, "Aspects of the *Descent from the Cross* from Lippi to Cigoli," doctoral dissertation, University of Iowa, 1978.

79 The effect was perceptively described by Justi, 1909, 121: *"Bei Michelangelo ist jene Schaustellung nur ein zufälliges, ganz transitorisch momentanes Ergebnis des mechanischen Vollzugs: . . .Christus ist nur für uns, die Betrachter des Gemäldes, in diese Stellung gebracht worden."*

CHAPTER THREE. HUMANISM AND THE ALTAR IMAGE

1 Paul Kristeller, *Holzschnitte im königlichen Kupferstichkabinett zu Berlin, Graphische Gesellschaft,* XXI, Berlin: Cassirer, 1915, n. 89.

2 Even the other aspects of Michelangelo's composition, such as the kneeling figures in the foreground, find precedents within the Man of Sorrows tradition: An engraving by the Housebook Master (Lehrs, n. 22), for example, shows the Man of Sorrows supported by God the Father and adored by the kneeling figures of the Virgin and St. John.

3 The rarity of the Man of Sorrows as the main subject of altarpieces was noted, with some exceptions, by Braun, 1924, II, 451. See also Von der Osten, 1935, 33, who observed, *"Selten zeigt er sich an den Altarflügen und an der Rückseite, fast gar nicht im Schrein"* and also noted exceptions on p. 34, n. 54. A few further exceptions in Italy may be noted. An altarpiece by Taddeo Gaddi in the Yale University Art Gallery features a Christ in the tomb with the Virgin that shows distinct affinities with Man of Sorrows images; a similar arrangement is found in an altarpiece by Mariotto di Cristofano in the parish church of Carda di Castelfocognano (Arezzo). The figure appears in more distinctly recognizable form in an early fifteenth-century panel showing the *Man of Sorrows between the Virgin and St. Lucy* in the church of Santa Lucia in San Giovanni Valdarno (illustration in Frederick Antal, *Florentine Painting and its Social Background,* London: K. Paul, 1948, pl. 120A); in Lorenzo Monaco's Accademia panel (Figure 35); and in a panel by Niccolò di Pietro Gerini derived from Lorenzo Monaco's, originally in Santissima Annunziata and now in the Uffizi (illustration in Luisa Marcucci, *Gallerie nazionali di Firenze: i dipinti toscani del secolo 14,* Roma: Istituto poligrafico dello Stato, 1965, pl. 75). There is also the Angelico-school triptych of the *Man of Sorrows between St. Francis and St. Jerome* in the Archiepiscopate of Florence. It may be objected that it is not certain whether the London *Entombment* is an

altarpiece at all. I argue below that it did originate in an altarpiece commission for the church of Sant' Agostino in Rome in 1500, but apart from this external evidence, the internal evidence of the panel is paramount. The panel's design is the result of a conscious adherence to altarpiece traditions and paradigms. It would be a statement about the category and institution of altarpieces even in the unlikely instance that it did not officially belong to the category; indeed, in that case it would be an even more overt statement.

4 Frey, 1956, 122: *"Vielleicht war es eine Sheu gerade vor der zu großen und unmittelbaren Realität, die dem 'Bilde' durch die enge Verknüpfung mit der realen Gegenwart Gottes im Meßopfer verleihen wurde, die sich der Verwendung des Schmerzensmannes im Schrein entgegenstellte."* This idea, only suggested here, is one application of the more elaborate theory articulated in Frey's fascinating essay, "Der Realitätscharakter des Kunstwerkes," *Festschrift Heinrich Wölfflin,* Munich: Schmidt, 1935, 30–67.

5 In some representations of the scene Christ's appearance takes the place of the altarpiece, almost as if the living reality were substituting the altar image. Three examples among many: the *Mass of St. Gregory* formerly in Paris attributed to Andrea di Niccolò by Berenson, 1970, II, n. 838; the *Mass of St. Gregory* by Bernt Notke in the Marienkirche in Lübeck of 1501–4 (illustration in Wiltrud Mersmann, *Der Schmerzensmann,* Düsseldorf: Schwann, 1952, pl. 31); and the Rhenish *Mass of St. Gregory* of ca. 1500 in the Augsburg Gallery (illustration in Berliner, 1945, Fig. 16). The issue appears to have been a special concern for Israhel van Meckenem, in whose engravings of the *Mass of St. Gregory* (B. 100, 101, and 102) the Man of Sorrows is placed in sensitive and ambiguous relationships with the altarpiece structure. For illustrations see *The Illustrated Bartsch,* IX, New York: Abaris, plates 99, 100, and 101. The Man of Sorrows also makes an appearance as a sort of paradigmatic altar image in other scenes of miracles involving altars. In Taddeo di Bartolo's predella panel of the *Miraculous Mass at Greccio,* for example, the altar is mounted by a triptych with the Man of Sorrows in the central panel. (For an illustration, together with a reconstruction of the entire altarpiece, see Gail E. Solberg, "A Reconstruction of Taddeo di Bartolo's Altarpiece for S. Francesco a Prato, Perugia," *Burlington Magazine,* CXXXIV, 1992, 646–54, Fig. 30.) The fact that in such scenes the Man of Sorrows could figure as the altar image par excellence gives more pointed significance to the fact that it only very rarely figured as such in reality.

6 Frey, 1956, 120.

7 Other examples include the *Man of Sorrows – Trinity* panel by Jan Polack in Blutenberg of 1491 (brought to my attention in a graduate seminar paper by Rosa Berland); a large late fifteenth-century German *Man of Sorrows – Trinity* panel in the sacristy of Sant' Alessandro in Colonna, Bergamo; and a Lübeck School retable of the same subject in Hald, Denmark (illustration in Steinberg, 1996, fig. 250). In a notable case of literal archaism, in 1473 an earlier (ca. 1400?) Man of Sorrows sculpture was introduced into the main corpus of an altarpiece in Breslau (discussion and illustration in Von der Osten, 1935, 33, n. 54, Fig. 80).

8 See, for example, the triptych by Francesco dai Libri in SS. Nazaro e Celso, illustrated in Berenson, 1970, II, n. 1286, as well as the relief sculpture in San Lorenzo attributed to Girolamo Benaglio, and the canvas in the Museo d'Arte in Castelvecchio, both illustrated in Rudolf Berliner, "Arma Christi," *Münchener Jahrbuch der Bildenden Kunst,* 6, 1955, Figs. 26 and 27. See also the Man of Sorrows altarpiece in San Lorenzo in Vicenza; for an illustration, see Peter Humfrey, "The

Bellini, the Vivarini, and the Beginnings of the Renaissance Altarpiece in Venice," in Borsook and Superbi Gioffredi, 1994, Fig. 101, who ascribes it to a Paduan sculptor and dates it to the late fifteenth century. A *Man of Sorrows* panel by Benedetto Diana in the Museo Correr in Venice measures about 1 meter in height and thus could also have served on an altar. For a slightly later example, see the wood sculpture by Stefano Lamberti in the parish church of Condino, dated 1530 (illustration in *Imago Lignea: Sculture lignee nel Trentino dal XIII al XIV secolo,* ed. Enrico Castelnuovo, Trent: Temi, 1989, cat. 35). Other solutions were closer to Michelangelo's in offering a historiated scene organized around a Man of Sorrows-like Christ. We see deliberate and rather awkward efforts to preserve the Man of Sorrows at the center of a narrative scene in, for example, a lost *Lamentation* by Polidoro da Caravaggio formerly in San Silvestro in Rome whose composition is preserved in a drawing in Chantilly (see Lanfranco Ravelli, *Polidoro a San Silvestro al Quirinale,* Bergamo:Edizioni dell'Ateneo di scienze, lettere ed arti, 1987, figure 3). Another example is a never-executed *Lamentation* by Baccio Bandinelli, the preparatory drawings for which show an extremely theatrical staging; see, most dramatically, the drawing in the Uffizi, Annamaria Petrioli Tofani, *Gabinetto disegni e stampe degli Uffizi. Inventario.* III. *Disegni di figura,* Florence: Olschki, 1991, inv. n. 539F, p. 229; the drawing is discussed in relation to the commission by Philippe Costamagna, "La création de l' ordre des théatins et ses répercussions sur l'art de Rosso Fiorentino et de ses contemporains," in *Pontormo e Rosso,* eds. Roberto P. Ciardi and Antonio Natali, Venice, Marsilio, 161, n. 17. I discuss the case of Rosso's *Dead Christ* in Boston in chapter 5.

9 For the trend of placing tabernacles, traditionally kept on side walls, on altars toward the late fifteenth century, see Braun, 1924, II, 349 and 589. See also Otto Kurz, "A Group of Florentine Drawings for an Altar," *Journal of the Warburg and Courtauld Institutes,* 18, 1955, 35–53; Hans Caspary, *Das Tabernakel in Italien bis zum Konzil von Trient,* Munich: Inaugural-Dissertation, Ludwig-Maximilians-Universität, 1964, 68–88, van Os, 1984–90, II, 207–12; and Humfrey, 1993, especially 73–4. The strength of the trend can be gauged by listing only the Italian cathedrals that saw sacrament tabernacles placed on their high altars in this period: in Florence (1496, under Savonarola, see n. 11), Aquileia (ca. 1500), Siena (1506), Vicenza (1532), Verona (1535). At San Marco in Venice (not a cathedral at this time, of course), the *Pala d'Oro* was unremovable, but in 1517 a sacrament altar by the Bregno shop was placed in the apse directly behind it.

10 Humfrey, 1993, 72. For examples of the contractual manifestations of these private interests, and their manifestation in a saint-oriented piety, see Hope, 1990.

11 The diarist Luca Landucci reported an episode that reveals a clear link between Savonarolan policy and the placement of a sacrament tabernacle on the high altar of Florence Cathedral; *A Florentine Diary from 1450 to 1516,* trans. Alice de Rosen Jervis, London: Dent, New York: Dutton, 1927, 128–9: "29th November [1496]. The crucifix was taken off the high altar at Santa Maria del Fiore, and put down below, where the canons sit; and on the high altar was placed instead a carved wooden tabernacle for the host, not yet gilt but beautiful to see." And then, in 1498, after the fall of Savonarola (141): "2nd May. The tabernacle which had been placed on the high altar in Santa Maria del Fiore to contain the host was taken away again, and the crucifix replaced there as before." It was a standard feature of Gian Matteo Giberti's pastoral visits to demand that sacrament tabernacles be

restored, cleaned, removed from their traditional obscure locations, and placed on the high altar of the church. An entirely typical example appears in his early pastoral visit within the city of Verona in 1529, on a visit to the church of Santa Maria della Rocca Maggiore: ". . .*ubi factis debitis officiis et exequiis pro defunctis iuxta solitum, primo se contulit ad locum sacratissimi Corporis Domini nostri Iesu Christi, quo viso, mandavit vas seu tabernaculum restaurari et poni in eo frustum corporalis, ut mundius conservetur et reponi in medio altaris maioris ut in aliis imposuit.*" *Riforma Pretridentina della Diocesi di Verona: Visite Pastorali del Vescovo G. M. Giberti, 1525–42,* ed. Antonio Fasani, III, Vicenza: Istituto per le Ricerche di Storia Sociale e di Storia Religiosa, 1989, 1557. On Giberti's Christocentric emphasis, see Prosperi, 1969, 270–1. Giberti's most spectacular intervention, of course, occurred in the choir of Verona Cathedral, where a sacrament tabernacle was placed on the high altar and surrounded by Michele Sanmicheli's *tornacoro* in 1534.

12 Panofsky, 1953, 250–8; Belting, 1994, 432–42; Bernhard Decker, *Das Ende des mittelalterlichen Kultbildes und die Plastik Hans Leinbergers,* Bamberger Studien zur Kunstgeschichte und Denkmalpflege, ed. R. Suckale and A. Hubel, III, Bamberg, 1985; idem, "Reform within the Cult Image: The German Winged Altarpiece before the Reformation," in Humfrey and Kemp, 1990, 90–105; Joseph Koerner, *The Moment of Self-Portraiture in German Renaissance Art,* Chicago: University of Chicago Press, 1993, 80–126.

13 Matz, 1969, n. 171. On this type of *thiasos* sacrophagus, see Erwin Pochmarski, *Dionysische Gruppen: Eine typologische Untersuching zur Geschichte des Stützmotivs,* Vienna: Österreichischen Archäologischen Instituts, 1990, 157–8. The known drawings by Renaissance artists after this work are: Pisanello (sometimes attributed to Gentile da Fabriano), Milan, Biblioteca Ambrosiana, inv. F. 214 inf., n. 15 *r.*; Girolamo da Carpi, "Contraffazioni," Turin, Biblioteca Reale, T. 91, fol 15 *r.*; Guglielmo della Porta, "Della Porta Sketchbook," Düsseldorf, Kunstmuseum, fol. 7*r.* I am grateful to the *Census of Ancient Works of Art Known to the Renaissance,* Humboldt University, Berlin, for this information, and I wish to thank Professor Horst Bredekamp for facilitating my access to it. The relief also appears to have been known to Lorenzo Ghiberti; see Richard Krautheimer and Trude Krautheimer-Hess, *Lorenzo Ghiberti,* Princeton, NJ: Princeton University Press, 1956, 349 and Fig. 144.

14 Hind, V, 232, n. 7; see also Oberhuber, 1973, 494, n. 179, and Emmerling-Skala, 1994, 387. The print is based on a sarcophagus now in Blenheim palace; see Matz, 1969, n. 45, and Bober-Rubinstein, 1986, n. 80.

15 See, for example, Matz, 1969, ns. 3, 4, 35, 40, 77, and 278.

16 Bacchic subjects did not have a monopoly on this figure type, and Michelangelo would have seen it in other ancient works. Hirst, 1981a, 588, in arguing for an early dating for the London panel, pointed out similarities between the figure style in the painting and the famous drawing of a nude figure seen from behind in the Casa Buonarroti, which Wilde, 1932–34, had shown to be based on a Hercules relief, a version of which now exists in the Vatican. Wilde also argued, on the basis of Jacopino del Conte's 1541 *Baptism* in San Giovanni Decollato in Rome and a *Flagellation* by another Michelangelo student now in the Prado, that Michelangelo has also made a study of the figure in the profile view, a view that brings it very close to the female arching figure in the London painting. Another *Flagellation,* by Marten van Heemskerk, from the St. Lawrence altar in Alkmaar, now in Linköping, shows the same figure and bears an even more

striking resemblance, in reverse, to the figure in the London painting: It shows the arching back and the downturned head, and even supplies the far leg in the act of stepping up. In both this and the Prado *Flagellation* cited by Wilde, the figure is positioned on one side of a nude Christ, flanked on the other side by a figure seen from in front. More recently, Andrew Butterfield, "A Source for Michelangelo's National Gallery *Entombment*," *Mitteilungen des Kunsthistorisches Institutes in Florenz*, 33, 1989, 390, has adduced a similarly posed figure from a *Hunt of Meleager* sarcophagus – one of the dancing figures in the "procession" behind Meleager – as a model for this same figure in the painting. All of these figures share an ecstatic quality most consistently found in bacchic representations, and the further bacchic models to be discussed below suggest that in the case of the London *Entombment* the bacchic associations were paramount and colored Michelangelo's response even to sarcophagi without explicitly bacchic themes.

17 On the gem, see Antonino Giuliano, "Catalogo delle gemme che recano l'iscrizione: LAV. R. Med.," in *Il Tesoro di Lorenzo il Magnifico. Repertorio delle gemme e delle vasi*, Florence: Sansoni, 1980, 61–2, n. 33, Fig. 26. Condivi, 1911, 11 specifically mentions that Lorenzo de' Medici showed Michelangelo his gem collection. Vasari, VI, 11, states that Lorenzo's son Piero often called on Michelangelo's opinion regarding the gems in the Medici collection. On Michelangelo and antique gems, see Agosti and Farinella, 1987, 37–42. For the Medici palace medallions, see Nicole Dacos, "La fortuna delle gemme medicee nel Rinascimento," in *Il Tesoro*, (supra), 85–114, esp. 106–8. The cycle reveals a strong bacchic orientation (three, and possibly four, of the medallions represent bacchic subjects) and thus shows a significant bacchic strain in both the art and thought of Michelangelo's milieu in Florence. There was a bacchic atmosphere in other Medici homes besides that of Lorenzo the Magnificent; an antichamber of the house of Lorenzo di Pierfrancesco was festooned with *"uno panno lino depinctoni* [sic] *l'istoria di Bacho, apicatone intorno a le mura. . ."* (see John Shearman, "The Collections of the younger branch of the Medici," *Burlington Magazine*, 117, 1975, 25, n. 40).

18 Christopher Lloyd, "A Short Footnote to Raphael Studies," *Burlington Magazine*, 119, 1977, 113–14, proposed this engraving as a source for a drawing by Raphael made in preparation for his Baglioni *Entombment* (Figure 65), discussed in ch. 4 of this book. He suggested, further, that it might have acted as a common source for both Raphael's and Michelangelo's paintings.

19 Quoted by Edgar Wind, "The Maenad under the Cross," *Journal of the Warburg and Courtauld Institutes*, 1, 1937–38, 70.

20 Aby Warburg, *La Rinascita del Paganesimo Antico*, Florence: La Nuova Italia, 1966, 303, Fig. 120. This essay, "Der Eintritt des antikisierenden Idealstils in die Malerei der Frührenaissance," appears only as a précis in Warburg, 1932, 175–6. See also Friedrich Antal, "Some Examples of the Role of the Maenad in Florentine Art of the Later Fifteenth and Early Sixteenth Centuries," *Journal of the Warburg and Courtauld Institutes*, 1, 1937–38, 71–3.

21 Hirst, 1981a, 588.

22 Philostratus, *Imagines*, trans. A. Fairbanks, Cambridge, MA: Harvard University Press, 1979, 9 (1.2.7–9).

23 Erika Tietze-Conrat, *Mantegna*, London: Phaidon, 1955, 243.

24 Hirst, 1981a. For the letter, see *Carteggio*, I, letter I, 1.

25 Dvořák, 1989, 80–1 called it *"das erste heidnisch gedachte Bildwerk seit der Antike."* Wind, 1968, 177–90, also stressed the relationship of the *Bacchus* to the antique in the context of Renaissance debates *de imitatione,* although with dubious conclusions as to Michelangelo's position in the debate. One wonders, of course, also about the colossal marble *Hercules* that Michelangelo made between 1492 and 1494, which was first recorded in the Strozzi family and was later sent to France. See Tolnay, 1949, 197–8, Paul Joannides, "Michelangelo's Lost Hercules," *Burlington Magazine, CXIX,* 1977, 550–4, and idem, "A supplement to Michelangelo's lost Hercules," *Burlington Magazine, CXXIII,* 1981, 20–3. Michael Hirst, "Michelangelo, Carrara and the Marble for the Cardinal's Pietà," *Burlington Magazine, CXXVII,* 1985, 154–9 suggested that Piero de' Medici originally commissioned this work; see also his remarks in *Carteggio Indiretto,* II, App. 2, n. 1, 497–500.

26 Wind, 1968, 178. See also Gesing, 1988, 44–5.

27 On Dionysus as a "suffering god" and his relation to festivals of the dead, see Walter F. Otto, *Dionysus: Myth and Cult,* trans. Robert Palmer, Bloomington: Indiana University Press, 1965, chs. 9 and 17. On Dionysus' role in funerary contexts see also Pierre Boyancé, *Le culte des Muses chez les philosophes grecs: Études d'histoire et de psychologie religieuse,* Paris: Boccard, 1937, ch. 3; Susan Cole, "Voices from beyond the grave: Dionysos and the dead," in *Masks of Dionysos,* ed. Thomas Carpenter and Christopher Faraone, Ithaca, NY: Cornell University Press, 1993, 276–95; and Dirk Obbink, "Dionysos Poured Out: Ancient and Modern Theories of Sacrifice and Cultural Formation," in ibid., 65–86.

28 Marcel Detienne, *Dionysos at Large,* trans. Arthur Goldhammer, Cambridge, MA: Harvard University Press, 1989, 46–56 and 79–83.

29 I am grateful to John Shearman for having first pointed this out to me. Could it be that this departure from the antique was at the basis of Riario's decision to reject the work (see Hirst, 1994, 31)? Michelangelo came to Riario's notice through a convincing forgery (the lost *Sleeping Cupid*), and the work was returned to the artist when it was discovered not to be a true antique. In the *Bacchus,* Michelangelo openly declared his freedom from antique models, as has often been recognized, and it is likely that this pleased Riario even less. As Hirst noted, Riario's rejection of the *Bacchus* would explain the disparaging comments about the cardinal made in Condivi's biography (Condivi, 1911, 20: "Cardinal di San Giorgio understood little and was no judge of sculpture"). If rigid classicism was at the basis of Riario's aversion to "modern antiquities" (Hibbard, 1985, 42), then this episode may well constitute a "practical" instance of the debate *de imitatione*: Riario, in this case, represents the side of the strict Ciceronians and Michelangelo represents the side of those in favor of eclectic emulation, on the model of his recent advisor Angelo Poliziano. For the distinction between imitation and emulation, see G. W. Pigman, "Versions of Imitation in the Renaissance," *Renaissance Quarterly,* 33, 1980, 1–32. For the exchange between Poliziano and Paolo Cortesi, see *Prosatori Latini del Quattrocento,* ed. Eugenio Garin, Milan: Ricciardi, 1952, 902–10. For the later exchanges between Giovanni Pico della Mirandola and Ermolao Barbaro, and between Giovanfrancesco Pico and Pietro Bembo, see Giorgio Santangelo, *Le epistole "De imitatione" di Giovanfrancesco Pico della Mirandola e di Pietro Bembo,* Florence: Olschki, 1954, and idem, *Il Bembo critico e il principio d'imitazione,* Florence: Sansoni, 1950. See also Scott, 1910, which contains English translations of the Pico-Bembo letters, as

well as of Erasmus' *Ciceronianus.* For some applications of these debates to the visual arts see Eugenio Battisti, "Il concetto d'imitazione nel Cinquecento," in *Rinascimento e Barocco,* Turin: Einaudi, 1960, 175–215. On Riario's antiquarianism, see Margaret Daly Davis, "'Opus isodomum' at the Palazzo della Cancelleria: Vitruvian Studies and Archeological and Antiquarian Interests at the Court of Raffaelle Riario," in *Roma, centro ideale della cultura dell'Antico nei secoli XV e XVI: da Martino V al sacco di Roma, 1417–1527,* ed. Silvia Danesi Squarzina, Milan: Electa, 1989, 442–57. On Michelangelo's alliance with Poliziano in the imitation debate, see Giovanni Agosti's entry on the *Battle of Lapiths and Centaurs* in and Farinella, 1992, 25–7, which offers ample evidence against Wind's puzzling positioning of Michelangelo on the "intransigent" or "Ciceronian" side of the debate (1968, 182, n. 14).

30 For the emphasis on blood and gore in representations of the Passion, see Marrow, 1979. For the tradition of the "sweetness" of the Passion, see Friedrich Ohly, *Süsse Nägel der Passion: ein Beitrag zur theologischen Semantik,* Baden-Baden: Koerner, 1989.

31 Daniélou, 1944, 277 and *ff.*

32 *Phaedrus,* 244A–245B; 249E; 265A–B.

33 On Gregory of Nyssa, see Daniélou, 1944, esp. 275–308. On Ambrose, Augustine, and Jerome, see Lewy, 1929, 146–64. Lewy's patristic citations are often unreliable; where I cite from Lewy, I have corrected them.

34 St. Ambrose, *De fide libri V (ad Gratianum Augustum),* book 1, ch. 20; Migne, *PL, XVI,* 559 (excerpted and discussed in Lewy, 1929, 148): *"Ex hoc ergo botryone est vinum quod laetificat cor hominis, sobrietatem inebriat, crapulam fidei et verae religionis exhalat, crapulam castitatis infudit."*

35 St. Ambrose, *Expositio in Psalmum CXVIII,* sermo 15, 28; Migne, *PL,* XV, 1428 (cited in Lewy, 1929, 148, n. 2): "Hac ergo ebrietate corpus non titubat, sed resurgit; animus non confunditur, sed consecratur."

36 St. Ambrose, *De mysteriis,* ch. IX, paragraph 58; Migne, *PL,* XVI, 426. Here, too, Ambrose invokes Psalm 103:15.

37 St. Augustine, *Enarrationes in Psalmos,* Psalm 35, paragraph 14; Migne, *PL,* XXXVI, 351 (excerpted in Lewy, 1929, 161–2): *"Nolite mirari; ebrii erant. Unde ebrii erant? Videte: acceperunt calicem unde inebriarentur. . . . Ergo, fratres, simus filii hominum, et speremus sub tegmine alarum eius, et inebriemur ab ubertate domus eius."*

38 Savonarola, III, 1971, sermon XLVIII, 396–7.

39 The *Ovide Moralisé,* 118–19, interprets the myth of Semele as an example of what happens to a *"corps dissolu et plain d'yvresse et de glottonie."* After a conventional condemnation of the sins of drunkenness and luxury, the author then invoked the alternative reading: *"Autre sentence y peut on prendre comme il s'en suit, c'est assavoir que par Semele nous est signifié la voulenté devote de creature humaine qui est enyvree de divine amour et tousiours subgette et soubzmise à crainte de Dieu offenser. . . . De tel amour one esté enyvrez les glorieux saincts et sainctes, dont les ungs par force d'amour se sont voluntairement souffers martirez, et les autres sont es cieulx volez et colloquez en pardurable gloire."*

40 Giovanni Pico della Mirandola, *Oration on the Dignity of Man,* in *The Renaissance Philosophy of Man,* eds. Ernst Cassirer, Paul Oskar Kristeller, and John Hermann Randall, Chicago: Chicago University Press, 1948, 234.

41 See above all his *Commentarium in Phedrum,* part of his *Commentaria in Platonem* published in Florence in 1496; text and translation in Allen, 1981, 82–6. Ficino's

earliest treatment of the problem occurs in his epistolary tract of 1457, *De divino furore,* addressed to Peregrino Agli; see Ficino (1570), 1962, I, 612–15, and English translation in *The Letters of Marsilio Ficino,* trans. Members of the Language Department of the School of Economic Science in London, London: Shepheard-Walwyn, I, 1975, 44–8. For other accounts of the madnesses, see his *Epitome* of Plato's *Ion* in Ficino (1570), 1962, II, 1281–4, and his *In Convivium Platonis sive de amore* (7.14, 15), ed. and trans. Raymond Marcel as *Marsile Ficin: Commentaire sur le banquet de Platon,* Paris: Les Belles Lettres, 1956, 258–60. For Ficino's alterations to and elaborations on Plato's account of the madnesses, see Allen, 1984, 43–68. See also Chastel, 1954, 129–35. For our purposes, two things are interesting about Ficino's adaptation of the Platonic schema: The order is not stable, and the four forms of frenzy are often mingled. Ficino devoted a small chapter in his commentary on the *Phaedrus* to explaining why this mutual contamination of the frenzies must occur. It is an important passage, because in Michelangelo's preoccupation with the theme, especially in his late *Pietàs*, there is a mingling of love ecstasy and the religious or mysterious ecstasy associated with Bacchus, very much along the lines described by Ficino. Allen, 1981, 142–5, cap. XIIII (245A), "*How the four divine frenzies are joined together. The mundane gods. The divine and human souls:* In describing any one frenzy, Socrates in a way recalls the others: not unjustly so, for they are mutually joined (*coniugati*). In the intelligible world the illuminating power of Apollo possess the related inciting (*provocantem*) and, as it were, heating (*calefactoriam*) power of Bacchus. The power for prophecy and poetry flourishes in the illuminating power, the power for love and [priestly] prayer in the inciting power (*in provocatrice*). In the heavens there is a similar bond in the Sun and near the Sun. For light and heat refer to both Apollo and Bacchus. Furthermore, the Sun's power incites us via Mercury to the Muses [that is, to poetry], and via Venus to love. . . . Finally, in us the understanding and the will are kin: prophecy and poetry pertain to the former, but priestly prayer (*mysteriale votum*) along with love to the latter. Accordingly, we often flee from prophecy to prayers, and often from prayers we acquire prophecy. On the one hand we sing divine hymns with the Muse [that is, with poetry]; on the other we are incited to the love of divine things. In turn, by always loving such ardently, we prophesy many matters and perform mysteries effectively and sing hymns of admiration." See also Allen, 1984, 66–7.

42 The passage occurs in his *Epitome* of the second dialogue of Plato's *Republic*; Ficino (1570), 1962, II, 1399: "*Ebrietas ergo sit duplex: altera quidem sub Luna, letheo induct potu, per quam anima extra se posita, et infra se posita obliviscitur divinorum, circa terrena delirans: altera vero super Lunam, nectarea proveniens potione, per quam animus extra se positus, supra se positus, morborum mortalium obliviscitur: suscipiensque divina, quasi primo illorum splendore caligat. . .*" Giovanni Pico della Mirandola took over the distinction in his *Conclusiones; Opera omnia* (reprint of edition of Basel, 1572), Turin: Bottega d'Erasmo, 1971, I, 104, n. 6. Gesing, 1988, 78, argued that the distinction is acknowledged and respected in Mantegna's bacchic prints.

43 The passage, which occurs in Ficino's preface to the *Mystical Theology* of Pseudo-Dionysus (see Ficino [1570], 1962, 1013), is quoted by Wind, 1968, 62, whose translation I follow. Cf. Summa 10 from the *Commentarium in Phaedrus*; Allen, 1981, 138: "Finally since he [Socrates] has become ecstatic through Bacchus, perhaps the Apollonian demon enraptures him (for Apollo is closest to Bacchus)

with the result that he even exceeds the bounds of human behavior and thereafter treats of the divine love that excites us through some frenzy."

44 Ficino, *Theologia Platonica* (1474), ed. Raymond Marcel, Paris: Les Belles Lettres, 1964, 222 (XIII, 2): "Let us conclude now that by these seven types of presage the superiority of the human soul with regard to matter is so great that, when the body is dominated, softened and half-dead, its vision is much clearer, its activity is more remarkable than when the body operates, as if it did not need the cooperation of the body to realise all manner of marvels. This is how it is shown how great is the accord between the soul and the divine beings, how great is its relation to God, since every time that it turns in on itself, it participates in celestial mysteries and in divine providence." Allen, 1984, 59, n. 55 believed that Chastel, 1954, 44, drew an overly rigid distinction between the *vacationes mentis* described here and the *furores* described in the *Phaedrus* commentary and elsewhere, rightly pointing out the similarity between Ficino's descriptions of the two states. As Allen notes, the similarity was also observed by Frances Yates, *The French Academies of the Sixteenth Century,* London: Warburg Institute, 1947, 128–9.

45 O'Malley, 1968, 148. The passage is quoted and set into cultural context by Bober, 1977, 234 and passim. I have benefited greatly from exchanges with John O'Malley on these matters.

46 See Boyle, 1981, 51 and passim, and Screech, 1980, 35, 105, and passim. On some of these associations in Rabelais, see Florence Weinberg, *The Wine & the Will: Rabelais's Bacchic Christianity,* Detroit: Wayne State University Press, 1972.

47 Marrow, 1979, ch. 2, sec. G, 64–5: "Christ drunk."

48 Ghent, Bibliotheek der Rijksuniversiteit, MS 220, 113; quoted in Marrow, 1979, 64.

49 St. Augustine, *The City of God* (16.2), trans. John Healey, London: Dent, 1945, 100.

50 St. Jerome, *Tractatus sive homiliae in psalmos,* Psalm 80, in *Anecdota Maredsolana,* III, part 2, ed. Germain Morin, Oxford: Parker, 1897, 69–70 (excerpted in Lewy, 1929, 162, n. 1): *"Sicut ergo Dominus in passione inebriatus est, sic et sancti in ardore fidei cotidie inebriantur, et inebriantur Spiritu sancto. Tu qui die hesterna aurum colligebas, hodie procis: nonne apud ignotos videris insanus? Denique et apostoli, quoniam Spiritus sanctus descenderat super eos et inpleverat eos, et loquebantur linguis variis, propterea dicebantur musto pleni."* The two major sets of Jerome's Psalms homilies were not completely published until Morin's edition. This homily, which does not appear in Erasmus' 1516 Jerome edition, does not seem to have been known to Renaissance readers, although I hear a possible echo of Jerome's idea in Tullio Crispoldi's reference to the "pazzia della croce" in his *Historia della passione* of 1539 (see Prosperi, 1969, 274–5). The influence of Origen on these homilies has long been recognized and might well explain Jerome's ecstatic emphasis. Vittorio Peri, *Omelie Origeniane sui Salmi: Contributo all'identificazione del testo latino,* Città del Vaticano: Biblioteca Apostolica Vaticana, 1980, argued that these homilies were not merely influenced by Origen but were actually loose translations of some of Origen's lost homilies on the Psalms. I wish to thank Brian Daley for this reference and for his comments on this homily.

51 St. Augustine, *De genesi ad litteram,* book 12, ch. 5, paragraph 14; Migne, *PL,* XXXIV, 458. The passage, quoted and discussed by Screech, 1980, 49 and 197, comments on St. Paul's rapture to the third heaven (II Corinthians 12:1–4, 11). Augustine was interestingly undecided about the relation between soul and body

in such an ecstasy (I quote from Screech's translation): "The apostle . . . himself did not know whether, when he was caught up into the third heaven, he was still in the body as the soul is in the body when the body is said to be alive . . . or whether on the other hand it had entirely left his body, which lay dead until the soul came back to those dead limbs once the revelation was over. In that case he was not in a waking sleep, nor did he come back to his senses again [after] having been alienated in ecstasy, but, being dead, he was brought back to life again. . . . His mind was alienated from his body; but it is not certain whether his body was left quite dead or whether his soul [*anima*] remained there as it does when the body is alive. . . . That is no doubt why he said: 'Whether in the body, whether outside the body, I know not.'"

52 See n. 43.

53 See Allen, 1984, 45.

54 Cf. Erasmus, *The Praise of Folly,* in Erasmus, 1964, 172: "In this way the entire man will be outside of himself; and his happiness will be due to no other fact than that, so placed, he will share in the Highest Good which draws all to Itself. Although this happiness is perfected only when the souls are rejoined to their bodies, yet since in this mortal life there is, for the pious, a meditation and a foreshadowing of this, they occasionally have a foretaste of the reward to come."

55 See above all Belting, 1986.

56 Bernhard Jussen, "*Dolor* und *Memoria.* Trauerriten, gemalte Trauer und soziale Ordnungen im späten Mittelalter," in *Memoria als Kultur,* ed. Otto Gerhard Oexle, Göttingen: Vandenhoeck & Ruprecht, 1995, 207–52, made this important observation and connected the forms of expression adopted by the two artists to different "registers" in the late-medieval social code of lament. Using these criteria, Jussen was able to argue, quite convincingly, that a drawing in the Accademia of the *Man of Sorrows* (his Fig. 17), disputed in attribution between Bellini and Mantegna, should be attributed to Mantegna. True connoisseurship needs to be historically informed.

57 My reading adapts an oral communication from Leo Steinberg concerning a similar feature in the Christ of Caravaggio's Chiesa Nuova *Entombment,* now in the Vatican. See Steinberg, 1996, 81–94, 195–203. These visual solutions involve theological ideas not far from those at the basis of the long-held ritual of the Byzantine mass ceremony, the zēōn, in which warm water was mingled with the wine after consecration in recognition of the belief that they had issued warm from the body of Christ even after death, due to the vivifying presence of the holy spirit within the dead body. See Grondijs, 1941, ch. 3 and passim.

58 See Rumy Hilloowala and Jerome Oremland, "The St Peter's Pieta: A Madonna and Child? – An Anatomical and Psychological Reevaluation," *Leonardo,* 20, 1987, 87–92.

59 Dunkerton, 1994, 117.

60 According to Hirst, 1981a, 589, n. 59, the only historian to remark upon this feature was Venturi, 1925, 730: "*Eppure il nudo alabastrino non è piagato, non porta segni di martirio, di struggimento, di morte.*" Dunkerton, 1994, 118, confirmed that although the painting is unfinished in certain parts, these areas are brought to a level of finish such as to have shown wounds had Michelangelo intended to paint them.

61 Venturi, 1925, 731: "*. . .dopo il riposo, il corpo intatto, incorrotto e incorrottibile del Redentore balzerà catapulta contro il male e il peccato.*"

62 Raymond of Capua, *Vita Sanctae Catherinae,* ch. III, *Acta Sanctorum,* ed. Jean Carnandet, Paris: Palme, 1863–1940, XII, 889: "Quis enim putasset corpus meum, dum tam dure patiebatur et moriebatur in cruce, ac dum postea jacebat exanime, vitam habere semper in se latentem, et unione indivisibili unitam? Certe nedum extranei ac perversi, sed nec ipsi Apostoli mei, qui tanto fuerant mecum tempore, hoc credere potuerunt: omnes perdiderunt fidem et spem. Et tamen, licet verissime hoc corpus meum non viveret vita, quam percipiebat ab anima propria; habebat tamen secum unitam vitam interminatam, qua omnia viventia vivunt: cujus virtute, tempore quo ab aeterno fuit decretum, spiritus ei proprius fuit reunitus, cum longe majori vitae ac virtutis collatione quam prius: quia cum immortalitatis, impassibilitatis et aliarum dotium dono, quibus prius donatum non fuerat."

63 Pietro da Lucca, 1527, the section entitled "Contemplatione sopra le venerande exequie e la molto honorata sepoltura del nostro Signore," 117 *v.*: *"Cominciano ad apparire segni di gloria e di vittoria. Imperho che lo extinto e vulnerato e deformato corpo del signore in uno istante per respiro de la povera madre et de li circonstanti fu fatto tutto sano, candido, e bianco come se mai ferita ne battitura alcuna ricevesse."* And 118 *v.*: *". . .benche fusse morto e da l'anima separato, niente di meno sempre fu con la divinita unito e congionto."* Less theologically inventive, the simple idea that Christ was "asleep" rather than dead appears to have been rather widespread. The metaphor appears in Byzantine religious poetry (see Belting, 1994, 270), and is invoked virtually as a commonplace in Hartmann Schedel's *Liber chronicarum,* Nuremberg, Koberger, 1493 (reprint New York: Landmark Press, 1979), lxxxi *v.,* where in Jerusalem he mentions *"der Grab in dem der herr von unßern wegen geschlaffen hat."*

64 Hirst, 1981a, 588.

65 Dunkerton, 1994, 118.

66 Hirst, 1981a, 589, n. 59. On the relation between classical nude and Christian cult image in the statue, see also Wolfgang Lotz, "Zu Michelangelos Christus in S. Maria sopra Minerva," in *Festschrift für Herbert von Einem zum 16. Februar 1965,* eds. Gert von der Osten and Georg Kauffman, Berlin: Mann, 1965, 143–50, and Steinberg, 1996, 19–22 and 146–7.

67 Aspects of this culture that are especially relevant to my concerns are studied by O'Malley, 1979. See also idem, "The Theology Behind the Sistine Ceiling," in Carlo Pietrangeli et al., *The Sistine Chapel: the Art, the History, the Restoration* (New York: Harmony, 1986), esp. 108–22, and the essays collected in idem, 1981. See also D'Amico, 1983, Charles Stinger, *The Renaissance in Rome,* Bloomington: Indiana University Press, 1985, and most recently Rowland, 1998.

68 See Hirst, 1981a, Nagel, 1994, and Hirst, 1994, 59. Whether or not this hypothesis is accepted, the commission of an altarpiece from Michelangelo for this church, under the sponsorship of Jacopo Gallo (Hirst, 1981a, App. B, Doc. 5), establishes the connection between the artist, his friend Gallo, and Sant'Agostino, a connection that extended to Michelangelo's first Roman patron, Raffaelle Riario, who was Cardinal Protector of the Augustinian Order and was also involved in the Sant'Agostino commission (Hirst, 1981a, App. A, Doc. 1). An important and underappreciated link to the humanist milieu located at Sant'Agostino might well have been Cardinal Francesco Piccolomini, the future Pius III. He had a hand in the negotiations over the endowment for this chapel (Nagel, 1994, 166), and was a well-known patron to the humanists there. Aurelio Lippo Brandolini, the most prominent figure at the convent of Sant'Agostino before Giles of

Viterbo, dedicated both his *De ratione scribendi* and his *In sacram Hebraorum historiam Epithoma* to Piccolomini. (Both treatises are discussed below). Piccolomini was to commission fifteen statues from Michelangelo for his altar in the Siena cathedral only a year later in 1501, just after Michelangelo left Rome. The cardinal very probably entered into negotiations with Michelangelo about this project while the artist was still in Rome engaged in the Sant'Agostino commission, a commission in which, as I mentioned above, Piccolomini had a hand. It is almost certain that the cardinal knew the artist already before the Sant'Agostino commission. Piccolomini was the executor of the last will of Cardinal de Bilhères, the patron of the St. Peter's *Pietà,* and thus would have been aware of the artist from 1497; see Kathleen Weil-Garris, "Michelangelo's *Pietà* for the Cappella del Rè di Francia," in *'Il se rendit en Italie,' Études offertes à André Chastel,* Rome: Edizioni del Elefante, 1987, 97, n. 60. I thank John Shearman for first alerting me to this fact.

69 Wind, 1968, 177–90.

70 Giles of Viterbo, fols. 197*v.*–198*r.,* quoted and paraphrased by Wind, 1968, 187.

71 See Bober, 1977; and now, most importantly, Rowland, 1998.

72 Wilde, 1932–34, and Dvořák, 1989, 80: *"So war Michelangelo der erste unter den Künstlern der Neuzeit, der den grundsätzlichen Gegensatz zwischen der Antike und der Kunst seiner Zeit empfand und sich von dieser abwendend jener sich nicht nur wie seine Vorgänger in einzelnen formalen Vorzügen, sondern in der ganzen Auffassung der Kunst und ihres Verhältnisses zu den naturlichen Gegegebenheiten und zum christlichen Vorstellungsleben näherte."*

73 This is not to say that the type had not already been adapted in Italy (see Wolfgang Körte, "Deutsche Vesperbilder in Italien," *Kunstgeschichtliches Jahrbuch der Bibliotheca Hertziana,* I, 1937, 1–138), but given that Michelangelo's commission came from a French patron, it seems reasonable to assume a more direct relation to the northern tradition.

74 Milanesi, 1875, 614: "*. . .sarà la più bella opera di marmo che sia hoge in Roma, et che maestro nisuno lo faria megliore hoge.*"

75 Shearman, 1992, 236–7.

76 Vasari, VI, 16.

77 Burckhardt, 1988, 36. For a thoroughgoing study of the group, see Weil-Garris (as in n. 65). Her reconstruction has been contested by William Wallace, "Michelangelo's Rome *Pietà*: Altarpiece or Grave Memorial?" in *Verrocchio and Late Quattrocento Italian Sculpture,* eds. Steven Bule, Alan Phipps Darr, Fiorella Superbi Gioffredi, Florence: Le Lettere, 1992, 243–255, who proposed that the group originally stood on the ground and was not associated with the altar. The issue will most likely not be settled until further evidence comes to light.

78 On Andrea Sansovino's sculpture and its context, see Virginia Anne Bonito, "The Saint Anne Altar in Sant' Agostino, Rome: A New Discovery," *Burlington Magazine,* CXXII, 1980, 805–12; idem, "The Saint Anne Altar in Sant'Agostino: Restoration and interpretation," *Burlington Magazine,* CXXIV, 1982, 268–76; and idem, 1983. For more on its cultural context, see also Bober, 1977. My thinking about Sansovino's group has benefited greatly from a 1997 graduate seminar paper by Elisabeth Neumann, "The Saint Anne Altar in Sant'Agostino Reconsidered." On Jacopo's *Madonna* see Bruce Boucher, *The Sculpture of Jacopo Sansovino,* I, New Haven, CT; Yale University Press, 1991, 25–28, and II, cat. 10. Jacopo's remarkable figure of *St. James* for the church of San Giacomo degli

Spagnuoli (original now in Santa Maria di Monserrato) is also part of this trend and is notable particularly for reviving the antique type of the standing figure in the context of a Christian altar.

79 Giles of Viterbo, 197v. Under the heading *"Scriptorum sacrorum elegantia,"* the passage assesses the writings of the church fathers and culminates in the present century, *"quo post eversam aurei seculi veram elegantiam nulla aetas pervenit."* He mentioned Pontano's hymns and Sannazzaro's *De partu Virginis* and then the fact that *"ad Divae Annae aram meo in templo per Coricium erectam: certamen Poetarum visum"* (a reference to the poems of the *Coryciana*), and asserted that these sacred celebrations were the chaste successors of the poetic contests of antiquity: *"cessit venus virgini, impudicitia* [unreadable], *luxuria castitati."* A fuller description of these celebrations is given in the published edition of these poems, *Coryciana,* ed. Blossius Palladius, Rome: Ludovicus Vicentinus and Lautitius Perusinus, 1524, iv–v; see Bonito, 1983, 21–22. Giles expressed similar sentiments when discussing the greatest artistic project of the period, the new St. Peter's (193*r.*–194*v.*), where he asserted that Julius II *"soli posuit tabernaculum huius saeculi ultimus . . . quod in maioris templis ut sol noctis syderibus comparatur."* On Giles's reform thought, see O'Malley, 1968, and "Giles of Viterbo, a reformer's thought on Renaissance Rome," in O'Malley, 1981, 1–11. For an excellent study of the relation between this papal culture and the visual arts see Ingrid Rowland, "Render unto Caesar the Things which are Caesar's: Humanism and the Arts in the Patronage of Agostino Chigi," *Renaissance Quarterly,* 39, 1986, 673–730, and also Rowland, 1998.

80 On the *Coryciana* and Goritz's feasts, see Bober, 1977, Bonito, 1983, Jozef Ijsewijn, "Poetry in a Roman Garden: The Coryciana," in *Latin Poetry and the Classical Tradition: Essays in Medieval and Renaissance Literature,* ed. Peter Godman and Oswyn Murray, Oxford: Clarendon, 1990, 211–31, and Julia Haig Gaisser, "The Rise and Fall of Goritz's Feasts," *Renaissance Quarterly,* 48, 1995, 41–55.

81 I quote from the more easily accessible selection provided by Bonito, 1983, where Sadoleto's epigram appears on p. 240: *"Doctum, et nobile te simul cöegit, / Has Iane ingenii locare formas / Illa est Nobilitas quae unus audes / Nostro aeuo veteres referre vultus. . ."* (The critical edition of the *Coryciana* by Jospeh Ijsewijn [Rome: Herder, 1997] did not become accessible to me in the preparation of this study.)

82 See the poems by Blossius Palladius, B. Dardanus, Castiglione, and Delius Hieronymus Alexandrinus; Bonito, 1983, 251–3, 261, 285–6, 300–03, respectively. See also Bober, 1977, who shows that in Goritz's circle the cult of St. Anne was associated with the cult of the nymph Corycia, the virgin bride who presided over a grotto-fountain. Bober stresses the dionysiac orientation of this cult, and of the assemblies held at the villas of Goritz, Angelo Colocci and, until his death in 1505, Jacopo Gallo.

83 On the pilgrimage to the Fair Virgin at Regensburg (1519–21), see David Freedberg, *The Power of Images: Studies in the History and Theory of Response,* Chicago: University of Chicago Press, 1989, 100–04; Belting, 1994, 453–7; and Christopher Wood, "Ritual and the Virgin on the Column: The Cult of the Schöne Maria at Regensburg," *Journal of Ritual Studies,* 6, 1992, 87–107.

84 In a poem by Panhormitanus; Bonito, 1983, 280: *"Inter naturam atque artem cum facta fuissent / Haec tria signa, fuit mens nova de statuis."* It is interesting to observe that a split emerged between this high-level humanist "cult" and more popular cultic traditions. Jacopo Sansovino's *Madonna del Parto* was to become one of the

most popular cult statues in Rome, as can be seen from the *ex votos* that still surround it. What was projected as a revival of the antique under sophisticated Christian humanist auspices was, at a lower social level, taken up into living cult practices. The sculpture's popular audience responded with familiar forms of Christian image worship, and it is likely that the overt references to antique models touched a still-vital pagan undercurrent latent in popular piety. By contrast, Andrea Sansovino's *St. Anne* group, with its more contrived artistic references and involved figural structure, does not seem ever to have made much of an impression on popular audiences. Conceived in a sophisticated scholarly and artistic ambient, it remains the concern of scholars to this day.

85 In Michelangelo, typically, we find some ambivalence over this departure, Wilde, 1978, 41, noticed that the *Pietà,* though freestanding, is finished only in front, a feature that led him to suggest that it should be called "a high-relief rather than a free-standing group." Despite the highly plastic treatment and the references to freestanding antique sculpture, therefore, the group shows a continuing attachment to a tradition of relief sculpture more common to Christian altars. On the traditional attachment of Christian sculptures to columns, tabernacles, and niches, see Walter Paatz, "Von den Gattungen und vom Sinn der gotischen Rundfigur," in *Sitzungsberichte der Heidelberger Akademie der Wissenschaften, Philosophisch-historische Klasse,* 38, 1951, 6–32.

86 Hirst, 1994, 42–6, offered an acute analysis of these features and a cogent comparison to Granacci's panel. He also argued, convincingly, that the Manchester *Madonna* prepares, rather than reflects, the solution found in the Bruges *Madonna.*

87 The related case of the *Doni Tondo* is discussed in chapter 7 of this book.

88 In the *Bruges Madonna* the motif of the Child stepping onto the fold of the Virgin's robe, and in the *Medici Madonna* the turn of the Virgin's shoulders.

89 Sheryl E. Reiss, "A medieval source for Michelangelo's Medici Madonna," *Zeitschrift für Kunstgeschichte,* L, 1987, 394–400. Reiss pointed out (400, n. 25) that the icon, known as the *Madonna di San Zanobi,* would have had special significance for Giulio de' Medici, Michelangelo's patron, both because Cardinal Giulio, as archbishop of Florence, was Saint Zenobius's spiritual successor and because Giulio, who was born on May 27, shortly after Saint Zenobius's feast day, was himself given the middle name of Zanobi.

90 For Pietro da Lucca's text, see n. 63. For Michelangelo's contract for the Piccolomini altar, see Milanesi, 1875, 616–19.

91 The distinction was evidently also a concern for Erasmus. See the *Enarratio in Psalmum XXXIII* ASD, I, 3, 101: *"Haec eo pluribus inculcare visum est, quo simul et illorum errori mederemur, qui non multo religiosius legunt sacras historias, quam Herodotum aut Titum Livium, et eorum fidem ac vigilantiam excitarem, quibus persuasum est in omnibus scripturis divino spiritu proditis latere Christum. Littera occidit, inquit Paulus, spiritus vivificat."*

92 *Delle virtù mostrateci nella Passione dal nostro signor Gesù Cristo,* Rome Stamperia Ermateniana, 1767, 22–4: *"Non enim nunc aut Gavianam crucem, ut Tullius; aut Cesarem necem, ut Maro; aut principis alicujus mortem, ut veteres saepe fecere, deploramus aut describimus: sed eam Crucem, in qua Christus Rex Regum, Princeps Principium, verus Deus, Deique Filius, ab iis ipsis, quos creaverat, quos legibus erudierat, quos innumeris beneficiis affecerat, quorum denique caussa factus Homo, ad homines venerat, contra jus fasque omne crucifixus est. . . . Hanc vero quum nulla vis eloquentiae attingere, nullum*

ingenii acumen penetrare, nullius mentis amplitudo comprehendere, aut complecti queat." Not all the humanist preachers observed Brandolini's sense of Christian decorum, as Erasmus made devastatingly clear in the *Ciceronianus,* where he described another Good Friday sermon at the Sistine Chapel (given by a Ciceronian whom he refrains from naming) who deplored the death of Christ "as he would have the death of Socrates or Phocion, who, though they had committed no crime, were compelled through the ingratitude of their fellow-citizens to drink the hemlock; or of Epaminondas who on account of his brilliant campaigns was compelled to plead for his life before the people; or of Scipio who after so many services to the Republic went out to exile. . . . I ask what could be more unconvincing or inappropriate than this?" (I quote from Scott, 1910, 64.)

93 O'Malley, 1979.

94 The treatise, *De ratione scribendi libri tres,* is discussed by O'Malley, 1979, 45–51. It was dedicated to Cardinal Francesco Piccolomini, who became Michelangelo's patron in 1501 and who very likely knew the artist at least from the time of the commissioning of the Vatican *Pietà,* i.e., 1497 (see n. 68).

95 O'Malley, 1979, 49.

96 O'Malley, 1979, 63.

97 Savonarola, II, 1971, sermon XVIII, 21: *"Il culto divino esteriore t'ho detto altre volte che è ordinato allo interiore, e tutto l'ordine di questo è ordinato a Dio. . . . Le cerimonie della Chiesa sono ordinate alli sacramenti, li sacramenti sono ordinati a l'uomo e l'uomo al ben e beato vivere, il ben e beato vivere a perfezione del universo, e quella è ordinata a Dio. . . . Ma li tepidi hanno fatto tutto a rovescio, perché dove ogni cosa è ordinata e debbasi fare per gloria di Dio, eglino hanno convertito ogni cosa in gloria loro e hanno fatto sua ogni cosa che doveva essere di Dio. Li tepidi preti e religiosi ordinano là quelle belle feste e uccellano a pane, danari e candele, e poco si curano dello onore di Dio."* These are some of the fiercest sermons that Savonarola gave, and they include his famous tirades against the errors of the painters. For Condivi's statement that Michelangelo kept "always in mind the memory of [Savonarola's] living voice," see Condivi, 1911, 76. It is perhaps worth noting that of all the sermons that Savonarola gave while he was in power these are the only ones that Michelangelo could have heard: In Bologna from October 1494, he did not return to Florence before late 1495; he left again for Rome in June of 1496 and remained there until 1501.

98 Savonarola, III, 1971, sermon XLVIII, 390: *"E non consiste el vivere bene nelle cerimonie, ma nello essere drento bene regulato verso di Dio e verso il prossimo. Revocate adunque la mente vostra a Dio, e non dite: – Noi siamo ricchi –, non sperate in paramenti né in cappelle né in cose esteriori, perché io vi avviso che queste cose vi sono a peccato. . . . [391] Lasciate dunque andare tante ipocresie e atendete al culto interiore e fate penitenzia."*

99 See Eugenio Garin, *La cultura filosofica del Rinascimento italiano: ricerche e documenti,* Florence: Sansoni, 1961, 166–82, for the relation between humanist reform concerns and critiques of institutional religon in Quattrocento Italy.

100 Erasmus, 1964, 65.

101 Trinkaus, II, 1970, 648–9. The view is closely related to the humanists' "rhetorical critique of scholastic theology," for which see Trinkaus, I, 1970, 150–70, and II, 563–721, and passim, and Salvatore Camporeale, "Renaissance Humanism and the Origins of Humanist Theology," in *Humanity and Divinity in the Renaissance and Reformation: Essays in honor of Charles Trinkaus,* ed. John O'Malley, Thomas Izbicki, and Gerald Christianson, Leiden: Brill, 1993, 101–24. One example of such a critique comes in the polemical preface to Aurelio Brandolini's "literary"

retelling of the Old Testament, *In sacram Hebraorum historiam Epithoma* (Biblioteca Apostolica Vaticana, Ottob. Lat. 438), where he appeals to his dedicatee cardinal Francesco Piccolimini to support him in a typically humanist battle against the scholastic guardians of biblical exegesis, pleading for a more direct contact to Christian truth through a rhetorical, rather than theological, exposition of the Bible. The text is discussed in Trinkaus, II, 1970, 601–13, and D'Amico, 1983, 146–7.

CHAPTER FOUR. THE ALTARPIECE IN THE AGE OF HISTORY PAINTING

1 Benedetto Croce, *Estetica,* 2nd ed., Bari, 1902, 40. Quoted by Hans Robert Jauss, "Theory of Genres and Medieval Literature," in Jauss, 1982, 78.

2 Jauss, "Theory of Genres," as in n. 1, 80.

3 Charles Rosenberg, "Raphael and the Florentine *Istoria,*" in *RbR,* 175–87, argues persuasively that Raphael deliberately followed Alberti's precepts in this painting and offers some suggestions as to how Raphael might have obtained knowledge of Alberti's treatise.

4 This point was clearly perceived by Locher, 1994, 109: *"Diese Konzeption wird in ein Bildmedium übertragen, in dem sie nicht entstanden ist, wo sie sich aber bewährt und durch die Leistung des Künstlers mit der tradition dieses Bildmediums harmonisiert ist."* Although he sees it as an important innovation and turning point, therefore, Locher tends to place the work within a continuous altarpiece tradition: It effected an *"Ausdrucksweiterung und Modernisierung"* (119) of the *Aufgabe* of the altarpiece; 119–20: *"Das neue Konzept wäre der Idee nach eine konsequente Weiterführung der Entwicklung, die mit der Erfindung des Quadro und der Einführung der Perspektive im Altarbild zu Beginn des 15. Jahrhunderts ihren Anfang genommen hat."* This leads Locher, in turn, to see the Baglioni altarpiece as part of a harmonious development that is continued in Raphael's own later altarpieces. I approach the work, instead, as an instance of generic tension and conflict. The problem was addressed by Belting, 1987. An analogous case is the typological disruption that occurred in early sixteenth-century Italian villa architecture, studied by Manfredo Tafuri, "Commitenza e tipologia nelle ville palladiane," *Bollettino del C.I.S.A.* 11, 1969, 120–36. Although Raphael's later altarpieces lie beyond the scope of this book, within the logic of the argument presented here they represent a mature reaction against the youthful experiment embodied in the *Entombment*: The *Madonna of Foligno,* the *Sistine Madonna,* and, most important, the *Transfiguration* represent, in my view, a deliberate effort to reinstate values proper to the altar-piece tradition, now consciously distinguished from the emerging institution of the gallery picture.

5 See Jack M. Greenstein, *Mantegna and Painting as Historical Narrative,* Chicago: Chicago University Press, 1992, 39.

6 The most global effort to date to study the changing status of easel painting in the sixteenth and early seventeenth centuries is Stoichita, 1993.

7 Many aspects of the situation in the Venetian context have been accurately observed by Humfrey, 1993, especially the section "Altarpieces and Non-Altarpieces," 79–86. See also my review in *Art Bulletin,* 77, 1995, 139–42.

8 According to Irma A. Richter, "The Drawings for the Entombment," *Gazette des Beaux-Arts* 6 ser. 28, 1945, 344–5 the change of subject from lamentation to entombment "may have been influenced . . . by Mantegna's famous engraving of

that subject." According to Pope-Hennessey, 1970, 52, "with the change of subject, Raphael turned to a new source of inspiration, a classical sarcophagus with the death of Meleager."

9 Vasari, IV, 164: *"Immaginossi Raffaello nel componimento di quest' opera il dolore che hanno i più stretti ed amorevoli parenti nel riporre il corpo d'alcuna più cara persona, nella quale veramente consista il bene, l'onore e l'utile di tutta una famiglia."*

10 Jacob Burckhardt, *The Civilization of the Renaissance in Italy,* trans. S. G. C. Middlemore, I, New York: Harper & Row, 1958, 48.

11 See, for example, von Salis, 1947, 61–73.

12 *Cronache,* 103. For the purposes of readability, I quote longer passages from the English translation (*Chronicles*).

13 *Cronache,* 104: *"...dove era una sala nella quale erano pente tutti li capitanee che mai ebbe peroggia sino a quel dì, e similmente tutti li dottore famose, ciascuno de propio."* This palace had been built by Braccio, Grifonetto's grandfather. The inscriptions under the portraits of famous men were written by the young Matarazzo himself; they are fondly remembered in a letter from his friend Jacopo Antiquari. See Giovanni Battista Vermiglioli, *Memorie di Jacopo Antiquari,* Perugia: Baduel, 1813, 2, who claimed (100) that the two humanists were related, and Guglielmo Zappacosta, *Francesco Maturanzio umanista perugino,* Bergamo: Minerva Italica, 1970, 11. From a letter written in 1428 from Bologna by the sculptor Jacopo della Quercia we learn that this castlelike palace was built by the Bolognese architect Fioravante Fioravanti: "...and it is true that there is another architect here in Bologna, who is called Fioravante, ... and he did the castle of Braccio in Perugia..." Gilbert, 1980, 4; original text in James Beck, *Jacopo della Quercia e il Portale di San Petronio a Bologna,* Bologna: Alfa, 1970, 103.

14 *Chronicles,* 135–6.

15 *Chronicles,* 138–9.

16 *Chronicles,* 139.

17 *Chronicles,* 113.

18 *Chronicles,* 125.

19 *Chronicles,* 139.

20 Ibid.

21 Paris, Louvre, inv. 3865; Pen over stylus and black chalk, 33.4 × 39.7 cm.

22 The *Cronache,* 125, said that Guido, Astorre, and Sigismondo *"furno portato, senza lume nè altra solennità, quelli tre a San Francisco, e el corpo del nobile Simonetto a Santo Domenico."* Alison Luchs, "A Note on Raphael's Perugian Patrons," *Burlington Magazine,* CXXV, 1983, 29–31, stated that there is no firm sixteenth-century evidence to support the hypothesis that Grifonetto was buried in the family chapel in San Francesco and pointed out that he is not mentioned among those buried there in Cesare Crispolti's *Perugia Augusta* of 1648. As evidence for the opposite view, Locher, 1994, 131, n. 48, quoted a document discussed without citation by Astur, 1964, 137, n. 1: *"Un anno prima della tragedia il giovane Grifonetto ed i suoi, senza certo prevedere gli eventi, avevano già disposto il luogo della sua e loro sepoltura: Con atto del 5 marzo 1499 il Capitolo di S. Francesco concedeva a Grifonetto Baglioni che accettava a nome proprio e di sua madre Atalanta, la cappella di S. Matteo, per sè, per l'ava Angela d'Acquaviva, per Atalanta e i loro eredi."* Locher, 1994, 159, n. 56 also quoted an eighteenth-century *Dizionario dell Famiglie Perugine* (Archivio di Stato di San Pietro, Perugia, C.M. 220, vol. II, f. 143), which says about Grifonetto: *"fu con gran solennità fatto il Funere a San Fran[ces]co del Convento, ove fu sepolto, secondo alcuni, e*

secondo altri a S. Maria Nuova." The wording of this document unfortunately leaves unclear whether the uncertainty has to do with where he was buried or with where the funeral services took place.

23 Aby Warburg, "Francesco Sassetti's letztwillige Verfügung" (1907), in Warburg, 1932, 131–2. See also Eve Borsook and Johannes Offerhaus, *Francesco Sassetti and Ghirlandaio at Santa Trinita, Florence,* Doornspijk, Holland: Davaco, 1981, 15–18.

24 I owe this observation to John Shearman.

25 The question of the attribution of the *cimasa* and the frieze, and their original position on the altarpiece, is treated by Francesco Santi, *Galleria Nazionale dell'Umbria: Dipinti, sculture e oggetti dei secoli XV–XVI,* Rome: Istituto Poligrafico dello Stato, 1985, cat. nos. 101–02. The autograph drawing in Lille, Musée des Beaux-Arts, inv. 465, for the figure of God the Father appears to belong to the earliest phase of the project.

26 Locher, 1994, 79–80, also connected the figure of Charity to Atalanta's role as mother.

27 Oxford, Ashmolean Museum, n. 529; pen over stylus with traces of black chalk, 17.8 × 20.5 cm. I therefore concur with the opinion of Pope-Hennessy, 1970, 52, that this sheet, the nude study of the right-hand group (Oxford Ashmolean, Parker no. 530), and the clothed study of the same group in the British Museum (no. 1895-9-15-636) precede, rather than follow, the Louvre composition. For a different reconstruction of the sequence, see Joannides, 1983, 163.

28 The influence of the Mantegna print already at this stage was observed by Crowe and Cavalcaselle, 1882, 301; Mitsch, 1983, 93; Rosci, 1991, 35–6, and Locher, 1994, 75. The figure of St. John is most often singled out in comparisons with the Mantegna print, above all because he appears to stand alone on the right side of the sheet. This point needs to be refined, first of all because the figure's main provenance is certainly the Perugino repertoire: In the Pitti *Lamentation* two figures stand in a similar pose. The pose can, however, be interpreted as an adaptation of the more strictly Peruginesque stance in the previous composition sheet (Ashmolean, n. 529), via the nude study on Ashmolean, n. 530, in the direction of the statuesque solidity of Mantegna's St. John. Moreover, the figure's solitude is misleadingly reinforced by photographic reproduction: There is a head just sketched in behind and another figure drawn lightly in chalk in front. The St. John figure was, evidently, intended to be surrounded by those other figures that appear on the sheet of nude studies just mentioned. It remains significant, however, that only this figure was brought up to the level of finish that characterizes the rest of the sheet: This specific decision might have been affected by Mantegna's example. Further evidence of Raphael's knowledge of Mantegna's print in this period is offered by drawings after the print preserved in a sketchbook in Venice, which also includes motifs from Raphael's early works. As Silvia Ferino Pagden, *Disegni umbri del Rinascimento da Perugino a Raffaello,* Florence: Olschki, 1982, 158–62, Figs. 164 and 165, argued, the references to Raphael's early works in the sketchbook imply a date in the period before Raphael left definitively for Rome, i.e., before 1508. If her attribution of the sketchbook to Domenico Alfani, the artist who oversaw the Baglioni commission from Perugia, proves to be correct, it strongly reinforces the connection of these drawings to the Perugian commission. Although the evidence is not conclusive as to the exact date, the references to Raphael's early works suggest that the sketches after Mantegna as well were already in existence at the time the Baglioni commission was undertaken. The connection to Mantegna via the

Venetian sketchbook was also discussed by Locher, 1994, 75. That the young Raphael grew up with a close awareness of Mantegna is also indicated by the extended passage which Raphael's father, Giovanni Santi, wrote in praise of Mantegna in his *Cronaca Rimata,* book 22. For an English translation, see Gilbert, 1980, 95*ff.*

29 A connection to Signorelli's Orvieto *Lamentation* fresco has been seen by many scholars in a drawing by Raphael of the carrying of a dead body, sometimes described as the *Death of Adonis,* now in the Ashmolean (see discussion in Parker, 1956, n. 539*r*). For the young Raphael's relations to Signorelli see Creighton Gilbert, "Signorelli and Young Raphael," in *RbR,* 109–24. Tom Henry, "Signorelli, Raphael and a 'Mysterious' Pricked Drawing in Oxford," *Burlington Magazine,* CXXXV, 1993, 612–19, has recently strengthened the connection between Raphael and Signorelli – particularly the Signorelli of the Orvieto frescoes – in the years when Raphael was involved in the *Entombment.* He demonstrated that a Raphael pen drawing at Oxford, probably dating to 1506, was made on a sheet of paper that had also been used by Signorelli, as a cartoon for a figure in the *Resurrection of the Flesh* at Orvieto (Parker, 1956, n. 523). He was unable to identify the subject or purpose of the nude figure studies on the verso of this sheet, which have been connected to Michelangelo's *David* by Anna Forlani Tempesti, *Raffaello: L'Opera, Le Fonti, La Fortuna,* Novara, 1968, II, 337. To my eye, they more closely resemble his studies for carrying figures, for example those found in the Oxford drawing (Parker, 1956, n. 539*r*) just mentioned. The similarity between the figures on these two sheets, beyond confirming the attribution of these nude studies to Raphael (which some have doubted, see Henry, supra, 612, n. 2), also confirms a dating to the period ca. 1506.

30 The Signorelli banner is mentioned by Mitsch, 1994, 96, and Locher, 1994, 76, in relation to the later Oxford drawing discussed below (see Figure 69).

31 Von Salis, 1947, 72, for example, mentioned the possible connection between the use of the Meleager motif in the final painting and *"vielleicht schon der Klang des seltenen Namens Atalanta."* Joannides, 1983, 165, mentioned that "(t)he coincidence of names with Atalanta Baglione may have had some significance." Rosci, 1991, 39, repeated the suggestion but also left it undeveloped. Kurt Forster, review of Pope-Hennessey, 1970, in *Art Quarterly,* 35, 1972, 426–7, mentioned "the uncanny parallel to the mythical story of Atalanta [sic] and her son Meleager" but did not develop it into a thoroughgoing analysis of the drawings and painting. Locher, 1994, 92–3, also addressed the problem, noting some of the above-cited opinions; his own analysis did not, however, go further than pointing to the parallels drawn in the *Ovide Moralisé* between Christ and Meleager. These parallels are, however, somewhat generic. They do not, as I point out below, place interpretative emphasis on those aspects of the Meleager story most relevant in the context of Atalanta's commission, above all Althaea's moral crisis. It is my intention to show how the three thematic levels – biblical narrative, ancient myth, and personal and political history – combine in this work to produce a unique set of associations, beyond those offered in the allegorical tradition.

32 See Bodo Guthmüller, "Lateinische und volksprachliche Kommentare zu Ovid's *Metamorphosen,*" in A. Buck and O. Herding, *Der Kommentar in der Renaissance,* Boppard: Boldt, 1975, 119–39.

33 On Spirito, see Giovanni Battista Vermiglioli, *Biografia degli scrittori perugini e notizie delle opere loro,* Perugia: Bartelli, II, 1829, 300. Giulia Baglioni, née Vitelli, married

Gentile Baglioni (brother of the murdered Astorre) in 1513; see Astur, 1964, 213. On Ovid in the Perugian context generally, see Bodo Guthmüller, *Ovidio Metamorphoseos Vulgare,* Boppard: Boldt, 1981, 143–64.

34 I quote from Ovid, *Metamorphoses,* trans. Frank Justus Miller, 2nd ed., 2 vols., Cambridge, MA: Harvard University Press, 1960–64.

35 *Ovidii Metamorphosis cum commentariis Raphaelis Regii,* Venice, 1497, unpaginated (8.497): *"Videtur stulte esse dictum. Quo namque modo quis pius possit impietate? Sed pia videtur fuisse Althaea fratrum caedem ulciscendo; impia filium necando."*

36 See, for example, *Ovide Moralisé,* 232: *"Quant Dieu le Père ot envoyé czá jus son seul Filsz pour y devenir homme et homme rachapter de la prinson d'enfer, il fut tant chault et alumé du tyson et du feu de charité, qu'il voulut en son humanité souffrir la mort."* Locher, 1994, 93, cited an edition of the *Ovide Moralisé* in which the Fates are likened to the three theological virtues that figured in the predella of Raphael's altarpiece.

37 See "Francesco Sassetti's letztwillige Verfügung" (1907) and "Bildniskunst und florentinisches Bürgertum" (1902), in Warburg, 1932, 127–63, 353–65, and 89–126, 340–52, respectively.

38 Oxford, Ashmolean, no. 531; pen, 218 × 307 cm. Mitsch, 1983, 94, interpreted the figures to be lowering the body into a grave represented by the dark shaded area on the ground. This reading is supported by the activity of the figures in the mortuary study on British Museum 1963-12-16-1*v.*

39 London, British Museum, inv. no. 1963-12-16-1; pen, 21.3 × 32.0 cm. Until 1963 this drawing was known only through an engraved copy, in reverse direction, made by the Comte de Caylus when it was in the collection of Crozat. For a reproduction see Oskar Fischel, *Raphaels Zeichnungen,* IV, Berlin, 1923, n. 170.

40 This drawing also incorporates features of Meleager sarcophagi: The arms of the left carrier are shown extended and straight, as in the sarcophagi, and not in the implausible position shown in Mantegna's print. My attention was drawn to this detail by the observations of Gilbert, "Signorelli and young Raphael," in *RbR,* 122–3, who plausibly believes this drawing shows Raphael's interest in Signorelli's grisaille in the lamentation scene at Orvieto and Meleager sarcophagi and, less plausibly, that "Mantegna is not yet a major source" at this stage in the drawing process. The right carrier shows, I believe, Raphael's absorption of all these models. My point about the British Museum sheet was most closely anticipated by Charles M. Rosenberg, "Raphael and the Florentine *Istoria,*" in *RbR,* 177: "This composition is the least successful of the series, suggesting an almost schizophrenic division between the movement and tension of an Entombment and the static emotionality of a *Pietà*. It is as though Raphael were somehow trying to fulfill two commitments in a single composition, one to himself to exploit the possibilities of the Florentine narrative, and another to his patroness, to reflect her personal loss." See also the following note.

41 Oxford, Ashmolean, n. 539; pen, 26.5 × 33.0 cm. The drawing corresponds to no known Meleager composition and in fact turns the entire group in the opposite direction from those examples that are known. A significant antique precedent for the carrying of a dead body in this direction is the scene of the carrying of Hector in the "Tabula Iliaca" in the Capitoline Museum in Rome. See Von Salis, 1947, 67. It is not certain that the drawing comes at precisely this point in the development of the *Entombment* composition; indeed, Parker, 1956, n. 539, believed it to be entirely unrelated to the drawings for the *Entombment.* I introduce it merely to

point out that in this drawing and in the drawing under discussion the figures of the carriers are understood in a similar fashion. In the British Museum sheet, however, Raphael attempted to integrate the carrying motif into the more static lamentation or *pietà*-derived composition.

42 Cf. Mitsch, 1983, 95.

43 Oxford, Ashmolean Museum, n. 532; pen over rubbed black chalk, Christ's body in red chalk, 28.2 × 24.6 cm; and London, British Museum, Department of Prints and Drawings, inv. n. 1855-2-14-1; pen over black chalk, 23 × 31.9 cm.

44 This point, noted already by Crowe and Cavalcaselle, I, 1882, 307, is generally agreed upon by scholars, but its implications for an early trip by Raphael to Rome have, unaccountably, not been fully drawn. John Shearman, "Raphael, Rome and the Codex Escurialensis," *Master Drawings* 15, 1977, 133, has presented strong arguments for two visits by Raphael to Rome before his definitive arrival in 1508.

45 The Roman provenance of the painting has been discussed by Hirst, 1981a, who proposed a connection between the panel and the commission of an altarpiece from Michelangelo for the church of Sant'Agostino in Rome in 1500. See also Nagel, 1994.

46 Christopher Lloyd, "A Short Footnote to Raphael Studies," *Burlington Magazine,* 119, 1977, 113–14, has proposed that the Oxford sheet is derived from the central carrying group in Mantegna's *Bacchanal with Silenus* (Fig. 3.9). I believe this model, if it is relevant, was transmitted through Michelangelo's panel. I argued in chapter 1 that Mantegna's print was an important inspiration, not only in composition but also in theme, for Michelangelo's composition. On the Oxford sheet, Raphael abandoned the frontal motif but adapted the mechanics and trajectory of the carrying group, using motifs that show a much more specific, point-by-point resemblance to Michelangelo's group. The features that appear most to resemble Mantegna's group – the presence of three carrying figures, the stepping motion of the left carrier, and above all the tight compression of the group – are all, I believe, transmitted through the London painting.

47 Interestingly, in the worked-up and squared *modello* in the Uffizi, Raphael switched the pose of the legs – that is, *back* to the pose for that carrier which he knew from Mantegna's *Entombment* print and which he had already used in the earlier drawing in the British Museum discussed above. In following this detail we can virtually measure the impact that Michelangelo's conception first made on Raphael and then witness Raphael's efforts to absorb and control it.

48 This head is the only one for which there exists an elaborate head study, in Chantilly, Musée Condé FR. VIII, 44*v.* In this drawing, Raphael has turned the eyes so that they look back toward the left, thus increasing the pathos of the expression. The pose now comports a triple reversal: The body is oriented toward the left, the head turns back toward the right, and the eyes turn back again toward the left. The pose of the head and the investigation of expressive qualities seem to be a direct response to the challenge of the *Laocoön* and thus further support the idea that Raphael had been in Rome in the year 1506.

49 A similarity first pointed out to me by John Shearman.

50 Berenson, 1938, I, 181. The appearance of this study at this stage would seem to indicate that Michelangelo sculpted the *St. Matthew* in 1506, during his time in Florence between April and November. A letter of Soderini dated November 1506 states that Michelangelo had begun work on the apostles for the cathedral. See Giovanni Gaye, *Carteggio Inedito d'Artisti dei Secoli XIV, XV, XVI,* II, Florence:

Molini, 1840, 92, cited in Barocchi, II, 1962, 227. Tolnay, 1975, 175–6, has identified it with the *St. Matthew,* because it is the only one of which we have any trace. One thus imagines Raphael confronting it upon returning to Florence. Raphael's drawings after Michelangelo's works in this period tended to be made soon after their appearance. Indeed, one has the impression that in these years Raphael was deliberately stalking Michelangelo, determined to incorporate as quickly as possible every new step taken by the older artist. This behavior was to continue through the period of the Sistine ceiling. Michelangelo never quite forgot it, and decades later it was to provoke his bitter comment, in a letter of October 1542, *Carteggio,* IV, 155: "*ciò che* [Raphael] *haveva dell'arte, l'aveva da me.*" By this reasoning, the appearance of a figure adapted from the Virgin in the *Doni Tondo* in Raphael's final painting would suggest that the tondo, like the *St. Matthew,* is to be dated to 1506. Certainly there is more room in Michelangelo's chronology for these two works in 1506 than in the period before leaving Florence, in March 1505.

51 Locher, 1994, 101–03, offered a sensitive analysis of Raphael's *"Trennungsgedanken"* and *"Kontrastregie."*

52 John Shearman, "The Chigi Chapel in Santa Maria del Popolo," *Journal of the Warburg and Courtauld Institutes* XXIV, 1961, 129–60.

53 The general phenomenon in images as well as in devotional literature has been studied by Büttner, 1983.

54 The principal documentation surrounding Scipione Borghese's acquisition of the painting has been collected by Paola della Pergola, *Galleria Borghese. I Dipinti,* II, Rome: Istituto poligrafico dello Stato, Libreria dello Stato, 1959, 195–215. One letter (201) protests the loss of *"una nobilissima et rarissima pittura celebrata da varii autori, et di una gioia incomparabile, la quale erano andati più volte varii Cardinali et principii a vagheggiare. . ."* Another (208), testifying to the importance of printed books in these developments, complains of *"il dolore di veder levato Tesoro si pretioso, lodato dal Vasari, dal Borghini, e da altri Autori stampati. . ."*

55 This point is confirmed by Silvia Ferino Pagden, "From Cult Image to the Cult of Images," in *AR,* 165–89, who showed that the transformation of Raphael's altarpieces into aesthetic monuments began at the very earliest stages of their reception.

56 The problem has been most directly addressed by Stoichita, 1993, although with minimal reference to Italian art. For Italy, the best starts in this direction have been made above all in studies of Venetian painting. See Patricia Fortini Brown, *Venetian Narrative Painting in the Age of Carpaccio,* Princeton, 1988, and Humfrey, 1993.

57 Paul Hills, "The Renaissance Altarpiece: A Valid Category?" in *AR,* 48.

58 See Jurj Tynyanov, "On Literary Evolution," in *Readings in Russian Poetics: Formalist and Structuralist Views,* eds. Ladislav Matejka and Kristina Pomorska, Cambridge, MA: M.I.T. Press, 1971, 66–77. Cf. Jakobson, 1971, 85: "The hierarchy of artistic devices changes within the framework of a given poetic genre; the change, moreover, affects the hierarchy of poetic genres, and simultaneously, the distribution of artistic devices among the individual genres. Genres which were originally secondary paths, subsidiary variants, now come to the fore, whereas the canonical genres are pushed toward the rear."

59 John Shearman, *Pontormo's Altarpiece in Santa Felicita,* Newcastle upon Tyne: University of Newcastle upon Tyne, 1971, and idem, 1992, 87–94, has interpreted

what we see in the painting as a rotating movement of Christ's body downward, toward the real altar in the chapel. Leo Steinberg, "Pontormo's Capponi Chapel," *Art Bulletin,* 56, 1974, 385*ff.*, interpreted the two carrying figures as angels poised to lift the body of Christ toward God the Father in the cupola above.

CHAPTER FIVE. PASSIONATE WITHDRAWAL

1 See Paul de Man, "Criticism and Crisis," in De Man, 1983, 3–19.

2 See O'Malley, 1968, especially ch. 5, Bober, 1977, and Rowland, 1998.

3 The clearest exponent of the new ethos was perhaps the Bolognese bishop Gabriele Paleotti, who argued in his 1582 *Discorso intorno alle imagini sacre e profane* for the superiority of Western alphabets over ancient and non-Western hieroglyphs (1961, 142–9). Gianfranco Cantelli, *Mente corpo linguaggio: Saggio sull'interpretazione vichiana del mito,* Florence: Sansoni, 1985, 346–57, saw Paleotti's position as an initial step in the early modern overturning of the belief in archaic symbolic wisdom. His thesis is discussed by Anthony Grafton, "The Rest vs. The West," *New York Review of Books,* XLIV, 6, April 10, 1997, 63. Fragnito, 1988, 31ff. studied the "technico-juridical culture" that replaced the refined humanist culture of the papal court beginning with the pontificate of Paul IV (1555–59). She also shows that already by the late 1550s the earlier period was being mythologized as a heydey of intellectual refinement and cultural freedom by its survivors, such as Ludovico Beccadelli, who had been closely connected to both Bembo and Pole. On the changing relation between humanists and the curia during this period, see also the classic studies of Carlo Dionisotti, "Chierici e laici," and "La letteratura italiana nell'età del concilio di Trento," in idem, 1967, 47–73 and 183–204 respectively.

4 Quoted after the translation in Buonarroti, 1965, 276. *Carteggio,* IV, 299: *"Al prete di' che non mi scriva piùa Michagniolo scultore', perché io non ci sono conosciuto se non per Michelagniolo Buonarroti, e che se un cictadino fiorentino vuol fare dipigniere una tavola da altare, che bisognia che e' truovi un dipintore: ché non fu' mai pictore né scultore come chi ne fa boctega. Sempre me ne sono guardato per l'onore di mie padre e de' mia frategli, ben io abbi servito tre papi, che é stato forza."* For a fine discussion of this letter and its implications, see William Wallace, *Michelangelo at San Lorenzo: The Genius as Entrepreneur,* Cambridge, MA: Cambridge University Press, 1994, Introduction.

5 These associations are studied in chapter 6.

6 The estimate, perhaps exaggerated, was made by Pier Paolo Vergerio; see Fontanini, 1972, 444.

7 Ginzburg and Prosperi, 1975, 187: *"Nel 1480 (per usare una data simbolica) il rapporto dell' individuo con Dio passava attraverso tutta una serie di istituzioni in cui era difficile distinguere le componenti religiosi da quelle civili. Nel 1540 (altra data simbolica) queste mediazioni si erano logorate, lasciando insoddisfata una domanda religiosa che la crisi generale della società aveva reso più acuta."*

8 Vienna, Albertina, inv. n. 103; *Corpus* 432*r.* Black and red chalk, 40.4 × 23.3 cm. The relationship between the drawing and the painting received the most consistent attention in a flurry of letters on the London panel written to the London *Times* throughout the month of September 1881. The debate, involving J. C. Robinson, E. J. Poynter, F. W. Burton and an anonymous R. A., was usefully summarized by Richter, 1883, 41–4.

9 Thode, 1908, 484–485, and idem, 1912, 174.

10 This procedure is foreign enough from what we know of Michelangelo's working methods to instill legitimate doubts about the authorship of the drawing. Michelangelo's other studies for *Pietàs* and *Lamentations* all reconceive the pose of the body; familiar postures, even from quite early in his career, reappear in the process, but this process does not begin, as this drawing has, with an act of direct copying. A similar point was made by Hirst, 1988, 20, in discussing Michelangelo's use of his own drawings: "Michelangelo must have been the readier to destroy his drawings because, unlike artists as diverse as Andrea del Sarto or Rubens, he did not reuse them. It is difficult to find a single case where we can point to his having picked up, for example, a study made from life, and re-employed it for a subsequent work. . . For every invention, Michelangelo started, as it were, from scratch." His example is the *Leda,* which, though deriving from the pose of the Medici Chapel *Night* made shortly before, was designed on the basis of new drawings, rather than on the reuse of the ones made for the sculpture. Condivi, 1911, 76, stressed Michelangelo's conscious avoidance of self-imitation: "Michael Angelo had a most retentive memory, so that although he has painted so many thousand figures, as may be seen, he has never made one like to another, or in the same pose; indeed, I have heard him say that if he ever draws a line which he remembers to have drawn before, he rubs it out if it is to come before the public." (The point was repeated and amplified by Vasari, VI, 114–15.) The importance of the issue for Michelangelo is demonstrated by his own comment on the Condivi passage, which was noted in the margin of the printed text by a contemporary; Ugo Procacci, "Postille contemporanee in un esemplare della vita di Michelangelo del Condivi," *Atti del convegno di studi Michelangioleschi,* Rome: Edizioni dell' Ateneo, 1966, 293: *"Dissemi [Michelangelo] è vero, e se tu voi far bene, varia sempre e fa più tosto male."* [Paraphrase: It is better to risk failure innovating than to play it safe by copying oneself.] These claims to absolute originality, like Michelangelo's Condivi's assertion that Michelangelo had never had a teacher, have rightly been contested by modern scholars, who point to his abundant reliance on previous models and techniques. The point here, however, is not whether Michelangelo was always able to avoid *unconscious* imitation and self-imitation but that his *conscious* aim was to avoid doing so. He might, despite himself, repeat a pose; it is far less likely that he would make a drawing directly copied after his own work and then proceed carefully to work it up. In any case, this would be an extremely rare instance of such a procedure in Michelangelo's work. Sylvia Ferino Pagden's entry on the drawing, in *VC,* cat no. IV.47, 454, also raised some doubts about the drawing's authorship and also suggested a date toward the early 1530s.

11 The difference in posture between painting and drawing was observed by the anonymous R. A. in his letter to the London *Times,* September 12, 1881, but because he believed the drawing to be preparatory to the painting, he was led to believe that the *painting* was the awkward variation on the authentic drawing. My position was most clearly anticipated by Richter, 1883, 43–44, who wrote in response to R. A.'s letter: ". . .a close comparison [of picture and drawing] . . . seems to me to point to a totally different conclusion about the importance of the drawing. I would only draw attention to the weakness in the outline of the thigh and the calf of the right leg, and to the want of anatomic accuracy in the outline of the corpse near the hip, deficiencies in the drawing which are not to be met within the picture. Therefore if the drawing, as seems to be the case, proves to be not only a later work, but also an inferior production to the picture, which I maintain to be

by Michelangelo, it would follow that the drawing is one of the finest *pasticcios* ever produced after the great Florentine master, and perhaps copied direct from the painting."

12 These features have, I believe, important implications for the attribution question. In the drawing the unity of the London Christ figure is disrupted but not reconceived as a new whole. Instead, the parts are dislocated from one other: One could imagine the torso being moved without occasioning any shift in the legs, or the left arm being raised or lowered without its affecting the posture of the torso. Such "regional autonomy" is essentially foreign to what we know of Michelangelo's figural (as well as architectural) style.

13 Inv. n. 1896-7-10-1*r.*, Wilde 64*r.*, *Corpus* 270*r.*

14 Cf. Dvořák, 1989, 130 (comparing the Florence *Pietà* to the Vatican *Pietà*): *"Nicht die Madonna, sondern der tote Christus ist die Hauptfigur – wie er hier aufgerichtet gezeigt wird, entspricht mehr dem Trecento und frühen Quattrocento – nicht als süße Last, sondern als der Gottessohn, der Helfer and Erlöser, der für die Menschheit gestorben ist."* Frederick Hartt, "Power and the Individual in Mannerist Art," in *The Renaissance and Mannerism: Studies in Western Art* (Acts of the Twentieth International Congress of the History of Art), II, Princeton: Princeton University Press, 1963, 222–38, saw this sacramental emphasis as a general trend in the depiction of *Pietàs* in the years after 1517.

15 See the classic essay by Wilhelm Pinder, "Die dichterische Würzel der *Pietà*," *Repertorium für Kunstwissenschaft,* 42, 1920, 145–63. These devotional parallels are recapitulated in the formal derivation of the *Pietà* from the image of the Virgin and Child. See Panofsky, 1927, 266, and Hanns Swarzenski, "Quellen zum deutschen Andachtsbild," *Zeitschrift für Kunstgeschichte,* 4, 1935, 142. The structural parallel between the image of the Virgin and Child and that of the *Pietà* is on occasion made explicit by their pairing in a pendant relationship. See, for example, the two frescoes painted by Perugino in the church of Santa Maria Maggiore at Spello.

16 For Christocentric trends in the visual arts and their relation to reform agendas, see Humphrey, 1993, 73–6, and idem, "Altarpieces and Altar Dedications in Counter-Reformation Venice and the Veneto," *Renaissance Studies,* 10, 1996, 371–87. See also Adriano Prosperi, "The Religious Crisis in Early Sixteenth-Century Italy," in David Alan Brown, Peter Humfrey, and Mauro Lucco, *Lorenzo Lotto: Rediscovered Master of the Renaissance,* ex. cat., New Haven: Yale University Press, 1997, 21–6.

17 See chapter 3, second section.

18 Florence, Casa Buonarroti 69*r.*; *Corpus* 91*r.* Black pencil; 39.9 × 28.2 cm.

19 The first record of this commission appears in a letter of December 1533, which itself refers to an earlier agreement probably dating to June of the same year. See Michael Hirst, "Sebastiano's *Pietà* for the Comendador Mayor," *Burlington Magazine,* 114, 1972, 587.

20 See Julius Schlosser, "Über einige Antiken Ghibertis," *Wiener Jahrbuch für Kunstgeschichte* 24, 1904, 125–40, and *Ghibertis Denkwürdigkeiten,* II, Berlin: Bard, 1912, 172 for the textual documentation. To Christian Huelsen, "Il Letto di Policleto," *Jahreshefte des österreichischen archäologischen Institutes,* 28, 1915, 130–7, goes the credit for identifying the relief type to which Ghiberti's belonged. Michelangelo made a drawing after the sleeping figure in the mid-1520s while he was working on the Medici projects in San Lorenzo (Windsor Castle, Popham-

Wilde, 1949, 422*r.*; *Corpus* 99*r.*), and incorporated the entire composition in the inlay decoration of the floor of the Biblioteca Laurenziana. See also the pen sketch which reproduces the entire group, Casa Buonarroti 53*r.*, reproduced in Dussler, 1959, 438*r.*, pl. 184.

21 Paris, Louvre, Inv. n. 716; *Corpus* 92*r.* Black chalk; 25.5 × 32 cm. Again, although this drawing is much loved, I believe the attribution to Michelangelo is questionable. The first dubious fact about it is that, like the Vienna sheet discussed above (see Figure 78), it is directly copied from another work: It follows the Casa Buonarroti sheet quite precisely (the figures in the two sheets are almost identical in size). Please see n. 10 for a discussion of such a practice of copying in relation to Michelangelo's known working habits. The second point is that the lines of the Louvre drawing copy the Casa Buonarroti sheet in a dutiful, almost myopic manner. This procedure led to difficulties where different parts of the figure meet, as noted by Perrig, 1960, 140. The right profile of the torso (to our left) is followed down to the hip area; there it arrives too close to the upper profile of the right thigh: The buttock, a round and ample form in the Casa Buonarroti sketch, is here virtually omitted in the conjunction of hip and thigh. Precisely this sort of flattened treatment of the hip area occurs in Sebastiano's drawing of God the Father for the Chigi chapel in Windsor (Popham-Wilde, 1949, n. 924; Hirst, 1981b, pl. 174). This specific sort of problem does not occur in known Michelangelo drawings: Exaggerations and distortions of proportion certainly do occur, and quite often, but not this sort of anatomical omission. The draftsman of the Louvre sheet attempted to correct his error by simply drawing another contour for the thigh a little farther up and another for the buttock a little farther down. Is it likely that Michelangelo would have lavished such attention on the modeling of a figure whose contours show such obvious miscalculations? Once the possibility is entertained that Sebastiano was the draftsman of the Louvre sheet, certain features fall into place. The legs, which were not included in the model sketch in the Casa Buonarroti, repeat a formula adapted (ultimately from the Sistine *Adam* [see Figure 83]) for the figure of *Lazarus* in Sebastiano's altarpiece now in London. One immediately feels the loss of Michelangelo's guidance in these looping, anatomically indifferent forms. A cursory comparison of this rounded knee with the quickly sketched but anatomically sensitive knees on the verso of the Casa Buonarroti sheet (for figures in the *Last Judgment*) shows a difference so marked as to make it difficult to attribute them to the same hand. The two arm studies at the corners of the sheet are, however, not so easily dismissed. As I point out below, I believe these small sketches are Michelangelo's efforts to demonstrate how problems in the treatment of the figure could be resolved by changing the pose of the arm.

22 This point was stressed by Perrig, 1960, 139.

23 Further similarities reinforce the hypothesis. The seated posture, the blocklike tomb seat shrouded in drapery, and the Virgin supporting Christ from behind – all of these features are also present in the Úbeda *Pietà*. The British Museum composition mentioned above (see n. 13) is formally very distinct, but it, too, may be an earlier idea, also superseded, for the Úbeda commission, especially when we consider that Sebastiano himself initially proposed to make a composition "similar to the *Pietà* in St. Peter's" [*"a guisa di quella dela febre"*, see Hirst, "Sebastiano's *Pietà,*" as in n. 19, 587]. This hypothesis is independent of the attribution question. If the drawings are Michelangelo's, then they are earlier efforts superseded by the final

Bed of Polycleitus – based composition. If the drawings are by Sebastiano, then they represent his efforts, before Michelangelo's arrival in Rome in Autumn 1533, to fashion a composition by his own lights, using the two most thematically related works by Michelangelo (the *Entombment* and the *Pietà*) then available to him in Rome. (For the Roman provenance of the London painting, see Hirst, 1981a, and Cecil Gould, "Some Addenda to Michelangelo Studies," *Burlington Magazine,* XCIII, 1951, 279–82.) We will probably never find proof of the connection of these drawings to the Úbeda commission, but in the end it is not really necessary. If the drawings are by Michelangelo and to be dated circa 1530, then they are related to the drawings for the Úbeda painting by their shared thematic problems and should be understood in relation to one another and to the conception of the Úbeda *Pietà* whether they were made expressly "for" that commission or not. If the drawings are by Sebastiano, then it is difficult to avoid the conclusion that they are directly related to the Úbeda commission.

24 Bober and Rubinstein, 1986, 127. The work's Renaissance reception is brilliantly studied by Leonard Barkan in *Unearthing the Past,* New Haven, CT: Yale University Press, forthcoming. I thank him for an advance viewing of this section.

25 As Hirst, 1981b, 131, put it, "Berenson's strictures cannot be gainsaid." I would add only that this "woodenness" is not merely a matter of a simple weakness in Sebastiano's ability to depict figures. It stems from a difference in conception, a tendency to see the dead Christ merely as an inert and pathetic corpse. Sebastiano's painting is a sentimental *Andachtsbild,* of the kind later – and partly on Sebastiano's model – to be turned into an industry in Spain by Luis de Morales.

26 Shearman, 1966.

27 Connections between Rosso's investigations and contemporary debates over the interpretation of the Eucharist have been proposed by Regina Stefaniak, "Replicating Mysteries of the Passion: Rosso's *Dead Christ with Angels,*" *Renaissance Quarterly,* 45, 1992, 677–738.

28 The description comes in a document requesting that the panel, left in Rome during the Sack, be returned to him in Borgo San Sepolcro. It was published by David Franklin, "New Documents for Rosso Fiorentino in Sansepolcro," *Burlington Magazine,* CXXXI, 1989, Document 5, 827: "*. . .et specialiter unum quadrum lignaminis, ornatum picturis, et in quo inest picta figura domini nostri Iesu Christi in forma Pietatis, cum quibusdam Angelis circumcircha dictam figuram.*" The terms *pietà* or *immagine della pietà,* it should be noted, were more often used to describe what we would call a Man of Sorrows, the *imago pietatis* proper, than the configuration that the term is now generally understood to describe, i.e., the *Vesperbild.* This is the way, for example, Neri di Bicci used the term; e.g., *Le ricordanze,* ed. Bruno Santi, Pisa: Marlin, 1976, 60 (f. 26r.): "*. . .e nella predella la Piatà e quattro meze fighure da lato.*" See also the illuminating chapter on the meaning of the word *pietàs* in relation to the Man of Sorrows image in Belting, 1981, Excursus A, 281–8. On the specific tradition of the Man of Sorrows with angels, or *Engelpietà,* see Georg Swarzenski, "Insinuationes divinae pietatis," *Festschrift Heinrich Wölfflin,* Munich: Schmid, 1924, 65–74; Hubert Schrade, "Beitrag zur Erklärung des Schmerzensmannbildes," *Deutschkundliches – Friedrich Panzer zum 60. Geburtstag überreicht,* Heidelberg: Winter, 1930, 178–9; and Gert von der Osten, "Engelpietà," *Reallexikon zur Deutschen Kunstgeschichte,* V, Stuttgart: Druckenmüller, 1960, 603. It should be noted that Rosso's image – like Michelangelo's *Pietà* for Vittoria Colonna to be discussed below – conforms particularly to an Italian tradition of

the Man of Sorrows with angels, in which Christ is flanked by angels rather than supported from behind by one, as observed by Panofsky, 1927, 268. Early examples of this type include the relief by Giovanni Pisano in Berlin and the predella of the stone altarpiece by Tommaso Pisano in San Francesco at Pisa (illustrations in Belting, 1981, Figs. 31 and 35). The two types were combined in Andrea del Sarto's lost Puccini *Pietà* (see John Shearman, *Andrea del Sarto,* II, Oxford: Clarendon, 1965, 229–30), which Shearman, 1966, proposed as a source for Rosso's Boston panel.

29 The similarity was noted by Shearman, 1966, 170, n. 30; and by Sydney Freedberg, *Painting in Italy 1500–1600,* Middlesex: Penguin, 1979, p. 201, n. 31, who seems to believe that the relation goes the other way around: "There is a dense complex of references to Michelangelo in the Christ [of Rosso's Boston panel], but the most exact is to the drawing (Paris, Louvre), disputed in attribution between Michelangelo and Sebastiano del Piombo. . ." There is good reason to believe that Sebastiano was aware of Rosso's panel, which had been left in Rome during the Sack (see Franklin, "New Documents," as in previous note).

30 Julia Kristeva, *Black Sun: Depression and Melancholia,* trans. Leon S. Roudiez, New York: Columbia University Press, 1989, 110.

31 The best analysis of Dostoyevsky's reception of the panel is by Victor Stoichita, "Ein Idiot in der Schweiz: Bildbeschreibung bei Dostoiewsky," in *Beschreibungskunst – Kunstbeschreibung,* eds. Gottfried Boehm and Helmut Pfotenhauer, Munich: Prestel, 1995, 425–44.

32 See, for example, John Rowlands, *Holbein. The Paintings of Hans Holbein the Younger. Complete Edition.* Oxford: Phaidon, 1985, 52–3, and Oskar Bätschmann and Pascal Griener, *Hans Holbein,* London: Reaktion, 1997, 89.

33 Francesco Bocchi, *Le bellezze della citta di Fiorenza: doue a pieno di pittura, di scultura, di sacri tempij, di palazzi i piu notabili artifizij, & piu preziosi si contengono,* Florence, 1591; facs. ed. with an introduction by John Shearman, Farmborough: Gregg, 1971, 223–4. Quoted by Thomas Frangenberg, "The Art of Talking about Sculpture: Vasari, Borghini and Bocchi," *Journal of the Warburg and Courtauld Institutes,* 58, 1995, 130, whose translation I follow.

34 Colonna, 1979, 423: *"Ultra che essendovi la divinità che non lo lassò mai, credo haveva la solita Maestà et grande, anzi molto maggiore, perchè la morte che ne li altri usa violentia et perhò rimangono come persone offese, in Christo che con tanta dolcezza l'haveva chiamata et desiderata, penso ne rimase un atto tanto dolce suave et pietoso che reinteneriva ogni duro core, et accendeva ogni fredda mente, la brutezza della morte era non solo bella nel bellissimo volto ma la fierezza se convertì in dolcezza grande."* I discuss Colonna's Passion tract at length in the following chapter.

35 Gilio, 1961, 39–41.

36 Hirst, 1988, 116.

37 Hirst, 1981b, 131, has observed that the figure of Christ for the Úbeda *Pietà* was conceived with an eye to Sebastiano's Venetian sensibilities, in particular by incorporating the "Venetian tradition of representing the dead Christ, supported from behind and depicted to the knees" exemplified in Giovanni Bellini's treatments of the subject.

38 The resulting arrangement bears a striking resemblance to the strange *Lamentation* painted by the young Ghirlandaio in the Vespucci chapel in the church of Ognissanti in Florence.

39 Hirst, 1988, 116.

40 See Wind, 1968, 152–90. Hirst, 1988, 116, emphasized the dark and funereal aspects of the *Children's Bacchanal.* On the association of Bacchus with death and funerary contexts, see Walter F. Otto, *Dionysus: Myth and Cult,* trans. Robert Palmer, Bloomington: Indiana University Press, 1965, chs. 9 and 17; Pierre Boyancé, *Le culte des Muses chez les philosophies grecs: Études d'histoire et de psychologie religieuse,* Paris: Boccard, 1937, ch. 3; Susan Cole, "Voices from beyond the Grave: Dionysos and the Dead," in *Masks of Dionysos,* ed. Thomas Carpenter and Christopher Faraone, Ithaca, NY: Cornell University Press, 1993, 276–95; and Dirk Obbink, "Dionysos Poured Out: Ancient and Modern Theories of Sacrifice and Cultural Formation," in ibid., 65–86.

41 Erwin Panofsky, *Studies in Iconology* (1939), New York: Harper, 1962, 222. This allusion lends further credence to the idea, proposed above, that Michelangelo was recalling Raphael's painting in the closely contemporary Bayonne sheet (see Figure 86).

42 Hirst, 1988, 115.

43 See the liturgical texts, Passion dramas, and devotional literature studied in E. Parker, "The Descent from the Cross: Its Relation to the Extra-Liturgical Deposition Drama," doctoral dissertation, New York University, 1975.

44 Haarlem, Teylers Museum, n. A 25; *Corpus* 89r. Red chalk; 26.1 × 18.5 cm.

45 In Nagel, 1996, I argued that a drawing of disputed date in Oxford (see Figure 99) was one of the condensed formulas drawn from the Haarlem *Deposition* drawing at this time. The central group was then, I proposed, reworked by Michelangelo in the 1540s, and it played an important role in the conception of the Florence *Pietà.* The drawing is accordingly discussed in ch. 7.

46 Paris, Louvre, Inv. n. 1016*r.*; *Corpus* 268*r.* Red chalk; 11 × 9.3 cm.

47 Steinberg, 1970.

48 Vienna, Albertina, Sc.R. 136, Inv. n. 102*r*; *Corpus* 269*r.* Red chalk; 32 × 25.1 cm.

49 These qualities frustrated Berenson enough for him to take the sheet away from Michelangelo. He found the drawing distasteful because it does not satisfy Albertian expectations of purposeful activity. Having no other criteria by which to assess these qualities, he could see the drawing only as an example of outrageously bad artistic judgment. Even if couched in negative terms, the description of the sheet succeeds in drawing attention to some of its most important features; Berenson, I, 1938, 241: "The Florentine [Michelangelo] would have treated this subject as a study of weight and support. Rapidly as he might have done it, he would have jotted down no limb which did not serve this purpose. Still less would he have sketched out whole figures which do nothing, or worse than nothing, while forming part of the same compact group. Not only is the dead figure badly constructed, but it is too boneless and limp for artistic treatment, there being apparently no part of it which does not require separate outside support. And of this support it gets little if any, except by way of flourish and alarum. The author of this sketch had of course seen studies by Michelangelo for this theme, but had so little understood their purpose that he supposed it to consist in a pell-mell of figures and limbs of any proportions, any attitudes, any shapes, provided they formed an agitated mass."

50 Vittoria Colonna, *Rime e lettere di Vittoria Colonna,* Rome: Barbera, 1860, sonnet 21, 171.

51 I say "architectonic" because the clearest analogies to this solution appear in Michelangelo's architectural designs. A compressed merging between two vertically arranged forms characterizes, for example, the design of the doors of the

New Sacristy: The cornice of the doors serves also as the base of the tabernacles above; the volutes, which hang, not unlike Christ's lower arms, to either side, are both corbels to the door and "knees" to the tabernacles. Michelangelo, after some difficulty, arrived at a similar solution in his model for the two-story façade for San Lorenzo: An indeterminate middle zone acts both as entablature for the lower order and as *basamento* for the upper order.

CHAPTER SIX. ARTWORK AND CULT IMAGE

1 On the question of drawings as finished works in their own right, see Wilde, 1978, 147–58, and Hirst, 1988, chapter X, "The Making of Presents." I follow Wilde and Hirst in describing this type of work as a presentation drawing, and thus distinct from a *modello,* which is a finished design for a project yet to be realized, more often than not in another medium. This is, of course, not to deny the fact that *modelli* were often deemed worthy of being collected in their own right. I follow Robinson, Tolnay, and Hirst, among others, in identifying the Colonna *Pietà* with the drawing now in the Isabella Stewart Gardner Museum in Boston (*Corpus* 426r. Black chalk; 29.5 × 19.5 cm.). An especially strong argument in favor of this attribution is Tolnay's observation of a *pentimento* in the left foot of the left-hand angel (see *Corpus,* III, 77). None of the arguments made here, however, depend on this attribution.

2 See, for example, the negotiations involved in the making of Francesco Pesellino's *Trinity* altarpiece, now in the London National Gallery, which can be reconstructed from the documentation published by Pèleo Bacci, *Documenti e commenti per la storia dell'arte,* Florence: Le Monnier, 1944, 113–51. An informative account of the situation in the Venetian context is offered by Peter Humfrey, 1993, part 1, ch. 2, "Purposes and Uses." See also Gilbert, 1977, and Hope, 1990. On the development of the private mass in the late Middle Ages, see Jungmann, I, 1986, 103*ff.,* John Bossy, "The Mass as a Social Institution 1200–1700," *Past and Present,* C, 1983, 29–61, and Jacques Chiffoleau, "Sur l'usage obsessionnel de la messe pour les morts à la fin du Moyen Age," in *Faire Croire: Modalités de la diffusion et de la reception des messages religieux du XIIe au XVe siècle,* Rome: École française de Rome, 1981, 238–45. On its place within the economy of late-medieval piety generally, see John Bossy, *Christianity in the West 1400–1700,* Oxford: Oxford University Press, 1985, especially 3–75. For the specific case of Florence, see Richard Trexler, "Ritual Behavior in Renaissance Florence: The Setting," *Medievalia et Humanistica: Studies in Medieval and Renaissance Culture,* n.s., IV, 1973, 125–44.

3 See Fenlon, 1972, 70–71. On the northern Italian Benedectine reform movement, with which Pole had early associations (Fenlon, 1972, 30 *ff.*), see Barry Collett, *Italian Benedictine Scholars and the Reformation: The Congregation of Santa Giustina of Padua,* Oxford: Clarendon, 1985.

4 For Catarino's text see Fontanini, 347–422. For the date of Flaminio's revisions, see Ginzburg and Prosperi, 1975, 69–70, where they also entertain the hypothesis that the manuscript of the *Beneficio* reached Catarino's hands through Vittoria Colonna herself. Although the historical reliability of de Hollanda's dialogues is still debated, especially with regard to the opinions attributed to Michelangelo, it seems that he would be least likely to invent these matters of setting and circum-

stance. The strongest arguments in favor of de Hollanda's reliability as a recorder of Michelangelo's views have been offered by Bury, 1981.

5 Manzoni, 1870, 269: *"Non mi ricordo che si sia parlato nè trattato tra noi et quella signora d'altro dogma che della giustificazione per la fede, et ne anch' questo saprei dire a punto con che circonstantie ella se tenesse, ma basta che l'attribuiva molto alla gratia et alla fede in suoi ragionamenti. Et d'altra parte nella vita et nelle attioni suoe mostrava di tenere gran conto dell'opere, facendo grand'elemosine, et usando charità universalmente con tutti, nel che veniva a osservare et seguire il conisglio che ella diceva haverli dato il Cardinale* [Pole], *al quale ella credeva come un oracolo, cioè che ella dovesse attendere a credere come se per la fede sola s'havesse a salvare, et d'altra parte attendere ad operare come se la salute sua consestesse nelle opere."*

6 The evidence comes in a well-known letter from the bishop of Fano to Cardinal Ercole Gonzaga; Karl Frey, *Michelangelo: Quellen und Forschungen,* Berlin: K. Curtis, 1907, 139: *"Monsignor Polo ha per notizia, ch'ella desidera un Cristo di mane di Michelangelo, et ammè imposto che io intenda secretamente la verità di cotal suo desiderio: perchè, essendo in effetto, egli ne ha uno di mano propria del detto, che volentieri glielo manderebbe; ma è in forma di Pietà, pure se gli vede tutto il corpo. Dice che questo non sarebbe un privarsene, percioché dalla marchesa di Pescara* [i.e., Vittoria Colonna] *ne può avere un altro."* On the meaning of the expression *"in forma di Pietà"* or *"in forma pietatis"* see ch. 5, n. 28. Here the reference is quite clear, as the author felt it necessary to specify that Christ is shown in full length, as opposed to the half-length type of the Man of Sorrows commonly found in Italy. Thomas Mayer, who has consulted the original letter in Mantua, has kindly informed me that the author of this letter was not Cosimo Gheri, as Frey suggests, but Pietro Bertano, his successor, and that it is to be dated ca. 1546.

7 Quoted after the translation in Gleason, 1981, 159. Fontanini, 1972, chap. VI, f. 67*v.*, 81: *"Mi dirai: – Io credo bene la remissione de' peccati e so che Dio è verace, ma dubito di non esser degno di tanto dono –. Ti rispondo che la remissione de' peccati non sarebbe dono e grazia, ma mercede, se Dio te la concedesse per la dignità delle opere tue: ma ti replico che Dio ti accetta per giusto e non ti imputa il peccato per i meriti di Cristo, i quali ti sono donati e diventano tuoi per la fede. Adunque, seguendo il santo consiglio di san Bernardo, non creder solamente in generale la remissione de' peccati, ma applica questo credere al tuo particolare, credendo indubitatamente che per Cristo to sono perdonate tutte le tue iniquità."*

8 I quote examples as the argument proceeds. To take one example, however, in a letter of 1541 to Cardinal Pole, Colonna toyed, not entirely playfully, with the analogy; Pagano and Ranieri, 1989, 95: *"La supplico che con la sua carità anzi de Chisto* [sic] *con la quale ogni molestia suffre, me perdoni se 'l molesto in mandarle certe frascarie, et se ben con San Paulo V.S. suol dire che è più beata cosa el dare che 'l recevere, contentise dare ad me questa beatitudine."* Another case of Colonna's semiserious theological punning is discussed by Fenlon, 1972, 214–15.

9 *Carteggio,* IV, 122: *"Volevo, Signiora, prima che io pigliassi le cose che Vostra S[igniori]a m'à più volte volute dare, per riceverle manco indegniamente ch'i' potevo, fare prima qualche cosa a quella di mia mano; dipoi riconosciuto e visto che la gratia d'Iddio non si può comperare, e che'l tenerla a disagio è pechato grandissimo, dico mie colpa, e volentieri dette cose accecto. E son certo, quando l'arò, non per ave[r]le in casa, ma per essere io in casa loro, mi parrà essere in paradiso. . ."* Creighton Gilbert, in Buonarroti, 1965, 267, missing the analogy between divine grace and gift giving, offered what I believe to be a flawed translation of the passage: "[T]hen, having realized and seen that

the grace of God is not to be bought and it is a great sin to keep you in suspense. . ." E. H. Ramsden, *The Letters of Michelangelo,* II, London: Owen, 1963, 4, offered a largely similar reading: "Then I came to realize that the grace of God cannot be bought, and that to keep you waiting is a grievous sin." My reading of the text, where the pronoun *la* refers to *la grazia di Dio* and not to Colonna, is borne out by the poem included in the letter, which I discuss below. My thanks to Leonard Barkan, Stefano Cracolici, and Brian Stock for discussing the translation of this letter with me.

10 Vasari, VI, 112: *"nè voleva presenti di nessuno, perchè pareva, come uno gli donava qualcosa, d'essere sempre obligato a colui."* William Wallace, "Friends and Relics at San Silvestro in Capite, Rome," *Sixteenth Century Journal,* 30, 1999, 439, has proposed that the gift of Colonna's that so burdened Michelangelo in the letter and sonnet under discussion was a chance to view the "Veronica" cloth with the miraculous image of Christ, a prize relic of the church of San Silvestro in Capite, where Colonna resided when in Rome. This would be the image referred to in the closing of the same letter; *Carteggio,* IV, 122: "L'aportatore di questa sarà Urbino che sta meco, al quale Vostra S(igno)ria potrà dire quando vuole ch'i' venga a vedere la testa di Cristo che Sua Gratia disse mostràmi." Wallace has made an exciting discovery in connecting the head of Christ mentioned in Michelangelo's letter to the Veronica at San Silvestro, but his further claim, identifying the gift referred to earlier in the letter and in the sonnet with this special viewing opportunity, is difficult to sustain. First, Michelangelo refers to gifts in the plural ("*Le cose che Vostra S(igno)ria m'à più volte dare*"), and, second, he refers to their being in his house, an arrangement that is difficult to imagine in the case of the San Silvestro relic.

11 Flaminio introduced the simile in a letter to Gasparo Contarini, probably from 1538, in an effort to clarify a debate over whether the act of faith was itself the result of divine grace or of free will. Quoted in Pastore, 1981, 97: *"Dico che sono due opinioni, l'una delle quali par che dica che la gratia del Signore sia come il sole, il quale quanto è in sé illumina egualmente ognuno et che cosi il non por come il porre obstacolo a questo superceleste lume è mera operatione del nostro libero arbitrio. La altra opinione dice che senza particolar gratia et aiuto de Dio lo huomo non se astiene di mettere oppositione a quella luce beata. La prima opinione è difesa da V.S.; la seconda da Ms. Tullio [Crispoldi]."* (Flaminio was on Crispoldi's side of the debate.) In a letter to Marguerite d'Angoulême (Ferrero and Müller, 1892, letter CXII, 186–7), Colonna spoke in similar terms of an internal resistance to grace, and like Michelangelo she invoked the divine parallel in the context of an interpersonal relationship of courtesy (in this case, the issue is a hoped-for personal visit). Marguerite's generosity and wisdom is like the celestial manna to the Hebrews, *"et se a quelli l'effetto della grazia superò di gran lunga ogni loro aspettatione, a me similmente l'utilità di vedere la M. V. credo che avanzarà ogni mio desiderio. . ."* She warned, however, that it will require great charity, *"perchè in me troverà resistenza a saper ricever le sue gratie."*

12 Marcel Mauss, *The Gift: Forms and Functions of Exchange in Archaic Societies,* trans. Ian Cunnison, New York: Norton, 1967.

13 Jacques Derrida, *Given Time: 1. Counterfeit Money,* trans. Peggy Kamuf, Chicago: Chicago University Press, 1992, and esp. 1–83. See also the discussion of the gift's "increase" in Hyde, 1979, 25–39.

14 Derrida, 1995, 95.

15 Derrida, 1995, is essentially an extended commentary on Søren Kierkegaard's conception of faith.

16 See Natalie Zemon Davis, *Gifts and Bribes in Sixteenth-Century France,* Lancaster, UK, 1995.

17 Seneca, *Moral Essays,* trans. John W. Basore, III, London and Cambridge, MA: Harvard University Press, 1935, book 1, ch. 2, sec. 3, 10–11: *"Beneficiorum simplex ratio est: tantum erogatur; si reddet aliquid, lucrum est, si non reddet, damnum non est. Ego illud dedi, ut darem."* Seneca's text, which was edited by Erasmus in 1515 and 1529, was translated into Italian by Michelangelo's correspondent and commentator Benedetto Varchi. It is interesting to find that in his version Varchi stresses the "unidirectionality" of the gift and generalizes the message in what could be read as a reformist direction; Benedetto Varchi, *Seneca De Benifizii,* Florence: Torrentino, 1554, 4: *"Il modo di dare i benifizii è un solo, perche si danno solamente, se poi te n'è renduto alcuna, questo si chiama guadagno: se nò, non si chiama danno, perchè i benifizii si danno per dare, non per ricevere il cambio."* On Varchi's reformist sympathies and affinities with the Viterbo circle, see the very fine analysis of Simoncelli, 1979, 330–95, which proves Varchi to have been a very close reader of the *Beneficio di Cristo.*

18 Gleason, 1981, 128. Fontanini, 1972, 29r.–v., 41: *"E che cosa può operare l'uomo, che meriti un tanto dono e tesoro quanto è Cristo? Questo tesoro si dà solamente per grazia e favore e misericordia di Dio, e la fede sola è quella che riceve cotal dono, e ci fa godere della remissione de' peccati. . . . Le quali cose tutte le opere, che possono fare tutti li uomini insieme, non potrano conseguire nè fare."*

19 The parallel between the gift and the work of art – the idea that works of art are not like other commodities but are giftlike in that their value is irreplaceable and incommensurable – is by now taken quite for granted. Hyde, for example, took it as the premise of his study. It is, I believe, necessary to historicize this premise and attempt a genealogy of the identification. Hyde's own examples, and his guiding conception of what constitutes art, implicity suggest that the identification is a feature of post-Kantian aesthetics. One might argue, in fact, that the very project of marking off and defining the realm of the work of art as such by stressing, as Immanuel Kant did in the *Critique of Judgment,* its disinterested quality or generally by claiming its exemption from conceptual logic or the logic of "economic" relations – a project served especially well by the notion of the gift – is perhaps the most peculiarly modern feature of modern aesthetics. The case here under study offers one early, experimental moment in the history of this identification, before it received theoretical elaboration, and thus stands as a warning against adopting it as a universal premise.

20 See the variant in Buonarroti, 1960, 342–3: *"Per esser manco almen, signiora, indegnio."*

21 Buonarroti, 1960, 86, 343–44: *"S'alcun legato è pur tal piacer molto, / come da morte altrui tornare in vita, / qual cosa é che po' paghi tanta aita, / che rende il debitor libero e sciolto? / É se pur fusse, ne sarebbe tolto / il soprastar d'una mercé infinita / al ben servito, onde sarie 'mpedita / da l'incontro servire, a quella volto. / Dunche, per tener alta vostra grazia, / donna, sopra 'l mie stato, in me sol bramo / ingratitudin più che cortesia: / chè dove l'un del-l'altro al par si sazia, / non mi sare' signor quel che tant' amo: / ché 'n parità non cape signoria."* The sentiment is echoed in a letter from Vittoria Colonna to Marguerite d' Angoulême in 1540; Colonna, 1892, 185: *"Sereniss. Regina. Le alte et religiose parole della humanissima lettera di V. Maestà mi dovriano insegnare quel sacro silentio, che in vece di lode s'offerisce alle cose divine; ma temendo che la mia riconoscentia non si potesse riputare ingratitudine, ardirò, non già di rispondere, ma di non tacere in tutto. . ."*

22 Ralph Waldo Emerson, "Gifts," in *The Works of Emerson,* vol. 1, New York: Tudor, n.d., 344.

23 The expression appears in Buonarroti, 1960, 136: *"Non è più bassa o vil cosa terrena."* In the terms of Flaminio's letter (Pastore, 1981, 97) quoted above, this would put Michelangelo in the more radical camp.

24 *Carteggio,* IV, 102. Michelangelo was, of course, speaking idealistically and was quite capable of treating artistic gifts in a calculating spirit in his practical life. One example is the dagger that he offered to Filippo Strozzi in 1507 after it had been rejected by its original comissioner. As William Wallace has argued ("Manoeuvring for Patronage: Michelangelo's Dagger," *Renaissance Studies,* 11, 1997, 20–26), Michelangelo was careful to offer it as a gift – he instructed his brother Buonarroto: "make him a present of it, as from yourself, and do not say anything to him about the cost" – and in this way to maintain good relations with the Strozzi, who proved to be important sources of support in Buonarroto's rise to a position of prominence in Florentine politics. Closer to the time of the Colonna *Pietà,* Michelangelo revealed a quite calculating conception of gift exchange when writing epitaphs for the tomb of Cecchino Bracci for Luigi del Riccio. Each variant epitaph appears to have been extorted by a gift (usually of delicacies) from del Riccio, so that Michelangelo felt compelled to account semifacetiously for each one: "For the salded mushrooms" (Saslow, 1991, n. 198); "For the fennel" (Saslow, 1991, n. 199); "the trout and truffles would compel heaven" (Saslow, 1991, n. 194). Sometimes his return gifts included drawings: "I'm paying you back for the melons with a scribble, but not yet the drawing; but I'll certainly do it, since I can draw better" (Saslow, 1991, n. 206).

25 On the "discourse of secrecy" surrounding the presentation drawings, see Barkan, 1991, 82.

26 The association was noted, but not pursued, by Hirst, 1988, 107: "The real parallel for these drawings of Michelangelo is love poetry, above all sonnets, actuated by profound personal feeling."

27 Barkan, 1991, 81.

28 Hyde, 1979, 48–9.

29 *Carteggio,* IV, 102. Michelangelo is quoting from sonnet 206, *"S' i' 'l dissi mai, ch' i' vegna in odio a quella,"* in Francesco Petrarca, *Le rime,* eds. Giosuè Carducci and Severino Perrari, Florence: Sansoni, 1956, 292–4, where it is noted that the *canzone* was adapted to sonnet form in the sixteenth century by Francesco Maria Molza, as well as by Michelangelo's friend Claudio Tolomei. The metaphors invoked by Michelangelo in this letter-poem do not end there. The poem included in the letter is written at a right angle to the body of the letter, between it and Michelangelo's signature. In other words, it forms a calligram of the *"crocifisso"* itself. Moreover, his signature is written upside down, making the entire page a gloss on the theme of the included poem, *"Or in su l'uno, ora in su l' altro piede/ variando. . ."* (Buonarroti, 1960, 87–8), which describes the poet's disoriented soul, so topsy-turvy he can no longer see the heavens.

30 Cropper, 1995, 159–205. These ideas were developed by Cropper in earlier articles, "On Beautiful Women: Parmigianino, Petrarchismo, and the Vernacular Style," *Art Bulletin,* LVIII, 1976, 374–94, and more recently, "The Beauty of Woman: Problems in the Rhetoric of Renaissance Portraiture," in *Rewriting the Renaissance: The Discourses of Sexual Difference in Early Modern Europe,* ed. Margaret W. Ferguson, Maureen Quilligan, Nancy J. Vickers, Chicago: University of Chicago Press, 1986,

175–90. For a cogent summary of these views, see also Elizabeth Cropper and Charles Dempsey, *Nicolas Poussin: Friendship and the Love of Painting,* Princeton, NJ: Princeton University Press, 1996, 177–82.

31 On the secularization of traditional categories of religious images toward 1500, see above all Belting, 1994, especially ch. 20: "Religion and Art: The Crisis of the Image at the Beginning of the Modern Age." For more in-depth accounts of the genres of portraiture and landscape along these lines, see Joseph Leo Koerner, *The Moment of Self-Portraiture in German Renaissance Art,* Chicago: University of Chicago Press, 1993, especially ch. 4, "The Artist as Christ," and Christopher S. Wood, *Albrecht Altdorfer and the Origins of Landscape,* Chicago: University of Chicago Press, 1993, especially ch. 1, "Independent Landscape." In Nagel, 1993b, I argued that through devices such as *sfumato* painting "internalized" modes of concealing and revealing traditionally associated with the presentation of cult images, and with the mysteries of religious cult generally. Painting thus acquired a quasi-religious mystique in its own right, quite apart from the religiousness of its subject matter – a development that was later to be fundamental to Kantian philosophical aesthetics and Romantic conceptions of the artist and the work of art.

32 Girolamo Savonarola, *Sermoni sopra il salmo "Quam bonus,"* in *Sermoni e prediche di F. Girolamo Savonarola,* Prato: Guasti, 1846, sermon 16, 434–5 (excerpted in French translation in Gustave Gruyer, *Les illustrations des écrits de Jérôme Savonarole publiés en Italie au XVe at au XVIe siècle et les paroles de Savonarole sur l'art,* Paris: Firmin-Didot, 1879, 199): *"L'amore è come un dipintore. Un buono dipintore, se e' dipigne bene, tanto delettano gli uomini le sue dipinture, che nel contemplarle rimangon sospesi, e qualche volta in tal modo che e' pare che e' sieno posti in estasi e fuora di loro, e pare che e' si dimentichino di loro medesimi. Così fa l'amore di Gesù Cristo quando è nell' anima. . . . Domanda uno che sia innamorato d'una donna, che cosa gli dipinga l'amore nella camera della fantasia; risponderà, la faccia sua, gli occhi e gesti, le veste e simili cose; e tanto bene gliele dipigne, che tutte le potenze dell'anima sua rimangono sospese a tali pitture, e non si diletta di pensare ad altro, nè di contemplare altro che quelle pitture. . . . E se questo fa l'amore carnale, molto più l'amore spirituale, cioè di Gesù Cristo."* Not surprisingly, this passage is followed by a commentary on the Song of Songs.

33 *Carteggio,* IV, 104: *"Certo io non potrei mai exsplicar quanto sottilmente et mirabilmente è fatta, per il che son risoluta de non volerlo de man d'altri. Et però chiaritimi: se questo è d'altri, patientia; se è vostro, io in ogni modo vel torrei. Ma in caso che non sia vostro et vogliate farlo fare a quel vostro, ci parlaremo prima, perchè cognoscendo io la difficultà che ce è di imitarlo, più presto mi resolvo che colui faccia un'altra cosa che questa."* The question of the making of copies raised by this letter (as well as by the letter mentioning Pole's version of the *Pietà* drawing, quoted in n. 6, is, unfortunately, not at all clear. It is one of those instances in these letters where, as Hirst, 1988, 117, put it, "their language is difficult to interpret." Alexander Perrig, *Michelangelo's Drawings: The Science of Attribution,* trans. Michael Joyce, New Haven, CI: Yale University Press, 1991, 48, also admitted that "their contents are filled with riddles." The narrative he offered (48) to solve these riddles – which attempts to establish their sequence, the works to which they refer, the purpose of the unfinished drawing mentioned in the letter quoted above, and finally their date – is filled with dramatic supplementation not substantiated by the evidence.

34 The point corresponds to an assertion of Lodovico Dolce, elucidated by Cropper, 1995, 177: "Though Alberti had said that invention by itself could be beautiful, Dolce insists that, no matter how beautiful the invention, it requires equally beau-

tiful drawing. In other words, invention must appear, not just in words addressed to the mind but also embodied in visible representation in order to become beautiful to the eye." Cf. Nagel, 1993b, 18.

35 *Carteggio,* IV, 105.

36 Campi, 1994, 75–6, stressed the fact that the miracle happened after the apostles' failed efforts and thus interpreted the quotation as an expression of Colonna's Christocentrism. He also believed that this letter, which mentions a *"Christo"* rather than a *"Crucifixo,"* refers specifically to the drawing of the *Pietà.* Hirst, 1988, 117, believed that this and the other letters refer to the British Museum *Christ on the Cross.*

37 William West, "Nothing as Given: Economies of the Gift in Derrida and Shakespeare," *Comparative Literature,* 48, 1996, 11.

38 See Colonna's letter to Giulia Gonzaga of December 8, 1541, which gives a strong sense of the connections between Valdés and Viterbo; Colonna, 1892, 240: *"Ho inteso che V.S. ha mandato la espositione sopra San Paolo ch'era molto desiderata, et più da me che n'ho più bisogno."* Our understanding of Vittoria's connection to the thought of Valdés, independently and through the mediation of Ochino, has now been significantly enriched by Campi, 1994.

39 Juan de Valdés, *La Epistola de San Pablo a los Romanos, i la I. a los Corintios,* Madrid: Impresora de Alegria, 1856 *(Comentario ó declarazion breve i compendiosa sobre la epístola de San Pablo Apóstol á los romanos,* Venice: Juan Philadelphio, 1556), XV: *"Es bien verdad que el conozimiento que tienen de que Cristo es Hijo de Dios, los que no se sienten reconziliados con Dios, no se puede llamar propriamente conozimiento: porque si fuese conozimiento, haria en ellos el efecto que haze en los otros zertificándoles de su reconziliazion con Dios, i dándoles paz en sus conszienzias."*

40 *Le cento e dieci divine considerazioni del Giovanni Valdesso,* Halle: Ploeta, 1860, Considerazione CII, *"Che la fede Cristiana ha necessitá d'esser confermata con la esperienza; quale è la esperienza e come s'acquista,"* 376: *"Onde intendo che il primo e principale intento che debbiamo avere noi che accettiamo l'Evangelio, credendo che in Cristo Dio ha castigato tutti li nostri peccati, è acquistare la esperienza di questo, affinechè essendo così confermata la nostra fede, non sia bastante uomo alcuno di appartarci da essa nè di farci dubitare nè titubare in essa, come sono bastanti mentre la nostra fede non sta confermata con la esperienza."* According to Pietro Carnesecchi (Manzoni, 1870, 495), during Colonna's residence at Viterbo, Flaminio had with him Valdés's *Considerations,* which he was translating from Spanish into Italian for Giulia Gonzaga – again reinforcing the connection between Viterbo and Valdés.

41 A theme taken up in the *Beneficio,* Fontanini, 1972, ch. IV, 30–30*v*., 41–42: *"E però niun s'inganni . . . che la vera fede consista nel credere alla istoria di Iesú Cristo nella maniera che si crede a quella di Cesare e di Alessandro. Questo modo di credere è una fede istorica, fondata in mera relazione di uomini e di scritture e impressa leggiermente nell' animo per una certa usanza. . . . Questa cosí fatta fede é una immaginazione umana, che non innova niente il cuor dell'uomo, né lo riscalda dell' amor divino. . ."* It was a distinction typical of the thinking of Christian humanists and provoked by the fact that as humanists with a developed interest in the study of secular history they were compelled to give renewed critical attention to the question of what made sacred history different. In ch. 3 I present a fuller discussion of the humanist views and argue that Michelangelo grappled pictorially with this issue in the London *Entombment,* in attempting to adapt the principles of history painting to the demands of altar images.

42 Cf. José C. Nieto, *Juan de Valdés and the Origins of the Spanish and Italian Reformation,* Geneva: Droz, 1970, 253: "Valdés' hermeneutical principle is rooted in the experience of the word of God as it affects human self-consciousness. Thus, the ultimate hermeneutical question addressed by Valdés to the biblical text is preconditioned by the redemptive and soteriological quest for the text's effect upon his consciousness. The hermeneutical organon is therefore man's own conscience, and whatever does not touch him is passed over with the hope that in some other occasion it will speak to his conscience."

43 A point aptly emphasized by Susanna Peyronel Rambaldi, "Ancora sull'Evangelismo italiano: categoria o invenzione storiografica?" *Società e Storia,* 18, 1982, 951: *"Una cultura fondata su una esperienza interiore, aristocratica come più volte è stata definita, e individuale, i cui cardini erano la giustificazione per fede da una parte e l'odio per la superstizione, le pratiche non spirituali, dall'altra, non era una cultura che potesse esser facilmente divulgata e divenire patriminio comune della Chiesa della Controriforma."* The point is close to that made long ago by Cantimori, 1939, 24, who observed that in Valdesianism *"il motivo della riforma interiore conduceva a una religiosità puramente individuale o di piccoli gruppi, non adatta a produrre o a guidare un movimento largo e radicato in tutti i ceti della popolazione, come doveva essere un movimento di riforma generale."* This passage was quoted and discussed by Massimo Firpo, *Tra Alumbrados e "Spirituali": Studi su Juan de Valdés e il Valdesianesimo nella crisi religiosa del '500 italiano,* Florence: Olschki, 1990, 16, n. 23, and 13–43. He specifically made the point (28) that the "reserve" typical of the group around Valdés was due not simply to fear of persecution but rather to the nature of the piety they practiced: *"Mi pare lecito individuare in questa teorizzazione della prudenza (di cui risultano evidenti le implicazioni nicodemitiche) non solo la consapevolezza della necessità di erigere una sorte di flessibile schermo protettivo contro sospetti e accuse, che del resto non tarderanno farsi sentire, ma anche uno strumento funzionale a un' opera d'insegnamento, di iniziazione graduale dei nuovi adepti a dottrine religiose diverse da quelle tradizionali e via via più approfondite e riposte, scandite a livelli successivi di radicalismo dottrinale e destinate quindi a essere communicate poco per volta, passo per passo, accompagnando sapientemente il processo di 'esperientia' e progressiva rigenerazione cristiana che si veniva sviluppando nell' animo dei discepoli."*

44 In 1545, Benedetto Varchi noted with amused exasperation that the question of free will was debated *"non solamente dai teologi e filosofi, ma da tutte le sorti di letterati, anzi pure da qualunche idiota e volgare uomo; ed io mi ricordo essendo in Padova, che infino i ciabattini e fruttaroli, non che i sarti ed i calzolai, erano venuti a tale, dopo le prediche di non so che frate degli Scappuccini* [he is feigning not to remember Bernardino Ochino], *che mai non ragionavano d'altro, ma sempre disputavano della libertà dell' arbitrio e conseguentemente della predestinazione di Dio, della grazia e dell' opre, di maniera che . . . sono venute quelle dissensioni che ciascuno sa."* Benedetto Varchi, *Lezioni sul Dante e Prose Varie,* ed. Giuseppe Aiazz and Lelio Arbib, I, Florence: Società Editrice delle Storie del Nardi e del Varchi, 1841, 49–50. Quoted by Simoncelli, 1979, 342–3. In a letter of 1540 to the bishop of Modena Giovanni Morone, his vicar Giovanni Domenico Sigibaldi reported with great alarm: *"Tutta questa cità (per quanto è la fama) è maculata, infetta del contagio di diverse heresie come Praga. Per le botege, cantoni, case etc. ognuno (intendo che) disputa de fede, de libero arbitrio, de purgatorio et eucharistia, predestinazione."* Quoted in Massimo Firpo, "Gli 'spirituali', l'accademia di Modena e il Formulario di Fede del 1542: Controllo del dissenso religioso e nicodemismo," *Rivista di Storia e Letteratura Religiosa,* XX,

1984, 47. Already in 1538 Gasparo Contarini, earlier a defender of the public dissemination of reforming doctrine, saw the danger of *"alcuni predicatori li quali havevano predicato libero arbitrio, della predestinazione, onde havevano fatto gran confusione, havendo posto in capo a molti che la salute e la dannatione fussero necessarie e non contingente, et però che si poteva far male et compiacersi a suo modo."* Letter to Ercole Gonzaga, 19 January, 1538, in Walter Friedensburg, "Der Briefwechsel Gasparo Contarinis mit Ercole Gonzaga nebst einem Briefe Gian Pietro Carafas," in *Quellen und Forschungen aus italienischen Archiven und Bibliotheken,* II, 1899, 185.

45 The relevance of the treatise to the drawing was observed by Nagel, 1993a, 222–30, and by Campi, 1994, 49–51. The treatise has been set into the context of reformist writing and concerns over images by Adriano Prosperi, "Zwischen Mystikern und Malern: Überlegungen zur Bilderfrage in Italien zur Zeit Vittoria Colonnas," in *VC,* 283–92. It is written in the form of a letter addressed to a certain "Padre," whose authority is invoked at various points in the course of the text. Simoncelli, 1979, 211–13, showed that several passages, and those in particular that make reference to the "Padre," contain remarkably close allusions to Bernardino Ochino's *Prediche Nove.* On the basis of this evidence, he argued convincingly that Ochino, Colonna's spiritual advisor from 1534 to 1541, was the addressee of the text. This in turn helps to determine its date: Ochino's *Prediche Nove* were delivered in Venice during Lent of 1539 and were published in 1541; in August 1542 he fled to Geneva. Vittoria Colonna thus probably composed her text between 1539 and 1542 – that is, in the same period to which scholars usually date Michelangelo's drawings for her, and the correspondence that mentions them. Prosperi, supra, 292, noted that many of these arguments were also made by Eva Maria Jung, "Il Pianto della Marchesa di Pescara" (1957), *Archivio Italiano per la Storia della Pietà,* X, 1997, an article I have not been able to consult. On Colonna's relations with Ochino, who was himself heavily under the influence of Valdés, see Alfred von Reumont, *Vittoria Colonna, marchesa di Pescara: Vita, fede e poesia nel secolo decimosesto,* trans. Ermanno Ferrero and Giuseppe Müller, 2nd ed., Turin, 1892, 151–72, and Campi, 1994, 21–54.

46 Colonna, 1979, 423.

47 Colonna, 1979, 423: *"far del suo corpo quasi morto una sepoltura in quella hora."* For Colonna, as for Michelangelo, the lap was the very seat of love. And it was not exclusive to women. In a letter to Pietro Bembo (Colonna, 1892, 174), for example, she stated, *"veggo il grande affetto suo verso me, che da ogni parte soprabonda alla verità et si spande con la piena falda del suo caldo amore. . ."*

48 Colonna, 1979, 423: *"quel fuoco de amor et de tormento che se era desdignato per la grandezza sua mostrarsi tutto di fore, haveva consumato et penetrato l'intimo del'anima, hora nel toccar el sacro Corpo de Christo se allargò con maxima abondantia, et uscì per li occhi con più amare lacrime, et per la bocca con più accesi suspiri."*

49 Colonna, 1979, 423.

50 Colonna, 1979, 423.

51 Colonna, 1979, 424: *"queste virtù ancor che se ne andassero con l'anima . . . ne restò col santo corpo la impressione in sin la sua resurrettione per viver poi con lui glorificato in meglior vita, sì che tutte rilucevan in quello aspetto visibil più a li altri a la Madonna perchè più ardentemente languisse."* [Although these virtues had left with his soul . . . they left imprints on the holy body until his resurrection when they were again united with him glorified in a better life, so that they all shone in that visible aspect and especially to the Madonna who yearned all the more ardently.]

52 Colonna, 1979, 425.
53 Colonna, 1979, 425.
54 Colonna, 1979, 426.
55 Colonna, 1979, 426.
56 Colonna, 1979, 426.
57 Colonna, 1979, 427.
58 Colonna, 1979, 427: *"così la Madonna vedendo che non vi era la beata anima de Christo, qual sola era sufficiente ad honorar l'immensa grandeza de la divinità, li pareva che a lei sola appartenesse el grand' offitio de supplire a tanto debito, onde havria voluto liquefarsi, consumarsi anzi farsi ultima nel fuoco del'amore et ne le lacrime de la compassione per toglier al mondo et a se stessa l'ingratitudine, et render a Dio lo ossequio et il colto che li convenia."*
59 Colonna, 1979, 428.
60 Colonna thus preserved a role for the Virgin but subsumed it firmly within a Christocentric orientation, thus offering a "reformed" version of the Catholic tradition of Marian piety, and of medieval Passion literature. Campi, 1994, 48–54, offered a sustained analysis of this *"silenzioso ma vasto ridimensionamento mariologico,"* in both the *Pianto* and in the *Rime,* and its relations to the thought of Valdés and Ochino. I have attempted to show, both in the analysis of the drawings offered above, and more broadly in Nagel, 1993a, 8–89 and 182–247, that the corollary of this shift of emphasis, in the arena of visual traditions, was Michelangelo's shift from the Marian *Vesperbild* to the Christocentric *imago pietatis.*
61 Dante Alighieri, *The Divine Comedy,* trans. Charles S. Singleton, Princeton, NJ: Princeton University Press, 1975, 329.
62 *"Wer 15 Jahre lang täglich 100 Paternoster und Ave Maria betet, hat nach Ablauf der 15 Jahre jedem tropfen ein Paternoster gebetet. So viele Tropfen habe ich für dich und alle Mencshen vergossen:"* The text, from a prayer book belonging to the convent of Unterlinden in Colmar, is published and discussed in Thomas Lentes, *Gebetbuch und Gebärde: Religiöses Ausdrucksverhalten in Gebetbüchern aus dem Dominikanerinnen-Kloster St. Nikolaus in Undis zu Strassburg (1350–1550),* University of Münster, 1997, 550 and 1094–7. On the medieval "piety of counting" more generally, see Arnold Angenendt, Thomas Braucks, Rolf Busch, Thomas Lentes, and Hubertus Lutterbach, "Gezählte Frömmigkeit," *Frühmittelalterliche Studien,* 29, 1995, 1–71.
63 See Emile Mâle, *L'art religieux à la fin du moyen âge en France,* Paris, 1908, 93: In the fourteenth century seven *Pater Nosters*, seven *Ave Marias*, and seven short prayers called the "prayers of Saint Gregory" obtained a true pardon of 6,000 years from time in Purgatory; by the fifteenth century the sum had been inflated to 46,000 years. An intermediate stage in this inflationary process is represented by a highly informative mid-fifteenth-century indulgence panel of the *Man of Sorrows – Gregory Mass* in the Wallraf-Richartz Museum in Cologne (reproduced in Belting, 1981, Fig. 108), whose inscription reads that the 14,000 years of true pardon traditionally accorded to worshippers who say the prescribed prayers before this image has since been increased to 27,036 years.
64 In the *Praise of Folly* (1964, 129), Erasmus has Folly exclaim: "Then what shall I say about those who happily delude themselves with false pardons for their sins? They calculate the time to be spent in Purgatory down to the year, month, day, and hour as if it were a container that could be measured accurately with a mathematical formula."

65 This part of my discussion has benefited greatly from conversations with Thomas Lentes.

66 The ground drop that accommodates the lower half of Christ's body was interpreted as a tomb in several copies after the design, beginning with the relief in the Vatican. This point was made by Leo Steinberg, 1970, 266–7, who also emphasized the collapsing of the narrative span from birth to entombment.

67 Steinberg, 1970, interpreted the motif of Christ between the parted legs of the Virgin as a metaphor of parturition and progeniture in the Colonna *Pietà,* as well as in Michelangelo's other works and in Renaissance art generally. The interpretative context adduced here serves, I believe, to confirm, and nuance, Steinberg's observations on this and on a number of other points to be noted.

68 See also Ÿrjo Hirn, *The Sacred Shrine: A Study of the Poetry and Art of the Catholic Church,* London: Faber, 1958, 162–3, for the theological tradition of comparing Christ's tomb and the Virgin's womb.

69 A feature noted by Steinberg, 1970, 267, who interpreted it in this sense.

70 From the "Viaggio dell'anima al porto celeste," a letter-treatise addressed to Alvise Priuli attributed to Vittoria Colonna by B. Fontana, "Nuovi documenti vaticani intorno a Vittoria Colonna," *Archivio della società romana di storia patria,* X, 1887, 616.

71 A point made repeatedly and effectively by Campi, 1994, who made the important caveat (74): *"Tutto ciò non implica certamente l'esclusione di Maria dall'orizzonte della fede. In una linea di pensiero evidentemente affine al giudizio di Ochino e, in buona parte, della Colonna, la madre del Signore è raffigurata* [in the drawing] *non nell'atto di intercedere per l'umanità, ma di chi affida se stessa umilmente all'iniziativa salvifica di Dio e fedelmente cutodisce nel proprio cuore la parola divina ascoltata."*

72 "Beyond the Market: Books as Gifts in Sixteenth-Century France," *Transactions of the Royal Historical Society,* 5th series, 33, 1983, 72.

73 Condivi, 1911, 73.

74 See Daniel E. Bornstein, *The Bianchi of 1399: Popular Devotion in Late Medieval Italy,* Ithaca, NY: Cornell University Press, 1993. For images of their crosses, see the illustrations to Giovanni Sercambi's chronicle, in *Le illustrazioni delle croniche nel codice Lucchese,* II, Genoa, 1978, 190–1 and 195–202.

75 Cantimori, 1939, especially 22–23, "Umanesimo e religione nel Rinascimento," in idem, 1975, especially 277–80, and "Il circolo di Juan de Valdés e gli altri gruppi evangelici," in idem, 1975, 193–203. Much literature since Cantimori has labored to show the relations between reform ideas and institutions (rather than distinguished individuals) and their diffusion beyond the elite studied by Cantimori, a reevaluation that in turn has shed light on continuities in reformist thought and practice throughout the Cinquecento and thus has drawn emphasis away from the "crisis" of the reform movement traditionally dated to 1542. The literature of the last generation is usefully summarized by Anne Jacobson Schutte, "Periodization of Sixteenth-Century Italian Religious History: The Post-Cantimori Paradigm Shift," *Journal of Modern History,* 61, 1989, 269–84, who however somewhat overstates their revisionist implications. Many of the contributions cited by Schutte – for example Massimo Firpo's and Dario Marcatto's account of the war over the control of the Church that began in the 1530s, and the complementary accounts offered by Gigliola Fragnito, Adriano Prosperi, and Vincenzo de Caprio of the demise of the influence of the *spirituali* in the Church around the middle of the century – reveal that the new contributions broaden and refine rather than "over-

turn" the picture offered by Cantimori. Much of the new literature has, in fact, served better to contextualize the situation of the *spirituali* as described by Cantimori. For example, Ronald K. Delph, "From Venetian Visitor to Curial Humanist: The Development of Agostino Steuco's 'Counter'-Reformation Thought," *Renaissance Quarterly,* 47, 1994, 102–39, has revealed contemporary resistance to reform-minded critiques of external ceremony, on the grounds that they risked undermining the principles of civic humanism, that is, the celebration of the virtue of the active life and of the beneficent effects of good political and religious institutions. Steuco was not against an inner spiritual piety that approached God without ritual and ceremony – indeed, he acknowledged it as a more exalted path – but he argued that only a small number of sensitive and intelligent people were capable of such a spiritual relationship with God, while the "ignorant" needed ceremonies, the usefulness of which he celebrated with great humanist gusto. Steuco's two-tiered system was in many ways opposed to the beliefs of the Viterbo circle, and yet the positions were not unrelated in that they both presupposed a critical distance from Church tradition and ritual. The *spirituali* were distanced from and dissatisfied by Church ceremony, and they withdrew from it or in various ways adapted it to a more private piety. Steuco's distance from it, instead, promoted a quasi-anthropological appreciation of its social usefulness, a critical and practical approach that he shared with Machiavelli.

CHAPTER SEVEN. SCULPTURE AS RELIC

1 *"Padre santo, noi non habbi[a]mo in collegio di bisogno di huomini che sappiano fare i sonetti."* The comment, reported in Niccolò Franco's life of Carafa from the late 1550s, is quoted in Massimo Firpo, "Pasquinate romane del Cinquecento," *Rivista Storica Italiana,* XCVI, 1984, 614. My attention was drawn to it by Fragnito, 1988, 29, who went on to discuss the replacement of the refined humanist culture with a technico-juridical culture at the papal court under Paul IV and after. Her description of the situation largely corroborates the account of Carlo Dionisotti, "Chierici e laici," and "La letteratura italiana nell'età del concilio di Trento," in idem, 1967, 47–73 and 183–204 respectively. The view has come under revision recently, for example by Frederick McGinness, *Right Thinking and Sacred Oratory in Counter-Reformation Rome,* Princeton: Princeton University Press, 1995, who has argued that humanist ideals and oratorical practices continued to play a vital role in the post-Tridentine papal court. Nonetheless, the remark of Gian Pietro Carafa with which I begin this chapter does signal an emerging battle for control of the Church that the humanistically-inspired *spirituali* with whom Bembo was associated were to lose. This battle has been sharply illuminated by Massimo Firpo's and Dario Marcatto's critical edition of the Inquisition trial of Giovanni Morone, *Il processo inquisitoriale del cardinal Giovanni Morone: Edizione critica,* I-VI, Rome: Istituto storico italiano per l'eta moderna e contemporanea, 1981–1989. See also, more synthetically, Adriano Prosperi, "Un'esperienza di ricerca nell' Archivio del Sant'Uffizio," *Belfagor,* 53, 1998, 309–45.

2 See Fragnito, 1988.

3 Quondam, 1991, 271.

4 Quondam, 1991, 278–9: *"dopo Trento sembra non esservi più spazio per dialoghi 'spirituali' e per rime 'cristiane' di questo tipo."*

5 The text is discussed in Fragnito, 1988, 45–6.

6 *Lettere volgari di diversi nobilissimi huomini, et eccelentissimi ingegni scritte in diverse materie,* Venice: Figliuoli di Aldo, 1551, libro secondo, 113–113*v*.: *"Ho ricevutoli versi di Marcantonio, & quando ne habbia ricuperati alcuni altri che sono in mano d'uno amico mio, io vi manderò anchor quelli, che vi satisferan molto piu à mio giudicio, perche son tanto piu vaghi et piu venusti, quanto che trattano di materie piu capaci di vaghezza che per la verità queste materie della religione à trattarle vagamente si fanno spesso di sante prophane: & credo che sia difficil cosa à farlo bene, & con dignità. Queste altre materie sono pastorali, et amorose: ma guarderetevi di gratia di mostrarli poi à certi Stoici che si scandalizano di ogni cosa. . ."* On della Torre's activities as secretary of Gian Matteo Giberti, see Adriano Prosperi, *Tra Evangelismo e Controriforma: Gian Matteo Giberti (1495–1543).* Rome: Edizioni di storia e letteratura, 1969, xv, 150, 164, 184, 188, 196, and passim. Deswarte-Rosa, 1997, 358, noted that on January 30, 1540, seven days after della Torre's letter quoted above, della Torre wrote Carlo Gualteruzzi asking to be sent some recent sonnets by Vittoria Colonna, about which he had heard from Lattanzio Tolomei (one of the interlocutors in de Holanda's dialogues), suggesting that his skepticism about the possibility of an elegant religious poetry did not dampen his enthusiasm for it. On Rullo, see Carlo de Frede, *La restaurazione cattolica in Inghilterra sotto Maria Tudor nel carteggio di Girolamo Seripando,* Naples: Libreria scientifica editrice, 1971, 27–31, 128, and J. Ignacio Tellechea Idigoras, *Fray Bartolomé Carranza y el Cardenal Pole: un navarro en la restauración católica de Inglaterra,* Pamplona: Diputación Foral de Navarra, 1977, 124–5. The connections between Rullo and Flaminio and Pole were described by Pietro Carnesecchi at his trial; Manzoni, 1870, 198: *"Venendo da Napoli il Flaminio et io verso Roma nel 1540, o 1541, salvo il vero* [later in his testimony (211) Carnesecchi confirmed that it was in the month of May 1541], *s'accompagnó con noi per terzo questo Rullo, come già conosciuto del Flaminio a Venetia o a Padua o Verona che si sia, perchè faceva professione di esser molto servitore di Giberto vescovo di Verona et Cardinal Polo, ambedui patroni del detto Flaminio; et giunti che fumo a Roma, il detto Rullo restò appresso il Cardinale d'Inghilterra* [Pole] *come hospite. . . . Essendo poi il detto Flaminio et io andati in Viterbo . . . ce ritrovamo di nuovo insieme col prelibato Rullo."* The split alluded to in this letter was, of course, not new to writers. Writing to Arnold of Bost in 1486, Ermolao Barbaro declared: "*Duo agnosco dominos, Christum et litteras.*" For Eugenio Garin, "Lo spirito cristiano di Pico della Mirandola," in *Pensée humaniste et tradition chrétienne aux Xve et XVIe siècles,* Paris: Centre national de recherche scientifique, 1950, 172ff., the letter signaled an emerging split, one that is not yet evident in Coluccio Salutati and Lionardo Bruni, and that Pico della Mirandola, with typical flair and idealism, did his best to heal.

7 Quoted and translated by Barnes, 1998, 78.

8 Ulrich Oelschläger, "Der Sendbrief Franz von Sickingens an seinem Verwandten Dieter von Handschuchsheim," *Blätter für pfalzische Kirchengeschichte und religiöse Volkskunde,* 37/38, 1971–72, 723: *"wenn aus falschem Glauben die selben* [images] *angebetet wurden, wäre es Abgötterei und offensichtlich gegen das Gebot Gottes, wenn man aber in deren Anschauung ihr standthaftes Leben und ihren festen Glauben in Christum betrachtet, und wir von daher ein Ebenbild ihres Leben und Wirken nähmen und uns befleissigten, denselben nachzufolgen, wären sie uns fruchtbar and desto besser zu dulden. Ich sorge mich aber, dass solches wenig geschieht, sondern mehr die Kunst und Schönheit und Pracht in ihnen angesehen wird und dadurch das Gemüt und die rechte innerliche Betrachtung im Gebet vom rechten hohen aufsteigenden Weg in Gott abgezogen wird, weshalb sie beinahe meines Erachtens in schönen Gemächern zur Zierde nützlicher wären*

als in der Kirche, damit nicht der Aufwand und die vergebene Mühe unnütz verloren wären." The passage was quoted and discussed by Martin Warnke, "Durchbrochene Geschichte? Die Bilderstürme der Wiedertaüfer in Münster 1534/35," in *Bildersturm: Die Zerstörung des Kunstwerks,* ed. Martin Warnke, Munich: Hanser, 1973, 73, who believed the suggestion to remove art from the church to the secular sphere of the private room *"markiert den künftigen Weg des Kunstwerkes im grossbürgerlichen Haushalt und zugleich die Doppelrolle, die es dort als Verwertungs – und Verinnerlichungsgegenstand spielen wird."* My attention was drawn to the passage by Belting, 1994, Appendix 42B, 552, where part of it is excerpted.

9 Jean Calvin, *Institutio Christianae Religionis* (1559 ed.), ed. A. Tholuck, Edinburg: Clark, 1874, Book I, ch. 11, section 12, 81: *"Neque tamen ea superstitione teneor ut nullas prorsus imagines ferendas censeam. Sed quia sculptura et pictura Dei dona sunt, purum et legitimum usum requiro: ne quae Dominus in suam gloriam et bonum nostrum nobis contulit, ea non tantum polluantur praepostero abusu, sed in nostram quoque perniciem convertantur."* This and other relevant passages from the *Institutes* are collected in Belting, 1994, Appendix 41, although with unreliable citations. The best account of Calvin's views on images is Scavizzi, 1992, 9–29. On the secularizing consequences of the Protestant polemic on images, see also Werner Hofmann, "Die Geburt der Moderne aus dem Geist der Religion," in *Luther und die Folgen für die Kunst,* ed. Werner Hofmann, Munich: Prestel, 23–71.

10 *"Vorressimo anche ne facesti fare a Sebastianello Venetiano pittore un quadro di pittura a vostro modo, non siano cose di sancti, ma qualche pitture vaghe et belle da vedere."* Published by Alessandro Luzio, *La galleria dei Gonzaga veduta all'Inghilterra nel 1627–1628* (1913), Milan: Bardi, 1974, 28. Quoted by Hirst, 1981, 158.

11 Vasari, III, 273–4. On Vasari's periodization and his use of the words *goffo* and *rozzo* with medieval art, see Patricia Rubin, *Giorgio Vasari: Art and History,* New Haven, CT: Yale University Press, 1995, 281–4. Vasari's description of a split between the piety of a rough medieval art and the impiety of modern artistic elegance echoes the wording adopted by Gilio, 1961 (for which see Introduction). Gilio's treatise appeared only a few years before Vasari's second edition and was dedicated to Vasari's patron Alessandro Farnese.

12 For an English version, see Klein and Zerner, 1966, 122–4. See Barnes, 1998, 80–8, for the echoes of Aretino's position in later Counter-Reformation critics.

13 On the authenticity of the *Dialogues* as a record of Michelangelo's views, see Bury, 1981. Summers, 1981, 332 *ff.,* implicitly endorsed the authenticity of the passage discussed here. Barnes, 1998, 89, explicitly defended it. The further context adduced here also, I believe, corroborates the reliability of this passage as a representation of Michelangelo's opinions.

14 Hollanda, 1911, 240.

15 For Catarino's criticism of the *Last Judgment,* see below. For Catarino's polemic against the *Beneficio,* which prompted Marcantonio Flaminio to make revisions of the text while in Viterbo in 1542, see Fontanini, 1972, 347–422. Ginzburg and Prosperi, 1975, 69–70, entertained the hypothesis that the first manuscript of the *Beneficio* reached Catarino's hands through Vittoria Colonna herself. For more on the personages and setting of Hollanda's *Dialogues,* see Deswarte-Rosa, 1997, esp. 358. See also ch. 6 of this book for more on the connections between Michelangelo, the Viterbo circle, and the *Beneficio di Cristo.*

16 For the full text, see ch. 1, n. 2.

17 See Garin, 1961, 166–82, and Trinkaus, II, 1970, 674–82.

18 See, for example, Lucien Febvre, *The Problem of Unbelief in the Sixteenth Century: The Religion of Rabelais,* trans. Beatrice Gottlieb, Cambridge, MA: Harvard University Press, 1982, 39–40, 79, 159, 171–3, 304, 312, and passim.
19 Vasari, VI, 117. When attempting to dissuade Sebastiano del Piombo from including the portrait of a friar in the chapel of San Pietro in Montorio, Michelangelo quipped that those who have ruined the whole world will have no trouble ruining a small chapel. This anecdote is followed by another, in which Michelangelo feigned not to recognize a former friend who has become a monk and appears in Rome decked out in an elaborate habit. Forced to recognize him, Michelangelo feigned pleasant surprise and delivered a thoroughly Erasmian dressing down: "*'O, voi siete bello! Se fossi così drento come io veggio di fuori, buon per l'anima vostra.'*"
20 de Hollanda, 1911, 240.
21 See "Francesco Sassetti's letztwillige Verfügung" (1907) and "Bildniskunst und florentinisches Bürgertum" (1902), in Warburg, 1932, 127–63, 353–65, and 89–126, 340–52, respectively.
22 de Hollanda, 1911, 240. See also the discussion of this passage in Summers, 1981, 332*ff.* As pointed out by Summers, 1981, 550, Michelangelo's position vis-à-vis Flemish art as described by de Hollanda is corroborated by the *letterato* Giovan Batttista Gelli. Defending Dante, he argued that whereas other poets write with *leggiadria* and elegance, Dante displays both *"grandezza dei concetti"* and *"l'arte nel sapere exprimergli."* He then compared those who prefer other poets to Dante to those who prefer Flemish painting to the painting of Michelangelo: they are charmed by the *"vaghezza de' colori e per la varietà de paesi che sono in quelle."* Giovanni Battista Gelli, *Letture edite e inedite . . . sopra la Commedia di Dante,* ed. Carlo Negroni, I, Florence: Bocca, 1887, 330. The passage was also adduced by Barocchi, BVM, IV, 1985.
23 Vasari, V, 101–02: *". . .finalmente disse che non voleva farla se non a fresco, e che il colorire a olio era arte da donna e da persone agiate et infingarde, come fra' Bastiano."* Vasari stressed the extreme offense taken by Michelangelo over this episode, which caused a permanent falling out between the two artists. See also Hirst, 1981b, 123–4.
24 Hollanda, 1911, 240. One of course wonders what Michelangelo thought about the hermit landscape frescoes by Polidoro da Caravaggio at San Silvestro.
25 See Dunkerton, 1994, 95–99, 111–13. See also the analysis by Ezio Buzzegoli in *Il Tondo Doni di Michelangelo e il suo restauro,* exh. cat., Florence: Uffizi, 1985, 57–70. That the tempera technique was considered archaic at least by Vasari's time is suggested by his account of the lost panel of *St. Francis* in San Pietro in Montorio. The first edition of Vasari, VI, 13, said Michelangelo *"[d]ipinse nella maniera antica una tavola a tempera d'un San Francesco con le stimite. . ."* In the second edition, Vasari specified that it was designed by Michelangelo but painted by his barber, who only knew how to color in tempera, again suggesting that tempera was the less advanced medium. Vasari's wording allows for the possibility that beyond being carried out in an old-fashioned medium the very design of the panel was archaizing. So much is also allowed by the phrasing of Varchi's mention of the panel in his funeral oration; Benedetto Varchi, *Orazione funerale di M. Benedetto Varchi fatta, e recitata da lui pubblicamente nell'essequie di Michelagnolo Buonarroti in Firenze, nella Chiesa di San Lorenzo,* Florence, Giunti, 1564, 16 (reported by BVM, 158): *"Lascierò indietro una tavola, che egli dipinse a tempera secondo la maniera antica*

dove è un devotissiomo San Francesco. . ." In his own life, Vasari, VI, 392, noted that he painted a room in his house in the tempera technique to preserve the memory of the old technique: "*E perché adorava sempre la memoria e le opere degli antichi, vedendo tralasciare il modo di colorire a tempera, mi venne voglia di risuscitare questo modo di dipignere, e la feci tutta a tempera; il qual modo per certo non merita d'esser affatto dispregiato o tralasciato.*"

26 See Lorne Campbell, "Memlinc and the followers of Verrocchio," *Burlington Magazine,* CXXV, 1983, 675*ff.*

27 Vasari, VI, 32. As Cossa died in 1477, I assume that Vasari meant Costa, who was still alive at the time of this purported remark. It is likely that Tura's more sculptural style escaped Michelangelo's criticism, a point suggested by the fact that Michelangelo emulated his drapery style in the figure of St. Petronius for the altar of St. Dominic in Bologna, as observed by Wilde, 1978, 29.

28 Cf. Barnes, 1998, 82 (paraphrasing Aretino): "Art and religion are set against each other, as though they are mutually exclusive. By valuing art so highly, Michelangelo has proved himself to be without religion." And 84: "That Michelangelo put art before religion became a leitmotif of the opposition."

29 Ambrogio Catarino Politi, *Commentaria in omnes divi Pauli epistolas et alias septem canones,* Venice, 1551, 645. The passage is discussed by Romeo de Maio, "Michelangelo e Pio IV," in *Riforme e miti della Chiesa del Cinquecento,* Naples: Guida, 1973, 98, and idem, *Michelangelo e la Controriforma,* Rome-Bari: Laterza, 1978, 19–20. See also Deswarte-Rosa, 1997, 358, and n. 62.

30 Gilio, (1564) 1961, 39, 38, and 55, respectively. See also my discussions of Gilio's medievalism in the introduction, in chapter 2, third section, and in chapter 5, second section, above.

31 See, for example, the accounts of Lomazzo and Comanini, studied by Barnes, 1998, 86–7, and 100–01.

32 Gilio, 1961, 55–6, 110–11.

33 Cf. Gianluigi Colalucci, "Tecnica e Metodologia Operativa di Michelangelo sul Giudizio Universale," in *Michelangelo: La Capella Sistina. Documentazioni e interpretazioni,* II, Vatican City: Musei Vaticani, 1999, 71: "*I cartoni sono stati tutti trasferiti a spolvero ma la pelle appessa alla mano di San Bartolommeo, pur essendo di grandi dimensioni, non reca tracce né di spolvero né di incisione.*"

34 Buonarroti, 1960, n. 285.

35 This point is in part inspired by Warburg's analysis of the use of grisaille in the works of Domenico Ghirlandaio, which Warburg interpreted as a sort of "*Verfremdungseffekt,*" a means of neutralizing the disturbing effect of pathos formulas, or, as he put it, "*sub adumbratione . . . die Antike in typologischer Distanz [zu] halten.*" See Charlotte Schoell-Glass, "Warburg über Grisaille: Ein Splitter über einen Splitter," in *Aby Warburg: Akten des internationalen Symposions Hamburg 1990,* ed. Horst Bredekamp, Michael Diers, and Charlotte Schoell-Glass, Weinheim: VCH, 1991, 199–212.

36 Vasari, VI, 9: "*Dolendosi adunque Lorenzo, che amor grandissimo portava alla pittura et alla scultura, che ne' suoi tempi non si trovassero scultori celebrati e nobili, come si trovavano molti pittori di grandissimo pregio e fama, deliberò, come io dissi, di fare una scuola.*" On the rise of panel painting as a rival to sculpture in Christian settings during the Duecento and Trecento, see Belting, 1981, ch. 1. See also Collareta, 1988. Cf. Burckhardt, (1898) 1988, 41: "Does the battle between painting and

sculpture in the context of altar decoration perhaps reflect in microcosm a larger battle within the history of western art that was eventually to result in the victory of painting?"

37 See Simoncelli, 1979, 330–95, which showed Varchi to have been a close reader of the *Beneficio di Cristo.*

38 Castiglione, 1960, 83. Adducing the same point, Bronzino concludes (*BT,* I, 64): *"adunque è più utile che la pittura."*

39 Bronzino, in *BT,* I, 65–6. The final phrase reads: *". . .dove della pittura non può farsi altro che cose finte e di niuna utilitade, altro che di piacere; e per questo essere più utile la scultura."* I follow the English translation in Klein and Zerner, 1966, 11–12. Bronzino's unfinished letter does not offer an answer on this particular point from the painter's side.

40 da Vinci, 1956, 38, 40.

41 Bronzino, in *BT,* I, 66; Klein and Zerner, 1966, 13.

42 Castiglione, 1960, 84. Paolo Pino, *Dialogo di Pittura,* in *BT,* I, 127–8.

43 See the excellent discussion by Summers, 1981, part 1, II: "*Quello che non è sia.*"

44 da Vinci, 1956, 36. In his 1549 treatise *Disegno,* Anton Francesco Doni offered a description of two (invented) visual figures of the sister arts, wherein the "pleasant" image of Painting, who is brightly colored, gay, ornamental, and graceful, is contrasted to the grave, severe, and pure image of Sculpture. See the discussion in Leatrice Mendelsohn, *Paragoni: Benedetto Varchi's* Due Lezzioni *and Cinquecento Art Theory,* Ann Arbor, MI: UMI Research Press, 1982, 71. On the feminine gendering of oil painting in period art theory, see Philip Sohm, "Gendered Style in Italian Art Criticism from Michelangelo to Malvasia," *Renaissance Quarterly,* 48, 1995, esp. 785–91.

45 Gilio, 1961, 97–8.

46 Gilio, 1961, 110.

47 Francesco Bocchi, *Eccellenza del San Giorgio di Donatello, dove si tratta del costume, della vivacità e della bellezza di detta statua* (1584), in *BT,* III, 188–9. Bocchi's retrospective sensibility and his distaste for trends in contemporary painting also come through in his *Discorso sopra l' eccellenza dell'opere d' Andrea del Sarto pittore fiorentino* of 1567, published and discussed by Robert Williams, "A Treatise by Francesco Bocchi in Praise of Andrea del Sarto," *Journal of the Warburg and Courtauld Institutes,* LII, 1989, 111–39.

48 Thode, 1912, 697. The passage is worth quoting in full: *"Nichts anderes nun, als was den Stil jener Zeichnungen bestimmte, bestimmt den Eindruck der unvollendeten Skulpturen. In ihnen erscheint die einzelne Form nicht scharf ausgebildet, sondern nur angedeutet, wie aus der Ferne gedacht. . . . Und dies besagt eben so viel als eine Überführung des Plastischen in das Malerische zu Gunsten der Vorstellung eines zart vibrirenden, reich bewegten Lebens."*

49 Ernst Steinmann, "Kompositionen Michelangelos in seltenen Stichen," in *Festschrift Paul Clemen,* Bonn: Cohen, 1926, 422–3.

50 Thode, 1912, 57: *"Die Kunst Michelangelos ist der letzte heroische Akt der Tragödie der christlichen Plastik."*

51 Vasari, VI, 77: *". . .ancora che egli avessi avuto animo che la dovessi servire per la sepoltura di lui, e pié di quello altare dove e' pensava di porla."* The group is mentioned in Vasari's first edition and was thus begun before 1550. That the figure of Christ was already well defined by this time is suggested by the fact that it provided the

model for Jacopo Salviati's figure of *Jonah* in the Cappella del Pallio in the Palazzo della Cancelleria, painted between 1548 and 1550, a point made by Nagel, 1996, 563, n. 33. (For the dating of the Cappella del Pallio, see Patricia Rubin, "The Private Chapel of Cardinal Alessandro Farnese in the Cancelleria, Rome," *Journal of the Warburg and Courtauld Institutes,* 50, 1987, 82–112.) This is not incompatible with the argument of Perrig, 1960, 37–9, that Vasari did not see it before leaving Rome in October 1546 (he was not to return until February 1550) and that his somewhat laconic passage on the piece in the first edition was probably interpolated into his manuscript on the basis of a report by one of the Roman readers shortly before January 1548 – thus placing the beginning of work on the sculpture in 1547. From Condivi's quite detailed description of the work it is evident that the most intensive work on the group was done before 1553. I concur with the dominant view that the group was mutilated not long before the death of Michelangelo's assistant Urbino in December 1555.

52 Oxford, Ashmolean Museum, Parker, 1956, n. 342 *r.*; *Corpus* 431*r.* Red chalk worked over with a darker red in the central area; 37.5 × 28 cm.

53 Daniele da Volterra, also in the 1540s, made a worked-up drawing based on this same sketch, Uffizi 1138E, in preparation for his fresco altarpiece in the Trinità de' Monti, which was begun in 1541. Another copy by Daniele from the Haarlem sheet, London British Museum 1946-7-13-326, is a study of the man climbing the ladder. Another sheet in the Louvre reproducing the group around the fainting Virgin in the Haarlem sheet, although closer to Michelangelo in style, is attributed to Daniele by Charles de Tolnay, "La Deposizione di Cristo, Disegno attribuito a Michelangelo a Haarlem," *Pantheon,* 25, 1967, 20. The first two examples, at least, indicate that the Haarlem sheet was, still in the 1540s, available for study in Michelangelo's shop.

54 Nagel, 1996, 565–6.

55 Parker, 1956, n. 342*r.*; Robinson, 1870, n. 37; Frey, 1909–11, n. 150.

56 Steinberg, 1972.

57 I am not convinced by the attempt to switch the identities of the Virgin and the Magdalene made by Moshe Arkin, "'One of the Marys. . .': An Interdisciplinary Analysis of Michelangelo's Florentine Pietà," *Art Bulletin,* 79, 1997, 493–517.

58 Wolfgang Stechow, "Joseph of Arimathea or Nicodemus?" in *Studien zur toskanischen Kunst: Festschrift für Ludwig Heinrich Heidenreich,* Munich: Prestel, 1964, 289–302, offered the most comprehensive survey of the depictions and legends involving these two personages and concluded that "the scales seem to be tipped" in favor of identifying Michelangelo's figure as Nicodemus. Schleif, 1993, especially 611–12, offers an array of supporting evidence for this identification.

59 See Schleif, 1993.

60 Vasari, VI, 93.

61 Vasari, VI, 120. This visit, which occurred during Julius III's pontificate (1550–1555), must have taken place before Vasari left Rome at the end of 1553. Leo Steinberg, "Michelangelo's Florentine *Pietà*: The Missing Leg," *Art Bulletin,* 50, 1968, 343–53, offered the hypothesis that beyond technical or "formal" considerations, Michelangelo's uneasiness with the leg derived from its thematic associations: The motif of the leg slung over the Virgin's thigh carried with it a strong charge of erotic associations, as is evident by its frequent use in amorous scenes. The spousal, amorous associations were an important part of Michelangelo's interpretation of the subject – as the works and texts discussed in

this book have served to confirm – but according to Steinberg they also produced acute psychic conflict, in the end causing him to destroy the group. The hypothesis that this conflict motivated Michelangelo's destructive act arose within a more encompassing discussion concerning Michelangelo's innovative use of amorous motifs in the context of the Passion (see Steinberg, 1970), but it is not necessary to this discussion. One can accept many of Steinberg's points concerning the significance of the motifs – and they have informed parts of my own argument – without accepting the hypothesis about the motive for destroying the group. In the end the hypothesis is unprovable, as it postulates unconscious processes.

62 Oxford, Ashmolean Museum, Parker 339*r.*; *Corpus* 433*r.* Black chalk; 10.8 × 28.1 cm. The date of 1552–53 was proposed by Baumgart, 1935, 44*ff.* Frey, 1956, 218–19, proposed the date 1552. Perrig, 1960, 93, concurred with this dating and placed the beginning of the work on the first version of the Rondanini *Pietà* in 1553 (82). Charles de Tolnay, "The Rondanini Pietà," *Burlington Magazine,* LXXIII, 1934, 285*ff.* dated the sheet to 1550–56. Vasari, VI, 93, mentioned that after the destruction of the group Michelangelo turned to *"un altro pezzo di marmo dove era stato già abbozzato un'altra Pietà, varia da quella, molto minore."* This statement has almost universally been taken as a reference to the Rondanini *Pietà,* but this is not so certain: the Palestrina *Pietà* is 253 cm tall; the Rondanini *Pietà* is 195 cm tall in its present state and was significantly taller in its first version; neither can be described as *"molto minore"* than the Florence *Pietà* (226 cm). Thus, either Vasari was wrong or he was referring to a work which we do not know. In Nagel, 1996, 570, n. 51, I agreed with Perrig that the Palestrina *Pietà* was a critique of the first version of the Rondanini *Pietà,* in turn superseded by Rondanini II. I would now not be so certain about the sequence; I would say simply that both Rondanini I and the Palestrina *Pietà* are responses to the frustrations of the Florence *Pietà* and that the conceptions for both came even before Michelangelo's destroyed the Florence group – that is, before 1555.

63 I disagree with the view of Wilde, 1978, 188–90, that in the Christ figure the right arm is all that remains of the first version and that the legs "on a smaller scale than the arm and too far removed from it" belong to a second version. The succession of "states" was clarified by Frey, 1956, 208–11, who observed in the legs and the right arm of Christ the remnants of the first version and then distinguished two states within the second version: one in which both the Virgin's head and Christ's are turned upward, and the second and final state, in which both heads are turned downward. We thus have Rondanini I and Rondanini II, a and b.

64 Private collection; formerly Newbury, Collection Gathorne-Hardy, n. 6; *Corpus* 426A*r.* Black chalk; 32.4 × 22 cm. Illustration in Hirst, 1988, pl. 146. There is also a copy in reverse in the Stedelik Museum in Amsterdam, reproduced in *Corpus,* text illustration to 427–30. The figure of Christ was also studied in two autograph figure studies, originally part of the same sheet, now in a Swiss private collection and in the Casa Buonarroti in Florence, as was demonstrated by Hirst, 1988, 69. There is also a series of studies (*Corpus* 427–30) for the figures of the forward-striding carriers.

65 The compositional similarity to the London painting was also noted by Tolnay, *Corpus* 426A*r.*

66 See Catherine Monbeig-Goguel, "Giulio Clovio 'nouveau petit Michel-Ange': à propos des dessins du Louvre," *Revue de l'Art,* 80, 1988, 41 and 46, n. 44.

67 Wilde, 1978, 184 and 192, n. 26 believed this series of "carrying" studies to be connected to the Palestrina *Pietà*. The carryings studied in these sheets do indeed show some similarities to the figure of the Magdalene in the sculpture, who is shown striding forward rather than simply standing, as in the Florence *Pietà*. However, the figure of Christ in the Palestrina *Pietà* is clearly supported by the single figure of the Virgin behind, an idea that is absent from the "carrying" studies discussed here, which without exception explore a lateral, two-carrier system. This is not simply a formal difference but an important thematic difference, for in removing the Virgin they also remove the intense amorous gestures that connect her to Christ. Much closer in every respect to the Palestrina group is a drawing in the Teylers Museum (Inv. A 35*r*.; *Corpus* 434*r*.), which shows the Virgin passionately kissing Christ's head.

68 Hirst interpreted the motif in the "carrying" studies as one of entombment, as we see in the Clovio drawing, but the fact that there the direction of movement is reversed might suggest otherwise. The forward-striding movement shown in the "carrying" drawings might involve another episode, such as the presentation of the body to the Virgin after the deposition, as we see it in a panel of the subject by the Master of the Virgo inter Virgines in the St. Louis Art Museum.

69 The date of the beginning of work on the second version was established by Baumgart, 1935, 48, on the basis of Taddeo Zuccaro's *Dead Christ with Angels* in the Borghese Gallery in Rome, which is based on the first version of the sculpture and datable to ca. 1560. Perrig's arguments, 1960, 80, n. 25, against the connection between the two works are not convincing. Equally unconvincing on the other chronological end is Tolnay's citation, 1960, 154–5, of Daniele da Volterra's famous letter of June 11, 1564, in which Daniele says that he saw Michelangelo working on the sculpture six days before his death, as evidence that the new version of the Rondanini *Pietà* was begun only at the very end of the artist's life. This letter establishes only that Michelangelo was *still* working on it at that time. Thus we cannot date Rondanini II any more precisely than 1560–64. I am inclined to believe that the great shift to the new conception occurred toward the beginning of this period and that the work that preoccupied Michelangelo just before his death (as recorded by Daniele) concerned precisely those more local changes to the head of the Virgin and the head of Christ observed by Frey, 1956, 208–11.

70 Frey, 1956, 212: *"Es ist, als ob aus dem ständigen schmerzlichen Erleben der Zerstörung für ihn eine treibende, schöpferische Kraft augegangen wäre, als ob die Vernichtung wie ein Nein-Sagen, wie eine asketische Absage an das Vergangene erlebt wurde, die er sich immer wieder zu vergegenwärtigen suchte, um in ihrer Überwindung ein Letztes und Endgültiges zu gestalten."*

71 Wilhelm Worringer, "Die *Pietà* Rondanini," *Kunst und Künstler,* 7, 1909, 356.

72 Vincenzo Borghini, *Modo di salvare il Bembo,* in Pozzi, 1988, 742: *". . .che le lingue ne' lor principii, come le altre opere della natura, sono imperfette, rozze, acerbe, ecc. e che il tempo le dirozza, matura e affinisce."* See the discussion of this and other passages in the introduction.

Abbreviations and Frequently Cited Sources

AR	*The Altarpiece in the Renaissance.* Eds. Humfrey, Peter and Martin Kemp. Cambridge, MA: Cambridge University Press, 1990.
ASD	*Opera Omnia Desiderii Erasmi Roterodami,* I –. Amsterdam: Elsevier Science, 1969 –.
B.	Bartsch, Adam von. *Le peintre-graveur.* I–XXI. Vienna: Degen, 1803–21.
BT	*Trattati d'Arte del Cinquecento.* Ed. Paola Barocchi. I–III. Bari: Laterza, 1960–62.
Carteggio	*Il Carteggio di Michelangelo.* Eds. Giovanni Poggi, Paola Barocchi, and Renzo Ristori. I–III. Florence: Sansoni, 1965–73.
Carteggio Indiretto	*Il Carteggio indiretto di Michelangelo.* Eds. Paola Barocchi, Kathleen Loach Bramanti, and Renzo Ristori. I–II. Florence: S.P.E.S., 1988 –.
Corpus	Tolnay, Charles de. *Corpus dei disegni di Michelangelo.* I–IV. Novara: Istituto Geografico De Agostini, 1975–80.
Hind	Hind, Arthur M. *Early Italian Engraving; A Critical Catalogue with Complete Reproduction of All the Prints Described.* I–VII. London: Quaritch, 1970.
Lehrs	Lehrs, Max. *Geschichte und kritischer Katalog des deutschen, niederländischen und französischen Kupferstiches im XV. Jahrhundert,* I–IX. Vienna: Gesellschaft für Vervielfältigende Kunst, 1908–34.
Migne, *PL*	Migne, Jacques-Paul. *Patrologiae cursus completus [microform]: sive biblioteca universalis, integra, uniformis, commoda, oeconomica, omnium SS. Patrum, doctorum scriptorumque eccelesiasticorum qui ab aevo apostolico ad usque Innocentii III tempora floruerunt . . . / [series Latina, in qua prodeunt Patres, doctores scriptoresque Ecclesiae Latinae, a Tertulliano ad Innocentium III].* I–CCXXI. Paris: Garniere, 1844–96.
RbR	*Raphael before Rome,* ed. James Beck, in *Studies in the History of Art,* Washington: The Gallery, 1986.
VC	*Vittoria Colonna: Dichterin und Muse Michelangelos.* Exh. cat., Kunsthistorisches Museum. Vienna: Kunsthistorisches Museum, 1997.
Vasari	Vasari, Giorgio. *Le vite de' più eccellenti pittori, scultori e archittetori nelle redazioni del 1550 e 1568.* Ed. Rosanna Bettarini, with comments by Paola Barocchi. I–VIII. Florence: Studio per Edizioni Scelte, 1966–87.

Agosti, Giovanni, and Vincenzo Farinella. *Michelangelo e l'arte classica.* Florence: Cantini, 1987.

Alberti, Leon Battista. *On Painting.* Trans Cecil Grayson. London: Penguin; New York: Viking Penguin, 1991.

Allen, Michael. *Marsilio Ficino and the Phaedran Charioteer.* Berkeley, CA: University of California Press, 1981.

———. *The Platonism of Marsilio Ficino: A Study of his Phaedrus Commentary, Its Sources and Genesis.* Berkeley, CA: University of California Press, 1984.

Astur, Baloneus. *I Baglioni.* Florence: Olschki, 1964.

Auerbach, Erich. *Mimesis: The Representation of Reality in Western Literature* (1946), Princeton, NJ: Princetion University Press, 1968.

———. "Figura." In *Scenes from the Drama of European Literature.* Minneapolis: University of Minnesota Press, 1984.

Barkan, Leonard. *Transuming Passion: Ganymede and the Erotics of Humanism.* Stanford, CA: Stanford University Press, 1991.

Barnes, Bernadine. *Michelangelo's Last Judgment: The Renaissance Response.* Berkeley, CA: University of California Press, 1998.

Barocchi, Paola. *La Vita di Michelangelo di Giorgio Vasari nelle redazioni di 1550 e 1568.* I–V. Milan and Naples: Ricciardi, 1962.

Bauerreis, Romuald. *Pie Jesu. Das Schmerzensmann-Bild und sein Einfluss auf die mittelalterliche Frömmigkeit.* Munich: Widman, 1931.

Baumgart, Friedrich. "Die Pietà Rondanini." *Jahrbuch der Preußischen Kunstsammlungen,* LV, 1935, 44*ff.*

Belting, Hans. *Das Bild und sein Publikum im Mittelalter: Form und Funktion früher Bildtafeln der Passion.* Berlin: Mann, 1981.

———. *Giovanni Bellini, Pietà: Ikone und Bilderzählung in der venezianischen Malerei.* Frankfurt: Fischer, 1986.

———. "Vom Altarbild zur autonomen Tafelmalerei." In *Kunst: Die Geschichte ihrer Funktionen.* Ed. Werner Busch and Peter Schmock. Weinheim/Berlin: Quadriga, 1987, 128*ff.*

———. *Likeness and Presence: A History of the Image in the Era before Art.* Trans. Edmund Jephcott. Chicago: Chicago University Press, 1994.

Berenson, Bernard. *The Drawings of the Florentine Painters.* 2nd ed. I–III. Chicago: Chicago University Press, 1938.

———. *Italian Pictures of the Renaissance. Florentine School.* I–II. London: Phaidon, 1963.

———. *Italian Pictures of the Renaissance. Central Italian Schools.* I–III. London: Phaidon, 1970.

Berliner, Rudolf. "The Freedom of Medieval Art." *Gazette des Beaux-Arts,* ser. 6, 28, 1945, 263–88.

———. "Bemerkungen zu einigen Darstellungen des Erlösers als Schmerzensmann." *Das Münster,* 9, 1956, 97–117.

Bober, Phyllis Pray. "The *Coryciana* and the Nymph Corycia." *Journal of the Warburg and Courtauld Institutes,* 40, 1977, 223–39.

———, and Ruth Rubinstein, with contributions by Susan Woodford. *Renaissance Artists & Antique Sculpture: A Handbook of Sources.* London: Harvey Miller, 1986.

Bonito, Virginia Anne. "The Saint Anne Altar in Sant'Agostino, Rome." Doctoral dissertation, New York: New York University, 1983.

Borsook, Eve, and Fiorella Superbi Gioffredi, eds. *Italian Altarpieces 1250–1550: Function and Design.* Oxford: Clarendon Press; New York: Oxford University Press, 1994.

Boyle, Marjorie O'Rourke. *Christening Pagan Mysteries: Erasmus in Pursuit of Wisdom.* Toronto: University of Toronto Press, 1981.

Braun, Joseph. *Der christliche Altar in seiner geschichtlichen Entwicklung.* I–II. Munich: Koch, 1924.

Buonarroti, Michelangelo. *Rime.* Ed. Enzo Noè Girardi. Bari, Italy: Laterza, 1960.

———. *The Complete Poems and Selected Letters of Michelangelo.* Ed. Robert Linscott, trans. Creighton Gilbert. New York: Modern Library, 1965.

Burckhardt, Jacob. *The Altarpiece in Renaissance Italy.* Ed. and trans. Peter Humfrey. Cambridge, MA, and New York: Cambridge University Press, 1988.

———. *The Altarpiece in the Renaissance* (1898). Trans. Peter Humfrey. New Haven, CT: Yale University Press, 1988.

Bury, John Bagnell. *Two Notes on Francisco de Hollanda.* London: Warburg Institute Surveys, 1981.

Büttner, Frank O. *Imitatio Pietatis: Motive der christlichen Ikonographie als Modelle zur Verähnlichung.* Berlin, 1983.

Campi, Emidio. *Michelangelo e Vittoria Colonna: Un dialogo artistico-teologico ispirato da Bernardino Ochino, e altri saggi di storia della Riforma.* Turin: Claudiana, 1994.

Cantimori, Delio. *Eretici italiani del Cinquecento.* Florence: Sansoni, 1939.

———. *Umanesimo e Religione nel Rinascimento.* Turin: Einaudi, 1975.

Castiglione, Baldassare. *Il Libro del Cortigiano* (1528). In *Opere di Baldassare Castiglione, Giovanni della Casa, Benvenuto Cellini.* Ed. Carlo Cordié. Milan and Naples: Ricciardi, 1960.

Cennini, Cennino. *The Craftsman's Handbook: The Italian "Il libro dell' arte."* Trans. Daniel V. Thompson. New York: Dover Publications, 1960.

Chastel, André. *Marsile Ficin et l'art.* Geneva: Droz, 1954.

Chronicles of the City of Perugia. Trans. Edward Strachen Morgan. London: Dent, 1905.

Collareta, Marco. "Le 'arti sorelle': Teoria e pratica del 'paragone'" In *La pittura in Italia: Il Cinquecento.* II. Milan: Electa, 1988.

Colonna, Vittoria. *Carteggio.* Eds. Ermanno Ferrero and Giuseppe Müller. 2nd ed. Turin: Loescher, 1892.

———. *Pianto sopra la Passione di Cristo.* In Simoncelli, 1979, App., Document 1, 423–8.

———. *Rime.* Ed. Alan Bullock. Roma: Laterza, 1982.

Condivi, Ascanio. *The Life of Michelangelo.* Trans. Charles Holroyd. In Michael Holroyd, *Michael Angelo Buonarroti, with translations of the life of the master by his scholar, Ascanio Condivi, and three dialogues from the Portuguese by Francisco Hollanda.* London: Duckworth, 1911.

Cronache perugine (attributed to Francesco Matarazzo). In *Archivio Storico Italiano,* XVI, 1851, 103 *ff.*

Cropper, Elizabeth. "The Place of Beauty in the High Renaissance and Its Displacement in the History of Art." *Medieval and Renaissance Texts and Studies,* 132, 1995, 159–205.

Crowe, J. A., and G. B. Cavalcaselle. *Raphael: His Life and Works.* I–II. London: Murray, 1882.

D'Amico, John. *Renaissance Humanism in Papal Rome: Humanists and Churchmen on the Eve of the Reformation.* Baltimore: Johns Hopkins University Press, 1983.

da Lucca, Pietro. *Arte del ben pensare e contemplare la passione del nostro Sinor Jesu Christo con un singular trattato dello imitar di Christo ni nouo corretta historiata.* Venice: N. da Aristotele da Ferrara detto il Zoppino, 1527.

da Vinci, Leonardo. *Treatise on Painting.* Ed. and trans. A. Philip McMahon. Princeton, NJ: Princeton University Press, 1956.

Daniélou, Jean. *Platonisme et Théologie Mystique: Essai sur la doctrine spirituelle de Saint Grégoire de Nysse.* Paris, Aubier, 1944.

de Hollanda, Francisco. *Three Dialogues on Painting.* Trans Charles Holroyd. In Charles Holroyd, *Michael Angelo Buonarroti, with Translations of the Life of the Master by his Scholar, Ascanio Condivi, and Three Dialogues from the Portuguese by Francisco Hollanda.* London: Duckworth, 1911.

de Man, Paul. *Blindness and Insight: Essays in the Rhetoric of Contemporary Criticism.* 2nd ed. Minneapolis: University of Minnesota Press, 1983.

Derrida, Jacques. *The Gift of Death.* Trans. David Wills. Chicago: Chicago University Press, 1995.

Deswarte-Rosa, Sylvie. "Vittoria Colonna und Michelangelo in San Silvestro al Quirinale nach den Gesprächen des Francisco de Holanda." In *VC,* 349–73.

Dionisotti, Carlo. *Geografia e storia della letteratura italiana.* Turin: Einaudi, 1967.

Dunkerton, Jill, in *The Young Michelangelo: The Artist in Rome 1596–1601.* London: National Gallery, 1994.

Dussler, Luitpold. *Die Zeichnungen des Michelangelo. Kritischer Katalog.* Berlin: Mann, 1959.

Dvořák, Max. *Studien zur Kunstgeschichte.* Leipzig: Reclam, 1989.

Emmerling-Skala, Andreas. *Bacchus in der Renaissance.* Hildesheim; New York: Olms, 1994.

Erasmus, Desiderius. *The Essential Erasmus.* Ed. John P. Dolan. New York and Scarborough, Ontario: Meridian, 1964.

Fenlon, Dermot. *Heresy and Obedience in Tridentine Italy: Cardinal Pole and the Counter Reformation.* Cambridge, MA: Cambridge University Press, 1972.

Ficino, Marsilio. *Opera omnia* (reprint Basel, 1570). Turin: Bottega d'Erasmo, 1962.

Fontanini, Benedetto (with revisions by Marcantonio Flaminio). *Il Beneficio di Cristo, con le versioni del secolo XVI, documenti e testimonianze.* Ed. Salvatore Caponetto. Florence: Sansoni, 1972.

Fragnito, Gigliola. *In museo e in villa: saggi sul rinascimento perduto.* Venice: Arsenale, 1988.

Frey, Dagobert. "Die Pietà-Rondanini und Rembrandts 'Drei Kreuze.'" In *Kunstgeschichtliche Studien für Hans Kauffmann.* Berlin: Mann, 1956.

———. "Ikonographische Bemerkungen zur Passionsmystik des späten Mittelalters." *Neue Beiträge zur Archäologie und Kunstgeschichte Schwabens Julius Baum zum 70. Geburtstag Gewidmet.* Stuttgart: Kohlhammer, 1952.

Frey, Karl. *Die Handzeichnungen Michelagniolos Buonarroti.* I–III. Berlin: Bard, 1909–1911.

Gardner von Teuffel, Christa. "Lorenzo Monaco, Filippo Lippi und Filippo Brunelleschi: die Erfindung der Renaissance-pala." *Zeitschrift für Kunstgeschichte,* 45, 1982, 1–30.

———. "From polyptych to pala: some structural considerations." In *La pittura nel XIV e XV secolo: il contributo dell'analisi tecnica alla storia dell'arte.* Eds. Henk van Os and J. R. J. Asperen de Boer. *Atti del XXIV Congresso Internazionale di Storia dell'Arte, 1979,* III. Bologna, 1983, 323–30.

Gelli, Giovanni Battista. *Sopra que' due sonetti del Petrarcha che lodano il ritratto della sua M. Laura.* Florence: Torrentino, 1549.

Gesing, Martin. *Triumph des Bacchus: Triumphidee und bacchische Darstellungen in der italienischen Renaissance im Spiegel der Antikenrezeption.* Frankfurt am Main, 1988.

Gilbert, Creighton. "Peintres et menuisiers au début de la Renaissance en Italie." *Revue de l'Art,* 35, 1977, 9–28.

———. *Italian Art: 1400–1500.* Englewood Cliffs: Prentice Hall, 1980.

Giles of Viterbo. *Historia viginti saeculorum.* Biblioteca Angelica, Rome, MS 502.

Gilio, Giovanni Andrea. *Dialogo nel quale si ragiona de gli errori de pittori circa l'historie: con molte annotationi fatte sopra il giuditio di Michelangelo, et in che modo vogliono esser dipinte le sacre imagini.* In *BT,* II, 1–115.

Ginzburg, Carlo, and Adriano Prosperi. *Giochi di pazienza: un seminario sul Beneficio di Cristo.* Turin: Einaudi, 1975.

Gleason, Elizabeth. *Reform Thought in Sixteenth-Century Italy.* Chico, CA: Scholar's Press, 1981.

Goldschmidt, Adolph. Intervention on Michelangelo's London Entombment. Sitzungsbericht Dezember 11, 1903. *Sitzungsberichte der Kunstgeschichtliche Gesellschaft Berlin,* 8, 1903, 56–8.

Grondijs, L. H. *L'iconographie Byzantine du crucifié mort sur la croix.* Bruxelles: Editions de Byzantion, 1941.

Hirst, Michael. "Michelangelo in Rome: An Altar-piece and the 'Bacchus.'" *Burlington Magazine,* 123, 1981, 581–93 [1981a].

———. *Sebastiano del Piombo.* Oxford: Clarendon, 1981. [1981b]

———. *Michelangelo and his Drawings.* New Haven and London: Yale University Press, 1988.

———. "The Artist in Rome 1496–1501." *The Young Michelangelo: The Artist in Rome 1596–1601.* London: National Gallery, 1994.

Hood, William. *Fra Angelico at San Marco.* New Haven, CT: Yale University Press, 1993.

Hope, Charles. "Altarpieces and the Requirements of Patrons." In *Christianity and the Renaissance: Image and Religious Imagination in the Quattrocento.* Ed. Timothy Verdon and John Henderson. Syracuse, NY: Syracuse University Press, 1990, 536–71.

Hyde, Lewis. *The Gift: Imagination and the Erotic Life of Property.* New York: Random House, 1979.

Humfrey, Peter. *The Altarpiece in Renaissance Venice.* New Haven: Yale University Press, 1993.

Jähnig, Karl W. "Die Beweinung Christi vor dem Grabe von Rogier van der Weyden." *Zeitschrift für Bildende Kunst,* n.s. 29, 1918, 171–6.

Jakobson, Roman. "The Dominant" (1935). In *Readings in Russian Poetics: Formalist and Structuralist Views.* Eds. Ladislav Matejka and Kristina Pomorska. Cambridge, MA: M.I.T. Press, 1971, 82–7.

Jauss, Hans Robert. *Toward an Aesthetic of Reception.* Minneapolis: University of Minnesota Press, 1982.

Joannides, Paul. *The Drawings of Raphael.* Oxford: Clarendon, 1983.

Jungmann, Joseph. *The Mass of the Roman Rite: Its Origins and Development.* I–II. Trans. Francis A. Brunner. Westminster, MD: Christian Classics, 1986.

Justi, Carl. *Michelangelo. Neue Beiträge zur Erklärung seiner Werke.* Berlin: Grote, 1909.

Kitzinger, Ernst. *The Art of Byzantium and the Medieval West: Selected Studies.* Ed. W. Eugene Kleinbauer. Bloomington, IN: Indiana University Press, 1976.

Klein, Robert, and Henri Zerner. *Italian Art 1500–1600.* Englewood Cliffs, NJ: Prentice-Hall, 1966.

Koch, Guntram. *Die mythologischen Sarkophage.* XII, 6. *Meleager.* Berlin: Mann, 1975.

Kris, Ernst, and Otto Kurz. *Legend, Myth, and Magic in the Image of the Artist: A Historical Experiment.* Trans. Alistair Lang and Lottie Newman. New Haven, CT: Yale University Press, 1979.

Levenson, Jay, Konrad Oberhuber, and Jacquelyn L. Sheehan. *Early Italian Engravings from the National Gallery of Art.* Washington: The Gallery, 1973.

Lewy, Hans. *Sobria ebrietas: Untersuchungen zur Geschichte der antiken Mystik.* Giessen, Germany: 1929.

Locher, Hubert. *Raffael und das Altarbild der Renaissance: Die "Pala Baglioni" als Kunstwerk im sakralen Context.* Berlin: Akademie, 1994.

Emile Mâle. *L'Art religieux à la fin du moyen âge en France.* Paris: Colin, 1908.
Mango, Cyril. *The Art of the Byzantine Empire, 312–1453.* Englewood Cliffs, NJ: Prentice-Hall, 1972.
Manzoni, Giacomo, Ed. "Estratto del Processo di Pietro Carnesecchi." *Miscellanea di Storia Italiana,* X, 1870, 187–573.
Marrow, James. *Passion Iconography in Northern European Art of the Late Middle Ages and Early Renaissance.* Kortrijk, Belgium: van Ghemmert, 1979.
Matz, Friedrich. *Die antiken Sarkophagreliefs.* IV. *Die Dionysischen Sarkophage.* Berlin: Mann, 1969.
Meditations on the Life of Christ. Isa Ragusa and Rosalie B. Green, eds. Princeton, NJ: Princeton University Press, 1961.
Milanesi, Gaetano, Ed. *Le Lettere di Michelangelo Buonarroti, coi ricordi ed i contratti artistici.* Florence: Successori di Monnier, 1875.
Millet, Gabriel. *Recherches sur l'iconographie de l'Evangile.* Paris: Fontemoing, 1916.
Minnich, Nelson. "Concepts of Reform Proposed at the Fifth Lateran Council," *Archivum Historiae Pontificiae,* 7, 1969, 163–251. Reprinted with new appendices in idem, the *Fifth Lateran Council (1512–17): Studies on its Membership, Diplomacy and Proposals for Reform,* London:Variorum Reprints, 1993, essay IV.
Mitsch, Erwin. "Florentinische und frühe römische Jahre." In *Raphael: Die Zeichnungen.* Stuttgart: Mayer, 1983.
Müntz, Eugene, *Les Collections des Medicis au XVe Siecle.* Paris: Rouam, 1888.
Nagel, Alexander. "Michelangelo, Raphael and the altarpiece tradition." Doctoral dissertation, Cambridge, MA: Harvard University, 1993 (1993a).
———. "Leonardo and *sfumato.*" *Res: Anthropology and Aesthetics,* 24, 1993b, 7–20.
———. "Observations on Michelangelo's late *Pietà* drawings and sculptures." *Zeitschrift für Kunstgeschichte,* LIX, 1996, 548–72.
Neri di Bicci. *Le ricordanze (10 marzo 1453–24 aprile 1475).* Ed. Bruno Santi. Pisa: Marlin, 1976.
Nussbaum, Martha. *The Fragility of Goodness: Luck and Ethics in Greek Tragedy and Philosophy,* Cambridge, MA: Cambridge University Press, 1986.
Oberhuber, Konrad, Jay Levenson, and Jacquelyn L. Sheehan. *Early Italian Engravings from the National Gallery of Art.* Washington, D.C: National Gallery of Art, 1973.
O'Malley, John. *Giles of Viterbo on Church and Reform: A Study in Renaissance Thought,* Leiden, the Netherlands Brill, 1968.
———. *Praise and Blame in Renaissance Rome: Rhetoric, Doctrine, and Reform in the Sacred Orators of the Papal Court, c. 1450–1521.* Durham, NC: Duke University Press, 1979.
———. *Rome and the Renaissance: Studies in Culture and Religion.* London: Variorum Reprints, 1981.
Ovide Moralisé en Prose. Ed. C. de Boer. Amsterdam: North-Holland, 1954.
Pagano, Sergio M., and Concetta Ranieri. *Nuovi Documenti su Vittoria Colonna e Reginald Pole.* Vatican City: Archivio Vaticano, 1989.
Paleotti, Gabriele. *Discorso intorno alle imagini sacre e profane* (1582). In *BT,* II, 117–509.
Panofsky, Erwin. "'Imago Pietatis.' Ein Beitrag zur Typengeschichte des 'Schmerzensmanns' und der 'Maria Mediatrix.'" In *Festschrift für Max J. Friedländer zum 60. Geburtstage.* Leipzig: Seeman, 1927, 261–308.
———. *Early Netherlandish Painting: Its Origins and Character.* Cambridge, MA: Harvard University Press, 1953.
———. "The First Page of Giorgio Vasari's *'Libro'*" (1930). In *Meaning in the Visual Arts.* Harmondsworth, UK: Penguin, 1970, 206–76

Parker, Karl. *Catalogue of the Collection of Drawings in the Ashmolean Museum. II. Italian Schools.* Oxford: Clarendon, 1956.

Pastore, Alessandro. *Marcantonio Flaminio: Fortune e sfortune di un chierico nell'Italia del Cinquecento.* Milan: Angeli, 1981.

Perrig, Alexander. *Michelangelos letzte Pietà-Idee.* Bern: Francke, 1960.

Pocock, J. G. A. *The Machiavellian Moment: Florentine Political Thought and the Atlantic Republican Tradition.* Princeton, NJ: Princeton University Press, 1975.

Pope-Hennessy, John. *Raphael.* New York: New York University Press, 1970.

Popham, Arthur E., and Johannes Wilde. *The Italian Drawings of the XV and XVI Centuries in the Collection of his Majesty the King at Windsor Castle.* London: Phaidon, 1949.

Pozzi, Mario, ed.. *Discussioni linguistiche del Cinquecento.* Turin: Unione tipografico-editrice torinese, 1988.

Prosperi, Adriano. *Tra Evangelismo e controriforma: G. M. Giberti (1495–1543).* Roma: Edizioni di storia e letteratura, 1969.

Quondam, Amedeo. *Il naso di Laura: Lingua e poesia lirica nella tradizione del Classicismo.* Ferrara, Italy: Panini, 1991.

Richter, Jean-Paul. *Italian Art in the National Gallery.* London, 1883.

Ringbom, Sixten. *Icon to Narrative.* Åbo, Finland: Åbo Akademie, 1965.

Robinson, J. C. *A Critical Account of the Drawings by Michel Angelo and Raffaello in the University Galleries, Oxford.* Oxford: Clarendon, 1870.

Rosci, Paolo, *Raffaello Deposizione,* Turin: Lindau, 1991.

Rowland, Ingrid. *The Culture of the High Renaissance in Italy.* Cambridge, MA: Cambridge University Press, 1998.

Saslow, James. *The Poetry of Michelangelo: An Annotated Translation.* New Haven, CT: Yale University Press, 1991.

Savonarola, Girolamo. *Prediche sopra Amos e Zaccaria* (Lent 1496). Ed. Paolo Ghiglieri. I–III. Rome: Angelo Belardetti, 1971.

Schapiro, Meyer. "Words and Pictures: On the Literal and the Symbolic in the Illustration of a Text." In *Words, Script, and Pictures: Semiotics of Visual Language.* New York: Braziller, 1996.

Schleif, Corine. "Nicodemus and Sculptors: Self-Reflexivity in Works by Adam Kraft and Tilman Riemenschneider." *Art Bulletin,* 75, 1993, 599–626.

Scott, Izora. *Controversies over the imitation of Cicero as a Model for Style, and Some Phases of Their Influence in the Schools of the Renaissance.* New York: Teachers College, 1910.

Screech, Michael. *Ecstasy and the Praise of Folly.* London: Duckworth, 1980.

Shearman, John. "The 'Dead Christ' by Rosso Fiorentino." *Bulletin of the Boston Museum of Fine Arts,* 64, 1966, 148–72.

———. *Pontormo's Altarpiece in Santa Felicita.* Westerham, UK: Westerham Press, 1971.

———. *Only Connect. . . Art and the Spectator in the Italian Renaissance.* Princeton, NJ: Princeton University Press, 1992.

Simoncelli, Paolo. *Evangelismo italiano del Cinquecento,* Rome: Istituto Storico Italiano di Storia Moderna e Contemporanea, 1979.

Steinberg, Leo. "The Metaphors of Love and Birth in Michelangelo's *Pietàs.*" In *Studies in Erotic Art.* Eds. Theodore Bowie and Cornelia Christenson. New York: Basic Books, 1970, 231–335.

———. *The Sexuality of Christ in Renaissance and in Modern Oblivion.* 2nd ed.. Chicago: Chicago University Press, 1996.

Stoichita, Victor. *L'instauration du tableau: Métapeinture à l'aube des Temps modernes.* Paris: Méridiens Klincksieck, 1993.

Summers, David. *Michelangelo and the Language of Art.* Princeton, NJ: Princeton University Press, 1981.

Thode, Henry. *Michelangelo und das Ende der Renaissance.* I. *Das Genie und die Welt.* Berlin: Grote, 1902.

———. *Michelangelo und das Ende der Renaissance.* II. *Der Dichter und de Ideen der Renaissance.* Berlin: Grote, 1903.

———. *Michelangelo und das Ende der Renaissance.* III. *Der Künstler und seine Werke.* Berlin: Grote, 1912.

———. *Kritische Untersuchungen.* I–II. Berlin: Grote, 1908.

———. *Kritische Untersuchungen.* III. *Verzeichniss der Zeichnungen, Kartons und Modelle.* Berlin: Grote, 1913.

Tolnay, Charles de. *Michelangelo I: The Youth of Michelangelo.* 2nd ed. Princeton, NJ: Princeton University Press, 1947.

———. *Michelangelo V: The Final Period.* Princeton, NJ: Princeton University Press, 1960.

———. *Michelangelo: Sculptor, Painter, Architect.* Princeton, NJ: Princeton University Press, 1975.

Trinkaus, Charles. *In Our Image and Likeness: Humanity and Divinity in Italian Humanist Thought.* Chicago: University of Chicago Press, 1970.

van Os, Henk. *Sienese Altarpieces, 1215–1460.* I–II. Groningen: Bouma's Boekhuis, 1984–1990.

Venturi, Adolfo. *Storia dell'Arte Italiana.* IX, part 1. Milan: Hoepli, 1925.

Vetter, Ewald M. "La Iconografía del 'Varón de Dolores': Su Significado y Origen." *Archivo Español de Arte,* 36, 1963, 197–231.

von der Osten, Gert. *Der Schmerzensmann: Typengeschichte eines deutschen Andachtsbildwerkes von 1300 bis 1600.* Berlin: Deutscher Verein für Kunstwissenschaft, 1935.

von Einem, Herbert. "Bemerkungen zur florentiner Pietà Michelangelos." *Jahrbuch der Preußischen Kunstsammlungen,* 61, 1940.

von Salis, Arnold. *Antike und Renaissance.* Erlenbach-Zürich: Rentsch, 1947.

Warburg, Aby. Intervention on Michelangelo's London Entombment. Sitzungsbericht Dezember 11, 1903. *Sitzungsberichte der Kunstgeschichtliche Gesellschaft Berlin,* 8, 1903, 56–8.

———. *Gesammelte Schriften.* I–II. *Die Erneuerung der heidnischen Antike.* Ed. Gertrud Bing. Berlin: B. G. Teubner, 1932.

Wilde, Johannes. "Eine Studie Michelangelos nach der Antike." *Mitteilungen des Kunsthistorischen Institutes in Florenz,* 4, 1932–1934, 41–64.

———. *Italian Drawings in the Department of Prints and Drawings in the British Museum. Michelangelo and His Studio.* London: Trustees of the British Museum, 1953.

———. *Michelangelo. Six Lectures.* Oxford: Clarendon Press, 1978.

Wind, Edgar. *Pagan Mysteries in the Renaissance.* 2nd ed. New York: Norton, 1968.

Zeri, Federico. *Pittura e controriforma: L'arte senza tempo di Scipione da Gaeta.* Turin: Einaudi, 1957.

Index

Boldface numbers refer to illustration number; number following n refers to note number